DIPLOMA IN FINANCIAL MANAGEMENT

MODULE A

Subject Area 1

INTERPRETATION OF FINANCIAL STATEMENTS

Interactive text

DipFM

This Interactive Text

BPP is the **official provider** of training materials for the ACCA's DipFM qualification.

In this February 2006 edition

- The syllabus and study guide, cross-referenced to the Text
- Fully updated for International Accounting Standards and terminology, examinable from December 2006
- Plenty of activities, examples and quizzes to demonstrate and practise techniques
- Full index
- Layout designed to be easy on the eye and easy to use

FOR EXAMS FROM DECEMBER 2006

BPP
PROFESSIONAL EDUCATION

First edition 2001
Fifth edition February 2006

ISBN 0 7517 2585 4 (previous ISBN 0 7517 2333 9)

British Library Cataloguing-in-Publication Data
A catalogue record for this book
is available from the British Library

Published by

BPP Professional Education
Aldine House, Aldine Place
London W12 8AW

www.bpp.com

Printed in Great Britain by W M Print
45-47 Frederick Street
Walsall, West Midlands
WS2 9NE

We are grateful to the Association of Chartered Certified Accountants for permission to reproduce past examination questions. The answers to past examination questions have been prepared by BPP Professional Education.

Contents

How to use this interactive text

This is the fifth edition of the BPP textbook for the Diploma in Financial Management Module A, subject area 1 - *Interpretation of Financial Statements*. It has been specifically written to cover the Syllabus and Study Guide, and reflects subsequent comments and clarification by the examiner.

With effect from the December 2006 sitting, the DipFM exams will be set using international terminology and International Accounting Standards. This book has been fully updated to reflect this change.

To pass the examination you need a thorough understanding in all areas covered by the syllabus and study guide.

Recommended approach

(a) To pass you need to be able to answer questions on **everything** specified by the syllabus and study guide. Read the text very carefully and do not skip any of it.

(b) Learning is an **active** process. Do **all** the activities as you work through the text so you can be sure you really understand what you have read.

(c) After you have covered the material in the Interactive Text, work through the questions in the Practice and Revision Kit for Module A.

(d) Before you take the exam, check that you still remember the material using the following quick revision plan.

  (i) Read through the chapter learning objectives. Are there any gaps in your knowledge? If so, study the section again.

  (ii) Read and learn the key terms.

  (iii) Read and learn the key learning points, which are a summary of each chapter.

  (iv) Do the quick quizzes again. If you know what you're doing, they shouldn't take long.

  (v) Use the BPP Passcards to revise the key issues in each topic.

This approach is only a suggestion. You or your college may well adapt it to suit your needs.

Remember this is a **practical** course.

(a) Try to relate the material to your experience in the workplace or any other work experience you may have had.
(b) Try to make as many links as you can to subject area 2 of Module A, and also to Module B.

Further question practice

Practice and Revision Kit

A substantial further bank of questions including past exam questions is available in the BPP Practice and Revision Kit for this module. The February 2006 edition has been fully updated for international standards and terminology.

i-Pass CD Rom

A recent addition to the DipFM suite of products is the BPP i-Pass CD Rom. We produce one each for Module A and Module B. These interactive CD Roms provide numerous multiple choice and data response questions for each of the two subject areas in the module. Ideal for question practice and revision, they are designed to test knowledge and perfect exam technique.

You can order all our products by telephoning 0845 0751 100 (within the UK) or +44 (0) 20 8740 2211 (from overseas) or order online at www.bpp.com.

Syllabus

The ACCA Diploma in Financial Management has two modules, A and B, each of which covers two subject areas.

Module A has the following two elements:

Subject area 1: *Interpretation of Financial Statements*

Subject area 2: *Performance Management*

This Interactive Text, and the separately published Practice and Revision Kit (for both subject areas of module A) cover the syllabus for subject area 1, Interpretation of Financial Statements.

A separate Interactive Text is available for the Performance Management part of Module A.

Subject Area 1 – Interpretation of Financial Statements

Aim

The overall aim of this paper is that candidates should be able to understand and interpret the financial statements produced by organisations for external users. Candidates should develop an understanding of the regulatory framework in which these statements are prepared and of the principles and methods which underlie their preparation.

Objectives

On completion of this paper candidates should be able to

- Describe the role and function of external financial reports and identify their users and the regulatory framework in which they are prepared
- Explain the accounting concepts and conventions present in generally accepted accounting practice
- Explain, supported by simple computations, the presentation, measurement and meaning of the primary financial statements and their contents
- Describe the informational role of the constituent parts of a corporate annual report usually presented in addition to the primary financial statements
- Compute, interpret and appraise financial performance, financial position and adaptability as revealed by financial statement analysis in particular by the use of financial and accounting ratios.

Syllabus content

		Chapter where covered in Text
1	**Regulation of Financial Statements**	
	The regulatory framework within which financial statements are prepared.	
	(a) The role of the International Accounting Standards Committee Foundation and constituent bodies	1
	(b) The role of the auditor and the meaning of fair presentation	1
2	**Financial Information**	
	(a) The objectives of financial statements and the needs of users	2
	(b) The reporting entity	2
	(c) The qualitative characteristics of financial information	4
	(d) The elements of financial statements	2, 3
	(e) Measurement in financial statements including an appreciation of the limitations of historical cost and the basic nature of current value accounting models	4
	(f) The basic features of accounting for public sector and non-profit organisations	4
3	**Financial Statements**	
	(a) The structure, features and content of the primary financial statements:	
	(i) Income statement	5
	(ii) Balance sheet	6
	(iii) Cash flow statement	11
	(iv) Statement of changes in equity	5
	(b) The major features, but not detailed contents of other elements of corporate annual reports:	
	(i) Notes to the accounts and additional financial statements	12
	(ii) Management report	12
	(iii) Chairman's statement	12
	(iv) Financial reviews	12
	(v) Environmental reports	12
	(vi) Interim accounts	12
	(vii) Preliminary announcements	12
	(c) The terminology and underlying accounting methods and principles used in preparing financial statements in respect of:	
	(i) Tangible non-current assets, including depreciation and the impact of revaluation	8
	(ii) Intangible non-current assets, including goodwill and research and development costs	8
	(iii) Current assets, in particular inventories and construction contracts	6
	(iv) Liabilities, including leases, contingencies and provisions	6
	(v) Share capital and reserves	9

		Chapter where covered in Text
(vi)	Events after the balance sheet date	6
(vii)	Reporting the substance of transactions	6
(viii)	Reporting financial performance, including segmental analysis	7
(ix)	Business combinations and other investments	10
(x)	Cash flow reporting	11
(xi)	The accounting implications of taxation, in particular current and deferred taxation	5

For all of the above computations may be required to support explanation, appraisal and justification of accounting policies and treatments.

4 **Analysis of Financial Statements**

(a) The computation, interpretation and appraisal of financial ratios in respect of:

(i)	Profitability, earnings, operating performance and efficiency	13
(ii)	Liquidity, solvency and working capital management	13
(iii)	Asset and capital structures, including gearing	13
(iv)	Cash flows and cash flow management	13
(v)	Stock market performance including earnings, dividend and price relationships	13

(b)	Common size statements, trend analysis, inter-firm analysis and failure prediction models.	14
(c)	The limitations of financial ratio analysis	13, 14

Excluded topics

The following topics are specifically excluded from the syllabus:

- The detailed process of double entry bookkeeping
- Foreign currency translation
- Accounting for pension costs and retirement benefits
- Related party disclosures
- Reporting for smaller entities
- SICS and IFRICS

Key areas of the syllabus

The key topics are:

- The regulatory framework
- The principles underlying financial statements
- The structure and content of the primary financial statements
- Financial statement analysis

Study Guide

1 **The Regulatory Framework of Accounting**

Syllabus reference la, b

- Outline the purpose and underlying assumptions of the ISAB Framework for the Preparation and Presentation of Financial Statements ('Framework')
- Explain the requirement for an audit of published financial statements and the role of the auditor
- Explain the nature of the 'fair presentation'
- Identify those entities which do not require audited published financial statements
- Explain the role and functions of regulatory bodies
  - International Accounting Standards Committee Foundation
  - International Accounting Standards Board (IASB)
- Explain the role and functions of the International Financial Accounting Reporting Interpretations Committtee

2 **Objectives of Financial Statements and the Reporting Entity**

Syllabus reference 2a, b

- Explain the objectives of decision usefulness and stewardship
- Identify the users of financial statements and their needs
- Explain the categories of financial information available to users and the role of general purpose financial statements
- Explain the need for information in respect of financial performance, financial position, generation of cash and financial adaptability
- Explain the principle of control in defining the boundary of the reporting entity

3 **Qualitative characteristics elements and related concepts**

Syllabus reference 2c, d

- Explain the need for relevance, reliability, comparability and understandability of financial information and constraints on these
- Define assets, liabilities, income, expenses, equity, contributions from owners and distributions from owners
- Explain and apply the concepts of accruals and going concern

4 **Measurement in financial statements**

Syllabus reference 2e

- Explain the need for a measurement basis to be used in financial statements
- Explain and apply the basic principles of historical cost accounting
- Explain the basic principles of current cost accounting

5 **Financial Statements I**

Syllabus reference 3a(i), 3a(ii)

- Explain how the basic accounting equation underlies the balance sheet and income statement and the relationship between these two statements

- Explain and apply the classification of asset and liability disclosure in the balance sheet
- Draft a balance sheet in vertical form
- Explain how and why revenue and expenses are disclosed in the income statement
- Draft an income statement in vertical form

6 **Financial statements II**

Syllabus reference 3a(iii), 3a(iv)

- Explain the difference between accruals based and cash based financial statements
- Explain the relationship of a cash flow statement to the other primary financial statements
- Explain the difference between realised and unrealised gains and losses and the purpose of comprehensive disclosure
- Draft a statement of changes in equity

7 **Financial statements III**

Syllabus reference 3b(i) – 3b(viii)

- Explain the need for additional information in the form of notes to the accounts and additional financial statements
- Identify the basic components of a management report
- Explain the purpose and usefulness of a chairman's statements
- Explain the need for summarised financial information and its limitations
- Identify the basic components of an operating and financial review
- Explain the need for preliminary announcements and interim statements
- Identify the fundamental differences between accounting for public sector and private sector entities

8 **Tangible non-current assets**

Syllabus reference 3c(i)

- Explain and apply accounting principles to the initial recognition and measurement of tangible assets
- Explain and apply the principal methods of depreciation and appraise their impact on the financial statements
- State and appraise the impact of the revaluation of non-current assets
- Explain the nature and effect of impairment of non-current assets

9 **Intangible non-current assets**

Syllabus reference 3c(ii)

- Discuss the nature of an intangible asset and in particular goodwill
- Explain and apply the accounting treatment of internally generated and purchased goodwill
- Distinguish between research expenditure and development costs
- Explain and apply the accounting treatment of research expenditure and development costs

10 **Current assets**

Syllabus reference 3c(iii)

- Explain and apply the basic inventory valuation principle of cost or net realisable value
- Explain and apply the stock valuation conventions of FIFO and weighted average

- Discuss the treatment of construction contracts
- Explain the need for assessment of receivables and receivables allowances

11 **Accounting for liabilities**

Syllabus reference 3c(iv)

- Explain the distinction between current and non-current liabilities
- Explain the difference between liabilities, provisions and contingent liabilities and apply the relevant accounting treatment of these to examples
- Explain the nature of finance and operating leases
- Explain and apply the accounting treatment of finance and operating leases

12 **Share capital, reserves and events after the balance sheet date**

Syllabus reference 3c(v), 3c(vi)

- Distinguish between different types of share capital and explain their characteristics
- Distinguish the different types of reserve (capital, revenue; realised/unrealised) and their uses
- Explain the nature of 'off-balance sheet finance' and the concept of substance over form
- Distinguish between adjusting and non adjusting events after the balance sheet date and explain their accounting treatment

13 **Reporting financial performance**

Syllabus reference 3c(vii), 3a(iv)

- Explain and appraise the meaning of a statement of financial performance (income statement) which identifies discontinuing operations, exceptional items, prior period adjustments and non-current assets held for resale
- Identify the items in the income statement which might be included in reported earnings per share
- Calculate reported earnings per share
- Explain the significance of earnings per share as a measure of performance
- Explain the link between the income statement and the statement of changes in equity
- Explain the purpose of segmental information (class of business, geographical) and appraise the usefulness of this information for interpretation of financial statements

14 **Accounting for investments, in particular groups including subsidiaries, associates and joint ventures.**

Syllabus reference 3c(viii), 3c(ii)

- Explain the treatment of investments held for resale
- Distinguish between subsidiaries, associates and joint ventures
- Describe the concept of a group and explain the terminology of accounting for groups
- Explain and apply consolidation accounting, equity accounting and the gross equity method
- Explain and apply the treatment of goodwill arising on acquisition
- Explain and apply impairment of goodwill

15 **Cash flow reporting**

Syllabus reference 3c(ix)

- Prepare a cash flow statement
- Appraise the usefulness of the information in a cash flow statement
- Interpret the information in a cash flow statement

16 **Accounting for taxation**

Syllabus reference 3c(x)

- Explain and apply the accounting treatment of current taxation
- Explain and apply the effect of timing differences on accounting and taxable profits
- Explain and apply the full provision method of accounting for deferred taxation
- Appraise the impact of current and deferred taxation on financial performance and financial position

17 **Analysis of financial statements: profitability, earnings, operating performance and efficiency**

Syllabus requirement 4a(i)

- Outline the basic methods of financial statement analysis, in particular common size statements and ratio analysis
- Calculate and interpret ratios which provides insights into financial performance
- Assess a company's financial performance in comparison with previous periods' financial statements, inter firm comparisons and industry averages
- Discuss the effect of accounting policy choice on the interpretation and assessment above

18 **Liquidity, solvency and working capital management**

Syllabus reference 4a(ii)

- Calculate and interpret ratios which provide insights into financial position and operating performance in respect of working capital
- Assess a company's financial position and working capital management in comparison with previous periods' financial statements, inter firm comparisons and industry averages
- Discuss the effect of accounting policy choice on the interpretation and assessment performance

19 **Assets and capital structure**

Syllabus reference 4a(iii)

- Calculate and interpret ratios which provide insights into financial position, financing and investment strategy and utilisation of resources
- Calculate and interpret ratios which indicate financial risk, in particular gearing
- Assess a company's financial position and financial risk in comparison with precious periods' financial statements, inter firm comparisons and industry averages
- Discuss the effect of accounting policy choice on the interpretation and assessment performance

20 **Cash flow and investment analysis**

Syllabus reference 4a(iv), 4a(v)

- Calculate and interpret ratios which provide insights into financial adaptability and generation and use of cash
- Calculate and interpret ratios which give an insight into earnings, dividend and price relationships which would be useful to an investor
- Assess a company's financial performance in relationship to its market price and in comparison with market averages and other market based data
- Discuss the effect of accounting policy choice on the interpretation and assessment above

21 **Comprehensive applications of financial statement appraisal and analysis**

Syllabus reference all of 1, 2, 3 and 4

- Explain the usefulness of multivariate ratio models, in particular with respect to failure prediction
- Discuss the limitations of financial statement ratio analysis techniques
- Analyse and interpret a comprehensive set of financial statements including all of those identified in 3(a) and (b)
- Critically evaluate the impact on the financial statements of accounting policies in respect of the items included in 3(c)
- Present an appraisal of the results of the financial statement analysis in a given context.

Reading list

The examiner has issued a reading list. It contains some suggestions for further and wider reading should you want to investigate any topics in greater depth, and it may be helpful when you are researching topics for the Module A Project.

- M Pendlebury, R Groves

  Company Accounts: Analysis, Interpretation and Understanding (5th Ed) 2001 Thomson Learning (ISBN 1-86152-595-8)

- G Holmes, A Sugden

  Interpreting Company Reports and Accounts (7th Ed) 1999
  Pearson (ISBN 0-273-64615-X)

- E McLavey, P Atrill

  Accounting: An Introduction (2nd Ed) 2002
  Prentice Hall (ISBN 0-273-65550)

The examination

The examination for each module will cover the two subject areas in that module. The examination for Module A will cover both 'Interpretation of Financial Statements' (subject area 1) and 'Performance Management' (subject area 2) topics.

The structure of the examination for Module A will be as follows.

Section A

20 multiple choice questions (10 covering subject area 1 and 10 covering subject area 2) of 2 marks each.

Section B

3 written questions of 20 marks each - covering subject area 1.

Section C

3 written questions of 20 marks each - covering subject area 2.

Candidates will be required to attempt all questions in Section A, one question from Section B, one question from Section C and one final question from either Section B or C.

The time allowed will be 3 hours.

The structure of the Module B examination follows the same format, but will cover financial strategy and risk management.

The pass mark for each examination is 50%.

Analysis of past papers

December 2006 will be the first sitting of the International version of this paper. However an analysis of past UK versions of this paper can give an indication of what we might expect.

December 2005

Section A

20 multiple choice questions of 2 marks each

Section B: Interpretation of financial statements

1 Types of share capital; impact of leases on gearing
2 Depreciation and impairment
3 Consolidated income statement

Section C: Performance management

4 Business process re-engineering; cellular manufacturing; quality improvement
5 Construction of production budgets; incentive schemes
6 Activity Based Costing; relevant costs and benefits

June 2005

Section A

20 multiple choice questions of 2 marks each

Section B: Interpretation of financial statements

1 Current and deferred taxation
2 Definitions and accounting treatment of liabilities, provisions and contingent liabilities
3 Auditors' and directors' responsibilities and reasons for audit

Section C: Performance management

4 Target cost pricing and pricing strategies
5 Relevant cost and limiting factor analysis
6 Supply chain management and outsourcing

December 2004

Section A

20 multiple choice questions of 2 marks each

Section B: Interpretation of financial statements

1 Operating and Financial Review and Five Year Summary
2 Cash flow statement
3 Acquisition of an associated undertaking

Section C: Performance management

4 Incentive schemes
5 Activity Based Costing: calculations and discussions
6 Cash budget for a new business

June 2004

Section A

20 multiple choice questions of 2 marks each

Section B: Interpretation of financial statements

1 Qualities of financial information; accounting treatments and policies
2 Accounting for a finance lease
3 Statement of Recognised Gains and Losses; earnings per share

Section C: Performance management

4 Transfer pricing
5 Decision making and relevant costs
6 Materials requirements planning; manufacturing resource planning; optimised production technology

December 2003

Section A

20 multiple choice questions of 2 marks each

Section B: Interpretation of financial statements

1 Accounting for associates; consolidated balance sheet
2 Post balance sheet events; calculation of retained profit and total net assets
3 Accounting for inventories and construction contracts

Section C: Performance management

4 Activity based costing: calculations and discussion
5 Variance analysis: identification of reasons for variances
6 Decision-making

June 2003

Section A

20 multiple choice questions of 2 marks each

Section B: Interpretation of financial statements

1 Cash flow statement with memo summarising key issues

2 GAAP on revaluation of freehold properties and need to provide depreciation, plus impact on financial statements

3 Criteria for classification as associate, accounting treatment and reconciliation of investment values between individual company balance sheet and consolidated balance sheet

Section C: Performance management

4 Supply chain management, Just in Time purchasing and the use of IT
5 Pricing policy, market skimming, market penetration
6 Budget preparation

December 2002

Section A

20 multiple choice questions of 2 marks each

Section B: Interpretation of financial statements

1 Inventory valuation methods: calculation and discussion
2 Reserve movements and share issues
3 Value for money concept

Section C: Performance management

4 Analysis and reasons for variances
5 Activity based costing: calculations; strengths and weaknesses
6 Non-financial methods of performance evaluation

June 2002

Section A

20 multiple choice questions of 2 marks each

Section B: Interpretation of financial statements

1 Common size statements and ratio analysis
2 Depreciation: discussion and calculations; revaluations
3 Stewardship and the needs of user groups; useful accounting ratios

Section C: Performance management

4 Return on Investment and Residual Income calculations; discussion of EVA®
5 Discussion of budgeting and suggestions for an appropriate budgeting system
6 Decision making and performance measures

Pilot Paper

Section A

20 multiple choice questions of 2 marks each

Section B: Interpretation of financial statements

1 Explanation of various accounting terms
2 Substance over form; discussion and calculations on leases
3 Calculation of inflation adjusted figures and commentary

Section C: Performance management

4 Calculations and comparisons of absorption costing and activity-based costing
5 Non-financial performance indicators and balanced scorecards
6 Transfer pricing

Projects

General

Candidates are required, as part of their assessment, to submit a project for each module of the Diploma in Financial Management qualification. Each project will cover the two subject areas in the module. The Module A project will therefore cover:

- subject area 1 (Interpretation of Financial Statements)
- subject area 2 (Performance Management)

The project will be an integrated assignment covering the two subject areas together; there will not be separate assignments.

The nature of the projects is such that they will not require extensive research and can be completed without reference to sensitive work situations. The projects will relate to the subject matter of the individual subject areas, and candidates who have studied the syllabus of each subject area should be able to have a good attempt at the project. Each project should be approximately 5,000 words in length, including appendices and tables, but excluding references and bibliographies. The project will involve a mixture of calculations and narrative tasks.

The BPP Project Guidance manual will help you to prepare for the Project element of Module A.

You can order by calling 0845 751 100 (within the UK), +44(0)20 8740 2211 (from overseas) or by visiting www.bpp.com.

Part A

Regulation of financial statements

1

Regulation of financial statements

Topic list
1 International Accounting Standards Committee (IASC) Foundation
2 International Accounting Standards Board (IASB)
3 International Financial Reporting Standards
4 International Financial Reporting Interpretations Committee (IFRIC)
5 Generally Accepted Accounting Practice (GAAP)
6 The IASBs *Framework*
7 Role of the auditor and fair presentation
8 Entities not requiring published financial statements

Introduction

This chapter introduces the regulatory framework for financial reporting. Of particular importance is the role of the IASB.

We also consider the role of the auditor and the fundamental concept of the true and fair view.

Learning objectives

	Syllabus reference
• outline the purpose and underlying assumptions of the IASB *Framework for the Preparation and Presentation of Financial Statements*	1a
• identify the role of the International Accounting Standards Committee Foundation and its constituent bodies	1a
• explain the role of the International Accounting Standards Board and the International Financial Accounting Reporting Interpretations Committee	1a
• discuss the role of the auditor	1b
• explain the nature of the 'true and fair view' and 'fair presentation'	1b
• identify types of entities that do not require audited published financial statements	1a, 1b

1 International Accounting Standards Committee (IASC) Foundation

1.1 Introduction

In March 2001, the International Accounting Standards Committee (IASC) Foundation was formed as a not-for-profit corporation incorporated in the USA. The IASC Foundation is the parent entity of the International Accounting Standards Board (IASB) (see section 2)

1.2 Objectives

The objectives of the IASC Foundation are:

(a) to develop, in the public interest, a single set of high quality, understandable and enforceable global accounting standards that require high quality, transparent and comparable information in financial statements and other financial reporting to help participants in the world's capital markets and other users make economic decisions;

(b) to promote the use and rigorous application of those standards

(c) in fulfilling the objectives associated with (a) and (b) to take account of, as appropriate, the special needs of small and medium-sized entities and emerging economies; and

(d) to bring about convergence of national accounting standards and International Accounting Standards and International Financial Reporting Standards to high quality solutions.

1.3 Structure

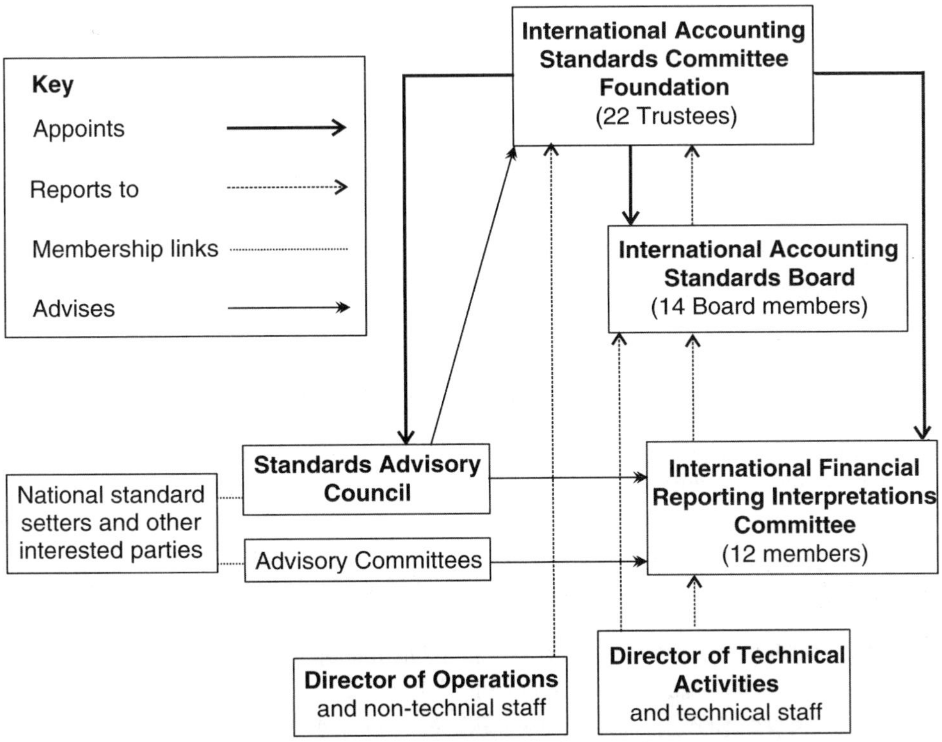

FAST FORWARD

The IASC Foundation Trustees appoint the IASB members, exercise oversight and raise the funds needed.

Trustees. The mix of trustees should broadly reflect the world's capital markets and a diversity of geographical and professional backgrounds. These are selected as follows:

(a) six from North America
(b) six from Europe
(c) six from the Asia/Oceania region; and
(d) four from any area, subject to establishing overall geographical balance

The IASC Foundation constitution also requires that the trustees should comprise an appropriate balance of professional backgrounds, including auditors, preparers, users, academics and other officials serving the public interest. To achieve this selection is normally after consultation with a range of organisations including the International Federation of Accountants (IFAC).

The Trustees appoint Members of the Board, the International Financial Reporting Interpretations Committee and the Standards Advisory Council. In addition to monitoring IASC Foundation's effectiveness and raising its funds the Trustees will approve IASC Foundation's budget and have responsibility for constitutional changes.

Standards Advisory Council. The Standards Advisory Council provides a formal vehicle for further groups and individuals with diverse geographic and functional backgrounds to give advice to the Board and, at times, to advise the Trustees.

2 International Accounting Standards Board (IASB)

FAST FORWARD

The IASB has sole responsibility for setting accounting standards (IFRSs).

2.1 Introduction

The International Accounting Standards Board (IASB) is an independent and privately funded accounting standard setter based in London. It has **sole responsibility** for setting accounting standards. Contributors include major accounting firms, private financial institutions, industrial companies throughout the world, central and development banks, and other international and professional organisations.

2.2 Structure of the IASB

The IASB has fourteen members selected by the IASC Foundation. They come from nine countries and have a variety of backgrounds with a mix of auditors, preparers of financial statements, users of financial statements and an academic. The Board consists of twelve full time members and two part-time members.

2.3 The IASB and current accounting standards

From April 2001 the IASB assumed its responsibilities from its predecessor body, the International Accounting Standards Committee (IASC). On that date it adopted all 41 of the International Accounting Standards (IASs) which had been issued by the IASC. It has also issued its own **International Financial Reporting Standards** (IFRS). So far 7 new IFRSs have been issued.

2.4 The IASB and IOSCO

The International Organisation of Securities Commissions (IOSCO) is the representative of the world's securities markets regulators. High quality information is vital for the operation of an efficient capital market, and differences in the quality of the accounting policies and their enforcement between countries leads to inefficiencies between markets. IOSCO has been active in encouraging and promoting the improvement and quality of IASs over the last ten years. Most recently, this commitment was evidenced by the agreement between IASC and IOSCO to work on a programme of 'core standards' which could be used by publicly listed entities when offering securities in foreign jurisdictions.

IOSCO spent a year reviewing the results of the project and released a report in May 2000 which recommended to all its members that they allow multinational issuers to use IASs, as supplemented by reconciliation, disclosure and interpretation where necessary to address outstanding substantive issues at a national or regional level.

IASB staff and IOSCO continue to work together to resolve outstanding issues and to identify areas where new IASB standards are needed.

2.5 European Commission and IASs

All listed entities in member states must use IASs in their consolidated financial statements from 2005.

To this end the IASB has undertaken an **improvements project**, dealing with **revisions to IAS**, for example in the area of materiality, presentation, leases, related parties and earnings per share. This has been matched in, for example, the UK, by a **convergence project**, bringing UK GAAP into line with IASs where these are better.

3 International Financial Reporting Standards

FAST FORWARD

You should be aware of the due process involved in producing international standards.

3.1 Authority

Requirements of International Financial Reporting Standards do not override national standards. However, there is growing harmonisation between national and international practices. For example in Europe the consolidated financial statements of many top multinationals are now prepared in conformity with national requirements, EC directives and IASs.

3.2 Due process

The overall agenda of the IASB will initially be set by discussion with the Standards Advisory Council. The process for developing an individual standard would involve the following steps.

Step 1 During the early stages of a project, IASB may establish an **Advisory Committee** to give advice on issues arising in the project. Consultation with the Advisory Committee and the Standards Advisory Council occurs throughout the project.

Step 2 IASB may develop and publish **Discussion Documents** for public comment.

Step 3 Following the receipt and review of comments, IASB would develop and publish an **Exposure Draft** for public comment.

Step 4 Following the receipt and review of comments, the IASB would issue a final **International Financial Reporting Standard**.

The period of exposure for public comment is normally 90 days. However, in exceptional circumstances, proposals may be issued with a comment period of 60 days. Draft IFRIC Interpretations are exposed for a 60 day comment period.

3.3 Current Standards

The current list is as follows.

International Accounting Standards		Date of issue
IAS 1 (revised)	Presentation of financial statements	Dec 2003
IAS 2 (revised)	Inventories	Dec 2003
IAS 7 (revised)	Cash flow statements	Dec 1992
IAS 8 (revised)	Accounting policies, changes in accounting estimates and errors	Dec 2003
IAS 10 (revised)	Events after the balance sheet date	Dec 2003
IAS 11 (revised)	Construction contracts	Dec 1993
IAS 12 (revised)	Income taxes	Nov 2000
IAS 14 (revised)	Segment reporting	Aug 1997
IAS 16 (revised)	Property, plant and equipment	Dec 2003
IAS 17 (revised)	Leases	Dec 2003
IAS 18 (revised)	Revenue	Dec 1993
IAS 19 (revised)	Employee benefits	Dec 2004
IAS 20	Accounting for government grants and disclosure of government assistance	Jan 1995

International Accounting Standards		Date of issue
IAS 21 (revised)	The effects of changes in foreign exchange rates	Dec 2003
IAS 23 (revised)	Borrowing costs	Dec 1993
IAS 24 (revised)	Related party disclosures	Dec 2003
IAS 26	Accounting and reporting by retirement benefit plans	Jan 1995
IAS 27 (revised)	Consolidated and separate financial statements	Dec 2003
IAS 28 (revised)	Investments in associates	Dec 2003
IAS 29	Financial reporting in hyperinflationary economies	Jan 1995
IAS 31 (revised)	Interests in joint ventures	Dec 2003
IAS 32 (revised)	Financial instruments: Presentation	Dec 2003
IAS 33 (revised)	Earnings per share	Dec 2003
IAS 34	Interim financial reporting	Feb 1998
IAS 36 (revised)	Impairment of assets	Mar 2004
IAS 37	Provisions, contingent liabilities and contingent assets	Sept 1998
IAS 38 (revised)	Intangible assets	Mar 2004
IAS 39 (revised)	Financial instruments: recognition and measurement	Dec 2004
IAS 40	Investment property	Dec 2003
IAS 41	Agriculture	Feb 2001
IFRS 1	First time adoption of International Financial Reporting Standards	June 2003
IFRS 2	Share-based payment	Feb 2004
IFRS 3	Business combinations	Mar 2004
IFRS 4	Insurance contracts	Mar 2004
IFRS 5	Non-current assets held for sale and discontinued operations	Mar 2004
IFRS 6	Exploration for and evaluation of mineral resources	Dec 2004
IFRS 7	Financial Instruments: Disclosures	Aug 2005

4 International Financial Reporting Interpretations Committee (IFRIC)

FAST FORWARD

IFRIC **interprets the application** of International Financial Reporting Standards.

The IASB has developed a procedure for issuing interpretations of its standards. This task is performed by the **International Financial Reporting Interpretations Committee** (IFRIC).

The duties of the IFRIC are:

(a) To interpret the application of International Financial Reporting Standards and provide timely guidance on financial reporting issues not specifically addressed in IFRSs or IASs in the context of the IASB's Framework, and undertake other tasks at the request of the Board.

(b) To have regard to the Board's objective of working actively with national standard setters to bring about convergence of national accounting standards and IFRSs to high quality solutions.

(c) To publish, after clearance by the Board, Draft Interpretations for public comment and consider comments made within a reasonable period before finalising an Interpretation.

(d) To report to the Board and obtain Board approval for final Interpretations.

In developing interpretations, the 12-person IFRIC will work closely with **similar national committees**. If no more than three of its members vote against an interpretation, the IFRIC will ask the Board to approve the interpretation for issue; as is the case for IASs, three-quarters of the Board must vote in favour of an interpretation. Interpretations will be formally published after approval by the Board.

5 Generally Accepted Accounting Practice (GAAP)

FAST FORWARD

The concept of what constitutes GAAP varies from country to country.

Key term

GAAP signifies all the rules, from whatever source, which govern accounting.

In individual countries this is seen primarily as a **combination** of:

- National company law
- National accounting standards
- Local stock exchange requirements

Although those sources are the basis for the GAAP of individual countries, the concept also includes the effects of **non-mandatory sources** such as:

- International accounting standards (but not after 2005 for listed entities in Europe)
- Statutory requirements in other countries

In many countries, like the UK, GAAP does not have any statutory or regulatory authority or definition, unlike other countries, such as the USA. The term is mentioned rarely in legislation, and only then in fairly limited terms.

There are different views of GAAP in different countries. In the UK it is seen as a dynamic concept. 'Generally accepted' does not simply mean 'generally adopted or used'. Any accounting practice which is legitimate in the circumstances should be regarded as GAAP based on factors including whether the practice is consistent with the fundamental concept of 'true and fair'.

This view is not held in all countries, however. In the USA particularly, the equivalent of a 'true and fair view' is 'fair presentation in accordance with GAAP'. Generally accepted accounting principles are defined as those principles which have 'substantial authoritative support'. Therefore accounts prepared in accordance with accounting principles for which there is not substantial authoritative support are presumed to be misleading or inaccurate.

The effect here is that 'new' or 'different' accounting principles are not acceptable unless they have been adopted by the mainstream accounting profession, usually the standard-setting bodies and/or professional accountancy bodies. This is much more rigid than the UK view expressed above.

6 The IASBs Framework

FAST FORWARD

The IASBs *Framework* provides a **conceptual** framework upon which IASs/IFRSs can be bared.

In July 1989 the old IASC produced a document, *Framework for the preparation and presentation of financial statements* (*'Framework'*). The *Framework* is, in effect, the **conceptual framework** upon which all IASs are based and hence which determines how financial statements are prepared and the information they contain.

The *Framework* consists of several sections or chapters, following on after a preface and introduction. These **chapters** are as follows.

- The objective of financial statements
- Underlying assumptions
- Qualitative characteristics of financial statements
- The elements of financial statements
- Recognition of the elements of financial statements
- Measurement of the elements of financial statements
- Concepts of capital and capital maintenance

We will look at the important details of the Framework in Chapter 3 and Chapter 4.

7 Role of the auditor and fair presentation

FAST FORWARD

The role of the auditor is to express an **opinion** as to whether the financial statements give a **true and fair view** or **present fairly**.

Without proper regulation, the directors of some companies might be tempted to produce accounts that are not properly prepared, and give a rosier or perhaps a misleading picture of the company's financial position. Compliance with accounting regulations needs to be monitored.

In most countries, audits are required under national statute in the case of a large number of undertakings including limited liability companies. The auditor, who must be professionally qualified, states expressly whether the accounts give a **true and fair view** or **present fairly**.

This opinion is given in the auditors' report. In other words, the role of the auditors is to provide **assurance** that, in their opinion, the accounts have been properly prepared. This gives the financial statement credibility.

Auditors must conduct an audit in accordance with standards set by an **International Audit and Assurance Standard Board (IAASB)**, which publishes International Standards on Auditing (ISAs).

Remember that the auditor furnishes a **report** that gives an **opinion** regarding the **truth and fairness** of the accounts. Beware of referring to the auditor's report as a certificate, as this implies that the auditor is certifying that the figures and disclosures are somehow correct. **In practice**, an audit will involve **checking samples** of **transactions** and **balances** that are designed to provide what is called '**reasonable assurance**'.

An auditor can provide two things that the shareholders of a business (and other users of company accounts) require:

(a) A knowledgeable review of the company's business and of its accounts

(b) An impartial view, since the accounts prepared by the company may not be impartially prepared by its directors

To provide a knowledgeable and impartial view, the auditor must be both properly qualified for the work, and also **independent**.

7.1 Small company audit exemption

Audits are expensive, and must be paid for by the company. There has been a lot of debate about whether the audit of small companies should be as extensive as the audit for larger companies. Small companies are often managed by their owner or owners, and the need to ensure that accounts give a true and fair view should not be as necessary. With larger companies, in contrast, the ownership (shareholders) and the management are much more likely to be different people, and the need to ensure true and fair reporting is therefore greater.

Whilst national legislation varies many countries have given small companies an exemption from the requirement to have an audit. This is the case in many EC countries where the exemption is based on the level of revenue of the companies. The maximum revenue of a company which qualifies as exempt under EC rules is £5.6m (in the UK).

7.2 True and fair/fair presentation

The auditor is required to report that the financial statements give a **true and fair view** or **present fairly** in all material respects the financial position, results and cash flows of the company concerned. (The terms true and fair and present fairly are equivalent).

The term 'true and fair' is not defined in law or audit guidance. Moreover, the courts have never tried to define it.

The application of the expression **'true and fair'** is therefore of a practical nature. Guidance gleaned from various sources suggests that certain factors should be taken into consideration:

- The concept of true and fair is dynamic and evolves in response to changes in **accounting** and **business practice**.
- It depends on the **financial reporting framework** used.
- The courts are unlikely to look for synonyms individually for the words 'true' and 'fair'. These should be **interpreted together** as a **single expression 'true and fair'.**

Key term

'True and fair' has no set definition. Broadly speaking it means 'reasonably accurate and not misleading'.

Under IFRS IAS 1 *Presentation of Financial Statements* defines fair presentation as follows.

Key term

Fair presentation requires the faithful presentation of the effects of transactions, other events and conditions in accordance with the definitions and recognition criteria for assets, liabilities, income and expenses set out in the *Framework for the Preparation and Presentation of Financial Statements.* The application of IFRSs with additional disclosure when necessary, is presumed to result in financial statements that achieve a fair presentation.

IAS 1 also states that the following are required for fair presentation:

- Selection and application of **accounting policies**
- Presentation of information in a manner which provides **relevant, reliable, comparable** and **understandable** information
- Additional **disclosure** where required

8 Entities not requiring published financial statements

FAST FORWARD

There is normally no legal requirement for businesses which are not companies to publish financial statements.

Generally, there is no direct legal requirement on businesses or organisations that are not companies to prepare financial statements. However, individuals who run their own business ('sole traders') or business partnerships need to prepare accounts in some form in order to prepare information for tax purposes.

Because these entities do not fall within the ambit of company legislation, they are not obliged to have a statutory external audit. However, a provider of finance, such as a bank or lender, may wish to see audited accounts from time to time

Key learning points

- The trustees of the **IASC Foundation** appoint members of the IASB.
- The IASB has sole responsibility for setting **accounting standards** (IFRSs).
- You should be aware of the **due process** involved in producing international standards.
- IFRIC **interprets the application** of International Financial Reporting Standards.
- The concept of what constitutes GAAP varies fro country to country.
- **GAAP** signifies **all the rules**, from whatever sources which govern accounting.
- The IASBs *Framework* provides a **conceptual framework** upon which IASs/IFRSs can be based.
- The role of the auditor is to express his **opinion** as to whether the financial statements give a **true and fair view** or **present fairly**.
- There is normally no legal requirement for businesses that are not companies to publish financial statements.

Quick quiz

1 What body currently produces International Financial Reporting Standards?

2 What is the relationship between the IASC Foundation and the IASB?

3 What do you understand by the term GAAP?

4 A conceptual framework is:

A A theoretical expression of accounting standards
B A list of key terms used by the IASB
C A statement of theoretical principles which form the frame of reference for financial reporting
D The proforma financial statements

5 Which of the following are chapters in the IASB *Framework?*

A Subsidiaries, associates and joint ventures
B Profit measurement in financial statements
C The objective of financial statements
D Accounting for interests in other entities
E Recognition of the elements of financial statements
F Presentation of financial information
G Substance of transactions in financial statements
H Qualitative characteristics of financial statements
I Quantitative characteristics of financial statements
J Measurement of the elements of financial statements
K Concepts of capital and capital maintenance
L The elements of financial statements.

6 What is the main reason why an audit is considered to be necessary?

Answers to quick quiz

1 International Accounting Standards Board (IASB).

2 The IASC Foundation appoints the members of the IASB. The IASB reports to the IASC Foundation.

3 GAAP is a combination of

- National company law
- National accounting standards
- Local stock exchange requirements
- International accounting standards
- Statutory requirements in other countries.

4 C

5 C, E, H, J, K and L.

6 The audit gives the financial statements credibility.

Part B
Financial information

Objectives of financial statements

Topic list
1 The purpose of financial statements
2 Assets and liabilities
3 The IASBs *Framework for the preparation and presentation of financial statements*
4 Accounting concepts: going concern and accruals

Introduction

This chapter introduces some key definitions and concepts. The IASBs *Framework* document is of particular importance as it forms the basis for all international accounting standards.

Learning objectives

On completion of this chapter you will be able to:

	Syllabus reference
• identify the nature of a business entity	2b
• explain the principle of control in defining the boundary of the reporting entity	2b
• describe the role of general purpose financial statements	2a
• define in broad terms the following elements of financial statements: profit, assets and liabilities	2d
• discuss the role of financial statements in assessing the stewardship of management	2a
• identify the users of financial statements and their information needs	2a
• describe the decision usefulness of financial statements	2a
• outline the types of financial information available to users	2d
• explain the need for information in respect of financial performance, financial position, generation of cash and financial adaptability	2a
• define assets and liabilities	2d
• describe and apply the concepts of going concern and accruals in preparing financial statements	2c, e

1 The purpose of financial statements

FAST FORWARD

Financial statements provide information about the **position** and **performance** of a business.

The main purpose of financial statements is to provide information about the **financial position** of a business entity, and about how it has **performed financially** over a given period of time. The individual financial statements, which will be explained in some detail later in this text, each provide particular information which could be of value to one or more interest groups.

1.1 What is a business entity?

FAST FORWARD

A reporting entity is a discrete, separately-identified unit or organisation that produces financial reports. A business entity may be a company, a group of companies, a business partnership or the business of a sole trader.

Financial statements are prepared for an 'entity' that makes money transactions. The term 'entity' can refer to non-business organisations and not-for-profit organisations, such as government departments, charities, clubs and societies. A '**business entity**' is involved specifically in business, usually for the purpose of making a profit: the term refers to companies, business partnerships and individuals running their own business ('sole traders').

An entity preparing financial statements (the '**reporting entity**') must be identifiable as a **distinct** and **discrete** unit or organisation; in other words, it should be a **cohesive** economic unit. To prepare financial statements, an entity must have a system of accounting for its transactions, because it is from the records of money transactions held in this system that financial statements are constructed. Such an accounting system is generally referred to as a 'book-keeping system'.

1.2 How does control define the boundary of the reporting entity

When beginning to study the interpretation of financial statements, it is convenient to think of the reporting entity as a single company. In reality, companies are more commonly linked together as a single **group**, with a **holding** or **parent company** and many subsidiary companies and sub-subsidiaries. A **subsidiary** is a company that is controlled by another company, for example through a controlling interest in its ordinary share capital.

1.3 Example

Suppose for example that Alpha Co owns 100% of the share capital of Beta Co, which in turn holds 100% of the share capital of Gamma Co.

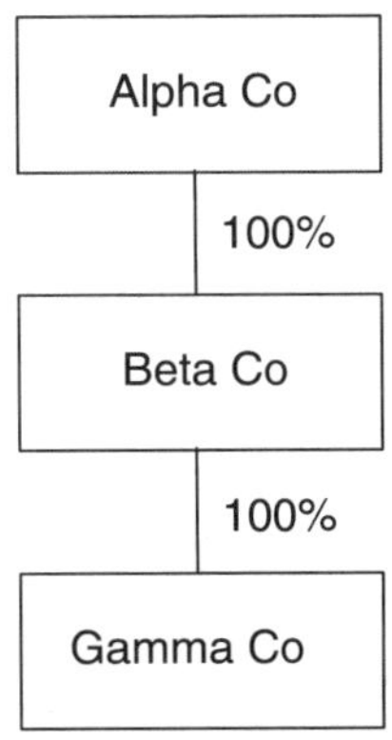

Alpha Co should provide statements about its financial performance and position (balance sheet, income statement, cash flow statement, and so on). But should it report exclusively on the performance of Alpha Co or should it report on the performance of Alpha, Beta and Gamma taken together, since Alpha Co controls the businesses of Beta and Gamma?

The view taken in financial reporting is that the reporting entity is not the individual company. **The reporting entity should be defined by the scope of control**. A parent company (holding company) of a group of companies should therefore present financial statements to its shareholders about the performance and position of the group as a whole. Published accounts are therefore usually '**group accounts**' or '**consolidated accounts**', which bring the performance and position of all the group companies together as a single entity.

Special features of group accounts are dealt with in chapter 10 of this text.

1.4 Financial performance

FAST FORWARD

Businesses of whatever size or nature exist to make a profit. A financial statement showing the profit or loss earned in a period is the income statement.

The purpose of a business is to make money for its owners. A business invests money in resources with the intention of making even more money. Business enterprises vary in character, size and complexity. They range from very small businesses (the local shopkeeper or plumber) to very large ones (eg Glaxo Smithkline, Marks and Spencer, Diageo). But the objective of earning profit is common to all of them.

Key term

Profit is the excess of income over expenditure. When expenditure exceeds income, the business is running at a loss.

One purpose of financial statements is to show whether a business has made a profit or a loss over a period of time from its operations. A statement showing the performance of a business has made in a given period of time is called a **income statement**.

Entities that do not exist to make a profit must nevertheless spend within their means. These organisations produce a performance statement disclosing their **income and expenditure** for a given period, rather than a statement of profit or loss.

The definition of profit above is slightly simplified. It is more correct to state that a profit or gain arises when the value of the owners' interest in a business rises, without the owners putting in any additional new capital. This definition might become clearer as you work your way through this text, but it is possible for a gain or a loss to arise without any transaction involving income or expenditure.

1.5 Financial position

FAST FORWARD

A statement of the financial position of an entity is a balance sheet. This shows the assets, liabilities and capital of the entity at a specific point.

Another purpose of financial statements is to show the financial position of an entity. In reality, the financial position of most businesses is always changing, and is not static. The financial position of a company next week is not going to be the same as its financial position now. However, a financial statement can only show the position of a business at a given point in time, and this 'snapshot' picture will hopefully give a fairly representative picture.

The main elements affecting the financial position of a business are:

(a) the economic resources it controls
(b) its financial structure
(c) its liquidity and solvency
(d) its capacity to adapt to changes in its environment

The financial position of a business (or any other entity) is largely concerned with what resources the business has and how much the business owes. This is reported in a statement known as a **balance sheet**, which shows the assets and liabilities of a business, and how much capital it has.

2 Assets and liabilities

2.1 Assets

FAST FORWARD

An **asset** is something valuable which a business owns or has the use of.

Examples of assets are factories, office buildings, warehouses, delivery vans, lorries, plant and machinery, computer equipment, office furniture, cash and also goods held in store awaiting sale to customers, and raw materials and components held in store by a manufacturing business for use in production.

Some assets are held and used in operations for a long time. An office building might be occupied by administrative staff for years. A machine might have a productive life of many years before it wears out. Other assets are held for only a short time. The owner of a newsagent shop, for example, will have to sell his newspapers on the same day that he gets them, and weekly newspapers and monthly magazines also have a short shelf life. The more quickly a business can sell the goods it has in store, the more profit it is likely to make, provided, of course, that the goods are sold at a higher price than the cost the business incurred to acquire them.

The definition of asset given above is somewhat simplified, although it is useful for introducing the idea of what an asset is. **A more formal definition is that an asset is a resource controlled by the business from which future economic benefits are expected to flow, arising out of a past transaction or event** (we will look at this definition in more detail in chapter 4).

(a) An item of office equipment is an asset. A company buying a **computer** will expect to **use it** over a **number of years**, and will derive **economic benefits** from it. The computer is an asset because it will provide economic benefits to the company in the future that have arisen out of a past event, the purchase of the computer.

(b) Money owed by a customer to a business is an asset of the business. For example, suppose that a company sells goods on credit to a customer for $3,000, and the customer is given 30 days to make the payment. Until the debt is paid, the customer is a 'debtor' of the company for $3,000. The **debt** is an **asset** because it gives the company **future economic** benefit (money income) arising out of a past transaction, the sale of the goods.

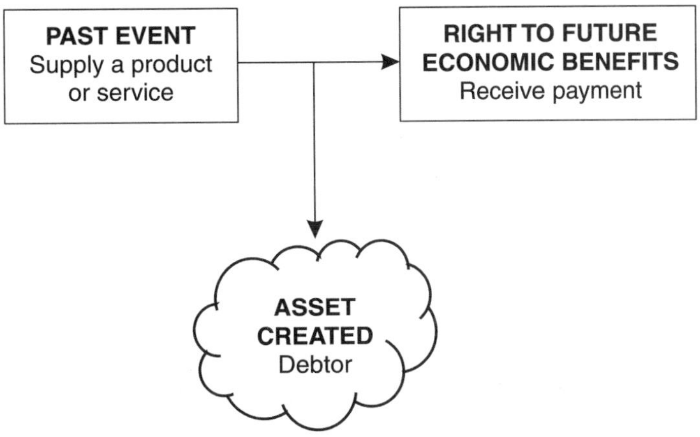

Key term

The customer who owes money is called a '**debtor**'. The balance owed in the business accounts will be referred to as a **'receivable'**.

2.2 Liabilities

FAST FORWARD

A **liability** is something which is owed to somebody else.

Key term

'Liabilities' is the accounting term for the debts of a business, what the business owes.

Some examples of liabilities are given below.

- A **bank loan** or bank **overdraft**. The liability is the amount which must eventually be repaid to the bank.
- **Amounts owed to suppliers** for goods purchased but not yet paid for. For example, a boat-builder might buy some sails on credit from a sail-maker, which means that the boat-builder does not have to pay for the sails until some time after they have been delivered. Until the boat-builder pays what he owes, the sail-maker will be his **creditor** for the amount owed. Note that the supplier who is owed money is called a **'creditor'**. The balance payable by the business will be referred to as a **'payable'**.
- **Taxation** owed to the government. A business pays tax on its profits but there is normally a gap in time between when a company declares its profits and becomes liable to pay tax and the time when the tax bill must eventually be paid.

Again, there is a more 'formal' definition of liability. A liability has been defined in the IASB's Framework as a **present obligation of the entity arising from past events, the settlement of which is expected to result in an outflow from the entity of resources embodying economic benefits** (we will look at this definition in more detail in chapter 4).

The ASB definitions are important and play a key role in financial reporting. Do try to memorise them.

Activity 2.1

What do you think the following items are, an asset or a liability?

Item	*Asset (A) or Liability (L)*
Money owed to a company by a customer for the provision of consultancy services	
Shares held by the company in another company, Dredge Co	
Sales Tax collected from customers and owed to the tax authority.	
Money held in a bank deposit	
Company car used by the chief executive	
Damages for unfair dismissal owed to a former employee	

3 The IASBs Framework for the preparation and presentation of financial statements

FAST FORWARD

There are various groups of people who need information about the activities of a business. You should be fully aware of these different user groups and their varying needs.

3.1 Role of general purpose financial statements

The IASBs *Framework* states that 'the objective of financial statements is to provide information about the reporting entity's financial position, performance and changes in financial position of an entity that is useful to a **wide range of users** for **making economic decisions**.'

Financial information about a company is of interest to a wide range of users. Some of these users are able to obtain special-purpose reports about a company specific to their information needs. Management can obtain internal management accounting reports, and on occasion, someone else, such as a lending bank or the tax authorities, can obtain specially-prepared reports. Many users of accounts, however, do not have access to special-purpose reports, and must rely for their information on **general purpose financial statements**, such as the company's published financial statements.

3.2 Users of financial statements

The following diagram depicts the users of financial statements.

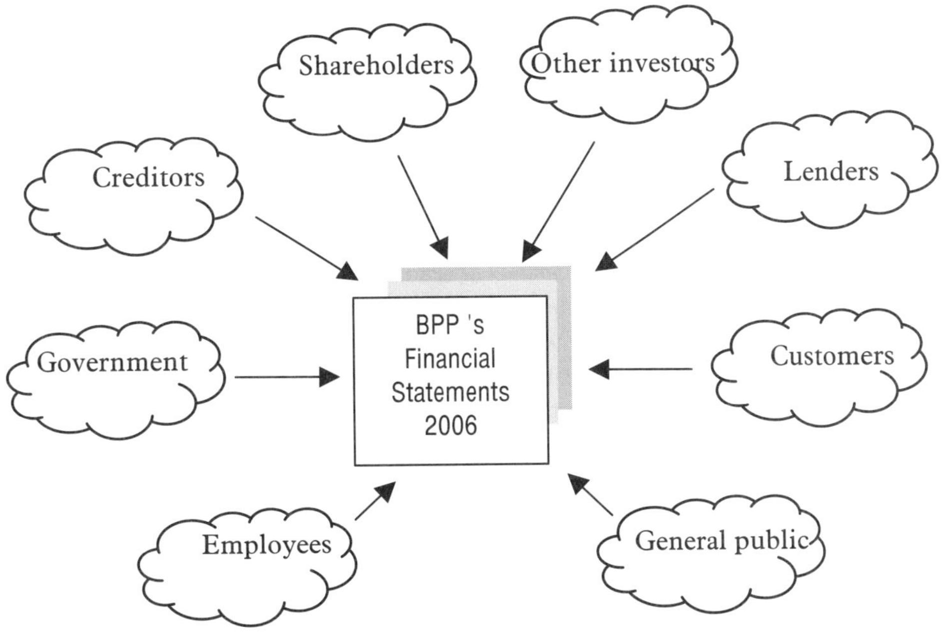

The IASB suggests that general purpose financial statements will meet the needs of most users.

3.3 Financial statements for assessing stewardship

Management is accountable to investors for the stewardship of the company. To understand this, you might find it useful to think of the stewardship of an estate, which involves looking after the assets and condition of the estate, and managing it in the interest of the owner. In much the same way, managers are responsible for the safeguarding of the assets and other resources of the company, and for putting these resources to an efficient and profitable use. Investors will be interested in any **information that helps them to judge how well management has carried out their stewardship responsibility**.

3.4 Decision usefulness of financial statements

Various groups make use of a company's financial statements to make economic decisions.

(a) Present and potential **investors** in the company will consider their investment decision. Should they buy shares in the company? Should they sell their shares? To make an investment decision, the investor needs information about profitability and the ability to generate cash to pay dividends, and also about the risks in the investment. Financial statements should help an investor to assess both the cash-generating capabilities of a company, and also its ability to respond to risks and change (its financial adaptability).

(b) **Lenders** to a company will be interested in any information that helps them to assess whether the company will have the ability to meet its obligations: to pay interest and repay the loan principal on time. Potential lenders need similar information to decide whether to lend to the company, and if so, how much and on what terms.

(c) **Suppliers** to the company and other **trade creditors** need to know how reliable the company will be in paying its debts, and how much credit can safely be given.

(d) **Employees** want information about the financial stability and profitability of their employer, particularly in the part of the company's business where they work. Their decision to remain with the company will depend to a large extent on the ability of the company to continue to offer them secure and well-paid employment. They will also be interested in how much the company is earning in order to reach a view on what remuneration levels should be.

(e) **Customers** are interested in the financial performance and position of a company in order to decide whether to continue buying from it. Where a customer relies on a long-term warranty, or expects to purchase replacement parts from the company over a long period, it will want reassurance that the company is financially stable, with good long-term future prospects.

(f) The **government** (and its agencies) can often obtain the information it needs from a company from special-purpose reports. Even so, general purpose financial statements can provide additional useful information. For example, the tax authorities are provided with specially-prepared information about the company's trading and profits to determine how much tax is payable. A comparison with general purpose financial statements can then help the tax authorities to asses whether the amounts payable in tax seem consistent with the published information. They would certainly be interested if a company declares profits of several million pounds but pays no corporation tax.

(g) Enterprises affect members of the **public** in a variety of ways. A major employer in a local community, for example, will help to boost the local economy and stimulate business and employment. Members of the general public might therefore use the financial statements of a company to assess trends and recent developments in its business, and the implications these might have in the future.

3.5 Types of financial information available to users

The information needs of different users are not the same. General purpose financial statements do not provide all the information that individuals need, or would like, to make their decisions, and the **limitations** of a company's report and accounts should be understood. Financial statements are **backward-looking**, reporting what has happened in the past, when users are more often concerned with the **future**. They also report on the company in purely **financial** terms, and do not properly address **non-financial** matters.

Managers responsible for the running of a business are likely to find **detailed management accounts** showing actual performance against budget, usually on a monthly basis, to be more useful than statutory financial statements. Moreover, these are likely to be used alongside **business plans** projected into the future usually over a period of three to five years.

3.6 Investor focus

The *Framework* states that 'As investors are providers of risk capital to the entity, the provision of financial statements that meet their needs will also meet most of the needs of other users that financial statements can satisfy'. Investors need information about the ability of a company to generate profits and cash flows from its operations and on the company's financial adaptability (ie its ability to respond to unexpected events and new opportunities). Essentially, other user groups are interested in the same information.

3.7 The information required by investors

Investors need information about a company's financial performance and financial position.

(a) **Financial performance** relates to the **return** that the company has made on the **resources** at its disposal. Information about performance provides an account of the **stewardship** by management, and can also be used to assess the ability of the company to **generate** cash from its **existing resources**. Information about historical performance can help investors to make judgements about future prospects.

(b) The **financial position** of a company relates to the assets that it owns (including its cash position), the liabilities it owes and the amount of capital invested. This information helps investors to assess the **stewardship of management**. It also helps them to understand how the **future cash flows** generated by the business will be distributed among those with an interest in or a claim on the company (eg lenders, trade creditors, employees and shareholders). Information about the cash position and liquidity helps investors to assess the **ability** of the company to **meet** its **financial obligations** as they fall due. Information about the **risk profile** of a company will help them to judge the **financial adaptability** of the company, and its ability to deal with **unexpected future setbacks and opportunities**.

(c) Information about **changes in the financial position** of an entity is useful in order to assess its investing, financing and operating activities during the reporting period. This information is useful in providing the user with a basis to assess the ability of the enterprise to **generate cash** and cash equivalents and the needs of the business to **utilise** those cash flows.

(d) The main general purpose financial statements are the **balance sheet** of a company, an **income statement** for the period under review and a **cash flow statement** for the same period. In broad terms, profits and cash flow information can be used to assess the **ability of the company to generate cash**. A balance sheet provides information about the **financial position**. Taken together, they provide information on **performance** and the **stewardship of management**.

Exam focus point

A question in the June 2002 UK exam required an explanation of the word 'stewardship', a discussion of the needs of user groups and the identification of accounting ratios that might be relevant for the users of financial statements.

Activity 2.2

It is easy to see how 'internal' people get hold of accounting information. A senior manager, for example, can just go along to the accounts department and ask the staff there to prepare whatever accounting statements he needs. But external users of accounts cannot do this. How, in practice, can (a) a business contact, (b) a financial analyst, (c) a bank or (d) an employee of the company obtain financial statements about the company?

4 Accounting concepts: going concern and accruals

In order to meet their objectives financial statements are prepared on the going concern and accruals basis.

4.1 Going concern

FAST FORWARD

The going concern concept requires assets to be valued on the assumption that the business will continue and will not be broken up or dissolved.

Key term

The entity is normally viewed as a **going concern**, that is, as continuing in operation for the foreseeable future. It is assumed that the entity has neither the intention nor the necessity of liquidation or of curtailing materially the scale of its operations. *(IASB Glossary)*

This assumption is based on the notion that, when preparing a normal set of accounts, it is always expected that the business will **continue to operate** in approximately the same manner for the foreseeable future (at least the next 12 months should be considered). In particular, the entity will not go into liquidation or scale down its operations in a material way.

The main significance of the going concern assumption is that the assets of the business **should not be valued at their 'break-up' value**, which is the amount that they would sell for if they were sold off piecemeal and the business were thus broken up.

Example: going concern

Suppose, for example, that Emma acquires a T-shirt printing machine at a cost of $60,000. The asset has an estimated life of six years, and it is normal to write off the cost of the asset to the income statement over this time. In this case a depreciation cost of $10,000 per year will be charged.

Using the going concern assumption, it would be presumed that the business will continue its operations and so the asset will live out its full six years in use. A depreciation charge of $10,000 will be made each year, and the value of the asset in the balance sheet will be its cost less the accumulated amount of depreciation charged to date. After one year, the **net book value** of the asset would therefore be $(60,000 – 10,000) = $50,000, after two years it would be $40,000, after three years $30,000 etc, until it has been written down to a value of 0 after 6 years.

Now suppose that this asset has no other operational use outside the business, and in a forced sale it would only sell for scrap. After one year of operation, its scrap value might be, say, $8,000.

The net book value of the asset, applying the going concern assumption, would be $50,000 after one year, but its immediate sell-off value only $8,000. It might be argued that the asset is over-valued at $50,000 and that it should be written down to its break-up value (ie in the balance sheet it should be shown at $8,000 and the balance of its cost should be treated as an expense). However, provided that the going concern assumption is valid, so that the asset will continue to be used and will not be sold, it is appropriate accounting practice to value the asset at its net book value.

(We will look at the treatment of assets in more detail in chapter 8).

Activity 2.3

A retailer commences business on 1 January and buys inventory of 20 washing machines, each costing $100. During the year he sells 17 machines at $150 each. How should the remaining machines be valued at 31 December if:

(a) He is forced to close down his business at the end of the year and the remaining machines will realise only $60 each in a forced sale?

(b) He intends to continue his business into the next year?

If the going concern assumption is not followed, that fact must be disclosed, together with:

(a) The basis on which the financial statements have been prepared; and
(b) The reasons why the entity is not considered to be a going concern.

4.2 Accrual basis of accounting

FAST FORWARD

The non-cash effect of transactions should be reflected in the accounting period in which they occur and not in the period any cash involved is received or paid.

The revised IAS 1 gives a definition of accruals based on recognition. However, for your exam the definition under the old IAS 1 is more relevant.

Key term

Accrual basis of accounting. The effects of transactions and other events are recognised when they occur (and not as cash or its equivalent is received or paid) and they are recorded in the accounting records and reported in the financial statements of the periods to which they relate. *(IAS 1, old version)*

Entities should prepare their financial statements on the basis that transactions are recorded in them, not as the cash is paid or received, but as the revenues or expenses are **earned or incurred** in the accounting period to which they relate.

According to the accrual assumption, then, in computing profit revenue earned must be **matched against** the expenditure incurred in earning it.

Example: accrual

Suppose that Emma (from Paragraph 4.1 above), prints 20 T-shirts in her first month of trading (May) at a cost of $5 each. She then sells all of them for $10 each. Emma has therefore made a profit of $100 by matching the revenue ($200) earned from the sale of 20 T-shirts against the cost ($100) of acquiring them.

If, however, Emma had only sold 18 T-shirts, it would have been incorrect to charge her income statement with the cost of 20 T-shirts, as she still has two T-shirts in inventory. If she intends to sell them in June she is likely to make a profit on the sale. Therefore, only the purchase cost of 18 T-shirts ($90) should be matched with her sales revenue, leaving her with a profit of $90. ($180 – $90).

The two remaining T-shirts would be carried forward in the balance sheet as assets (inventory) held at a cost of $10. (2 × $5).

If, however, Emma had decided to give up selling T-shirts, then the going concern assumption would no longer apply and the value of the two T-shirts in the balance sheet would be a break-up valuation rather than cost. Similarly, if the two unsold T-shirts were now unlikely to be sold at more than their cost of $5 each (say, because of damage or a fall in demand) then they should be recorded on the balance sheet at their net realisable value (ie the likely eventual sales price less any expenses incurred to make them saleable, eg paint) rather than cost. This also shows the application of the **prudence concept**, which we will look at chapter 4.

In this example, the concepts of going concern and accrual are linked. Because the business is assumed to be a going concern it is possible to carry forward the cost of the unsold T-shirts as a charge against profits of the next period.

Key learning points

- Financial statements provide information about the position and performance of a business.
- A reporting entity is a discrete, separately-identified unit or organisation that produces financial reports. A business entity may be a company, a group of companies, a business partnership or the business of a sole trader.
- Businesses of whatever size or nature exist to make a profit. A financial statement showing the profit or loss earned in a period is the income statement.
- A statement of the financial position of an entity is a balance sheet. This shows the assets, liabilities and capital of the entity at a specific point.
- An asset is something which a business owns or has use of.
- A liability is something which is owed to somebody else.
- There are various groups of people who need information about the activities of a business. You should be fully aware of these different user groups and their varying needs.
- The going concern concept requires assets to be valued on the assumption that the business will continue and will not be broken up or dissolved.
- The accruals basis of accounting requires the non-cash effect of transactions to be reflected in the accounting period in which they occur and not in the period any cash involved is received or paid.

Quick quiz

1. What is profit?
2. What are the main elements affecting the financial position of a business?
3. Do you think that petty cash held on the business's premises would be classified as an asset or a liability?
4. List three groups of people who might be interested in a company's financial statements.
5. Why might a bank be interested in the financial statements of a company?
6. What is the going concern concept?
7. Why is the accruals basis of accounting so important?

Answers to quick quiz

1. The excess of income over expenditure.
2. The economic resources it controls, its financial structure, its liquidity and solvency.
3. An asset.
4. Managers of the company, shareholders, trade contacts, providers of finance, tax authorities, employees, financial analysts and advisers, government agencies, the public.
5. In order to satisfy itself as to the company's financial position before giving it a loan.
6. The assumption in the preparation of the financial statements of an entity that it will continue in existence for the foreseeable future.
7. Because when financial performance for a period is being measured, items of income and expenditure should be included in the accounting period to which they actually relate rather than being shown in the period when the cash involved is received or paid.

Answers to activities

2.1

Item	*Asset (A) or Liability (L)*
Money owed to a company by a customer for the provision of consultancy services. (The customer owing money is called a debtor.)	A
Shares held by the company in another company, Dredge Co. (This is an investment.)	A
Sales Tax collected from customers and owed to the tax authority	L
Money held in a bank deposit	A
Company car used by the chief executive	A
Damages for unfair dismissal owed to a former employee	L

2.2 Any of these user groups could obtain the latest filed statutory accounts for the company from the Registrar of Companies or equivalent organisation. If the company is small or medium-sized, however, the accounts may be in an abbreviated form. Public companies whose shares are traded on the Stock Exchange are normally required to provide copies of their most recent published accounts to anyone who asks for them.

There is a greater problem in obtaining financial information from private companies. A trade contact, such as a supplier, can demand to see financial statements as a condition of doing business with the company. Similarly, a bank can demand to see financial information as a condition of granting a loan or overdraft facility.

Employees, as members of the public, are entitled to see the statutory accounts of their company employer. Some companies choose to provide financial statements prepared specifically for the benefit of their employees, but this is not normally a legal requirement.

2.3 (a) If the business is to be closed down, the remaining three machines must be valued at the amount they will realise in a forced sale, ie 3 × \$60 = \$180.

(b) If the business is regarded as a going concern, the inventory unsold at 31 December will be carried forward into the following year, when the cost of the three machines will be matched against the eventual sale proceeds in computing that year's profits. The three machines will therefore appear in the balance sheet at 31 December at cost, 3 × \$100 = \$300.

Assets, liabilities and the accounting equation

Topic list
1 Introduction: accounting fundamentals
2 The business as an entity separate from its owners
3 The accounting equation
4 The business equation
5 Payables and receivables
6 Double entry bookkeeping
7 The business equation as a link between profit and changes in the accounting equation

Introduction

This chapter looks at the way that business transactions are summarised to form financial information, particularly in the balance sheet. Whilst the syllabus does not require a detailed knowledge of double entry bookkeeping an understanding of the principles in this chapter is essential to your comprehension of the rest of this text.

Learning objectives

On completion of this chapter you will be able to:

	Syllabus reference
• identify the impact of simple business transactions on the assets, liabilities and capital of a business	2b, 2d
• explain the effect of simple business transactions on the profit of a business	2d
• interpret the accounting equation and business equation	2d
• acknowledge that every business transaction has a 'dual effect'	2d
• differentiate the nature of the accounting equation and the business equation	2d
• outline the elements of a balance sheet are assets, liabilities and capital, and the elements of an income statement are sales income and expenditure	2d
• describe the inter-relationship between the income statement and the balance sheet	3a(i), 3a(ii)

1 Introduction: accounting fundamentals

In order to understand financial statements properly, it is important to understand not only what the elements of financial statements are, but also how these elements interact. An accounting or book-keeping system is used to record business transactions. Financial statements are produced from the **accounting records** in the system at the end of a financial reporting period, and these records include all the transactions that have taken place since the previous financial statements were prepared.

Every business transaction has an effect on the financial position of a business. Business transactions involving income or expenditure affect both the profit of the business and its financial position. The effect of business transactions on the financial position of a business (on its assets, liabilities or its owners' capital) will be explained by means of the **accounting equation**. The effect of some transactions on profit will be explained with the **business equation**, and the link between profitability and changes in financial position will be explained by the relationship between the accounting and business equations.

2 The business as an entity separate from its owners

FAST FORWARD

In accounting a business is treated as an **entity that is separate from its owners**. Owners put capital into the business, including retained profits, and capital represents what the business 'owes' to its owner.

Before looking at the accounting equation, a key concept in accounting needs to be introduced. This is the **separate entity** concept. The preparation of accounts and financial statements starts from the assumption that the business is a separate entity, separate from its owners. For example, if Paula Bell sets up a hairdressing business, All Curls, the accounting records and financial statements of the business will be prepared on the assumption that the business, All Curls, is separate from its owner, Paula Bell. The owner is seen as 'putting money into the business'. The money put into a business by its owner or owners is called 'owners' capital'.

A **company** by law is a legal person, separate from its owners, the shareholders. For example, a company can make contracts in its own right, such as contracts to buy, to sell, to borrow and to employ people. The separation in the financial statements of the company as a business entity from its shareholders, who provide capital, is therefore supported in concept by legal reality.

Business partnerships and the businesses of sole traders are not legal persons. Even so, the separate entity concept is applied in accounting. Owners' capital is money the owners have invested in the business. The capital 'belongs' to the owners, and it could be said that the owners have a claim on the business for the capital they have invested, or that the business has an obligation to the owners for the capital they have provided.

2.1 Capital

The money put into a business by its owners is **capital**. As long as that money is invested, **accountants will treat the capital as money owed to the proprietor by the business**.

Key term

> **Capital** is an investment of money (funds) with the intention of earning a return. A business proprietor invests capital with the intention of earning **profit**. The business owes the capital and the profit to the proprietor.

Capital invested is therefore a form of **liability**. It represents a claim on the business, or an obligation of the business to someone else.

3 The accounting equation

FAST FORWARD

> An accounting equation can be used to show the value of the assets, liabilities and capital of a business at any point in time. Total assets are always equal to the sum of total liabilities plus owners' capital.

Since a business is a separate entity from its owners, it follows that:

(a) the business can 'owe money' to its owners, and capital should be treated as a form of liability

(b) the assets and liabilities of the business should be treated as belonging to the business, rather than its owners.

A fundamental rule of accounting, which flows from the separate entity concept, is that **the assets of a business will always be equal to the sum of its liabilities plus its owners' capital.** This is the accounting equation, and the practice of financial accounting is built on it.

FAST FORWARD

> An accounting equation is a balance sheet of a business.

Formula to learn

> **The accounting equation**
>
> Assets = Liabilities + Capital

This is the format in which the **balance sheet** of a business is shown. A balance sheet, like the accounting equation, is simply a statement of the assets, liabilities and capital of a business at a particular point in time. Both the accounting equation and the balance sheet of a business are altered by every business transaction, but the basic rule of 'Assets = Liabilities + Capital' always remains true.

Let's demonstrate this with an example, which we will build up as this chapter progresses.

3.1 Example: The accounting equation

On 1 July, Eliza Doolittle decides to open up a flower stall in the market, to sell flowers and potted plants. She has $2,500 to put into her business.

As soon as the business is set up, an 'accountant's picture' can be drawn of what it **owns** and what it **owes**. The business begins by **owning** the cash that Eliza has put into it, $2,500. Does it **owe** anything? The answer is **yes**.

The business is a separate entity in accounting terms. It has obtained its **assets**, in this example cash, from its owner, Eliza Doolittle. **It therefore 'owes' this amount of money to its owner.** The money is the owner's starting capital. If Eliza changed her mind and decided not to go into business after all, the business would be dissolved by the 'repayment' of the cash by the business to Eliza.

Capital invested is therefore a form of **liability.** Adapting this to the idea that liabilities and assets are always equal amounts, we can state the accounting equation as follows.

Formula to learn

The accounting equation 1

Assets = Liabilities + Capital

$2,500 (cash) = $0 + $2,500

3.2 Example continued: different assets

Eliza Doolittle purchases a market stall from Sanjay Patel for $1,800.

She also purchases some flowers and potted plants from a trader in the New Covent Garden wholesale market, at a cost of $650.

This leaves $50 in cash, after paying for the stall and goods for resale, out of the original $2,500. She is now ready for her first day of market trading on 3 July. How does the accounting equation look now?

Solution

The assets of the business have now changed. There is less cash, but the business now owns a stall and some flowers and plants. At 3 July, before trading begins, the state of her business is as follows.

Assets		=	*Liabilities*	+	*Capital*
	$				
Stall	1,800		$0		$2,500
Flowers and plants	650				
Cash	50				
	2,500				

There is no change in the capital of the business. There has simply been a reduction of $2,450 in one asset (cash) and a corresponding increase in two other types of asset.

3.3 Example continued: trading to make a profit

On 3 July Eliza has a very successful day. She sells all of her flowers and plants, for $900 cash.

Since Eliza has sold goods costing $650 to earn income (often referred to in accounting as 'revenue') of $900, we can say that she has earned a **profit** of $(900 – 650) = $250 on the day's trading.

Profit, like capital, belongs to the owners of a business. It's why they invest in their business in the first place. In this case, the $250 belongs to Eliza Doolittle. However, although the money is in Eliza's own hands, it is treated at the moment as remaining within the business. As long as a **business retains its profits, and does not pay anything out to its owners, the retained profits are accounted for as an addition to the proprietor's capital:** they become part of that capital.

This is how the accounting equation looks for Eliza's business after making the profit of $250. Notice that the total amount of assets and the owner's capital have increased by $250, the profit earned.

Assets	$	=	*Liabilities*	+	*Capital*	$
Stall	1,800				Capital introduced	2,500
Flowers and plants	0				Retained profit	250
Cash (50 + 900)	950					
	2,750		$0			2,750

So we could expand the accounting equation as follows.

Formula to learn

The accounting equation with retained profits

Assets = Liabilities + (Capital introduced + Retained profits)

3.4 Increase in net assets

Key term

Net assets = Total assets – Total liabilities

Another way of showing the accounting equation is as follows.

Assets – Liabilities	=	Capital
Net assets	=	Capital

At the beginning and then at the end of 3 July Eliza Doolittle's financial position was as follows.

	Net assets	=	*Capital*
(a) At the beginning of the day:	\$(2,500 – 0)	=	\$2,500
(b) At the end of the day:	\$(2,750 – 0)	=	\$2,750
Increase in net assets	250	= Retained profit for day	250

We can now state various principles.

(a) At any point in time, a business's **net assets** represent the **capital introduced** by the owner plus the business's **retained profit** to that point in time.

(b) At a later point in time, the **increase** in the business's net assets represents the additional **profit made** in the intervening period.

(c) **Total** net assets at that later point represent the capital introduced by the owner plus the business's **increased** retained profit.

For example:

		$m			$m			$m
1 Jan	Net assets	170	=	Capital introduced	20	+	Retained profit	150
1 Jan-31 Dec	Increase in net assets	34	=				Profit made in year	34
31 Dec	Total net assets	204	=	Capital introduced	20	+	Total retained profit	184

3.5 Drawings

FAST FORWARD

Profits earned by a business add to capital, and losses reduce capital. **Drawings** reduce capital. This means that the capital of a business is increased by the retained profits (profits earned minus drawings).

Key term

Drawings are amounts of money taken out of a business by its owner. The term 'drawings' is used for business partnerships and the businesses of sole traders. For companies, money taken out of the business by its owners is a **dividend**.

3.6 Example continued: drawings

Since Eliza Doolittle has made a profit of $250 from her first day's work, she feels justified in drawing some of the profits out of the business, for living expenses. She decides to pay herself $180, in what she thinks of as 'wages', as a fair reward for her day's work.

If Eliza had hired someone to do the work for her, and paid that person $180, the payment would be wages (or salary). The wages or salary would then be treated as an expense of the business, and deducted in calculating the amount of profit that the business has earned. In contrast, money paid out of profits to its owner is not salary or wages.

As Eliza is the **owner** of her business, the $180 is **not** an expense to be deducted before the figure of profit is arrived at.

Any amounts paid by a business to its proprietor are treated by accountants as withdrawals of profit (drawings), and not as expenses incurred by the business. In the case of Eliza's business, the position is that the profit **earned** is the $250 surplus on sale of flowers, but the profit **retained** in the business is $(250 – 180) = $70. In other words, the business made a profit of $250, of which $180 has been taken out as drawings and only $70 has been retained in the business.

	$
Profit earned by business	250
Less: profit withdrawn by Eliza	(180)
Profit retained in the business	70

The drawings are taken in cash, and so the business loses $180 of its cash assets. After the drawings have been made, the accounting equation would be restated as follows.

Assets		=	*Liabilities*	+	*Capital*	
	$					$
Stall	1,800				Capital introduced	2,500
Flowers and plants	0				Profit earned	250
Cash $(950 – 180)	770				Less drawings	(180)
	2,570	=	$0	+		2,570

The increase in net assets since trading operations began is now only $(2,570 – 2,500) = $70, which is the amount of the retained profits.

Profits are recorded in the accounting equation (and balance sheet) of a business because they are **capital as long as they are retained in the business**. When they are paid out as drawings, the business suffers a **reduction in capital**.

We can therefore restate the accounting equation again.

Formula to learn

The accounting equation adjusted for withdrawal of profit

Assets = Liabilities + Capital introduced + (Earned profit – Drawings)

3.7 Dual effect of all business transactions

FAST FORWARD

All business transactions have a **dual effect**. The dual effect of transactions is the basis of the **'double entry' system of book-keeping** that is used to record business transactions.

It is essential to remember that the basic equation (Assets = Liabilities + Capital) always holds good. This means, for example, that if a transaction has the effect of adding an asset to the resources of a business, there will be a reduction in another asset by an equal amount, or there will be an increase in capital, or an increase in a liability.

Any transaction affecting the business has a **dual effect**, as shown in the table below.

	Asset	=	*Capital*	+	*Liabilities*
	Increase		Increase		
or	Increase				Increase
or			Increase		Decrease
or			Decrease		Increase
or	Decrease		Decrease		
or	Decrease				Decrease

Activity 3.1

Consider each of the transactions below, and mark on the grid how assets, liabilities and capital will be increased or decreased by the transaction. We have done the first one for you.

(a) A business is informed by its bank that it no longer owes the bank $100 in bank charges.

(b) The business finds it has been overcharged $50 for some furniture it bought on credit.

(c) A gas bill of $200 is received by the business.

(d) The owner withdraws $500 from the business.

(e) Cash is introduced into the business by its owner.

(f) A car is bought by the business, for payment in one month's time.

Transaction	=	*Assets*	=	*Capital*	+	*Liabilities*
a				Increase		Decrease
b						
c						
d						
e						
f						

4 The business equation

FAST FORWARD

The increase in net assets during a period of time is explained by the retained profit for the period (profit earned minus drawings) plus any new capital introduced. This connection between profits and changes in net assets is an expression of the **business equation**.

The business equation is an elaboration of the accounting equation which gives a definition of profits earned. Whereas the accounting equation is a rudimentary balance sheet, the business equation is a way of showing the link between the income statement and the opening balance sheet at the start of a period and the closing balance sheet at the end. The example of Eliza Doolittle has shown that **the amount of profit earned** in a time period can be related to the **increase in the net assets** of the business, **the drawings of profits** by the proprietor and **the introduction of new capital**.

We know that

Assets	=	Liabilities	+	Capital

which is the same as

Assets	=	Liabilities	+	Capital introduced
			+	Retained profits

which is the same as

Assets	=	Liabilities	+	Capital introduced
			+	Retained profits
			–	Drawings

As time goes on, **retained profit** (profit earned less profit taken out in drawings) builds up the amount of capital in the business. At the start of an accounting period, retained profits will form **part of the 'opening balance' of capital**, i.e. the business capital at the start of the period. As we proceed through another period of trading, additional profit will (hopefully) be earned. So we should look at the accounting equation again.

Formula to learn

The accounting equation re-stated

Assets = Liabilities + Capital introduced
+ Profit retained in previous periods
+ Profit earned in current periods
– Drawings in current period

Let's see how this works in the case of Eliza Doolittle.

4.1 Example continued: earning more profits

The next market day is on 10 July, and Eliza purchases more flowers and plants for cash, at a cost of $740. She is not feeling well, because of a heavy cold, and so she accepts the offer of help for the day from her cousin, Charlie, whom she agrees to pay a wage of $40.

Eliza and Charlie sell all their goods for $1,100 cash. Eliza pays Charlie his wage of $40 and draws out $200 for herself. How do these transactions affect Eliza's capital?

Solution

The accounting equation before trading begins on 10 July, and after trading ends on 10 July, can be set out as follows.

(a) *Before trading begins*

Assets		=	*Capital*		+	*Liabilities*
	$			$		
Stall	1,800		Capital introduced	2,500		
Flowers and plants	740		Retained profit	70		
Cash $(770 – 740)	30					
	2,570			2,570		$0

(b) *After trading ends*

On 10 July, all the goods are sold for $1,100 cash, and Charlie is paid $40. The profit for the day is $320, computed as follows.

	$	$
Sales		1,100
Less: cost of goods sold	740	
Charlie's wage	40	
		780
Profit		320

Eliza withdraws $200 of this profit for her personal use.

Assets		=	*Capital*		+	*Liabilities*
	$			$		
Stall	1,800		At beginning of 10 July	2,570		
Flowers and plants	0		Profits earned on 10 July	320		
Cash (30 + 1,100 – 40 – 200)	890		Less drawings	(200)		
	2,690			2,690	+	$0

4.2 Introducing more capital

When a business is going well, the owner may decide to **invest more money** in it, in the expectation of generating even more profit. We need to include introductions of new capital into the accounting equation. In doing so, we will arrive at the **business equation**, which allows us to compute profit from analysing the increase in net assets of the business, drawings and new capital introduced.

4.3 Example: more capital introduced

On 10 July, in addition to all the other transactions, Eliza decides to hire a van at a cost of $50 to transport the flowers and plants, paying for the hire out of cash from her own purse. How would this affect the accounting equation at the end of 10 July?

Solution

After trading ends

On 10 July, all the goods are sold for $1,100 cash, Charlie is paid $40 and the van cost $50. Profit for the day is $270.

	$	$
Sales		1,100
Less: cost of goods sold	740	
Charlie's wage	40	
van hire	50	
		830
		270

Eliza withdraws $200 for her personal use.

Assets		=	*Capital*		+	*Liabilities*
	$			$		
Stall	1,800		At start of trading	2,570		
Goods	0		Capital introduced	50		
Cash (30 + 1,100 + 50 – 40 – 50 – 200)	890		Profits earned 10 July	270		
			Drawings	(200)		
	2,690			2,690		$0

New capital introduced to the business should also be brought into the accounting equation.

Formula to learn

The accounting equation re-stated

Assets = Liabilities + Capital introduced in previous periods
+ Profit retained in previous periods
+ Profit earned in current period
+ Capital introduced in current period
– Drawings in current period

If we put Eliza Doolittle's figures into this, we get

Assets	$		*Capital*		*Liabilities*
Stall	1,800	= Capital introduced in previous periods	2,500	+	0
Cash	890	+ Profit retained in previous periods	70		
		+ Profit earned in current period	270		
		+ Capital introduced in current period	50		
		– Drawings in current period	(200)		
	2,690		2,690		0

4.4 The business equation

We are now ready to see how profit earned in a period can be expressed simply in terms of transactions within the period.

PREVIOUS PERIODS	Assets at start of period	=	Capital introduced in previous periods + Profit retained in previous periods	+	Liabilities at start of period
	+				
CURRENT PERIOD	Increase/decrease in assets (I)	=	Profit earned in current period (P) + Capital introduced in current period (C) – Drawings in current period (D)	+	Increase/decrease in liabilities (I)
	=				
END OF CURRENT PERIOD	Total assets at end of period	=	Total capital at end of period	+	Liabilities at end of period

Concentrating on the current period box above, we can state the business equation as follows.

Formula to learn

The business equation

$P = I + D - C$

Where:

P = Profit earned in the current period

I = Increase (or decrease) in net assets during the period. (This is a net figure for the increase (or decrease) in assets minus the increase (or plus the decrease) in liabilities in the period)

D = Drawings in the current period

C = Capital introduced during the period

Let's see how Eliza's figures for 10 July go into this equation.

Profit = Increase in net assets + Drawings – Capital introduced
= $(2,690 – 2,570) + $200 – $50
= $270

You may be a little concerned about why the **capital introduced in the period** is a **negative figure** in the equation. When a business is given new capital, perhaps in the form of extra money paid in by the proprietor herself, there will be an increase in the net assets of the business without any profits being earned. This means that if a proprietor puts an extra $5,000 into his business, the profit from the transaction according to the business equation, would be P = $5,000 + 0 – $5,000 = $0.

Similarly we saw with Eliza Doolittle that the $50 cash introduced was added to assets (cash) in the accounting equation in Paragraph 4.3 but was also added to capital.

P = $50 + 0 – $50 = 0

5 Payables and receivables

FAST FORWARD

Many business transactions are made on credit. **Creditors** are owed money by a business and are **liabilities (payables)** of the business. **Debtors** owe money to the business, and are **assets (receivables)** of the business.

5.1 Credit transactions

We have been concentrating on **capital** (including retained profits) and **assets** (cash, goods for resale, non-current assets), where the transactions of a business have been in cash. In reality, many business transactions are made on credit. Goods or services are obtained without payment for cash on delivery. Instead, the customer takes credit, and undertakes to pay later. Businesses give credit to their customers, and they also take credit from their suppliers.

In addition, businesses do not rely entirely on owners' capital for their long-term funding. Sometimes they borrow.

We shall now look at business transactions involving credit, and **payables and receivables**.

5.2 Payables

Key terms

- A **creditor** is a person from whom a business has **purchased** items and to whom a business **owes** money. A **payables balance** is the **liability** of the business which arises. Examples of payables include bank loans (money owed to the bank) and unpaid telephone and electricity bills.
- A **trade creditor** is a person to whom a business owes money for debts incurred in the course of trading operations. The term might refer to amounts still outstanding which arise from the purchase from suppliers of materials, components or goods for resale. In the accounts the amount owed to suppliers will be recorded as **trade payables**.

It is a common business practice to make purchases on **credit terms**, with a promise to pay within 30 days perhaps, or two months or even three months of the date of the purchase. For example, Alpha might buys goods costing $2,000 on credit from Beta. Beta might send Alpha an invoice for $2,000, dated 1 March, with credit terms that payment must be made within 30 days. If Alpha chooses not to pay the invoice immediately and delays payment until 31 March, Beta will be a creditor of Alpha for $2,000, between 1 and 31 March. There will be a **trade payables** balance of $2,000.

5.3 Receivables

Key terms

- A **debtor** is a person to whom the business has **sold** items and by whom the business is **owed** money. A receivable is an **asset** of a business (the business 'owns' a right to receive payment).
- A **trade debtor** is a customer who owes the business money for amounts incurred in the course of trading operations, i.e. because the business has sold its goods or services on credit to the debtor.

  In the accounts the amount owed by customers will be recorded as **trade receivables**.

Just as a business might buy goods on credit, so too might it sell goods to customers on credit. For example, suppose that Gamma sells goods on credit to Delta for $6,000 on terms that payment is due within two months of the invoice date, 1 October. If Delta takes the credit and does not pay the $6,000 until 30 November, Delta will be a debtor of Gamma for $6,000 from 1 October until 30 November.

There will be a trade receivables balance of $6,000.

This might serve as a useful summary.

CREDIT TRANSACTIONS	
SALES by the business to a customer	PURCHASES by the business from a supplier
↓ creates a DEBTOR (a customer who owes money to the business)	↓ creates a CREDITOR (a supplier who is owed money by the business)
↓ recorded as an ASSET (receivable) of the business	↓ recorded as a LIABILITY (payable) of the business
↓ settled when the business RECEIVES CASH	↓ settled when the business PAYS CASH

5.4 Example continued: receivables and payables

Let's continue further the example of Eliza Doolittle's market stall, by looking at the consequences of the following transactions in the week to 17 July.

(a) Eliza realises that she is going to need even more money in the business and so she makes the following arrangements.

  (i) She invests immediately a further $250 of her own capital.

  (ii) She persuades her friend Professor Higgins to lend her $500 immediately. Professor Higgins tells her that she can repay the loan whenever she likes, but in the meantime she must pay him interest of $5 per week at the end of the market day. They agree that it will probably be quite a long time before the loan is eventually repaid.

(b) She decides to buy a second-hand van to pick up flowers and plants from her supplier and bring them to her stall in the market. She finds a car dealer, Laurie Loader, who agrees to sell her a van on credit for $700. Eliza agrees to pay for the van after 30 days' trial use.

(c) During the week, Eliza's Uncle Henry telephones her to ask whether she would be interested in selling him some garden gnomes and furniture for his garden. Eliza tells him that she will look for a supplier. After some investigations, she buys what Uncle Henry has asked for, paying $300 in cash to the supplier. Uncle Henry accepts delivery of the goods and agrees to pay $350 at a later date.

(d) Eliza buys flowers and plants costing $800. Of these purchases $750 are paid in cash, with the remaining $50 on seven days' credit. Eliza decides to use Charlie's services again as an assistant on market day, at an agreed wage of $40.

(e) On 17 July, Eliza sells all her goods, earning revenue of $1,250 (all in cash). She takes out drawings of $240 for her week's work. She also pays Charlie $40 in cash. She decides to make the interest payment to her Uncle Henry the next time she sees him.

(f) There were no van expenses.

First of all we can state the following accounting equations:

(a) After Eliza and Professor Higgins have put more money into the business

(b) After the purchase of the van

(c) After the sale of goods to Uncle Henry

(d) After the purchase of goods for the weekly market

(e) At the end of the day's trading on 17 July, and after drawings have been withdrawn from profit

Then we are going to state the business equation showing profit earned during the week ended 17 July.

Solution

There are a number of different transactions to deal with here. This solution deals with them one at a time in chronological order, highlighting the numbers that change each time in **bold type**. (In practice, as you can possibly imagine, it would be possible to do one set of calculations combining the results of all the transactions. The transactions are taken separately here to illustrate the effect of each on the accounting equation – and balance sheet – of the business.

(a) The addition of the extra capital by Eliza and the loan from Professor Higgins.

The loan from Professor Higgins is for the long term, but he is not an owner of the business, even though he has made a long-term loan to it. He would only become an owner if Eliza offered him a partnership in the business, or turned the business into a company and offered him some shares. She has not done so; therefore Professor Higgins is simply a long-term creditor. His loan is a **liability** of the business – it is not business capital.

The accounting equation after $(250 + 500) = $750 cash is put into the business will be as follows:

Assets		=	*Liabilities*		+	*Capital*	
	$			$			$
Stall	1,800		Loan	**500**		As at end of 10 July	2,690
Goods	0					Additional capital	**250**
Cash $(890 + **750**)	**1,640**						
	3,440			500			2,940

(b) The purchase of the van (cost $700) is on credit, so Eliza doesn't have to pay until later.

Assets		=	*Liabilities*		+	*Capital*	
	$			$			$
Stall	1,800		Loan	500		As at end of 10 July	2,690
Van	**700**		Payable	**700**		Additional capital	250
Cash	1,640						
	4,140			1,200			2,940

(c) The sale of goods to Uncle Henry is on credit ($350), the cost to the business being $300 (cash paid). This gives a profit of $50. Uncle Henry, because he is paying later, is shown as a receivable.

Assets		=	*Liabilities*		+	*Capital*	
	$			$			$
Stall	1,800		Loan	500		As at end of 10 July	2,690
Van	700		Payable	700		Additional capital	250
Receivable	**350**					Profit on sale	**50**
Cash (1,640 – **300**)	**1,340**						
	4,190			1,200			2,990

(d) After the purchase of goods for the weekly market ($750 paid in cash and $50 of purchases on credit).

Assets		=	*Liabilities*		+	*Capital*	
	$			$			$
Stall	1,800		Loan	500		As at end of 10 July	2,690
Van	700		Payable for van	700		Additional capital	250
Goods	**800**		Payable for goods	**50**		Profit on sale to Uncle Henry	50
Receivable	350						
Cash (1,340 – **750**)	**590**						
	4,240			1,250			2,990

(e) After market trading on 17 July, sales of goods costing $800 earned revenues of $1,250. Charlie's wages were $40 (paid), the interest charge on the loan from Professor Higgins is $5 (not paid yet) and drawings out of profits were $240 (paid). The profit for 17 July may be calculated as follows, taking the full $5 of interest as a cost on that day.

	$	$
Revenue		1,250
Cost of goods sold	800	
Wages	40	
Interest	5	
		845
Profits earned on 17 July		405
Profit on sale of goods to Uncle Henry		50
Total profit for the week		455

Assets		=	*Liabilities*		+	*Capital*	
	$			$			$
Stall	1,800		Loan	500		As at end of 10 July	2,690
Van	700		Payable for van	700		Additional capital	250
Goods	**0**		Payable for goods	50		Profit on sale to Uncle Henry	50
Receivable	350		Payable for interest	**5**			
Cash (590 + **1,250** – **40** – **240**)	**1,560**					Profit for the week	**405**
						Drawings	**(240)**
	4,410			1,255			3,155

The increase in the net assets of the business during the week was as follows.

	$
Net assets as at the end of 17 July $(4,410 – 1,255)	3,155
Net assets as at the end of 10 July	2,690
Increase in net assets in week	465

The business equation for the week ended 17 July is as follows. (Remember that extra capital of $250 was invested by Eliza.)

$$
\begin{aligned}
P &= I + D - C \\
&= \$465 + \$240 - \$250 \\
&= \$455
\end{aligned}
$$

This confirms the calculation of total profit.

Activity 3.2

Show the effect on the accounting equation of each of the following transactions.

1 A business buys goods for $800 for cash.

2 The business sells these goods on credit for $1,400.

3 The customer pays three weeks later.

4 The business receives an invoice for a telephone bill for $2,600, all relating to the current accounting period.

5 The business pays the bill.

Transaction	*Change in assets*	*Change in liabilities*	*Change in capital*
1			
2			
3			
4			
5			

6 Double entry bookkeeping

Since the **total of liabilities plus capital is always equal to total assets**, any transaction has a **dual effect** – if it changes the amount of total assets it also changes the total liabilities plus capital, and *vice versa*. Alternatively, a transaction might use up assets of a certain value to obtain other assets of the same value. For example, if a business pays $50 in cash for some goods, its total assets will be unchanged, but as the amount of cash falls by $50, the value of goods in inventory rises by $50.

We can say then that there are two sides to every business transaction. Out of this concept has developed the system of accounting known as the 'double entry' system of bookkeeping, so called because every transaction is recorded twice in the accounts.

Key term

Double entry bookkeeping is the system of accounting which reflects the fact that:

- every financial transaction gives rise to two accounting entries
- each entry shows one of the effects of the transaction on the accounting equation

FAST FORWARD

'Ledger accounts' in a system of book-keeping are used to record transactions and show the current total value of a category of assets, or a category of liabilities, or owners' capital, or revenue or a category of expenditure.

Each asset, liability, item of expense or item of income has a **ledger account** in which the effect of business transactions are recorded. At any time, provided the accounting records are kept up-to-date:

(a) The total 'balance' on an **asset account** shows the current value of those assets owned by the business. For example, the balance on an office equipment account shows the total value of office equipment owned by the business, the total balance on the inventories account shows the total value of inventories held by the business, and the balance on the receivables account shows the total amount owed to the business by its debtors.

Similarly, the total balance on a **liabilities account** shows the total amount owed by the business for that type of liability (e.g. bank loans, trade payables).

(b) The total balance on the **sales account** shows the total sales revenue to date for the period.

(c) The total balance on various **expenses accounts** shows the total expenditure to date for the period for the particular item of expense (e.g. wages and salaries, telephone costs, advertising expenditure, legal expenses, and so on).

At the end of an accounting period, the balances are taken from each of these accounts, and form the basis for calculating the profit or loss for the period, and constructing a balance sheet for the end of the period.

7 The business equation as a link between profit and changes in the accounting equation

It has already been stated that the accounting equation is similar to a balance sheet, showing the assets, liabilities and capital of the business at a given moment in time. This chapter has shown that the business equation explains the change in the net assets of a business at the start of a period (i.e. the accounting equation at the start of the period) and the net assets at the end of the period.

Although it is not a part of the statutory accounts of a company, this link between opening net assets, profit, drawings, new capital and closing net assets might be shown in the income statement of a business, as follows.

	$
Revenue	500,000
Expenditure	360,000
Profit earned in the period	140,000
Less: Drawings	110,000
Retained profit for the period	30,000
Net assets at the start of the period	850,000
New capital introduced	70,000
Net assets at the end of the period	950,000

Activity 3.3

Try to explain the dual effects of each of the following transactions.

(a) A business receives a loan of $5,000 from its bank
(b) A business pays $800 cash to purchase goods for resale
(c) The proprietor of a business removes $50 from the till to buy her husband a birthday present
(d) A business sells goods costing $300 at a profit of $140
(e) A business repays a $5,000 bank loan, plus interest of $270

Key learning points

- In accounting, a business is treated as an **entity that is separate from its owners**. Owners put capital into the business, including retained profits, and capital represents what the business 'owes' to its owners.
- An **accounting equation** can be used to show the value of the assets, liabilities and capital of a business at any point in time. Total assets are always equal to the sum of total liabilities plus owners' capital.
- An accounting equation is a **balance sheet** of a business.
- **Profits** earned by a business add to capital, and losses reduce capital. **Drawings** (dividends in the case of companies) reduce capital. This means that the capital of a business is increased by the retained profits (profits earned minus drawings).
- All business transactions have a **dual effect**. For example, an increase in the value of one category of assets must be matched by an equal reduction in the value of another category of assets, or by an increase in liabilities or by an increase in capital (or a combination of these). The dual effect of transactions is the basis for the **'double entry' system of book-keeping** that is used to record business transactions.
- The increase in net assets during a period of time is explained by the retained profits for the period (profit earned minus drawings) plus any new capital introduced. This connection between profits and changes in net assets is an expression of the **business equation**.
- Many business transactions are made on credit. **Creditors** are owed money by a business, and are liabilities (payables) of the business. **Debtors** owe money to a business, and are assets (receivables) of the business.
- '**Ledger accounts**' in a system of book-keeping are used to record transactions, and show the current total value of a category of assets, or a category of liabilities, or owners' capital, or revenue or a category of expenditure.

Quick quiz

1 What is a business's prime objective?

2 Define profit.

3 What is an asset?

4 What is a liability?

5 How does the accounting view of the relationship between a business and its owner differ from the strictly legal view?

6 State the basic accounting equation.

7 What is capital?

8 What are drawings? Where do they fit in the accounting equation?

9 What does the business equation attempt to show?

10 What is the main difference between a cash and a credit transaction?

11 What is a creditor? What is a debtor?

12 Define double entry book-keeping.

Answers to quick quiz

1 A business's prime objective is earning a profit.

2 Profit is the excess of income over expenditure.

3 An asset is something valuable which a business owns or has the use of.

4 A liability is something which is owed to someone else.

5 In accounting a business is always treated as a separate entity from its owners, even though in law there is not always a distinction (in the cases of a sole trader and a partnership).

6 Assets = Capital + Liabilities.

7 Capital is the investment of funds with the intention of earning a profit.

8 Drawings are the amounts of money taken out of a business by its owner. In the accounting equation drawings are a reduction of capital.

9 The business equation describes the relationship between a business's increase in net assets in a period, the profit earned, drawings taken and capital introduced.

10 The main difference between a cash and a credit transaction is simply a matter of time – cash changes hands immediately in a cash transaction, whereas in a credit transaction it changes hands some time after the initial sale/purchase takes place.

11 A creditor is a person from whom a business has purchased items and to whom it owes money. The business records a payable balance. A debtor is a person to whom the business has sold items and by whom it is owed money. The business records a receivable balance.

12 Double entry book-keeping is a system of accounting which reflects the fact that every financial transaction gives rise to two equal accounting entries (a 'debit' and a 'credit', although you will not need to learn these terms).

Answers to activities

3.1

Transaction	*Assets*	=	*Capital*	+	*Liabilities*
(a)			Increase		Decrease
(b)	Decrease				Decrease
(c)			Decrease		Increase
(d)	Decrease		Decrease		
(e)	Increase		Increase		
(f)	Increase				Increase

3.2

Transaction	*Change in assets*	*Change in liabilities*	*Change in capital*
1	+ Inventory $800 – Cash $800		
2	– Inventory $800 + Receivables $1,400		+ Profit $600
3	– Receivables $1,400 + Cash $1,400		
4		+ Payable $2,600	– Profit $2,600 (expenditures reduce profit)
5	– Cash $2,600	– Payable $2,600	

3.3 (a) Assets (cash) increase by $5,000, liabilities (amount owed to the bank) increase by $5,000.

(b) Assets (cash) decrease by $800, assets (inventories) increase by $800.

(c) Assets (cash) decrease by $50, capital decreases by $50 (the proprietor has taken $50 drawings for her personal use. In effect, the business has repaid her part of the amount it owed).

(d) Assets (cash) increase by $440, assets (inventory) decrease by $300, capital (the profit earned for the proprietor) increases by $140.

(e) Assets (cash) decrease by $5,270, liabilities (the bank loan) decrease by $5,000, capital decreases by $270 (the proprietor has made a 'loss' of $270 on the transaction).

Qualities of financial information and measurement

4

Topic list
1 Qualitative characteristics of financial information
2 The elements of financial statements
3 Recognition of the elements of financial statements
4 Revenue recognition
5 Measurement in financial statements
6 Basic principles of historical cost accounting
7 Capital maintenance
8 Current value models of accounting
9 Accounting for public sector organisations

Introduction

This chapter covers a range of topics. The link between them is that they are all concerned with the way in which elements in the financial statements are measured and the impact that this might have on the users of accounts.

Learning objectives

On completion of this chapter you will be able to:

		Syllabus reference
•	explain the need for relevance, reliability, comparability and understandability of financial information and constraints on these	2c
•	define assets, liabilities, income and equity	2d
•	identify the role of a measurement basis in financial reporting	2e
•	discuss and apply the basic principles of historical cost accounting	2e
•	describe the basic principles of current cost accounting	2e
•	explain the basic features of accounting for public sector and not for profit organisations	2f

1 Qualitative characteristics of financial information

FAST FORWARD

The *Framework* states that qualitative characteristics are the attributes that make the information provided in financial statements useful to users.

The four principal qualitative characteristics are

(1) understandability
(2) relevance
(3) reliability
(4) comparability.

1.1 Understandability

Users must be able to understand financial statements. The *Framework* however takes the view that preparers of financial statements can assume that users have some business, economic and accounting knowledge and are able to apply themselves to study the information properly. **Information about complex matters should not be left out** of financial statements simply due to its difficulty if it is relevant information.

1.2 Relevance

FAST FORWARD

Relevant information can have predictive and confirmatory value.

Key term

Relevance. Information has the quality of relevance when it influences the economic decisions of users by helping them evaluate past, present or future events or confirming, or correcting, their past evaluations. *(Framework)*

There are two ways in which information can influence decisions. It can have a **predictive** value and it can have a **confirmatory** value. The *Framework* states that the predictive and confirmatory roles of information are interrelated, in that the same information can have both predictive and confirmatory value. For example, an investor might have purchased shares in ABC Co some time ago, expecting the company to be profitable and pay high dividends. The annual financial statements of ABC Co published at a later date might both confirm the investor's expectations of what profits and dividends were likely to be and also help him to make a further assessment about what profits and dividends might be in future.

The *Framework* also explains that information does not need to be in the form of an explicit forecast to have predictive value. However the ability to make decisions is enhanced by the **manner** in which the information is presented eg by highlighting unusual items.

1.2.1 Materiality

FAST FORWARD

Materiality revolves around whether the information involved would have influenced the economic decisions made by users.

The relevance of information is affected by its **nature and materiality**.

Key term

Materiality. Information is material if its omission or misstatement could influence the economic decisions of users taken on the basis of the financial statements. *(Framework)*

The *Framework* states that information may be judged relevant simply because of its nature (eg share capital). In other cases, both the nature and materiality of the information are important. Materiality is not a primary qualitative characteristic itself (like reliability or relevance), because it is merely a threshold or cut-off point.

In practical terms materiality is a final test of what information should be included in the financial statements. If the inclusion of further information would not have a material effect on the usefulness of the financial information (in terms of relevance, reliability and so on) it need not be included. In preparing accounts it is important to assess what is material and what is not, so that time and money are not wasted in the pursuit of excessive detail.

Determining whether or not an item is material is a very **subjective exercise**. There is no absolute measure of materiality. It is common to apply a convenient rule of thumb (for example to define material items as those with a value greater than 5% of the net profit disclosed by the accounts). But some items disclosed in accounts are regarded as particularly sensitive and even a very small misstatement of such an item would be regarded as a material error. An example in the accounts of a limited liability company might be the amount of remuneration paid to directors of the company.

The assessment of an item as material or immaterial may **affect its treatment in the accounts**. For example, the income statement of a business will show the expenses incurred by the business grouped under suitable captions (heating and lighting expenses, rent and local taxes etc); but in the case of very small expenses it may be appropriate to lump them together under a caption such as 'sundry expenses', because a more detailed breakdown would be inappropriate for such immaterial amounts.

In assessing whether or not an item is material, it is not only the amount of the item which needs to be considered. The **context** is also important.

(a) If a balance sheet shows non-current assets of $2 million and inventories of $30,000 an error of $20,000 in the depreciation calculations might not be regarded as material, whereas an error of $20,000 in the inventory valuation probably would be. In other words, the total of which the erroneous item forms part must be considered.

(b) If a business has a bank loan of $50,000 and a $55,000 balance on bank deposit account, it might well be regarded as a material misstatement if these two amounts were displayed on the balance sheet as 'cash at bank $5,000'. In other words, incorrect presentation may amount to material misstatement even if there is no monetary error.

Users are assumed to have a reasonable knowledge of business and economic activities and accounting and a willingness to study the information with reasonable diligence.

1.3 Reliability

FAST FORWARD

Faithful representation, substance, neutrality and prudence are important aspect of reliability.

Information must also be reliable to be useful. The user must be able to depend on it being a **faithful representation**.

Key term

Reliability. Information has the quality of reliability when it is free from material error and bias and can be depended upon by users to represent faithfully that which it either purports to represent or could reasonably be expected to represent. *(Framework)*

Even if information is relevant, if it is very unreliable it may be **misleading to recognise it**, eg a disputed claim for damages in a legal action.

1.3.1 Faithful representation

Information must represent faithfully the transactions it purports to represent in order to be reliable. There is a risk that this may not be the case, not due to bias, but due to **inherent difficulties in identifying the transactions** or finding an **appropriate method of measurement or presentation**. Where measurement of the financial effects of an item is so uncertain, entities should not recognise such an item, eg internally generated goodwill.

1.3.2 Substance over form

Faithful representation of a transaction is only possible if it is accounted for according to its **substance and economic reality**, not with its legal form.

Key term

Substance over form. The principle that transactions and other events are accounted for and presented in accordance with their substance and economic reality and not merely their legal form. *(Framework)*

This is looked at in more detail in Chapter 6.

1.3.3 Neutrality

Information must be **free from bias** to be reliable. Neutrality is lost if the financial statements are prepared so as to influence the user to make a judgement or decision in order to achieve a predetermined outcome.

1.3.4 Prudence

Prudence means exercising a **reasonable degree of caution** when there is some **uncertainty** in order that gains and assets are **not overstated** in value and liabilities are not **under-stated**.

Uncertainties exist in the preparation of financial information, eg the collectability of doubtful receivables. These uncertainties are recognised through disclosure and through the application of prudence. Prudence does not, however, allow the creation of hidden reserves or excessive provisions, understatement of assets or income or overstatement of liabilities or expenses.

1.3.5 Completeness

Financial information must be complete, within the **restrictions of materiality and cost**, to be reliable. Omission may cause information to be misleading.

1.4 Comparability

FAST FORWARD

Disclosure of **accounting policies** aids comparability.

The usefulness of financial information increases enormously if it can be compared with similar information.

Users must be able to compare an entity's financial statements:

(a) **Through time** to identify trends

(b) **With other entities' statements**, to evaluate their relative financial position, performance and changes in financial position

The consistency of treatment is therefore important across like items over time, within the entity and across all entities.

The **disclosure of accounting policies** is particularly important here. Users must be able to distinguish between different accounting policies in order to be able to make a valid comparison of similar items in the accounts of different entities.

Comparability is **not the same as uniformity**. Entities should change accounting policies if they become inappropriate.

Corresponding information for **preceding periods** should be shown to enable comparison over time.

1.5 Constraints on relevant and reliable information

1.5.1 Timeliness

Information may become irrelevant if there is a delay in reporting it. There is a **balance between timeliness and the provision of reliable information**. Information may be reported on a timely basis when not all aspects of the transaction are known, thus compromising reliability.

If every detail of a transaction is known, it may be too late to publish the information because it has become irrelevant. The overriding consideration is how best to satisfy the economic decision-making needs of the users.

1.5.2 Balance between benefits and cost

This is a pervasive constraint, not a qualitative characteristic. When information is provided, its benefits must exceed the costs of obtaining and presenting it. This is a **subjective area** and there are other difficulties: others than the intended users may gain a benefit; also the cost may be paid by someone other than the users. It is therefore difficult to apply a cost-benefit analysis, but preparers and users should be aware of the constraint.

1.5.3 Balance between qualitative characteristics

A **trade off between qualitative characteristics** is often necessary, the aim being to achieve an appropriate balance to meet the objective of financial statements. It is a matter for **professional judgement** as to the relative importance of these characteristics in each case.

1.6 True and fair view/fair presentation

The *Framework* does not attempt to define these concepts directly. It does state, however, that the application of the **principal 'qualitative' characteristics** and of **appropriate accounting standards** will usually result in financial statements which show a true and fair view, or present fairly.

2 The elements of financial statements

FAST FORWARD

Transactions and other events are grouped together in broad **classes** and in this way their financial effects are shown in the financial statements. These broad classes are the elements of financial statements.

The *Framework* lays out these elements as follows.

Elements of financial statements

Measurement of financial position in the balance sheet

- **Assets**
- **Liabilities**
- **Equity**

Measurement of performance in the income statement

- **Income**
- **Expenses**

A process of **sub-classification** then takes place for presentation in the financial statements, eg assets are classified by their nature or function in the business to show information in the best way for users to take economic decisions.

2.1 Financial position

We need to define the three terms listed under this heading above. We looked at the basic definitions of assets and liabilities in Chapter 2.

Key terms

- **Asset**. A resource controlled by an entity as a result of past events and from which future economic benefits are expected to flow to the entity.
- **Liability**. A present obligation of the entity arising from past events, the settlement of which is expected to result in an outflow from the entity of resources embodying economic benefits.
- **Equity**. The residual interest in the assets of the entity after deducting all its liabilities. *(Framework)*

These definitions are important, but they do not cover the **criteria for recognition** of any of these items, which are discussed in the next section of this chapter. This means that the definitions may include items which would not actually be recognised in the balance sheet because they fail to satisfy recognition criteria particularly, as we will see below, the **probable flow of any economic benefit** to or from the business.

Whether an item satisfies any of the definitions above will depend on the **substance and economic reality** of the transaction, not merely its legal form. For example, consider finance leases (see Chapter 6).

2.2 Assets

We can look in more detail at the components of the definitions given above.

Key term

Future economic benefit. The potential to contribute, directly or indirectly, to the flow of cash and cash equivalents to the entity. The potential may be a productive one that is part of the operating activities of the entity. It may also take the form of convertibility into cash or cash equivalents or a capability to reduce cash outflows, such as when an alternative manufacturing process lowers the cost of production.

(Framework)

Assets are usually employed to produce goods or services for customers; customers will then pay for these. **Cash itself** renders a service to the entity due to its command over other resources.

The existence of an asset, particularly in terms of **control**, is not reliant on:

(a) **physical form** (hence patents and copyrights); *nor*

(b) **legal rights** (hence leases).

Transactions or events **in the past** give rise to assets; those expected to occur in the future do not in themselves give rise to assets. For example, an intention to purchase a non-current asset does not, in itself, meet the definition of an asset.

2.3 Liabilities

Again we can look more closely at some aspects of the definition. An essential characteristic of a liability is that the entity has a **present obligation**.

Key term

Obligation. A duty or responsibility to act or perform in a certain way. Obligations may be legally enforceable as a consequence of a binding contract or statutory requirement. Obligations also arise, however, from normal business practice, custom and a desire to maintain good business relations or act in an equitable manner. *(Framework)*

It is important to distinguish between a present obligation and a **future commitment**. A management decision to purchase assets in the future does not, in itself, give rise to a present obligation.

Settlement of a present obligation will involve the entity giving up resources embodying economic benefits in order to satisfy the claim of the other party. This may be done in various ways, not just by payment of cash.

Liabilities must arise from **past transactions or events**. In the case of, say, recognition of future rebates to customers based on annual purchases, the sale of goods in the past is the transaction that gives rise to the liability.

2.3.1 Provisions

Is a provision a liability?

Key term

Provision. A present obligation which satisfies the rest of the definition of a liability, even if the amount of the obligation has to be estimated. *(Framework)*

Activity 4.1

Consider the following situations. In each case, do we have an asset or liability within the definitions given by the *Framework?* Give reasons for your answer.

(a) Pat Co has purchased a patent for $20,000. The patent gives the company sole use of a particular manufacturing process which will save $3,000 a year for the next five years.

(b) Baldwin Co paid Don Brennan $10,000 to set up a car repair shop, on condition that priority treatment is given to cars from the company's fleet.

(c) Deals on Wheels Co provides a warranty with every car sold.

2.4 Equity

Equity is defined above as a **residual**, but it may be sub-classified in the balance sheet. This will indicate legal or other restrictions on the ability of the entity to distribute or otherwise apply its equity. Some reserves are required by statute or other law, eg for the future protection of creditors. The amount shown for equity depends on the **measurement of assets and liabilities.** It has nothing to do with the market value of the entity's shares.

2.5 Performance

Profit is used as a **measure of performance**, or as a basis for other measures (eg EPS). It depends directly on the measurement of income and expenses, which in turn depend (in part) on the concepts of capital and capital maintenance adopted.

The elements of income and expense are therefore defined.

Key terms

- **Income**. Increases in economic benefits during the accounting period in the form of inflows or enhancements of assets or decreases of liabilities that result in increases in equity, other than those relating to contributions from equity participants.
- **Expenses**. Decreases in economic benefits during the accounting period in the form of outflows or depletions of assets or incurrences of liabilities that result in decreases in equity, other than those relating to distributions to equity participants.

(Framework)

Income and expenses can be **presented in different ways** in the income statement, to provide information relevant for economic decision-making. For example, distinguishing between income and expenses which relate to continuing operations and those which do not.

Items of income and expense can be **distinguished** from each other or **combined** with each other.

2.6 Income

Both **revenue** and **gains** are included in the definition of income. **Revenue** arises in the course of ordinary activities of an entity.

Key term

Gains. Increases in economic benefits. As such they are no different in nature from revenue. *(Framework)*

Gains include those arising on the disposal of non-current assets. The definition of income also includes **unrealised gains**, eg on revaluation of marketable securities.

2.7 Expenses

As with income, the definition of expenses includes losses as well as those expenses that arise in the course of ordinary activities of an entity.

Key term

Losses. Decreases in economic benefits. As such they are no different in nature from other expenses. *(Framework)*

Losses will include those arising on the disposal of non-current assets. The definition of expenses will also include **unrealised losses**, eg exchange rate effects on borrowings.

2.8 Capital maintenance adjustments

A **revaluation** gives rise to an increase or decrease in equity.

Key term

> **Revaluation**. Restatement of assets and liabilities. *(Framework)*

These increases and decreases meet the definitions of income and expenses. They are **not included** in the income statement under certain concepts of capital maintenance, however, but rather in equity (see Section 8).

3 Recognition of the elements of financial statements

FAST FORWARD

> Recognition is based on the **definition** of an element, **probability** of future economic benefits and **reliability** of measurement.

The financial statements report the assets, liabilities and capital of a company in its balance sheet and the income and expenditure during an accounting period in the income statement. Rules are needed to establish exactly when an asset or liability comes into existence and so should be reported in the balance sheet. Similarly there must be rules when income is earned or expenditure incurred for inclusion in the income statement. These rules relate to the **'recognition'** of items in the financial statements and are closely linked to the accruals concept, materiality and to a lesser extent prudence.

Key term

> **Recognition**. The process of incorporating in the balance sheet or income statement an item that meets the definition of an element and satisfies the following criteria for recognition:
>
> (a) it **is probable** that any future economic benefit associated with the item will flow to or from the entity; and
>
> (b) the item has a cost or value that can be measured with **reliability**.
>
> *(Framework)*

3.1 Probability of future economic benefits

Probability here means the **degree of uncertainty** that the future economic benefits associated with an item will flow to or from the entity. This must be judged on the basis of the **characteristics of the entity's environment** and the **evidence available** when the financial statements are prepared.

3.2 Reliability of measurement

The cost or value of an item, in many cases, **must be estimated**. The *Framework* states, however, that the use of reasonable estimates is an essential part of the preparation of financial statements and does not undermine their reliability. Where no reasonable estimate can be made, the item should not be recognised, although its existence should be disclosed in the notes, or other explanatory material.

Items may still qualify for recognition **at a later date** due to changes in circumstances or subsequent events.

3.3 Recognition of items

We can summarise the recognition criteria for assets, liabilities, income and expenses, based on the definition of recognition given above.

Item	Recognised in	When
Asset	The balance sheet	It is probable that the future economic benefits will flow to the entity and the asset has a cost or value that can be measured reliably.
Liability	The balance sheet	It is probable that an outflow of resources embodying economic benefits will result from the settlement of a present obligation and the amount at which the settlement will take place can be measured reliably.
Income	The income statement	An increase in future economic benefits related to an increase in an asset or a decrease of a liability has arisen that can be measured reliably.
Expenses	The income statement	A decrease in future economic benefits related to a decrease in an asset or an increase of a liability has arisen that can be measured reliably.

4 Revenue recognition

FAST FORWARD

Revenue should be recognised when it is probable that future economic benefits will flow to the entity and when these benefits can be measured reliably.

4.1 Introduction

Accruals accounting is based on the **matching of costs with the revenue they generate**. It is crucially important under this convention that we can establish the point at which revenue may be recognised so that the correct treatment can be applied to the related costs. For example, the costs of producing an item of finished goods should be carried as an asset in the balance sheet until such time as it is sold; they should then be written off as a charge to the trading account. Which of these two treatments should be applied cannot be decided until it is clear at what moment the sale of the item takes place.

The decision has a **direct impact on profit** since under the prudence concept it would be unacceptable to recognise the profit on sale until a sale had taken place in accordance with the criteria of revenue recognition.

Revenue is generally recognised as **earned at the point of sale**, because at that point four criteria will generally have been met.

- The product or service has been **provided to the buyer**.
- The buyer has **recognised his liability** to pay for the goods or services provided. The converse of this is that the seller has recognised that ownership of goods has passed from himself to the buyer.
- The buyer has indicated his **willingness to hand over cash** or other assets in settlement of his liability.
- The **monetary value** of the goods or services has been established.

At earlier points in the business cycle there will not in general be **firm evidence** that the above criteria will be met. Until work on a product is complete, there is a risk that some flaw in the manufacturing process will necessitate its writing off; even when the product is complete there is no guarantee that it will find a buyer.

At later points in the business cycle, for example when cash is received for the sale, the recognition of revenue may occur in a period later than that in which the related costs were charged. Revenue recognition would then depend on fortuitous circumstances, such as the cash flow of a company's customers, and might fluctuate misleadingly from one period to another.

However, there are times when revenue is **recognised at other times than at the completion of a sale**. For example, in the recognition of profit on long-term construction contracts. Under IAS 11 *Construction contracts* (see Chapter 6) contract revenue and contract costs associated with the construction contract should be recognised as revenue and expenses respectively by reference to the stage of completion of the contract activity at the balance sheet date.

(a) Owing to the length of time taken to complete such contracts, to defer taking profit into account until completion may result in the income statement reflecting, not so much a fair view of the activity of the company during the year, but rather the results relating to contracts which have been completed by the year end.

(b) Revenue in this case is recognised when production on, say, a section of the total contract is complete, even though no sale can be made until the whole is complete.

4.2 IAS 18 *Revenue*

IAS 18 governs the recognition of revenue in specific (common) types of transaction. Generally, recognition should be when it is probable that **future economic benefits** will flow to the entity and when these benefits can be **measured reliably**.

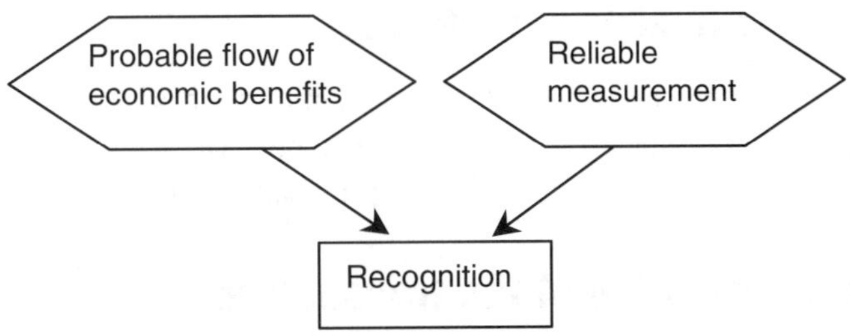

Income, as defined by the IASB's *Framework* document, includes both revenues and gains. Revenue is income arising in the ordinary course of an entity's activities and it may be called different names, such as sales, fees, interest, dividends or royalties.

4.3 Scope

IAS 18 covers the revenue from specific types of transaction or events.

- **Sale of goods** (manufactured products and items purchased for resale)
- **Rendering of services**
- Use by others of entity assets yielding **interest, royalties and dividends**

Interest, royalties and dividends are included as income because they arise from the use of an entity's assets by other parties.

Key terms

> **Interest** is the charge for the use of cash or cash equivalents or amounts due to the entity.
>
> **Royalties** are charges for the use of non-current assets of the entity, eg patents, computer software and trademarks.
>
> **Dividends** are distributions of profit to holders of equity investments, in proportion with their holdings, of each relevant class of capital.

The standard specifically **excludes** various types of revenue arising from leases, insurance contracts, changes in value of financial instruments or other current assets, natural increases in agricultural assets and mineral ore extraction.

4.4 Definitions

The following definitions are given in the standard.

Key terms

> **Revenue** is the gross inflow of economic benefits during the period arising in the course of the ordinary activities of an entity when those inflows result in increases in equity, other than increases relating to contributions from equity participants.
>
> **Fair value** is the amount for which an asset could be exchanged, or a liability settled, between knowledgeable, willing parties in an arm's length transaction. *(IAS 18)*

Revenue **does not include** sales taxes, value added taxes or goods and service taxes which are only collected for third parties, because these do not represent an economic benefit flowing to the entity. The same is true for revenues collected by an agent on behalf of a principal. Revenue for the agent is only the commission received for acting as agent.

4.5 Measurement of revenue

When a transaction takes place, the amount of revenue is usually decided by the **agreement of the buyer and seller**. The revenue is actually measured, however, as the **fair value of the consideration received**, which will take account of any trade discounts and volume rebates.

4.6 Identification of the transaction

Normally, each transaction can be looked at **as a whole**. Sometimes, however, transactions are more complicated, and it is necessary to break a transaction down into its **component parts**. For example, a sale may include the transfer of goods and the provision of future servicing, the revenue for which should be deferred over the period the service is performed.

At the other end of the scale, **seemingly separate transactions must be considered together** if apart they lose their commercial meaning. An example would be to sell an asset with an agreement to buy it back at a later date. The second transaction cancels the first and so both must be considered together.

4.7 Sale of goods

Revenue from the sale of goods should only be recognised when *all* these conditions are satisfied.

(a) The entity has transferred the **significant risks and rewards** of ownership of the goods to the buyer

(b) The entity has **no continuing managerial involvement** to the degree usually associated with ownership, and no longer has effective control over the goods sold

(c) The amount of revenue can be **measured reliably**

(d) It is probable that the **economic benefits** associated with the transaction will flow to the entity

(e) The **costs incurred** in respect of the transaction can be measured reliably

The transfer of risks and rewards can only be decided by examining each transaction. Mainly, the transfer occurs at the same time as either the **transfer of legal title**, or the **passing of possession** to the buyer - this is what happens when you buy something in a shop.

If **significant risks and rewards remain with the seller**, then the transaction is *not* a sale and revenue cannot be recognised, for example if the receipt of the revenue from a particular sale depends on the buyer receiving revenue from his own sale of the goods.

It is possible for the seller to retain only an **'insignificant' risk of ownership** and for the sale and revenue to be recognised. The main example here is where the seller retains title only to ensure collection of what is owed on the goods. This is a common commercial situation, and when it arises the revenue should be recognised on the date of sale.

The probability of the entity receiving the revenue arising from a transaction must be assessed. It may only become probable that the economic benefits will be received when an uncertainty is removed, for example government permission for funds to be received from another country. Only when the uncertainty is removed should the revenue be recognised. This is in contrast with the situation where revenue has already been recognised but where the **collectability of the cash** is brought into doubt. Where recovery has ceased to be probable, the amount should be recognised as an expense, *not* an adjustment of the revenue previously recognised. These points also refer to services and interest, royalties and dividends below.

Matching should take place, ie the revenue and expenses relating to the same transaction should be recognised at the same time. It is usually easy to estimate expenses at the date of sale (eg warranty costs, shipment costs, etc). Where they cannot be estimated reliably, then revenue cannot be recognised; any consideration which has already been received is treated as a liability.

4.8 Rendering of services

When the outcome of a transaction involving the rendering of services can be estimated reliably, the associated revenue should be recognised by reference to the **stage of completion of the transaction** at the balance sheet date. The outcome of a transaction can be estimated reliably when *all* these conditions are satisfied.

(a) The amount of revenue can be **measured reliably**

(b) It is probable that the **economic benefits** associated with the transaction will flow to the entity

(c) The **stage of completion** of the transaction at the balance sheet date can be measured reliably

(d) The **costs incurred** for the transaction and the costs to complete the transaction can be measured reliably

The parties to the transaction will normally have to agree the following before an entity can make reliable estimates.

(a) Each party's **enforceable rights** regarding the service to be provided and received by the parties

(b) The **consideration** to be exchanged

(c) The **manner and terms of settlement**

There are various methods of determining the stage of completion of a transaction, but for practical purposes, when services are performed by an indeterminate number of acts over a period of time, revenue should be recognised on a **straight line basis** over the period, unless there is evidence for the use of a more appropriate method. If one act is of more significance than the others, then the significant act should be carried out *before* revenue is recognised.

In uncertain situations, when the outcome of the transaction involving the rendering of services cannot be estimated reliably, the standard recommends a **no loss/no gain approach**. Revenue is recognised only to the extent of the expenses recognised that are recoverable.

This is particularly likely during the **early stages of a transaction**, but it is still probable that the entity will recover the costs incurred. So the revenue recognised in such a period will be equal to the expenses incurred, with no profit.

Obviously, if the costs are not likely to be reimbursed, then they must be recognised as an expense immediately. **When the uncertainties cease to exist**, revenue should be recognised as laid out in the first paragraph of this section.

4.9 Interest, royalties and dividends

When others use the entity's assets yielding interest, royalties and dividends, the revenue should be recognised on the bases set out below when:

(a) it is probable that the **economic benefits** associated with the transaction will flow to the entity; and

(b) the amount of the revenue can be **measured reliably**.

The revenue is recognised on the following bases.

(a) **Interest** is recognised on a time proportion basis that takes into account the effective yield on the asset

(b) **Royalties** are recognised on an accruals basis in accordance with the substance of the relevant agreement

(c) **Dividends** are recognised when the shareholder's right to receive payment is established

It is unlikely that you would be asked about anything as complex as this in the exam, but you should be aware of the basic requirements of the standard. The **effective yield** on an asset mentioned above is the rate of interest required to discount the stream of future cash receipts expected over the life of the asset to equate to the initial carrying amount of the asset.

Royalties are usually recognised on the same basis that they accrue **under the relevant agreement**. Sometimes the true substance of the agreement may require some other systematic and rational method of recognition.

Once again, the points made above about **probability and collectability** on sale of goods also apply here.

Activity 4.2

Given that prudence is the main consideration, discuss under what circumstances, if any, revenue might be recognised at the following stages of a sale.

(a) Goods are acquired by the business which it confidently expects to resell very quickly.
(b) A customer places a firm order for goods.
(c) Goods are delivered to the customer.
(d) The customer is invoiced for goods.
(e) The customer pays for the goods.
(f) The customer's cheque in payment for the goods has been cleared by the bank.

5 Measurement in financial statements

Measurement is defined as follows.

Key term

Measurement. The process of determining the monetary amounts at which the elements of the financial statements are to be recognised and carried in the balance sheet and income statement. *(Framework)*

This involves the selection of a particular **basis of measurement**. A number of these are used to different degrees and in varying combinations in financial statements. They include the following.

Key terms

- **Historical cost**. Assets are recorded at the amount of cash or cash equivalents paid or the fair value of the consideration given to acquire them at the time of their acquisition. Liabilities are recorded at the amount of proceeds received in exchange for the obligation, or in some circumstances (for example, income taxes), at the amounts of cash or cash equivalents expected to be paid to satisfy the liability in the normal course of business.
- **Current cost**. Assets are carried at the amount of cash or cash equivalents that would have to be paid if the same or an equivalent asset was acquired currently.

  Liabilities are carried at the undiscounted amount of cash or cash equivalents that would be required to settle the obligation currently.
- **Realisable (settlement) value**.
  - **Realisable value**. The amount of cash or cash equivalents that could currently be obtained by selling an asset in an orderly disposal.
  - **Settlement value**. The undiscounted amounts of cash or cash equivalents expected to be paid to satisfy the liabilities in the normal course of business.
- **Present value**. A current estimate of the present discounted value of the future net cash flows in the normal course of business. *(Framework)*

Historical cost is the most commonly adopted measurement basis, but this is usually combined with other bases, eg inventory is carried at the lower of cost and net realisable value.

5.1 Example

Suppose that a manufacturing company acquires a machine that has an expected useful life of four years. At the end of two years the company is preparing a balance sheet and has to decide what monetary amount to attribute to the asset.

Several valuations might be considered:

- The original cost (historical cost) of the machine
- Half of the historical cost, on the ground that half of its useful life has expired
- The amount the machine might fetch on the second-hand market ('disposal value')
- The amount it would cost now to replace the machine with an identical machine ('replacement cost')
- The amount it would cost to replace the machine with a more modern machine, incorporating the technological advances of the previous two years
- The machine's 'economic value', which is the amount of the profits the machine is expected to generate for the company during its remaining life.

All of these valuations have something to commend them, but a perceived advantage of the first two is that they are based on a figure (the machine's historical cost) which is objectively verifiable. The subjective judgement involved in the other valuations, particularly economic value, is so great as to lessen the reliability of any accounts in which they are used. The first two valuations are on a **historical cost** basis and the others are different **current value** measurements.

6 Basic principles of historical cost accounting

FAST FORWARD

Traditionally financial statements have been prepared using the **historical cost convention**. This maintains that items should be recorded in the accounts at their original cost. This has serious drawbacks particularly with regard to property valuations and in times of high inflation.

A long-established practice in accounting is that resources are normally, but not always, stated in accounts at their historical cost. The historical cost of an item is the amount that the business paid to **acquire** it. An important advantage of this procedure is that the objectivity of accounts is achieved: there is usually objective, documentary evidence to prove the amount paid to purchase an asset or pay an expense.

Traditionally, there have been two main reasons for the preparation of accounts:

(a) To meet the needs of the **owners** of a business for **information** about it

(b) To assist **management** in **controlling** the business and in **making decisions** about its future.

Although the information needs of internal and external users differ considerably, it has become clear that accounts prepared on a traditional historical cost basis can present financial information in a misleading manner. The greatest criticisms of **traditional accounting concepts** have stemmed from their **inability to reflect the effects of changing price levels**.

6.1 Non-current asset values are unrealistic

The most notable example is the valuation of **property** in financial statements. Businesses with freehold or long leasehold property often retain it for many years, and in the longer term, property values normally rise over time. (This has been a particular issue in the UK). A property purchased in 1960 for $100,000 could be worth much more now. Companies may gain from **rising property values** simply by **holding** on to the property, and should they ever decide to sell the property they will realise a **large gain** on the sale.

If assets such as property are valued in financial statements at their historical cost, **unrealised holding gains are not recognised**. This means that the total holding gain will be recorded as profit for the year in which the asset is eventually sold and the gain 'realised'. Arguably, it would be more appropriate to spread the holding gain over the period during which the asset was owned.

A further problem with historical cost values, for long-term assets (and even for shorter-term assets during a period of high inflation) is that the book values of different assets cease to provide comparability. For example, suppose that a company bought a freehold property for $500,000 in 1970, another property for $800,000 in 1980, a third property for $1,000,000 in 1990 and a fourth property for $1,200,000 in 2000. Using the historical cost convention, the property disclosures would be reported as $3,500,000 in total. However, given the different times at which the properties were bought, a total book value of $3,500,000 has no real meaning. It would certainly not reflect their current values.

This problem has been overcome to some extent because companies are permitted to re-value long-term assets such as property to a current market value. To this extent, provided revaluations are carried out regularly and by an independent valuer, reported asset values should be more meaningful. However, when some assets (but not others) are revalued to a current market value, the historical cost convention has been partially abandoned.

There are, in essence, two points to be considered.

(a) It has long been accepted that a balance sheet prepared under the historical cost concept is a historical record and not a statement of current worth. However, many people argue that the balance sheet of a company should at least give an **indication** of the **current value** of its assets.

(b) Traditionally, the prudence concept required that profits be recognised only when they are eventually realised. It may be argued that recognising unrealised holding gains on long-term assets, and permitting revaluations, is contrary to this traditional and conservative approach to applying prudence.

On balance, the weight of opinion is now in favour of restating asset values. It is felt that the criticism based on prudence can be met by ensuring that valuations are made as objectively as possible (e.g. in the case of property, by having independent expert valuations) and by not reporting unrealised gains (from upward revaluations of assets) within the income statement.

In a period of high inflation, profits may be seriously overstated

In principle, a business can distribute all its profits to its owners. For example, if a company makes a profit of $500,000 after taxation, it can pay out the full $500,000 in dividends to its shareholders. However, because of **inflation, paying out profits in full would leave the company with fewer net assets, in 'real terms', than it had before**. The money values of its net assets would not be reduced, but the actual quantity of assets that is represented by the money value would have eroded. For example, the company originally has $12,000 of inventory made up of 400 items of $30 each. If the price of an item goes up to $40, closing inventory of $12,000 would only comprise 300 items. A powerful argument, particularly during periods of high inflation, is that profit should be measured in such a way that if it were to be paid out in full to the business owners, the business would not lose any 'real' substance. Its **operating capability**, for example, should be **maintained**. In order to measure profits in this way, the historical cost convention would have to be abandoned.

6.2 Profits (or losses) on monetary items are not reported

In periods of inflation the purchasing power, and thus the value, of money falls. It follows that if a business has a money investment, such as a bank deposit, the investment will have a lower real value at the end of a period of time than it did at the beginning. In reality, a loss has been incurred. Similarly, the real value of a monetary liability will reduce over a period of time and a gain will be made. This is seen by private individuals as one of the benefits of a mortgage: over time, property values rise with inflation, but the amount owed on the mortgage does not. The same benefit applies to businesses that owe money, for example by borrowing from a bank or by issuing 'bonds' to raise money in the capital markets.

6.3 Comparisons over time are unrealistic

Using the historical cost convention tends to exaggerate the growth in profits of a business over time. For example, if a company's profit in 1984 was $200,000 and in 2004 it was $500,000, a shareholder's initial reaction might be that the company had done rather well. If, however, it was then revealed that with $200,000 in 1984 he could buy exactly the same goods as with $500,000 in 2004, the 150% growth in profits would seem less impressive.

Exam focus point

> A question in the UK pilot paper required the calculation of inflation adjusted figures for a five year summary, with comments on the results and the means of calculation.

7 Capital maintenance

FAST FORWARD

Current value accounting provides for the maintenance of the real value of the owner's capital in times of rising prices, whereas historical cost accounting does not.

The principle of **capital maintenance** is that a company should at least maintain the amount of **capital invested**, and (if there has not been a new issue of equity in the period) retained profit is measured by the amount by which capital (net assets) is increased in the period.

Under the historical cost accounting convention, capital maintenance is measured in nominal money values. If an item with a historical cost of $500 is sold for $500, there has been no profit, but capital has been maintained. Under the current cost accounting convention, capital maintenance is measured in terms of the physical maintenance of the operating capability of the company. If an item that cost $500 is sold for $500 when its replacement cost has risen to $510, there has been a loss in current cost terms, because the $500 earned from the sale would be insufficient to replace the item that has been sold. In the same way, the depreciation of non-current assets should be based on the current cost of the non-current assets, not their original cost, if the company is to **maintain** its **physical operating capability** over time.

Supporters of current value accounting argue that, in **a period of rising prices, historical cost accounting overstates real profit**, because it does not provide properly, in the measurement of profit, for maintaining the physical operating capability of the business.

7.1 The unit of measurement

Another way to tackle the problems of capital maintenance in times of rising prices is to look at the **unit of measurement** in which accounting values are expressed.

It is an axiom of conventional accounting, as it has developed over the years, that value should be measured in terms of money. It is also **implicitly assumed** that **money values are stable**, so that $1 at the start of the financial year has the same value as $1 at the end of that year. But when **prices are rising**, this assumption is invalid: **$1 at the end of the year has less value (less purchasing power) than it had one year previously**.

This leads to problems when aggregating amounts which have arisen at different times. For example, a company's non-current assets may include items bought at different times over a period of many years. They will each have been recorded in $s, but the value of $1 will have varied over the period. In effect the **non-current asset figure in a historical cost balance sheet is an aggregate of a number of items expressed in different units**. It could be argued that such a figure is **meaningless**.

Faced with this argument, one possibility would be to re-state all accounts items in terms of a stable monetary unit. There would be difficulties in practice, but in theory there is no reason why a stable unit ($ CPP = $s of current purchasing power) should not be devised. In this section we will look at a system of accounting (current purchasing power accounting, or CPP) based on precisely this idea.

7.2 Specific and general price changes

We can identify two different types of price inflation.

When prices are rising, it is likely that the **current value of assets will also rise**, but not necessarily by the general rate of inflation. For example, if the replacement cost of a machine on 1 January 20X2 was $5,000, and the general rate of inflation in 20X2 was 8%, we would not necessarily expect the replacement cost of the machine at 31 December 20X2 to be $5,000 plus 8% = $5,400. The rate of price increase on the machinery might have been less than 8% or more than 8%. (Conceivably, in spite of general inflation, the replacement cost of the machinery might have gone down.)

(a) There is **specific price inflation**, which measures price changes over time for a specific asset or group of assets.

(b) There is **general price inflation**, which is the average rate of inflation, which reduces the general purchasing power of money.

To counter the problems of specific price inflation some system of current value accounting may be used (such as current cost accounting). The capital maintenance concepts underlying current value systems do not attempt to allow for the maintenance of real value in money terms.

Current purchasing power (CPP) accounting is based on a different concept of capital maintenance.

8 Current value models of accounting

FAST FORWARD

Alternatives to historical cost accounting are different systems of current value accounting. These take into consideration the effect of inflation, and as a consequence, assets are revalued to current value, but the reported operating profits of a business exclude the effects of 'holding gains'.

The points mentioned in Section 6 should suggest that with the historical cost convention of accounting, problems arise with reporting asset values, the substance of debts and profits in times of severe and prolonged inflation. Various suggestions have been put forward, as alternatives to the historical cost accounting method. Of these various possible systems of 'accounting for price changes', most can be divided into one of two categories.

(a) **General price** change bases of accounting, and in particular current purchasing power (CPP)

(b) **Current value** bases. The basic principles of current value accounting are:

    (i) to show balance sheet items at some form of current value rather than historical cost

    (ii) to compute profits by matching the current value of costs at the date of consumption against revenue

The current value of an item will normally be based on replacement cost, net realisable value or economic value.

8.1 Current purchasing power accounting

Key term

CPP measures profits as the increase in the current purchasing power of equity. Profits are therefore stated after allowing for the declining purchasing power of money due to price inflation.

When applied to historical cost accounting, CPP is a system of accounting which makes adjustments to income and capital values to allow for the general rate of price inflation.

8.2 Example

Beep Co has non-current assets purchased on 1 January 20X1 held at historical cost of $60,000. The general price index includes the following information:

Year	Date	Price index
20X1	1 January	100
20X4	31 December	160

At 31 December 20X4 CPP cost of non-current assets would be:

$$60,000 \times \frac{160}{100} = \$96,000$$

8.3 Current cost accounting

Current Cost Accounting (CCA) reflects an approach to capital maintenance based on maintaining the **operating** capability of a business.

The conceptual basis of CCA is that assets should be valued at their '**value to the business**' (also known as 'deprival value'). This is usually the current replacement cost of the asset, although it will be the recoverable amount of the asset, if this is lower than replacement cost. **Recoverable amount** in turn, is the higher of net realisable value and value in use. **Value in use** is the economic value to the company of continuing to use the asset for the remainder of its expected useful life.

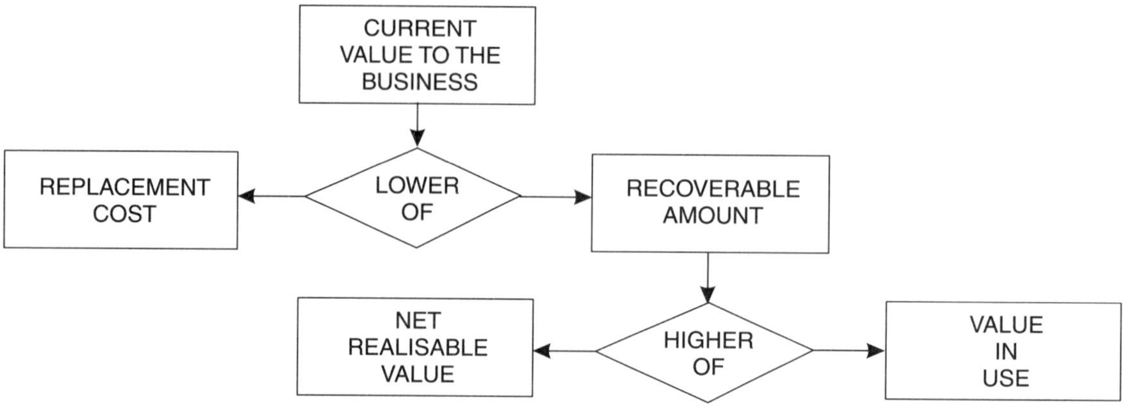

8.4 Example

A company has an item of equipment that has a replacement cost of $50,000. Its net realisable value is $25,000 and its value in use is $80,000. The current cost value of the asset is its replacement cost, $50,000, because this is lower than the recoverable amount of $80,000.

8.5 Holding gains

Holding gains are gains that are made simply by holding on to assets in a time of rising prices. They are equal to the difference between costs measured on a historical cost accounting basis and costs measured on a current cost accounting basis. For example, if the historical cost of an item of stock was $50, and its current value (replacement cost) is now $54, there has been a holding gain of $4.

A holding gain is *unrealised* as long as it remains in the ownership of the business. The holding gain is **realised** when the asset is sold or used in the period. For example, suppose that an inventory is purchased at the start of the year for $100, and when it is sold, its replacement cost has risen to $109. There is a realised holding gain of $9. The historical cost of sale is $100, but the current cost of sale is $109, to reflect the replacement cost of the sold item.

Holding gains also relate to non-current assets (and depreciation charges for the year) as well as the cost of inventories sold or consumed.

In a system of current cost accounting, both realised and unrealised holding gains are transferred to a special **current cost reserve** in the balance sheet. This segregates the holding gains from current cost profit.

8.6 Example

Fudge Co commenced business on 1 January 20X0. The balance sheets of the company at 31 December 20X0 have been prepared on two bases, the historical cost accounting basis and the current cost accounting basis. These balance sheets are given below:

Balance sheet as at 31 December 20X0

	Historical cost		*Current cost*	
	$	$	$	$
Tangible non-current assets		70,000		73,000
Less: Accumulated depreciation		(6,000)		(6,600)
		64,000		66,400
Current assets				
Inventory	8,000		9,000	
Cash	2,000		2,000	
		10,000		11,000
Total assets		74,000		77,400
Share capital		49,000		49,000
Profit for the year		20,000		15,000
Current cost reserve		-		8,400
		69,000		72,400
Loans		5,000		5,000
Total equity and liabilities		74,000		77,400

The current cost reserve is made up of unrealised holding gains of $3,400 and realised holding gains of $5,000.

The unrealised holding gains are the difference in non-current asset values ($2,400) plus the difference in the closing inventory values ($1,000). Since this is the first year of operation, the remaining $5,000 of the total current cost reserve must have arisen during trading this year, and will represent the difference in the historical profit and the current profit. A part of this difference is attributable to the difference in the depreciation charge for the year ($600). The remainder must be due to the difference between the historical cost and the current cost of the inventories sold.

The current cost accounting figures show that the company can distribute up to $15,000 in dividends without reducing the operating capability of the company below the level at the start of the year (when it began operating.)

9 Accounting for public sector organisations

FAST FORWARD

Public sector organisations are expected to achieve **value for money**. VFM is achieved through a combination of **effectiveness**, **efficiency** and **economy**.

Public sector organisations differ from companies in the private sector because:

(a) companies seek to earn a profit, and the directors are accountable to the shareholders

(b) public sector organisations are not-for-profit organisations, and have different objectives. They are also accountable to the public (or representatives of the public, in the form of a government representative).

9.1 Value for money regime

Whereas companies in the private sector are expected to make profits, public sector organisations have traditionally been expected to achieve **value for money.** Value for money has three elements:

(a) **Effectiveness**. This means success in achieving its not-for-money objectives. The objectives of a public sector organisation vary with the nature of the organisation. Hospitals have the objective of treating patients or reducing the incidence of certain illnesses. Schools have the objective of teaching numbers of students and achieving certain educational standards.

Effectiveness is judged by success in reaching any **identifiable** and **measurable** measure of achievement, or in making progress towards a **stated goal for achievement**.

(b) **Efficiency** means using resources well. Efficiency is a **measurement** of the **quantity** of **outputs** obtained per given quantity of **inputs**. In medicine, it might be the number of patients treated by each general practitioner. In education, it might be measured as a student: teacher ratio. Improvements in efficiency mean **getting more out of fewer input resources**, and so reducing costs per unit of output, and getting better value for money.

(c) **Economy** means keeping down the cost of input resources. Economy is achieved by **paying less for materials, labour, finance and other costs** such as accommodation. Whereas reducing over-staffing is a form of efficiency improvement, paying staff less to do a certain type of work would be an economy. In the hospitals, for example, switching the responsibility for a type of work from qualified doctors to trained nurses would be a form of economy, because nurses' time costs less than doctors' time. Similarly, switching responsibilities in the classroom from teachers to unqualified assistant helpers would be a form of economy.

Value for money is achieved by any combination of effectiveness, efficiency and economy. These factors are therefore likely to be the main focus of attention in the preparation and analysis of accounts for public sector organisations.

9.2 Best value framework

In some countries eg the UK, public sector organisations are required to review their services and set **challenging targets** for improving them.

There are various key elements to the best value approach.

- Continuous improvement
- Achieving a balance between quality and cost
- Improving accountability through better responsiveness to stakeholder needs.

The best value review process provides the opportunity to improve effectiveness, efficiency and economy by focusing on the so-called **four Cs**.

Challenge

- Why is the service provided?
- Can the service be provided in a better way?

Consult

- What do our customers think about the service?
- How do our employees believe we could improve the service?
- What do other service providing organisations think?

Compare

- How do our processes and practices compare with other similar organisations?
- Could we improve out services by adopting approaches used by others?

Compete

- How do our prices/charges, speed and quality compare with other service providers?
- Could the work be done more efficiently and effectively by another contractor?
- Could the service be improved by working in partnership with other organisations?

The overarching tool used to ensure delivery of best value in a public sector organisation is a **best value performance plan**. On a day-to-day level, performance management is driven by the use of **performance indicators** (or targets). (This is what public sector people are referring to when they appear on television discussing all the targets they have to meet.)

Activity 4.3

A report on the local library service of Seatown commented that the service had been successfully overhauled. The opening hours of the two libraries in the town had been reduced, with the result that some librarians were now employed part-time rather than full-time. In spite of this, the local council's intention to improve the reading habits of local residents seems to have improved, with the number of books taken out each year per head of the local population rising from 4.3 to 5.1, and the average period for which books were borrowed rising from 1.4 weeks to 1.75 weeks. The number of books borrowed per librarian employed (and per librarian hour) had risen substantially.

What elements of best value have been achieved in the local library service?

Key learning points

- The *Framework* states that qualitative characteristics are the attributes that make the information provided in the financial statements useful to users. These are understandability, relevancy, reliability, and comparability.
- Relevant information can have **predictive** and **confirmatory value**.
- **Materiality** revolves around whether the information involved would have influenced the economic decisions made by users.
- Faithful representation, substance, neutrality and prudence are important aspects of reliability.
- Disclosure of accounting policies aids comparability.
- Transactions and other events are grouped together in broad **classes** and in this way the financial effects are shown in financial statements. These broad classes are the **elements** of financial statements (assets, liabilities, equity, income and expenses.)
- **Recognition** is based on the definition of an element, probability of future economic benefits and reliability of measurement.
- Revenue should be recognised when it is probable that future economic benefits will flow to the entity and when these benefits can be measured reliability.
- Traditionally, financial statements have been prepared using the **historical cost convention**. This maintains that items should be recorded in the accounts at their original cost. This has serious drawbacks, particularly with regard to property valuations and in times of high inflation.
- Current value accounting provides for the maintenance of the real value of the owners' capital in times of rising prices, whereas historical cost accounting does not.
- Alternatives to historical cost accounting are different systems of **current value accounting**. These take into consideration the effect of inflation, and as a consequence, assets are revalued to current value, but the reported operating profits of a business exclude the effects of 'holding gains'.
- Public sector organisations are expected to achieve **value for money.** VFM is achieved through a combination of **effectiveness**, **efficiency** and **economy**.

Quick quiz

1 Define relevance.

2 In which two ways should users be able to compare an entity's financial statements?

3 What does prudence mean in the context of the preparation of accounts?

4 Is materiality essentially a numerical measure?

5 What is the historical cost of an item?

6 What are the drawbacks of historical cost accounting?

7 Name an alternative to historical cost accounting.

8 What are public sector organisations expected to achieve rather than making a profit?

Answers to quick quiz

1 Information has relevance when it influences the economic decisions of users by helping them evaluate past, present or future events or confirming (or correcting) their past evaluations.

2
- Through time to identify trends
- With other entity's statements

3 Exercising caution in circumstances where there is uncertainty. Should not be used as an exercise for setting up excessive provisions.

4 Assessing materiality is essentially a subjective exercise. Whilst relative size is important other factors such as nature and context should be considered.

5 The amount the business paid for it.

6 (a) Non-current asset values may be unrealistic.
(b) In a period of high inflation profits could be seriously overstated.
(c) Profits or losses on monetary items are not reported.
(d) Comparisons over time are unrealistic.

7 Current purchasing power accounting and current cost accounting.

8 Value for money.

Answers to activities

4.1 (a) This is an asset, albeit an intangible one. There is a past event, control and future economic benefit (through cost savings).

(b) This cannot be classified as an asset. Baldwin Co has no control over the car repair shop and it is difficult to argue that there are 'future economic benefits'.

(c) This is a liability; the business has taken on an obligation. It would be recognised when the warranty is issued rather than when a claim is made.

4.2 (a) A sale must never be recognised before the goods have even been ordered by a customer. There is no certainty about the value of the sale, nor when it will take place, even if it is virtually certain that goods will be sold.

(b) A sale must never be recognised when the customer places an order. Even though the order will be for a specific quantity of goods at a specific price, it is not yet certain that the sale transaction will go through. The customer may cancel the order, the supplier might be unable to deliver the goods as ordered or it may be decided that the customer is not a good credit risk.

(c) A sale will be recognised when delivery of the goods is made only when:

(i) the sale is for cash, and so the cash is received at the same time; or
(ii) the sale is on credit and the customer accepts delivery (eg by signing a delivery note).

(d) The critical event for a credit sale is usually the despatch of an invoice to the customer. There is then a legally enforceable debt, payable on specified terms, for a completed sale transaction.

(e) The critical event for a cash sale is when delivery takes place and when cash is received; both take place at the same time.

It would be too cautious or 'prudent' to await cash payment for a credit sale transaction before recognising the sale, unless the customer is a high credit risk and there is a serious doubt about his ability or intention to pay.

(f) It would again be over-cautious to wait for clearance of the customer's cheques before recognising sales revenue. Such a precaution would only be justified in cases where there is a very high risk of the bank refusing to honour the cheque.

4.3 The library service has clearly **consulted** users on opening houses and librarian service levels, probably by use of a survey or focus groups. The way the needs of users are satisfied has been **challenged** in terms of whether there is a better way the service can be provided.

Performance indicators have been set up to help the service managers monitor and measure performance.

- Annual average number of books borrowed per head.
- Average period for which books borrowed.
- Average number of books borrowed per librarian.

Effectiveness is therefore evident in the increase in the number of books borrowed per head of the population and the increase in the average length of book loans. **Efficiency** is evident in the increase in the number of books handled per librarian. **Economy** is evident in reducing library opening hours, and employing more part-time and fewer full-time staff.

Part C

Financial statements

5

Income statement

Topic list
1 The nature of limited companies
2 The financial statements of a limited company
3 Income statement
4 Changes in equity
5 Current tax
6 Deferred tax
7 IAS 33 *Earnings per share*

Introduction

This is an important practical area of the syllabus. Knowledge of the way in which an income statement is prepared is fundamental to success in this paper.

There are two aspects of income tax which must be accounted for: current tax and deferred tax. These will be discussed in Sections 5 and 6 respectively.

The purpose of any earnings yardstick is to achieve as far as possible clarity of meaning, comparability between one company and another, one year and another. IAS 33 *Earnings per share* goes some way to ensuring that these aims are achieved.

Learning objectives

On completion of this chapter you will be able to:

	Syllabus reference
• identify the nature of limited companies	3 a i
• explain the nature of dividends, how they are calculated and how they are reported in the income statement of a company	3 a i
• identify the component elements of a company's income statement, and the categories of expenses	3 a i
• identify the purpose of the statement of changes in equity	3 a iv, 3 c viii
• identify how the taxation charge in the income statement is made up, (in concept) the purpose of deferred taxation, and the methods of accounting for deferred taxation	3 a i, 3 c xi
• understand the meaning of earnings, earnings per share and fully diluted earnings per share, as reported on the face of the income statement	3 a i

1 The nature of limited companies

Limited companies are subject to extensive regulations in the preparation of their annual accounts. The form and content of the accounts may be regulated primarily by national legislation. This will often specify the minimum information that the accounts must show. The provisions of the legislation are normally supplemented by the requirements of the accounting standards. IAS1 *Presentation of financial statements* gives substantial guidance on the form and content of published financial statements.

The owners of a company are its **members** or **shareholders**, but a company is managed by its board of directors. In some companies, the directors are major shareholders. In larger companies, the directors may have some shares, but are not the major shareholders. Other shareholders use the annual accounts to assess the performance of their company and its management.

1.1 Share capital and dividends

FAST FORWARD

The ownership of a limited company is represented by shares. The owner of a company are its **members** or **shareholders.**

Exam focus point

Local rules and procedures may vary. The guidance below is based on the UK rules.

The owners' capital in a limited company is represented by **share capital**. When a company is set up for the first time, it issues shares. The shares are 'allotted' to investors, who pay for them and become shareholders of the company. Shares are denominated in units of 25 cents, 50 cents, $1 or whatever seems appropriate. The 'face value' of the shares is called their nominal value.

For example, when a company is set up with a share capital of, say, $100,000, the directors may decide to issue:

(a) 100,000 shares of $1 each nominal value, or
(b) 200,000 shares of 50 cents each, or
(c) 400,000 shares of 25 cents each, or
(d) 250,000 shares of 40 cents each etc

There may be several 'classes' of shares in a company.

(a) Preferred shares entitle their holders to a dividend each year. A preferred dividend is usually fixed, and expressed as a percentage amount each year on the nominal value of the shares. For example, a company with $1,000,000 of 5% preferred shares in issue will pay an annual preferred dividend of $50,000 to the holders of these shares.

(b) Ordinary shares represent the 'real' ownership of a company. Ordinary shareholders receive dividends out of profits, after preferred dividends have been paid. The amount of dividend in any year depends on the profitability of the company. Dividends are usually declared for ordinary shares in terms of 'x cents per share'. For example, if a company has 2 million ordinary shares of 50c each, and declares a dividend of 20 cents per share, the dividend payable will be $400,000 (2 million shares × 20c).

1.2 Declaring a dividend and paying a dividend

FAST FORWARD

Shareholders receive dividends out of profits. Dividends are commonly paid in two stages: an **interim dividend** and a **final dividend**.

Dividends are an appropriation of profit by the company's owners, and are similar to drawings by a sole trader or business partners from their business. Unlike dividends for sole traders and partnerships, however, company dividends are paid out of profits after the deduction of taxation. Companies are legal persons, and are liable to tax and shareholders 'own' the profits after tax.

Whilst some companies pay dividends annually, many companies pay dividends to their shareholders twice a year.

(a) An 'interim dividend' is paid in the middle of the financial year. For ordinary shares, the size of the interim dividend is decided by the board of directors. With preferred shares, shareholders receive one half of their fixed annual dividend.

(b) A 'final dividend' is paid after the end of the financial year. The final ordinary dividend is proposed to shareholders at the annual general meeting (AGM) of the company, which takes place some months after the end of the financial year. In this case the final proposed dividend is disclosed in the notes to the annual accounts of the company but under IAS10 *Events after the Balance Sheet Date* it is only recognised as a liability in the financial statements if it is declared on or before the balance sheet date.

1.3 Limited liability

Unlimited liability means that if a business runs up debts that it is unable to pay, the owners will become personally liable for the unpaid debts. They would be required, if necessary, to sell their private possessions in order to repay the debts of the business.

Sole traders and partners in most business partnerships have unlimited liability for the debts of their business. A new category of partnership, the 'limited liability partnership', has recently been introduced in some countries.

Limited companies offer limited liability to their owners.

Key term

Limited liability means that the maximum amount that an owner stands to lose in the event that the company becomes insolvent and cannot pay off its debts, is his share of the capital in the business. If the shares have been 'fully paid', the maximum that any investor stands to lose by investing in a company is the amount of his investment.

As a business grows, it needs more capital to finance its operations, and significantly more than the people currently managing the business can provide themselves. One way of obtaining more capital is to invite **investors from outside** the business to invest in the ownership or equity of the business. These new co-owners would not usually be expected to help with managing the business. To such investors, **limited liability is very attractive**.

Investments are always risky undertakings, but with limited liability the investor knows the maximum amount that he stands to lose when he puts some capital into a company.

1.4 Public and private companies

There are two classes of limited company.

(a) **Private companies**. Being private, they cannot invite members of the public to invest in their equity (ownership).

(b) **Public companies**. These are much fewer in number than private companies, but are generally much larger in size. Public limited companies can invite members of the general public to invest in their equity, and the shares of these companies may be traded on a public stock exchange, such as The London Stock Exchange in the UK.

2 The financial statements of a limited company

FAST FORWARD

IAS 1 covers the **form and content** of financial statements. The main components are:

- Balance sheet
- Income statement
- Statement of changes in equity/statement of recognised income and expenses
- Cash flow statement
- Accounting policies and explanatory notes to the financial statements

2.1 Overview

As well as covering accounting policies and other general considerations governing financial statements, IAS 1 *Presentation of financial statements* gives substantial guidance on the form and content of published financial statements. The standard looks at the balance sheet and income statement (the cash flow statement is covered by IAS 7). First of all, some general points are made about financial statements.

2.2 Profit or loss for the period

The income statement is the most significant indicator of a company's financial performance. So it is important to ensure that it is not misleading.

The income statement will be misleading if costs incurred in the current year are deducted not from the current year profits but from the balance of accumulated profits brought forward. This presents the current year's results more favourably.

IAS 1 stipulates that all items of income and expense recognised in a period shall be included in profit or loss unless a **Standard** or an **Interpretation** requires otherwise.

Circumstances where items may be excluded from profit or loss for the current year include the correction of errors and the effect of changes in accounting policies. These are covered in IAS 8 which we look at in chapter 7.

2.3 How items are disclosed

IAS 1 specifies disclosures of certain items in certain ways.

- Some items must appear on the **face of the balance sheet or income statement**
- Other items can appear in a **note to the financial statements** instead

- **Recommended formats** are given which entities may or may not follow, depending on their circumstances

Obviously, disclosures specified by **other standards** must also be made, and we will mention the necessary disclosures when we cover each statement in turn. Disclosures in both IAS 1 and other standards must be made either on the face of the statement or in the notes unless otherwise stated, ie disclosures cannot be made in an accompanying commentary or report.

2.4 Identification of financial statements

As a result of the above point, it is most important that entities **distinguish the financial statements** very clearly from any other information published with them. This is because all IASs apply *only* to the financial statements (ie the main statements and related notes), so readers of the annual report must be able to differentiate between the parts of the report which are prepared under IASs, and other parts which are not.

The entity should **identify each component** of the financial statements very clearly. IAS 1 also requires disclosure of the following information in a prominent position. If necessary it should be repeated wherever it is felt to be of use to the reader in their understanding of the information presented.

- **Name** of the reporting entity (or other means of identification)
- Whether the accounts cover a **single entity** only or a group of entities
- The **balance sheet date** or the period covered by the financial statements (as appropriate)
- The **reporting currency**
- The **level of precision** used in presenting the figures in the financial statements

Judgement must be used to determine the best method of presenting this information. In particular, the standard suggests that the approach to this will be very different when the financial statements are communicated electronically.

The **level of precision** is important, as presenting figures in thousands or millions of units makes the figures more understandable. The level of precision must be disclosed, however, and it should not obscure necessary details or make the information less relevant.

2.5 Reporting period

It is normal for entities to present financial statements **annually** and IAS 1 states that they should be prepared at least as often as this. If (unusually) an entity's balance sheet date is changed, for whatever reason, the period for which the statements are presented will be less or more than one year. In such cases the entity should also disclose:

(a) the **reason(s) why** a period other than one year is used; and

(b) the fact that the comparative figures given **are not in fact comparable** (in particular for the income statement, changes in equity, cash flows and related notes).

For practical purposes, some entities prefer to use a period which **approximates to a year**, eg 52 weeks, and the IAS allows this approach as it will produce statements not materially different from those produced on an annual basis.

2.6 Timeliness

If the publication of financial statements is delayed too long after the balance sheet date, their usefulness will be severely diminished. The standard states that entities should be able to produce their financial statements **within six months of the balance sheet date.** An entity with consistently complex operations cannot use this as a reason for its failure to report on a timely basis. Local legislation and market regulation imposes specific deadlines on certain entities.

IAS 1 looks at the balance sheet and the income statement. We will not give all the detailed disclosures as some are outside the scope of your syllabus. Instead we will look at a **'proforma' set of accounts** based on the Standard.

2.7 Disclosure of accounting policies

There should be a specific section for accounting policies in the notes to the financial statements. The following disclosure should be made:

(a) **Measurement bases** used in preparing the financial statements.

(b) Each specific **accounting policy** necessary for a proper understanding of the financial statements.

3 Income statement

FAST FORWARD

An income statement gives detailed information about information about income, expenses and profits of a business.

A useful starting point for an understanding of a company's income statement is to look at an example. The proforma income statements below are taken from IAS1.

Exam alert

IASs do not set out an obligatory format but it would be best practice to use the suggested format of IAS1.

3.1 Examples of income statements

IAS 1 offers two possible formats for the income statement, the difference between the two being the classification of expenses: by function or by nature.

XYZ GROUP
INCOME STATEMENT FOR THE YEAR ENDED 31 DECEMBER 20X8

Illustrating the classification of expenses by function

	20X8	*20X7*
	$'000	$'000
Revenue	X	X
Cost of sales	(X)	(X)
Gross profit	X	X
Other income	X	X
Distribution costs	(X)	(X)
Administrative expenses	(X)	(X)
Other expenses	(X)	(X)
Finance costs	(X)	(X)
Share of profit of associates	X	X
Profit before tax	X	X
Income tax expense	(X)	(X)
Profit for the period	X	X
Attributable to:		
Equity holders of the parent	X	X
Minority interest	X	X
	X	X

Illustrating the classification of expenses by nature

	20X8	20X7
	$'000	$'000
Revenue	X	X
Other operating income	X	X
Changes in inventories of finished goods and work in progress	(X)	X
Work performed by the entity and capitalised	X	X
Raw materials and consumables used	(X)	(X)
Employee benefits expense	(X)	(X)
Depreciation and amortisation expense	(X)	(X)
Impairment of property, plant and equipment	(X)	(X)
Other expenses	(X)	(X)
Finance costs	(X)	(X)
Share of profit of associates	X	X
Profit before tax	X	X
Income tax expense	(X)	(X)
Profit for the period	X	X
Attributable to:		
Equity holders of the parent	X	X
Minority interest	X	X
	X	X

3.2 Information presented on the face of the income statement

IAS 1 lists the following as the **minimum** to be disclosed on the face of the income statement.

(a) Revenue

(b) Finance costs

(c) Share of profits and losses of associates and joint ventures accounted for using the equity method (this relates to group accounts which we deal with in a later chapter).

(d) Pre-tax gain or loss recognised on the disposal of assets or settlement of liabilities attributable to discontinued operations

(e) Tax expense

(f) Profit or loss

The following items must be disclosed on the face of the income statement as allocations of profit or loss for the period.

(a) Profit or loss **attributable to minority interest**
(b) Profit or loss **attributable to equity holders of the parent**

The allocated amounts must not be presented as items of income or expense. There is a similar requirement for the statement of changes in equity or statement of recognised income and expense. (These relate to group accounts, covered later in this text.)

Income and expense items can only be **offset** when, and only when:

(a) It is permitted or required by an IFRS, or

(b) Gains, losses and related expenses arising from the same or similar transactions and events are immaterial, in which case they can be aggregated.

3.3 Information presented either on the face of the income statement or in the notes

An analysis of expenses must be shown either on the face of the income statement (as above, which is encouraged by the standard) or by note. This **sub-classification of expenses** indicates a range of components of financial performance; these may differ in terms of stability, potential for gain or loss and predictability.

When items of income and expense are material their nature and amount should be disclosed separately. This might include write downs of inventory or property, plant and equipment, disposals of property, plant and equipment or investments, discontinuing operations and litigation settlements.

3.4 Dividends

Dividends are not shown on the income statement. However, IAS 1 requires disclosure of the amount of **dividends per share** (declared or proposed) for the period covered by the financial statements. This may be shown either on the face of the income statement or in the statement of changes in equity. (See section 4.)

3.5 Other points to note

(a) Revenue excludes items of income such as income from investments and interest receivable.

(b) Companies are required to analyse their operating costs. IAS 1 allows expenses to be classified by function or by nature. (see 3.1)

The format classifying expenses by function is much more common in practice and should be used in your exam unless the question specifies otherwise.

Operating costs are split between cost of sales, distribution costs and administrative expenses. IAS 1 does not specify which costs should be allocated to which category. Typically, however distribution costs and administrative expenses would include the following:

- Distribution costs: Delivery costs, depreciation of warehouse, showroom, delivery vehicles and salesmen's cars, advertising, salesmen's salaries and commissions.
- Administrative expenses: rent, light and heat, director's remuneration, depreciation of officers and staff cars and other overheads.

(c) Gross profit is sales revenue minus the cost of sales.

4 Changes in equity

FAST FORWARD

IAS 1 requires a statement of changes in equity.

4.1 Statement of changes in equity

The statement can be in the format illustrated below (showing all changes in equity) or in the form of a statement of recognised income and expense.

XYZ GROUP
STATEMENT OF CHANGES IN EQUITY FOR THE YEAR ENDED 31 DECEMBER 20X8

	Attributable to equity holders of the parent						
	Share capital $'000	*Other reserves* $'000	*Translation reserve* $'000	*Retained earnings* $'000	*Total* $'000	*Minority interest* $'000	*Total equity* $'000
Balance at 31 December 20X7 brought forward	X	X	(X)	X	X	X	X
Changes in equity for 20X8							
Loss on property revaluation		(X)			(X)	(X)	(X)
Available-for-sale investments:							
Valuation gains (losses) taken to equity		(X)			(X)		(X)
Transferred to profit or loss on sale		X			X		X
Net income recognised directly in equity		(X)	(X)	–	(X)	(X)	(X)
Profit for the period		–	–	X	X	X	X
Total recognised income and expense for the period		(X)	(X)	X	X	X	X
Dividends				(X)	(X)	(X)	(X)
Issue of share capital	X	–	–	–	X	–	X
Balance at 31 December 20X8	X	X	(X)	X	X	X	X

4.2 Statement of recognised income and expense

This is an alternative method of presenting changes in equity. If this method is used, the notes to the financial statements must include a reconciliation of opening and closing balances of share capital, reserves and accumulated profit, as illustrated in the statement of changes in equity.

XYZ GROUP
STATEMENT OF RECOGNISED INCOME AND EXPENSE
FOR THE YEAR ENDED 31 DECEMBER 20X8

	20X8 $'000	*20X7* $'000
Gain/(loss) on revaluation of properties	(X)	X
Available-for-sale investments:		
Valuation gains/(losses) taken to equity	(X)	(X)
Transferred to profit or loss on sale	X	(X)
Net income recognised directly in equity	X	X
Net profit for the period	X	X
Total recognised income and expense for the period	X	X
Attributable to:		
Equity holders of the parent	X	X
Minority interest	X	X
	X	X
Effect of changes in accounting policy:		
Equity holders of the parent		(X)
Minority interest		(X)
		(X)

5 Current tax

FAST FORWARD

The tax charge for the year will include a estimate of the current year's tax and an adjustment for any under/over provisions from previous years.

5.1 Introduction

The **taxable profits** of an entity essentially comprise its net profit before dividends adjusted for certain items where the tax treatment differs from the accounting treatment.

The amount of tax to which a company is assessed on its profit for an accounting period is called its **tax liability** for that period. In general, an entity must pay its tax liability a certain amount of time after the period end (although in some countries, entities may have to make monthly or quarterly 'payments on account.')

In a simple situation the adjustment for tax would affect the financial statement as follows.

- introduce tax charge in the income statement (debit tax charge)
- create tax liability in the balance sheet (credit tax liability)

5.2 Recognition of current tax liabilities and assets

IAS 12 *Income taxes* requires any unpaid tax in respect of the current or prior periods to be recognised as a liability.

Conversely any excess tax paid should be recognised as an asset.

Activity 5.1

In 20X8 Darton Co had taxable profits of $120,000. In the previous year (20X7) income tax on 20X7 profits had been estimated as $30,000.

Required

Calculate tax payable and the charge for 20X8 if the tax due on 20X7 profits was subsequently agreed with the tax authorities as:

(a) $35,000; or
(b) $25,000.

Any under or over payments are not settled until the following year's tax payment is due.

Assume a corporate income tax rate of 30%.

5.3 Presentation

In the balance sheet, **tax assets and liabilities** should be shown separately from other assets and liabilities. (See chapter 6).

The tax expense/(income) should be shown on the face of the income statement.

6 Deferred tax

FAST FORWARD

Deferred tax is an accounts measure, used to match the tax effects of transactions with their accounting impact.

Exam focus point

You are unlikely to be asked any very complicated questions on deferred tax in this paper, so concentrate on understanding and being able to explain the purpose of deferred tax and to carry out basic calculations.

6.1 What is deferred tax?

When a company recognises an asset or liability, it expects to **recover or settle the carrying amount** of that asset or liability. In other words, it expects to sell or use up assets, and to pay off liabilities. What happens if that recovery or settlement is likely to make future tax payments larger (or smaller) than they would otherwise have been if the recovery or settlement had no tax consequences? In these circumstances, IAS 12 requires companies to recognise a **deferred tax liability** (or **deferred tax asset**).

6.2 Definitions

Don't worry too much if you don't understand the concept of deferred tax yet; things should become clearer as you work through this section. First of all, here are the definitions relating to deferred tax given in IAS 12.

Key terms

- **Deferred tax liabilities** are the amounts of income taxes payable in future periods in respect of taxable temporary differences.
- **Deferred tax assets** are the amounts of income taxes recoverable in future periods in respect of:
  - Deductible temporary differences
  - The carryforward of unused tax losses
  - The carryforward of unused tax credits
- **Temporary differences** are differences between the carrying amount of an asset or liability in the balance sheet and its tax base. Temporary differences may be either:
  - **Taxable temporary differences**, which are temporary differences that will result in taxable amounts in determining taxable profit (tax loss) of future periods when the carrying amount of the asset or liability is recovered or settled
  - **Deductible temporary differences**, which are temporary differences that will result in amounts that are deductible in determining taxable profit (tax loss) of future periods when the carrying amount of the asset or liability is recovered or settled
- The **tax base** of an asset or liability is the amount attributed to that asset or liability for tax purposes. *(IAS 12)*

We need to look at some of these definitions in more detail.

6.3 Tax base

We can expand on the definition given above by stating that the **tax base of an asset** is the amount that will be deductible for tax purposes against any taxable economic benefits that will flow to the entity when it recovers the carrying value of the asset. Where those economic benefits are not taxable, the tax base of the asset is the same as its carrying amount.

Activity 5.2

State the tax base of each of the following assets.

(a) A machine cost $10,000. For tax purposes, depreciation of $3,000 has already been deducted in the current and prior periods and the remaining cost will be deductible in future periods, either as depreciation or through a deduction on disposal. Revenue generated by using the machine is taxable, any gain on disposal of the machine will be taxable and any loss on disposal will be deductible for tax purposes.

(b) Interest receivable has a carrying amount of $1,000. The related interest revenue will be taxed on a cash basis.

(c) Trade receivables have a carrying amount of $10,000. The related revenue has already been included in taxable profit (tax loss).

(d) A loan receivable has a carrying amount of $1m. The repayment of the loan will have no tax consequences.

In the case of a **liability**, the tax base will be its carrying amount, less any amount that will be deducted for tax purposes in relation to the liability in future periods. For revenue received in advance, the tax base of the resulting liability is its carrying amount, less any amount of the revenue that will *not* be taxable in future periods.

Activity 5.3

State the tax base of each of the following liabilities.

(a) Current liabilities include accrued expenses with a carrying amount of $1,000. The related expense will be deducted for tax purposes on a cash basis.

(b) Current liabilities include interest revenue received in advance, with a carrying amount of $10,000. The related interest revenue was taxed on a cash basis.

(c) Current liabilities include accrued expenses with a carrying amount of $2,000. The related expense has already been deducted for tax purposes.

(d) Current liabilities include accrued fines and penalties with a carrying amount of $100. Fines and penalties are not deductible for tax purposes.

(e) A loan payable has a carrying amount of $1m. The repayment of the loan will have no tax consequences.

IAS 12 gives the following examples of circumstances in which the carrying amount of an asset or liability will be **equal to its tax base**.

- **Accrued expenses** have already been deducted in determining an entity's current tax liability for the current or earlier periods.
- A **loan payable** is measured at the amount originally received and this amount is the same as the amount repayable on final maturity of the loan.
- **Accrued expenses** will never be deductible for tax purposes.
- **Accrued income** will never be taxable.

6.4 Temporary differences

You may have found the definition of temporary differences somewhat confusing. Remember that accounting profits form the basis for computing **taxable profits**, on which the tax liability for the year is calculated; however, accounting profits and taxable profits are different. There are two reasons for the differences.

(a) **Permanent differences**. These occur when certain items of revenue or expense are excluded from the computation of taxable profits (for example, entertainment expenses may not be allowable for tax purposes).

(b) **Temporary differences**. These occur when items of revenue or expense are included in both accounting profits and taxable profits, but not for the same accounting period. For example, an expense which is allowable as a deduction in arriving at taxable profits for 20X7 might not be included in the financial accounts until 20X8 or later. In the long run, the total taxable profits and total accounting profits will be the same (except for permanent differences) so that temporary differences originate in one period and are capable of reversal in one or more subsequent periods. Deferred tax is the tax attributable to **temporary differences.**

6.5 Taxable temporary differences

FAST FORWARD

All taxable temporary differences give rise to a deferred tax liability.

Examples

The following are examples of circumstances that give rise to taxable temporary differences. However, don't worry too much about the detail. You just need to be aware of what might cause deferred tax to appear in the financial statements.

- **Interest revenue** received in arrears and included in accounting profit on the basis of time apportionment. It is included in taxable profit, however, on a cash basis.
- **Sale of goods revenue** is included in accounting profit when the goods are delivered, but only included in taxable profit when cash is received.
- **Depreciation** of an asset is accelerated for tax purposes. When new assets are purchased, allowances may be available against taxable profits which exceed the amount of depreciation chargeable on the assets in the financial accounts for the year of purchase.
- **Development costs** which have been capitalised will be amortised in the income statement, but they were deducted in full from taxable profit in the period in which they were incurred.
- **Prepaid expenses** have already been deducted on a cash basis in determining the taxable profit of the current or previous periods.
- Property, plant and equipment is **revalued** by an entity (under IAS 16), but no equivalent adjustment is made for tax purposes.

6.5.1 Example: taxable temporary differences

A company purchased an asset costing $1,500. At the end of 20X8 the carrying amount is $1,000. The cumulative depreciation for tax purposes is $900 and the current tax rate is 25%.

Required

Calculate the deferred tax liability for the asset.

Solution

Firstly, what is the tax base of the asset? It is \$1,500 – \$900 = \$600.

In order to recover the carrying value of \$1,000, the entity must earn taxable income of \$1,000, but it will only be able to deduct \$600 as a taxable expense. The entity must therefore pay income tax of \$400 × 25% = \$100 when the carrying value of the asset is recovered.

The entity must therefore recognise a deferred tax liability of \$400 × 25% = \$100, recognising the difference between the carrying amount of \$1,000 and the tax base of \$600 as a taxable temporary difference.

6.5.2 Timing differences

Some temporary differences are often called **timing differences**, when income or expense is included in accounting profit in one period, but is included in taxable profit in a different period. The main types of taxable temporary differences which are timing differences and which result in deferred tax liabilities are included in the examples given above.

- **Interest received** which is accounted for on an accruals basis, but which for tax purposes is included on a cash basis.
- **Accelerated depreciation** for tax purposes.
- Capitalised and amortised **development costs**.

Example: Current and deferred tax

Jonquil Co buys equipment for \$50,000 on 1 January 20X1 and depreciates it on a straight line basis over its expected useful life of five years. For tax purposes, the equipment is depreciated at 25% per annum on a straight line basis. Tax losses may be carried back against taxable profit of the previous five years. In year 20X0, the entity's taxable profit was \$25,000. The tax rate is 40%.

Required

Assuming nil profits/losses after depreciation in years 20X1 to 20X5 show the current and deferred tax impact in years 20X1 to 20X5 of the acquisition of the equipment.

Solution

Jonquil Co will recover the carrying amount of the equipment by using it to manufacture goods for resale. Therefore, the entity's **current tax** computation is as follows.

			Year		
	20X1	*20X2*	*20X3*	*20X4*	*20X5*
	\$	\$	\$	\$	\$
Taxable income*	10,000	10,000	10,000	10,000	10,000
Depreciation for tax purposes	12,500	12,500	12,500	12,500	0
Taxable profit/(tax loss)	(2,500)	(2,500)	(2,500)	(2,500)	10,000
Current tax expense/(income) at 40%	(1,000)	(1,000)	(1,000)	(1,000)	4,000

* ie nil profit plus \$50,000 ÷ 5 depreciation add-back.

The entity recognises a current tax asset at the end of years 20X1 to 20X4 because it recovers the benefit of the tax loss against the taxable profit of year 20X0.

The temporary differences associated with the equipment and the resulting deferred tax asset and liability and deferred tax expense and income are as follows.

			Year		
	20X1	*20X2*	*20X3*	*20X4*	*20X5*
	$	$	$	$	$
Carrying amount	40,000	30,000	20,000	10,000	0
Tax base	37,500	25,000	12,500	0	0
Taxable temporary difference	2,500	5,000	7,500	10,000	0
Opening deferred tax liability	0	1,000	2,000	3,000	4,000
Deferred tax expense/(income): bal fig	1,000	1,000	1,000	1,000	(4,000)
Closing deferred tax liability @ 40%	1,000	2,000	3,000	4,000	0

The entity recognises the deferred tax liability in years 20X1 to 20X4 because the reversal of the taxable temporary difference will create taxable income in subsequent years. The entity's income statement is as follows.

			Year		
	20X1	*20X2*	*20X3*	*20X4*	*20X5*
	$	$	$	$	$
Income	10,000	10,000	10,000	10,000	10,000
Depreciation	10,000	10,000	10,000	10,000	10,000
Profit before tax	0	0	0	0	0
Current tax expense/(income)	(1,000)	(1,000)	(1,000)	(1,000)	4,000
Deferred tax expense/(income)	1,000	1,000	1,000	1,000	(4,000)
Total tax expense/(income)	0	0	0	0	0
Net profit for the period	0	0	0	0	0

Notice that the charge (or credit) to the income statement for deferred tax is the difference between the opening and closing liability.

6.6 Deductible temporary differences

FAST FORWARD

All deductible temporary differences give rise to a deferred tax asset.

6.6.1 Examples

The deferred tax asset must also satisfy the **recognition criteria** given in IAS 12. These state that a deferred tax asset should be recognised for all deductible temporary differences to the extent that it is **probable that taxable profit will be available** against which it can be utilised. This is an application of prudence. Before we look at this issue in more detail, let us consider the examples of deductible temporary differences given in the standard. Again, don't worry too much about the detail. These examples are a useful aid in trying to understand the principles.

6.6.2 Transactions that affect the income statement

- **Retirement benefit costs** (pension costs) are deducted from accounting profit as service is provided by the employee. They are not deducted in determining taxable profit until the entity pays either retirement benefits or contributions to a fund. (This may also apply to similar expenses.)
- **Accumulated depreciation** of an asset in the financial statements is greater than the accumulated depreciation allowed for tax purposes up to the balance sheet date.
- The **cost of inventories** sold before the balance sheet date is deducted from accounting profit when goods/services are delivered, but is deducted from taxable profit when the cash is received.

- The **NRV** of inventory, or the **recoverable amount** of an item of property, plant and equipment falls and the carrying value is therefore **reduced**, but that reduction is ignored for tax purposes until the asset is sold.
- **Research costs** (or organisation/other start-up costs) are recognised as an expense for accounting purposes but are not deductible against taxable profits until a later period.
- Income is **deferred** in the balance sheet, but has already been included in taxable profit in current/prior periods.

6.6.3 Example: deductible temporary differences

Pargatha Co recognises a liability of $10,000 for accrued product warranty costs on 31 December 20X7. These product warranty costs will not be deductible for tax purposes until the entity pays claims. The tax rate is 25%.

Required

State the deferred tax implications of this situation.

Solution

What is the tax base of the liability? It is nil (carrying amount of $10,000 less the amount that will be deductible for tax purposes in respect of the liability in future periods).

When the liability is settled for its carrying amount, the entity's future taxable profit will be reduced by $10,000 and so its future tax payments by $10,000 × 25% = $2,500.

The difference of $10,000 between the carrying amount ($10,000) and the tax base (nil) is a deductible temporary difference. The entity should therefore recognise a deferred tax asset of $10,000 × 25% = $2,500 **provided that** it is probable that the entity will earn sufficient taxable profits in future periods to benefit from a reduction in tax payments.

6.7 Measurement and recognition of deferred tax

IAS12 requires the full provision method of accounting for deferred tax to be used.

There are various methods of accounting for deferred tax, only one of which is adopted by IAS 12.

- **Flow-through method**
- **Full provision method** (as under IAS 12)
- **Partial provision method** (as adopted in some countries, eg formerly the UK)

You must understand the differences between these methods and the conceptual reasons why **IAS 12 adopts the full provision method**.

Under the **flow-through method**, the tax liability recognised is the expected current tax liability for the period (ie no provision is made for deferred tax). The main **advantages** of the method are that it is straightforward to apply and the tax liability recognised is closer to many people's idea of a 'real' liability than that recognised under either full or partial provision. The main **disadvantages** of flow-through are that it can lead to large fluctuations in the tax charge and that it does not allow tax relief for non-current liabilities to be recognised until those liabilities are settled. In addition, profits may be overstated because there is no deferred tax charge leading to excessive dividend payments, distortion of earnings per share and of results in the eyes of shareholders.

The **full provision method** has the **advantage** that it recognises that each temporary difference at the balance sheet date has an effect on future tax payments. If a company claims an accelerated tax allowance on an item of plant, future tax assessments will be bigger than they would have been otherwise. Future transactions may well affect those assessments still further, but that is not relevant in assessing the position at the balance sheet date. The **disadvantage** of full provision is that, under certain types of tax system, it gives rise to large liabilities that may fall due only far in the future, if at all. Furthermore, it may be said to be less realistic than the partial provision method, if more objective.

The **partial provision method** addresses this disadvantage by providing for deferred tax only to the extent that it is expected to be paid in the foreseeable future. This has an obvious intuitive appeal, but its effect is that deferred tax recognised at the balance sheet date includes the tax effects of future transactions that have not been recognised in the financial statements, and which the reporting company has neither undertaken nor even committed to undertake at that date. It is difficult to reconcile this with the IASB's *Framework* document, which defines assets and liabilities as arising from past events. Where partial provision is required, the difference between the amount provided and the maximum (ie under the full provision method) should usually be disclosed.

Example: the three methods compared

Suppose that Girdo Co begins trading on 1 January 20X7. In its first year it makes profits of $5m, the depreciation charge is $1m and the tax allowances on those assets is $1.5m. The rate of corporation tax is 30%.

Solution: flow through method

The tax liability for the year is 30% × $(5.0 + 1.0 – 1.5)m = $1.35m. The potential deferred tax liability of 30% × ($1.5m – $1m) is completely ignored and no judgement is required on the part of the preparer.

Solution: full provision

The current tax liability is $1.35m again, but the debit in the income statement is increased by the deferred tax liability of 30% × $0.5m = $150,000. The total charge to the income statement is therefore $1.5m which is an effective tax rate of 30% on accounting profits (ie 30% × $5.0m). Again, no judgement is involved in using this method.

Solution: partial provision

Is a deferred tax provision necessary under partial provision? We need to look ahead at future capital expenditure plans. Will tax allowances exceed depreciation over the next few years? If *yes*, no provision for deferred tax is required. If *no*, then a reversal is expected, ie there will be a year in which depreciation is greater than tax allowances. The deferred tax provision is made on the maximum reversal which will be created, and any not provided is disclosed by note.

If we assume that the review of expected future capital expenditure under the partial provision method required a deferred tax charge of $75,000 (30% × $250,000), we can then summarise the position.

Summary

The methods can be compared as follows.

Method	*Provision* $	*Disclosure* $
Flow-through	-	-
Full provision	150,000	-
Partial provision	75,000	75,000

Exam focus point

> In the UK June 2005 exam candidates were required to explain both current tax and deferred tax and prepare some simple calculations of financial statement figures.

6.8 Section summary

- Deferred tax is an **accounting device**. It does *not* represent tax currently payable to the tax authorities.
- The **tax base** of an asset or liability is the value of that asset or liability for tax purposes.
- You should understand the difference between **permanent and temporary differences**.
- Deferred tax is the tax attributable to **temporary differences**.

7 IAS 33 *Earnings per share*

FAST FORWARD

Earnings per share is a measure of the amount of profits earned by a company for each ordinary share. Earnings are profits after tax and preferred dividends.

7.1 Significance of earnings per share

Earnings per share (EPS) is one of the most frequently quoted statistics in financial analysis. Because of the widespread use of the price earnings (P/E) ratio as a yardstick for investment decisions, it has become increasingly important. It is a measure of the amount of profit earned by a company during the financial year that can be attributed to each ordinary share.

7.2 Basic EPS

You need to know how basic EPS is calculated.

Basic EPS should be calculated by dividing the **net profit** or loss for the period attributable to ordinary shareholders by the **weighted average number of ordinary shares** outstanding during the period.

$$\text{Basic EPS} = \frac{\text{Net profit/(loss) attributable to ordinary shareholders}}{\text{Weighted average number of ordinary shares outstanding during the period}}$$

Earnings

Earnings includes **all items of income and expense** (including tax and minority interests) *less* net profit attributable to **preference shareholders**, including preference dividends.

Preference dividends deducted from net profit consist of:

(a) Preference dividends on non-cumulative preference shares declared in respect of the period

(b) The full amount of the required preference dividends for cumulative preference shares for the period, *whether or not* they have been declared (*excluding* those paid/declared during the period in respect of previous periods)

Per share

The number of ordinary shares used should be the weighted average number of ordinary shares during the period. By using this figure the corresponding EPS for the previous year will be comparable with the current year because as the weighted average number of shares has risen or fallen, there has been a **corresponding increase or decrease in resources**.

Example: weighted average

A Co has earnings of $200,000 and a year end of 31 December. On 1.10.X7 the company has 600,000 shares. On 1.10.X7 the company issued 300,000 shares at full market price.

Solution

In this case a weighted average number of shares would have to be calculated as follows:

1.1.X7	$600{,}000 \times \frac{9}{12}$	450,000
1.10.X7	$900{,}000 \times \frac{3}{12}$	225,000
		675,000

$$\text{Eps} = \frac{\$200{,}000}{675{,}000} = \$0.296$$

There are however other events which change the number of shares outstanding without a corresponding change in resources. These include bonus issues and rights issues. In these circumstances it is necessary to make adjustments so that the current and prior period EPS figures are comparable.

Activity 5.4

Flame Co is a company with a called up and paid up capital of 100,000 ordinary shares of $1 each and 20,000 10% preferred shares of $1 each. The company manufactures gas appliances.

The profit before tax was $150,000. Flame Co paid the required preferred share dividend and declared an ordinary dividend of 42c per share. Assuming an income tax rate of 30% on the given figures show the trading results and EPS of the company.

7.3 Example: earnings per share with a bonus issue

Greymatter Co had 400,000 shares in issue, until on 30 September 20X2 it made a bonus issue of 100,000 shares. Calculate the EPS for 20X2 and the corresponding figure for 20X1 if total earnings were $80,000 in 20X2 and $75,000 in 20X1. The company's accounting year runs from 1 January to 31 December.

Solution

	20X2		*20X1*	
Earnings	$80,000		$75,000	
Shares at 1 January	400,000		400,000	
Bonus issue	100,000		100,000	
	500,000	shares	500,000	shares
EPS	16c		15c	

The number of shares for 20X1 must also be adjusted if the figures for EPS are to remain comparable.

7.4 Rights issue

A rights issue of shares is an issue of new shares to existing shareholders **at a price below the current market value**. The offer of new shares is made on the basis of x new shares for every y shares currently held; eg a 1 for 3 rights issue is an offer of 1 new share at the offer price for every 3 shares currently held. This means that there is a bonus element included.

To arrive at figures for EPS when a rights issue is made, we need to calculate first of all the **theoretical ex-rights price**. This is a weighted average value per share, and is perhaps explained most easily with a numerical example.

7.5 Example: theoretical ex-rights price

Suppose that Egghead Co has 10,000,000 shares in issue. It now proposes to make a 1 for 4 rights issue at a price of $3 per share. The market value of existing shares on the final day before the issue is made is $3.50 (this is the 'with rights' value). What is the theoretical ex-rights price per share?

Solution

	$
Before issue 4 shares, value $3.50 each	14.00
Rights issue 1 share, value $3	3.00
Theoretical value of 5 shares	17.00

$$\text{Theoretical ex-rights price} = \frac{\$17.00}{5} = \$3.40 \text{ per share}$$

Note that this calculation can alternatively be performed using the total value and number of outstanding shares.

7.6 Procedures

The procedures for calculating the EPS for the current year and a corresponding figure for the previous year are now as follows.

(a) The **EPS for the corresponding previous period** should be multiplied by the following fraction. (*Note.* The market price on the last day of quotation is taken as the fair value immediately prior to exercise of the rights, as required by the standard.)

Formula to learn

$$\frac{\text{Theoretical ex - rights price}}{\text{Market price on last day of quotation (with rights)}}$$

(b) To obtain the **EPS for the current year** you should:

(i) Multiply the number of shares before the rights issue by the fraction of the year before the date of issue and by the following fraction

Formula to learn

$$\frac{\text{Market price on last day of quotation with rights}}{\text{Theoretical ex - rights price}}$$

(ii) Multiply the number of shares after the rights issue by the fraction of the year after the date of issue and add to the figure arrived at in (i)

The total earnings should then be divided by the total number of shares so calculated.

7.7 Example: earnings per share with a rights issue

Brains Co had 100,000 shares in issue, but then makes a 1 for 5 rights issue on 1 October 20X2 at a price of $1. The market value on the last day of quotation with rights was $1.60.

Calculate the EPS for 20X2 and the corresponding figure for 20X1 given total earnings of $50,000 in 20X2 and $40,000 in 20X1.

Solution

Calculation of theoretical ex-rights price:

	$
Before issue 5 shares, value × $1.60	8.00
Rights issue 1 share, value × $1.00	1.00
Theoretical value of 6 shares	9.00

Theoretical ex-rights price = $\frac{\$9}{6}$ = $1.50

EPS for 20X1

EPS as calculated before taking into account the rights issue = 40c ($40,000 divided by 100,000 shares).

EPS = $\frac{1.50}{1.60} \times 40c = 37\frac{1}{2}c$

(Remember: this is the corresponding value for 20X1 which will be shown in the financial statements for Brains Co at the end of 20X2.)

EPS for 20X2

Number of shares before the rights issue was 100,000. 20,000 shares were issued.

Stage 1:	$100{,}000 \times 9/12 \times \frac{1.60}{1.50} =$	80,000
Stage 2:	$120{,}000 \times 3/12 =$	30,000
		110,000

EPS = $\frac{\$50{,}000}{110{,}000}$ = $45\frac{1}{2}c$

The figure for total earnings is the actual earnings for the year.

7.8 Diluted EPS

FAST FORWARD

Diluted EPS is calculated by adjusting the net profit attributable to shareholders and the weighted average number of shares outstanding for the effects of all dilutive potential ordinary shares.

At the end of an accounting period, a company may have in issue some **securities** which do not (at present) have any 'claim' to a share of equity earnings, but **may give rise to such a claim in the future**. These securities include:

(a) A **separate class of equity shares** which at present is not entitled to any dividend, but will be entitled after some future date

(b) **Convertible loan stock** or **convertible preferred shares** which give their holders the right at some future date to exchange their securities for ordinary shares of the company, at a pre-determined conversion rate

(c) **Options** or **warrants**

In such circumstances, the future number of ordinary shares in issue might increase, which in turn results in a fall in the EPS. In other words, a **future increase** in the **number of ordinary shares will cause a dilution or 'watering down' of equity**, and it is possible to calculate a **diluted earnings per share** (ie the EPS that would have been obtained during the financial period if the dilution had already taken place). This will indicate to investors the possible effects of a future dilution.

Diluted EPS is complicated, but you only need to be able to deal with straight-forward situations.

Example: diluted EPS

In 20X7 Farrah Co had a basic EPS of 105c based on earnings of $105,000 and 100,000 ordinary $1 shares. It also had in issue $40,000 15% Convertible Loan Stock which is convertible in two years' time at the rate of 4 ordinary shares for every $5 of stock. The rate of tax is 30%. In 20X7 gross profit of $200,000 and expenses of $50,000 were recorded, including interest payable of $6,000.

Required

Calculate the diluted EPS.

Solution

Diluted EPS is calculated as follows.

Step 1 **Number of shares**: the additional equity on conversion of the loan stock will be 40,000 × 4/5 = 32,000 shares

Step 2 **Earnings**: Farrah Co will save interest payments of $6,000 but this increase in profits will be taxed. Hence the earnings figure may be recalculated:

	$
Gross profit	200,000
Expenses (50,000 – 6,000)	(44,000)
Profit before tax	156,000
Tax expense (30%)	(46,800)
Earnings	109,200

Step 3 **Calculation**: Diluted EPS = $\frac{\$109{,}200}{132{,}000}$ = 82.7c

Step 4 **Dilution**: the dilution in earnings would be 105c – 82.7c = 22.3c per share.

7.9 Presentation, disclosure and other matters

Basic and diluted EPS should be presented by an entity on the **face of the income statement** for each class of ordinary share that has a different right to share in the net profit for the period. The basic and diluted EPS should be presented with **equal prominence** for all periods presented.

Disclosure must still be made where the EPS figures (basic and/or diluted) are **negative** (ie a loss per share).

An entity may present **alternative EPS figures if it wishes**. However, IAS 33 lays out certain rules where this takes place.

Key learning points

- The ownership of a limited company is represented by shares. The owner of a company are its **members** or **shareholders.**
- Shareholders receive dividends out of profits. Dividends are commonly paid in two stages: an interim dividend and a final dividend.
- IAS 1 covers the form and content of financial statements. The main components are an income statement, a balance sheet, a cash flow statement, a statement of changes in equity/statement of recognised income and expenses and accounting policies and explanatory notes.
- An income statement gives detailed information about the income, expenses and profits of a business.
- IAS 1 requires a statement of changes in equity.
- The tax charge for the year will include an estimate of the current year's tax and an adjustment for any under/over provisions from previous years.
- Deferred tax is an accounts measure used to match the tax effects of transactions with their accounting impact.
- All taxable temporary differences give rise to a deferred tax liability.
- All deductible temporary differences give rise to a deferred tax asset.
- Earnings per share is a measure of the amount of profits earned by a company for each ordinary share. Earnings are profits after tax and preferred dividends. Basic EPS is calculated by dividing the net profit or loss for the period attributable to ordinary shareholders by the weighted average number of ordinary shares outstanding during the period.
- Diluted EPS is calculated by adjusting the net profit attributable to ordinary shareholders and the weighted average number of shares outstanding for the effects of all dilutive potential ordinary shares.

Quick quiz

1 Limited liability means that the shareholders of a company are not legally accountable.

True ☐

False ☐

2 What is gross profit?

3 Which of the following must be disclosed on the face of the income statement?

(a) Tax expense
(b) Analysis of expenses
(c) Net profit or loss for the period.

4 What is the alternative to the statement of changes in equity?

5 The tax expense related to the profit from ordinary activities should be shown on the face of the income statement.

True ☐

False ☐

6 Deferred tax liabilities are the amounts of income taxes payable in future periods in respect of ....

7 Give three examples of taxable temporary differences.

8 Which of the following methods of accounting for deferred tax is adopted by IAS 12?

A Flow-through method
B Differential method
C Full provision method
D Partial provision method

9 How is basic EPS calculated?

Answers to quick quiz

1 False. It means that if the company becomes insolvent, the maximum that an owner stands to lose is his share capital in the business.

2 Revenue less cost of sales

3 (a) and (c) only. (b) may be shown in the notes.

4 The statement of recognised income and expense.

5 True

6 Taxable temporary differences

7 Any three of:

- Interest revenue received in arrears
- Depreciation accelerated for tax purposes
- Development costs capitalised in the balance sheet
- Prepayments
- Sale of goods revenue recognised before the cash is received

8 C

9 $$\frac{\text{Net profit/(loss) attributable to ordinary shareholders}}{\text{Weighted average number of ordinary shares outstanding during the period}}$$

Answers to activities

5.1 (a)

	$
Tax due on 20X8 profits ($120,000 × 30%)	36,000
Underpayment for 20X7	5,000
Tax charge and liability	41,000

(b)

	$
Tax due on 20X8 profits (as above)	36,000
Overpayment for 20X7	(5,000)
Tax charge and liability	31,000

Alternatively, the rebate due could be shown separately as income in the income statement and as an asset in the balance sheet. An offset approach like this is, however, most likely.

5.2 (a) The tax base of the machine is $7,000.
(b) The tax base of the interest receivable is nil.
(c) The tax base of the trade receivables is $10,000.
(d) The tax base of the loan is $1m.

5.3 (a) The tax base of the accrued expenses is nil.
(b) The tax base of the interest received in advance is nil.
(c) The tax base of the accrued expenses is $2,000.
(d) The tax base of the accrued fines and penalties is $100.
(e) The tax base of the loan is $1m.

5.4 FLAME CO
TRADING RESULTS FOR YEAR TO 31 DECEMBER

	$	$
Profit before tax		150,000
Tax at 30%		(45,000)
Profit for the financial year		105,000
Less dividends		
Preferred *	2,000	
Ordinary	42,000	
		44,000
		61,000

EARNINGS PER SHARE

$$\frac{103{,}000\,*}{100{,}000} = 103\text{c}$$

*($105,000 – $2,000 preferred div = $103,000)

6

The balance sheet

Topic list
1 The format of a company balance sheet
2 Current assets
3 Inventory
4 Construction contracts
5 Liabilities
6 Accounting for leases
7 Provisions
8 Contingencies
9 Events after the balance sheet date
10 Reporting the substance of transactions

Introduction

We saw the income statement in the previous chapter. It is also of vital importance that you are familiar with the preparation of the balance sheet.

You should also pay particular attention to sections 3, 4 and 6 as there are very popular examination topics.

Learning objectives

On completion of this chapter you will be able to:

	Syllabus reference
• read a company's balance sheet and have an understanding of the key items of information shown	3 a ii
• describe the format of a company balance sheet, as suggested by IAS1	3 a ii
• explain the meaning and valuation of various current assets and current liabilities in the balance sheet	3 a ii, 3 c iii, 3 c iv
• explain the valuation of inventories and construction contracts.	3 c.iii
• discuss the accounting methods and principles used in accounting for leases	3 c iv
• identify the accounting methods and principles used in accounting for provisions	3 c iv
• identify the accounting methods and principles used in accounting for contingencies	3 c iv
• identify what events after the balance sheet date are, and how they are accounted for	3 c vi
• explain what is meant by 'reporting the substance of transactions' and in what ways this affects a company's balance sheet	3 c viii

1 The format of a company balance sheet

FAST FORWARD

IAS1 suggests a format for the balance sheet.

A balance sheet is a statement of the assets, liabilities and owners' capital of a business at a specific moment in time, typically at the end of the financial year. It is therefore a statement of the accounting equation for the business at that moment.

XYZ GROUP

BALANCE SHEET AS AT 31 DECEMBER 20X8

	20X8		*20X7*	
	\$'000	\$'000	\$'000	\$'000
Assets				
Non-current assets				
Property, plant and equipment	X		X	
Goodwill	X		X	
Other intangible assets	X		X	
Investments in associates	X		X	
Available-for-sale investments	X		X	
		X		X
Current assets				
Inventories	X		X	
Trade receivables	X		X	
Other current assets	X		X	
Cash and cash equivalents	X		X	
		X		X
Total assets		X		X

Equity and liabilities				
Equity attributable to equity holders of the parent				
Share capital	X		X	
Other reserves	X		X	
Retained earnings	X		X	
		X		X
Minority interest		X		X
Total equity		X		X
Non-current liabilities				
Long-term borrowings	X		X	
Deferred tax	X		X	
Long-term provisions	X		X	
Total non-current liabilities		X		X
Current liabilities				
Trade and other payables	X		X	
Short-term borrowings	X		X	
Current portion of long-term borrowings	X		X	
Current tax payable	X		X	
Short-term provisions	X		X	
Total current liabilities		X		X
Total liabilities		X		X
Total equity and liabilities		X		X

IAS 1 specifies various items which must appear on the **face of the balance sheet** as a minimum disclosure.

(a) Property, plant and equipment
(b) Investment property
(c) Intangible assets
(d) Financial assets (excluding amounts shown under (e), (h) and (i))
(e) Investments accounted for using the equity method
(f) Biological assets
(g) Inventories
(h) Trade and other receivables
(i) Cash and cash equivalents
(j) Trade and other payables
(k) Provisions
(l) Financial liabilities
(m) Current tax liabilities as in IAS 12
(n) Minority interests
(o) Issued capital and reserves

We will look at these items throughout the rest of the text.

Any **other line items**, headings or sub-totals should be shown on the face of the balance sheet when it is necessary for an understanding of the entity's financial position.

The example shown above is for illustration only (although we will follow the format in this Study Text). The IAS, however, does not prescribe the order or format in which the items listed should be presented. It simply states that they **must be presented separately** because they are so different in nature or function from each other.

1.1 Information presented either on the face of the balance sheet or by note

Further **sub-classification** of the line items listed above should be disclosed either on the face of the balance sheet or in notes to the balance sheet. The classification will depend upon the nature of the entity's operations. As well as each item being sub-classified by its nature, any amounts payable to or receivable from any **group company or other related party** should also be disclosed separately.

2 Current assets

FAST FORWARD

An entity must present current and non-current assets as separate classifications on the face of the balance sheet.

2.1 The current/non-current distinction

An entity must present **current** and **non-current** assets as separate classifications on the face of the balance sheet. A presentation based on liquidity should only be used where it provides more relevant and reliable information, in which case all assets and liabilities must be presented broadly **in order of liquidity**.

In either case, the entity should disclose any portion of an asset or liability which is expected to be recovered or settled **after more than twelve months**. For example, for an amount receivable which is due in instalments over 18 months, the portion due after more than twelve months must be disclosed.

The IAS emphasises how helpful information on the **operating cycle** is to users of financial statements. Where there is a clearly defined operating cycle within which the entity supplies goods or services, then information disclosing those net assets that are continuously circulating as **working capital** is useful.

This distinguishes them from those net assets used in the long-term operations of the entity. Assets that are expected to be realised and liabilities that are due for settlement within the operating cycle are therefore highlighted.

The liquidity and solvency of an entity is also indicated by information about the **maturity dates** of assets and liabilities. IFRS7: *Financial instruments: Disclosures* requires disclosure of maturity dates of both financial assets and financial liabilities. (Financial assets include trade and other receivables; financial liabilities include trade and other payables.) In the case of non-monetary assets, eg inventories, such information is also useful.

2.2 Current assets

Key term

An asset should be classified as a **current asset** when it:

- is expected to be realised in, or is held for sale or consumption in, the normal course of the entity's operating cycle; or
- is held primarily for trading purposes or for the short-term and expected to be realised within twelve months of the balance sheet date; or
- is cash or a cash equivalent asset which is not restricted in its use.

All other assets should be classified as non-current assets. *(IAS 1)*

Non-current assets includes tangible, intangible, operating and financial assets of a long-term nature. Other terms with the same meaning can be used (eg 'fixed', 'long-term').

The term 'operating cycle' has been used several times above and the standard defines it as follows.

Key term

> The **operating cycle** of an entity is the time between the acquisition of materials entering into a process and its realisation in cash or an instrument that is readily convertible into cash. *(IAS 1)*

Current assets therefore include inventories and trade receivables that are sold, consumed and realised as part of the normal operating cycle. **This is the case even where they are not expected to be realised within twelve months**.

Current assets will also include **marketable securities** if they are expected to be realised within twelve months of the balance sheet date. If expected to be realised later, they should be included in non-current assets.

Receivables represent the amounts owed to the business. Strangely, perhaps, the receivables shown as current assets may include debts that are not due to be paid within the next 12 months. Where there are long-term receivables, the balance sheet must show separately the amounts falling due within one year and the amounts falling due in over one year.

A note to the accounts itemises receivables in further detail. Categories of receivables that are shown include:

(a) Amounts receivable from trade customers (receivables arising in the course of the company's trading)

(b) Prepayments

(c) Other amounts

A **prepayment** is an amount of money that has been paid by the company for an expense that will not be chargeable against profits until the next financial year. For example, when a company pays rent of $20,000 in advance, for a rental period in the next financial year, the $20,000 is a prepayment, and included in receivables in the balance sheet. (In terms of the accounting equation, a prepayment reduces cash and increases prepayments, which are another asset.)

Accrued income relates to income that is properly attributable to the current financial year, but that has not yet been invoiced. Since there is no invoice yet, there is no amount receivable. For example, suppose that a company of consultants agrees to undertake a six-month contract for a client, and invoice the client for $500,000 when the job has been finished. If the job is half-finished at the end of the company's financial year, it might decide that $250,000 of income is properly attributable to the year just ended. If so, it will include $250,000 for the part-finished job in sales revenue, and accrued income of $250,000 as a receivable. (In terms of the accounting equation, profits (capital) and assets are both increased.) Accrued income is often included with prepayments.

A company might make an **allowance for receivables**. This is an amount set aside to provide for the fact that some current receivables may fail to pay what they owe. By making an allowance for these doubtful receivables, the company will recognise a loss before the bad debt actually occurs. The value of receivables in the balance sheet is the total receivables minus the allowance for debts. However, a company is not required to disclose the size of any allowance it has made.

2.3 Example

A company, which began trading on 1 January, Year 1, had trade receivables of $800,000 as at 31 December, Year 1. The allowance for debts was 2% of total trade receivables.

At 31 December Year 2 the company had total trade receivables of $1,000,000 and made an allowance of 3% for debts.

At 31 December Year 1, the trade receivables in the balance sheet should be $784,000:

	$
Trade receivables	800,000
Less allowance for debts (2%)	(16,000)
	784,000

There should be a charge against profits for the year of $16,000, which is the increase in the receivables allowance for the year.

At 31 December Year 2, the trade receivables should be $970,000:

	$
Trade receivables	1,000,000
Less allowance for debts (3%)	(30,000)
	970,000

There should be a charge in the income statement for Year 2 of $14,000, which is the increase in the allowance for debts in the year ($30,000 – $16,000).

3 Inventory

FAST FORWARD

Inventory must be valued at the lower of cost and net realisable value. The most commonly used methods to derive cost are FIFO and weighted average rate.

Note: Inventories are a popular exam topic.

The balance sheet includes an amount for inventories. This is the 'closing inventories' held by the company as at the end of its financial year. The valuation of closing inventory can be important, because the inventory value affects not just the balance sheet, but also the income statement.

The trading part of an income statement includes:

	£
Opening inventory	X
Plus purchases	X
Less closing inventory	(X)
Cost of goods sold	X

However, just writing down this formula hides two basic problems with inventories.

(a) How do you manage to get a **precise count** of inventory in hand at any given moment?
(b) Even once it has been counted, how do you **value** the inventory?

3.1 Inventory counting

Business trading is a continuous activity, but accounting statements must be drawn up at a particular date. In preparing a balance sheet it is necessary to **'freeze'** the activity of a business so as to determine its assets and liabilities at a given moment. However, a business buys inventory continually during its trading operations and either sells the goods onwards to customers or incorporates them as raw materials in manufactured products. This constant movement of inventories makes it difficult to establish what exactly is held at any precise moment. It is important that no inventory is subject to double/multiple counting or is missed out of the count.

Establishing proper '**cut off**' is a traditional problem with inventory counting eg Domeselec Co delivers a TV before the year end but only invoices the customer after the year end.

When a business holds easily-counted and relatively small amounts of inventory, quantities of inventories on hand at the balance sheet date can be determined by physically counting them in an inventory count.

The continuous nature of trading activity may cause a problem in that inventory movements will not necessarily cease during the time that the physical inventory count is in progress. Two possible solutions are:

(a) **Close down** the business while the count takes place; or
(b) Keep **detailed records** of inventory movements during the course of the inventory count.

Closing down the business for a short period for an inventory count (e.g. over a weekend or at Christmas) is the usual method preferred.

In more complicated cases, where a business holds considerable quantities of varied inventory, an alternative approach to establishing inventory quantities is to maintain a **continuous inventory counting process**. For example, a company may have a system whereby all inventory lines are counted at least once a year and agreed to the inventory records with (say) high value items being counted more frequently, especially towards the year end.

3.2 Valuing inventories

There are **several methods** which, in theory, could be used for the valuation of inventory items.

(a) Inventories might be valued at their **expected selling price**. However, the use of selling prices for inventory valuation is **ruled out**, because the inventory would be re-valued above its original cost, which would create a profit for the business before the inventory has been sold.

(b) Inventories might be valued at their expected selling price, less any costs still to be incurred in getting them ready for sale and then selling them. This amount is referred to as the **net realisable value** (NRV) of the inventories. Again, this may include a profit element.

(c) Inventories might be valued at their **historical cost** (i.e. the cost at which they were originally bought).

(d) Inventories might be valued at the amount it would cost to replace them. This amount is referred to as the **current replacement cost** of inventories. In traditional accounts, inventories are not valued in this way.

Historical cost is the normal basis of inventory valuation. Most inventory items are valued at their original cost. However, there may be occasions when the **net realisable value of inventory falls below its original cost** owing to reasons such as fall in market demand, deterioration or obsolescence. Where there is **uncertainty** as to whether cost will be recorded prudence will come into play. Consequently, when the net realisable value of an inventory item falls below its original cost, its value must be written down from cost to the lower amount.

The accounting treatment of inventory is governed by an accounting standard, IAS 2 *Inventories*. IAS 2 states that **inventory should be valued at the lower of cost and net realisable value**.

Activity 6.1

From the following figures, calculate the figure for inventory valuation, category by category (rather than item by item).

Inventory at 31 December 20X4			
Item	*Categories*	*Cost*	*Net realisable value*
1	A	560	660
2	A	880	740
3	A	780	960
4	B	340	500
5	B	420	620
6	C	800	700
7	C	1,720	1,200
8	D	1,140	1,320
9	D	1,540	1,980

Activity 6.2

The Great Flag Co has a 31 December year end. During September 20X6, the country hosted a major international sporting event and the accounts for the year ended 31 December 20X6 are likely to reflect a heightened profit blip, which is unlikely to be repeated in 20X7. However, demand is likely to pick up again in 20X8, when more tournaments are scheduled.

As at 31 December 20X6, the company had considerable inventories of flags costing $5 each of which the normal selling price is $12. The directors are considering writing down the value of the flags to $3 each so that the current year won't show such a big profit while allowing 20X7 sales to face a lower brought forward cost.

What comments would you have regarding the directors' proposals for carrying forward a low inventory figure in 20X7?

3.3 Determining the purchase cost

Inventory is valued at the lower of cost or net realisable value. But how is the *cost* of inventory established? This is a problem for all types of business, from retailers and companies in service industries to manufacturing organisations.

In a retail business, inventory will consist mainly of goods for resale. In a manufacturing company, inventory may be **raw materials** or **components** bought from suppliers, **finished goods** which have been made by the business but not yet sold, or work in the process of production and only part-completed (this type of inventory is called **work in progress** or WIP). It will simplify matters, however, if we begin by thinking about the historical cost of purchased raw materials and components, which ought to be their purchase price.

A business may be continually purchasing consignments of a particular inventory item, and may pay a different purchase price each time. As each consignment is received from suppliers the items are stored in the appropriate bin or on the appropriate shelf or pallet, where they will be mingled with previous consignments. When the storekeeper issues inventory to production he will simply pull out from the shelf or pallet the nearest items to hand, which may have arrived in the latest consignment or in an earlier consignment or in several different consignments. For accounting purposes, an inventory pricing technique is needed to attribute a cost to each of the components issued from stores. A technique has to be chosen because the purchase price of inventories varies from consignment to consignment. If prices did not vary, there would be no need to bother with choosing a valuation method.

There are several valuation methods that might be used.

Key terms

- **FIFO (First in, first out)**. Using this technique, we assume that inventories are used in the order in which they are received from suppliers and are costed accordingly.
- **LIFO (Last in, first out)**. This involves the opposite assumption, that the first stocks used up are the most recently acquired items.
- **Average cost**. Inventories are valued at their weighted average purchase cost. A new weighted average cost is calculated every time a new consignment of the inventory item is received.

Any or all of these methods might provide a suitable basis for valuing inventories. For financial accounts, it is usual to use either FIFO or average cost to value inventory for the balance sheet.

LIFO is not allowed under IAS 2.

3.4 Example

The purchases and consumption of an item of inventory during an accounting period were as follows.

Date	*Purchases*			*Consumed*
	units	$ per unit	$	units
1 February	300	10	3,000	
28 March	400	11	4,400	
25 April				200
8 May	300	12	3,600	
3 June				600
	1,000		11,000	800

Using the **FIFO valuation method**, the cost of the inventory used and the value of the closing inventory are as follows.

Date	*Units*		*Value*
			$
25 April	200	(200 × $10)	2,000
3 June	600	(100 × $10)	
		(400 × $11)	
		(100 × $12)	6,600
			8,600

The value of closing inventory is 200 units × $12 = $2,400.

Using the **LIFO valuation method**, the cost of the inventory used and the value of the closing inventory are as follows.

Date	*Units*		*Value*
			$
25 April	200	(200 × $11)	2,200
3 June	600	(300 × $12)	
		(200 × $11)	
		(100 × $10)	6,800
			9,000

The value of closing inventory is 200 units × $10 = $2,000.

Using an **average cost approach**, the average cost per unit for the period could be valued at $11,000/1,000 units = $11 per unit. The cost of the 800 units consumed would therefore be $8,800 and the value of the 200 units of closing inventory would be $2,200.

Each valuation method produces a different figure for an accounting period for the cost of inventory consumed/sold and the value of closing inventory. Inventory valuation therefore affects the reported profit in any one period, although not over the long term.

3.5 Inventory: IAS 2

The standard gives the following important definitions.

Key terms

- **Inventories** are assets:
  - held for sale in the ordinary course of business;
  - in the process of production for such sale; or
  - in the form of materials or supplies to be consumed in the production process or in the rendering of services.
- **Net realisable value** is the estimated selling price in the ordinary course of business less the estimated costs of completion and the estimated costs necessary to make the sale.

Inventories can **include** any of the following.

- **Goods purchased and held for resale**, eg goods held for sale by a retailer, or land and buildings held for resale
- **Finished goods** produced
- **Work in progress** being produced
- Materials and supplies awaiting use in the production process (**raw materials**)

3.5.1 Measurement of inventories

The standard states that '**Inventories should be measured at the lower of cost and net realisable value**.'

We introduced this rule earlier.

Exam focus point

> This is a very important rule and you will be expected to apply it in the exam.

The cost of inventories will consist of all costs of:

- **Purchase**
- **Costs of conversion**
- **Other costs** incurred in bringing the inventories to their **present location and condition**

The standard lists the following as comprising the costs of purchase of inventories:

- **Purchase price** *plus*
- **Import duties** and other taxes *plus*
- Transport, handling and any other cost **directly attributable** to the acquisition of finished goods, services and materials *less*
- **Trade discounts**, rebates and other similar amounts

Costs of conversion of inventories consist of two main parts.

(a) Costs **directly related** to the units of production, eg direct materials, direct labour

(b) Fixed and variable **production overheads** that are incurred in converting materials into finished goods, allocated on a systematic basis.

You may have come across the terms 'fixed production overheads' or 'variable production overheads' elsewhere in your studies. The standard defines them as follows.

Key terms

> - **Fixed production overheads** are those indirect costs of production that remain relatively constant regardless of the volume of production, eg the cost of factory management and administration.
> - **Variable production overheads** are those indirect costs of production that vary directly, or nearly directly, with the volume of production, eg indirect materials and labour. *(IAS 2)*

The standard emphasises that fixed production overheads must be allocated to items of inventory on the basis of the **normal capacity of the production facilities**. This is an important point.

(a) **Normal capacity** is the expected achievable production based on the average over several periods/seasons, under normal circumstances.

(b) The above figure should take account of the capacity lost through **planned maintenance**.

(c) If it approximates to the normal level of activity then the **actual level of production** can be used.

(d) **Low production** or **idle plant** will *not* result in a higher fixed overhead allocation to each unit.

(e) **Unallocated overheads** must be recognised as an expense in the period in which they were incurred.

(f) When production is **abnormally high**, the fixed production overhead allocated to each unit will be reduced, so avoiding inventories being stated at more than cost.

(g) The allocation of variable production overheads to each unit is based on the **actual use** of production facilities.

Any other costs should only be recognised if they are incurred in bringing the inventories to their **present location and condition**.

The standard lists types of cost which **would not be included** in cost of inventories. Instead, they should be recognised as an **expense** in the period they are incurred.

(a) **Abnormal amounts** of wasted materials, labour or other production costs

(b) **Storage costs** (except costs which are necessary in the production process before a further production stage)

(c) **Administrative overheads** not incurred to bring inventories to their present location and conditions

(d) **Selling costs**

3.5.2 Net realisable value (NRV)

As a general rule assets should not be carried at amounts greater than those expected to be realised from their sale or use. In the case of inventories this amount could fall below cost when items are **damaged or become obsolete**, or where the **costs to completion have increased** in order to make the sale.

In fact we can identify the principal situations in which **NRV is likely to be less than cost**, ie where there has been:

(a) An **increase in costs** or a **fall in selling price**

(b) A **physical deterioration** in the condition of inventory

(c) **Obsolescence** of products

(d) A decision as part of the company's marketing strategy to manufacture and sell products at a **loss**

(e) **Errors in production or purchasing**

A write down of inventories would normally take place on an item by item basis, but similar or related items may be **grouped together**. This grouping together is acceptable for, say, items in the same product line, but it is not acceptable to write down inventories based on a whole classification (eg finished goods) or a whole business.

The assessment of NRV should take place **at the same time** as estimates are made of selling price, using the most reliable information available. Fluctuations of price or cost should be taken into account if they relate directly to **events after the balance sheet date,** which confirm conditions existing at the end of the period.

The reasons why inventory is held must also be taken into account. Some inventory, for example, may be held to satisfy a firm contract and its NRV will therefore be the **contract price**. Any additional inventory of the same type held at the period end will, in contrast, be assessed according to general sales prices when NRV is estimated.

Net realisable value must be reassessed at the end of each period and compared again with cost. If the NRV has risen for inventories held over the end of more than one period, then the previous write down must be **reversed** to the extent that the inventory is then valued at the lower of cost and the new NRV. This may be possible when selling prices have fallen in the past and then risen again.

On occasion a write down to NRV may be of such size, incidence or nature that it must be **disclosed separately**.

3.6 Disclosure

This information is of great relevance to users of financial statements, particularly the change in assets from period to period. The standard lists common **classifications for inventories**.

- Merchandise
- Production supplies
- Materials
- Work in progress
- Finished goods

Accounting policies adopted in measuring inventories should also be disclosed.

4 Construction contracts

FAST FORWARD

Companies with construction contracts take credit for some of the anticipated profit before the contract has been completed. IAS 11 specifies how this should be dealt with.

4.1 Introduction

Imagine that you are the accountant at a construction company. Your company is building a large tower block that will house offices, under a contract with an investment company. It will take three years to build the block and over that time you will obviously have to pay for building materials, wages of workers on the building, architects' fees and so on. You will receive periodic payments from the investment company at various predetermined stages of the construction. How do you decide, in each of the three years, **what to include as income and expenditure** for the contract in the income statement?

This is the problem tackled by IAS 11 *Construction contracts.*

4.2 Example: construction contract

A numerical example might help to illustrate the problem. Suppose that a contract is started on 1 January 20X5, with an estimated completion date of 31 December 20X6. The final contract price is $1,500,000. In the first year, to 31 December 20X5:

(a) Costs incurred amounted to $600,000.

(b) Half the work on the contract was completed.

(c) Certificates of work completed have been issued, to the value of $750,000. (*Note.* It is usual, in a construction contract, for a qualified person such as an architect or engineer to inspect the work completed, and if it is satisfactory, to issue certificates. This will then be the notification to the customer that progress payments are now due to the contractor. Progress payments are commonly the amount of valuation on the work certificates issued, minus a precautionary retention of 10%).

(d) It is estimated with reasonable certainty that further costs to completion in 20X6 will be $600,000.

What is the contract profit in 20X5, and what entries would be made for the contract at 31 December 20X5 if:

(a) Profits are deferred until the completion of the contract?
(b) A proportion of the estimated revenue and profit is credited to the income statement in 20X5?

Solution

(a) If profits were deferred until the completion of the contract in 20X6, the revenue and profit recognised on the contract in 20X5 would be nil, and the value of work in progress on 31 December 20X5 would be $600,000. IAS 11 takes the view that this policy is unreasonable, because in 20X6, the total profit of $300,000 would be recorded. Since the contract revenues are earned throughout 20X5 and 20X6, a profit of nil in 20X5 and $300,000 in 20X6 would be contrary to the accruals concept of accounting.

(b) **It is fairer to recognise revenue and profit throughout the duration of the contract.**

As at 31 December 20X5 revenue of $750,000 should be matched with cost of sales of $600,000 in the income statement, leaving an attributable profit for 20X5 of $150,000.

The only balance sheet entry as at 31 December 20X5 is a receivable of $750,000 recognising that the company is owed this amount for work done to date. No balance remains for work in progress, the whole $600,000 having been recognised in cost of sales.

4.3 What is a construction contract?

A contract which needs IAS 11 treatment does not have to last for a period of more than one year. The main point is that the contract activity **starts in one financial period and ends in another**, thus creating the problem: to which of two or more periods should contract income and costs be allocated? In fact the definition given in the IAS of a construction contract is very straightforward.

Key term

Construction contract. A contract specifically negotiated for the construction of an asset or a combination of assets that are closely interrelated or interdependent in terms of their design, technology and function or their ultimate purpose or use. *(IAS 11)*

- Fixed price contract. A contract in which the contractor agrees to a fixed contract price, or a fixed rate per unit of output, which in some cases is subject to cost escalation clauses.
- Cost plus contract. A contract in which the contractor is reimbursed for allowable or otherwise defined costs, plus a percentage of these costs or a fixed fee.

Construction contracts may involve the building of one asset, eg a bridge, or a series of interrelated assets eg an oil refinery. They may also include **rendering of services** (eg architects) or restoring or demolishing an asset.

4.4 Contract revenue

Contract revenue will be the **amount specified in the contract**, subject to variations in the contract work, incentive payments and claims *if* these will probably give rise to revenue and *if* they can be reliably measured. The result is that contract revenue is measured at the **fair value** of received or receivable revenue.

4.5 Contract costs

Contract costs consist of:

- Costs relating **directly** to the contract
- Costs attributable to general contract activity which can be **allocated** to the contract, such as insurance, cost of design and technical assistance not directly related to a specific contract and construction overheads

- Any other costs which can be **charged to the customer** under the contract, which may include general administration costs and development costs

Costs that **relate directly** to a specific contract include the following.

- **Site labour costs**, including site supervision
- Costs of **materials** used in construction
- **Depreciation** of plant and equipment used on the contract
- Costs of **moving** plant, equipment and materials to and from the contract site
- Costs of **hiring** plant and equipment
- Costs of **design and technical assistance** that are directly related to the contract
- Estimated costs of **rectification and guarantee work**, including expected warranty costs
- **Claims from third parties**

Some costs **cannot be attributed** to contract activity and so the following should be **excluded** from construction contract costs.

- **General administration costs** (unless reimbursement is specified in the contract)
- **Selling costs**
- **R&D** (unless reimbursement is specified in the contract)
- **Depreciation** of idle plant and equipment not used on any particular contract

4.6 Recognition of contract revenue and expenses

Revenue and costs associated with a contract should be recognised according to the stage of completion of the contract at the balance sheet date, but *only when* the **outcome of the activity can be estimated reliably**. If a loss is predicted on a contract, then it should be recognised immediately. This is often known as the **percentage of completion method**.

The **percentage of completion method** is an application of the accruals assumption. Contract revenue is matched to the contract costs incurred in reaching the stage of completion, so revenue, costs and profit are attributed to the proportion of work completed.

We can **summarise** the treatment as follows.

- Recognise **contract revenue** as revenue in the accounting periods in which the work is performed

- Recognise **contract costs** as an expense in the accounting period in which the work to which they relate is performed

- Any **expected excess** of total contract costs over total contract revenue should be recognised as an expense immediately

- Any costs incurred which relate to **future activity** should be recognised as an asset if it is probable that they will be recovered (often called contract work in progress, ie amounts due from the customer)

- Where amounts have been recognised as contract revenue, but their **collectability** from the customer becomes doubtful, such amounts should be recognised as an expense, not a deduction from revenue

4.7 When can reliable estimates be made?

IAS 11 only allows contract revenue and costs to be recognised when the outcome of the contract can be predicted, ie when it is probable that the economic benefits attached to the contract will flow to the entity.

4.8 Determining the stage of completion

How should you decide on the stage of completion of any contract? The standard lists several methods.

- **Proportion of contract costs incurred** for work carried out to date
- **Surveys** of work carried out
- **Physical proportion** of the contract work completed

When the stage of completion is determined using the contract costs incurred to date, only contract costs reflecting the work to date should be included in costs incurred to date.

- Exclude costs relating to **future activity**, eg cost of materials delivered but not yet used
- Exclude payments made to subcontractors **in advance** of work performed

4.9 Outcome of the contract cannot be predicted reliably

When the contract's outcome cannot be predicted reliably the following treatment should be followed.

- Only recognise revenue to the extent of contract costs incurred which are expected to be **recoverable**
- Recognise contract costs as an **expense** in the period they are incurred

4.10 Recognition of expected losses

Any loss on a contract should be **recognised as soon as it is foreseen**. The loss will be the amount by which total expected contract revenue is exceeded by total expected contract costs. The loss amount is not affected by whether work has started on the contract, the stage of completion of the work or profits on other contracts (unless they are related contracts treated as a single contract).

4.11 Disclosures

The following should be disclosed under IAS 11

- Contract revenue recognised as **revenue in the period**
- **Methods used** to determine the **contract revenue**
- **Methods used** to determine **stage of completion** of contracts which are in progress

For **contracts in progress** at the balance sheet date, show the following.

- **Total costs incurred** and recognised profits (less recognised losses) to date
- **Advances** received
- **Retentions** (progress billings not paid until the satisfaction of certain conditions)

Amounts owed by customers and to sub-contractors for contract work must be **shown gross as an asset and a liability respectively**. These are determined by comparing the total costs incurred plus recognised profits to the sum of recognised losses and progress billings.

Any **contingent gains or losses**, eg due to warranty costs, claims, penalties or possible losses, should be disclosed in accordance with IAS 37 *Provisions, contingent liabilities and contingent assets.*

4.12 Summary of accounting treatment

The following summarises the accounting treatment for long-term contracts.

Income statement

(a) **Revenue and costs**

(i) Sales revenue and associated costs should be recorded in the income statement as the contract activity progresses.

(ii) Include an appropriate proportion of total contract value as sales revenue in the income statement.

(iii) The costs incurred in reaching that stage of completion are matched with this sales revenue, resulting in the reporting of results which can be attributed to the proportion of work completed.

(iv) Sales revenue is the value of work carried out to date.

(b) **Profit recognised in the contract**

(i) It must reflect the proportion of work carried out.

(ii) It should take into account any known inequalities in profitability in the various stages of a contract.

Balance sheet

(a) **Inventories**

	$
Costs to date	X
Less transfer to income statement	(X)
	X
Less foreseeable losses	(X)
	X
Less advances in excess of revenue	(X)
WIP	X

(b) **Receivables**

	$
Cumulative revenue recognised	X
Less advances	(X)
Amount recoverable on contracts	X

(c) **Payables**. Where progress billings exceed both cumulative revenue and net WIP the excess should be included in payables under 'payments on account'.

(d) **Provisions**. To the extent foreseeable future losses exceed WIP, the losses should be provided.

Activity 6.3

Haggrun Co has two contracts in progress, the details of which are as follows.

	Happy (profitable)	*Grumpy (loss-making)*
	$'000	$'000
Total contract price	300	300
Costs incurred to date	90	150
Estimated costs to completion	135	225
Progress payments invoiced and received	116	116

Required

Show extracts from the income statement and the balance sheet for each contract, assuming they are both:

(a) 40% complete; and
(b) 36% complete.

5 Liabilities

FAST FORWARD

Liabilities must be split in the balance sheet between current and non-current liabilities.

Key term

A liability should be classified as a **current liability** when it:

- is expected to be settled in the normal course of the entity's operating cycle; or
- is due to be settled within twelve months of the balance sheet date; or
- the entity does not have an unconditional right to defer settlement of the liability for at least twelve months after the balance sheet date.

All other liabilities should be classified as non-current liabilities. *(IAS 1)*

The categorisation of current liabilities is very similar to that of current assets. Thus, some current liabilities are part of the **working capital** used in the normal operating cycle of the business (ie trade payables and accruals for employee and other operating costs). Such items will be classed as current liabilities **even where they are due to be settled more than twelve months after the balance sheet date.**

There are also current liabilities which are not settled as part of the normal operating cycle, but which are due to be settled within twelve months of the balance sheet date. These include bank overdrafts, income taxes, other non-trade payables and the current portion of interest-bearing liabilities. Any interest-bearing liabilities that are used to finance working capital on a long-term basis, and that are not due for settlement within twelve months, should be classed as **non-current liabilities**.

As we saw in section 1 current liabilities include trade and other payables.

This is normally analysed in the accounts as follows:

(a) Trade payables
(b) Income tax payable
(c) Dividends payable
(d) Accrued expenses
(e) Other payables

An **accrual** represents an expense charged to the income statement for which an invoice has not yet been received, and so a debt is not yet payable. For example, there may be an accrual for four months' rental on a building where the rental is paid every six months in arrears. At the end of the accounting period, the company would have had the benefit of using the property for four months, but the rent is not payable for another two months.

Accrued expenses are charged to the income statement in order to apply the matching or accruals concept. The dual effect of making an accrual is to reduce capital/profit by the amount of the accrued expense, and to add to liabilities (since an accrual is a liability).

Deferred income arises when an organisation invoices a customer for goods or services, but some of the goods or services will not be provided until a future accounting period. For example, a training company might invoice a trainee for $500 for a course that runs for two weeks in December Year 1 and another two weeks in January Year 2. If the company's year-end is 31 December, it will include only half the price of the course ($250) revenue for Year 1. The remaining $250 of income will be deferred until Year 2. Deferred income is a liability, and the dual effect is + Assets (Cash received or Receivable invoiced) and + Liability (Deferred income). This would normally form part of accrued expenses.

6 Accounting for leases

FAST FORWARD

> Under finance leases
>
> – assets acquired should be capitalised
> – interest element of instalments should be charged against profit
>
> Operating leases are rental agreements and all instalments are charged against profit.

Businesses might acquire some of their non-current assets under a **finance lease** arrangement. (Some types of lease are called hire purchase agreements in some countries). In a leasing transaction there is a contract between the lessor and the lessee for the hire of an asset. The lessor retains legal ownership but conveys to the lessee the right to use the asset for an agreed period of time in return for specified rentals. IAS 17 defines a lease and recognises two types.

Key terms

- **Lease**. An agreement whereby the lessor conveys to the lessee in return for rent the right to use an asset for an agreed period of time.
- **Finance lease**. A lease that transfers substantially all the risks and rewards incidental to ownership of an asset. Title may or may not eventually be transferred.
- **Operating lease**. A lease other than a finance lease.

The essential distinction between a finance lease and an operating lease is that with a finance lease, the lessee obtains and uses the asset for most, if not all, of its useful economic life. In substance, the lessee obtains a long-term asset from the lessor, but pays for it in the form of lease rentals over the term of the lease agreement. In contrast, an operating lease is a short-term lease, and when the lease agreement ends, the owner takes back the asset and leases it to someone else.

The term 'lease' here does not refer at all to leasehold property, for which a full market price is paid when the asset is acquired. Finance leases refer to agreements where the lessee takes an asset without paying for it, and then makes periodic rental payments.

A *finance lease* is very similar in substance to a *hire purchase agreement*. (The difference in law is that under a hire purchase agreement the customer eventually, after paying an agreed number of instalments, becomes entitled to exercise an option to purchase the asset. Under a leasing agreement, ownership remains forever with the lessor.)

6.1 Accounting for operating leases: lessees and lessors

Operating leases do not really pose an accounting problem.

(a) The leased asset is the property of the lessor, and is a non-current asset in the lessor's balance sheet.

(b) Lease rental payments are income of the lessor and an expense of the lessee.

6.2 Substance over form in accounting for finance leases

For assets held **under finance leases (including hire purchase)** this accounting treatment would not disclose the reality of the situation. If a lessor leases out an asset on a finance lease, the asset will probably never be seen on his premises or used in his business again. It would be inappropriate for a lessor to record such an asset as a non-current asset. In reality, **what the lessor owns is a stream of future cash flows receivable from the lessee. The asset is a receivable rather than a non-current asset.**

Similarly, a lessee may use a finance lease to fund the 'acquisition' of a major asset which he will then use in his business, perhaps for many years. **The substance of the transaction is that the lessee has acquired a non-current asset, and this is reflected in the accounting treatment prescribed by IAS 17**, even though in law the lessee never becomes the owner of the asset.

Accounting for finance leases (and hire purchase agreements) is an example of showing the substance of a transaction in the accounts, rather than the 'legal form'. In other words, accounting for finance leases is an example of the principle of '**substance over form**'.

6.3 Accounting for finance leases: the basic rules for lessees

The basic rules in accounting for a finance lease or a hire purchase agreement are, from the perspective of the lessee, that:

(a) The asset acquired under the lease agreement is effectively a **non-current asset of the lessee**, and should be accounted for as such.

(b) The leased asset should be shown in the balance sheet at the lower of the fair value and the present value of the minimum lease payments.

(c) The leased asset, being a non-current asset, should be **depreciated** in the normal way, and there will be an annual charge for depreciation of leased assets in the lessee's income statement. The asset should be depreciated over the shorter of the lease term and the asset's useful life.

(d) In effect, the acquisition of the leased asset by the lessee is being financed by the lessor. The lessor should therefore be shown in the accounts of the lessee as a **long-term liability.**

(e) A finance lease commits the lessee to making a stream of future payments to the lessor. Since the lessor is effectively providing finance for the asset, the **rental payments** can be divided into two component elements: **interest on the debt** and **part-repayment of the debt**. Each year, there should be a charge in the income statement of the lessee for the interest element. The part-repayment of the debt reduces the outstanding debt to the lessor.

(f) By the end of the lease term, this debt will have reduced to zero, and the liability will have been settled in full.

The accounts of a company will therefore show leased assets as non-current assets, and there will be a payable for lease finance as a liability in the balance sheet. The income statement will include an 'interest charge' on the lease finance.

6.4 Accounting for finance leases: the basic rules for lessors

The same principles apply to accounting by lessors for finance leases. The lessor owns the asset legally, but in substance has surrendered ownership of the asset to the lessee. In return, the lessor has obtained a long-term receivable.

(a) A lessor cannot treat as non-current assets any items leased under a finance lease arrangement to a lessee.

(b) A lessor should show instead in its balance sheet a long-term receivable for the lease finance.

(c) Lease payments received should be divided into an interest element and a part-repayment of the debt element. The interest element should be treated as part of revenue in the income statement. The part-repayment of the lease finance debt will reduce the outstanding balance of the debt in the balance sheet. By the end of the lease period, the debt should be repaid in full.

6.5 Example

A company acquires a non-current asset under a finance lease agreement. The asset has an expected useful life of four years, after which it will have a nil residual value. The asset will be depreciated by the straight-line method.

The annual lease payments will be $30,000 for four years. The purchase cost of the asset would have been $100,000. It has been calculated that the interest element in the lease payments ($20,000 in total) will be as follows:

Year 1	$10,000
Year 2	$6,000
Year 3	$3,000
Year 4	$1,000

The finance lease is accounted for as follows.

(a) The asset is treated as a non-current asset costing $100,000, and depreciated accordingly.

(b) In the income statement, there will be charges for non-current asset depreciation and the interest element in the lease payments.

(c) When the non-current asset is acquired, a liability for the finance lease is also created, with a starting value of $100,000. The liability is gradually repaid over the term of the lease. The repayments are the annual lease payments minus the interest element, i.e. $20,000 in Year 1, $24,000 in year 2, $27,000 in year 3 and $29,000 in year 4.

Income statement

	Year 1	*Year 2*	*Year 3*	*Year 4*
	$	$	$	$
Depreciation	25,000	25,000	25,000	25,000
Interest	10,000	6,000	3,000	1,000

Balance sheet

	Start	*Year 1*	*Year 2*	*Year 3*	*Year 4*
		$	$	$	$
Non-current asset					
Cost	100,000	100,000	100,000	100,000	100,000
Accum. dep'n	-	25,000	50,000	75,000	100,000
Net book value	100,000	75,000	50,000	25,000	0
Payable for finance lease	100,000	80,000	56,000	29,000	0
Of which					
Current payables	$20,000	$24,000	$27,000	$29,000	
Non-current payables	$80,000	$56,000	$29,000	0	

6.6 Apportionment of rental payments

As we have already seen when the lessee makes a rental payment it will comprise two elements.

(a) An **interest charge** on the finance provided by the lessor. This proportion of each payment is interest payable and interest receivable in the income statements of the lessee and lessor respectively.

(b) A repayment of part of the **capital cost** of the asset. In the lessee's books this proportion of each rental payment must reduce the outstanding liability. In the lessor's books, it must reduce the amount owing.

The accounting problem is to decide what proportion of each instalment paid by the lessee represents interest, and what proportion represents a repayment of the capital advanced by the lessor. There are two apportionment methods you may encounter:

- The **actuarial method**
- The **sum-of-the-digits method**

Exam focus point

An examination question should always make it clear which method should be used. In theory, the aim is that the income statement finance charge should reduce over the lease term in line with the outstanding liability.

The **actuarial method** is the best and most scientific method. It derives from the common-sense assumption that the interest charged by a lessor company will equal the rate of return desired by the company, multiplied by the amount of capital it has invested.

(a) At the beginning of the lease the capital invested is equal to the fair value of the asset (less any initial deposit paid by the lessee).

(b) This amount reduces as each instalment is paid. It follows that the interest accruing is greatest in the early part of the lease term, and gradually reduces as capital is repaid. In this section, we will look at a simple example of the actuarial method.

The **sum-of-the-digits** method approximates to the actuarial method, splitting the total interest (without reference to a rate of interest) in such a way that the greater proportion falls in the earlier years. The procedure is as follows.

(a) Assign a digit to each instalment. The digit 1 should be assigned to the final instalment, 2 to the penultimate instalment and so on.

(b) Add the digits. A quick method of adding the digits is to use the formula $\frac{n(n+1)}{2}$ where n is the number of instalments. If there are twelve instalments, then the sum of the digits will be 78. For this reason, the sum of the digits method is sometimes called the **rule of 78**.

(c) Calculate the interest charge included in each instalment. Do this by multiplying the total interest accruing over the lease term by the fraction:

$$\frac{\text{Digit applicable to the instalment}}{\text{Sum of the digits}}$$

6.7 Example: apportionment methods

On 1 January 20X0 Bacchus Co, wine merchants, buys a small bottling and labelling machine from Silenus Co under a finance lease. The cash price of the machine was $7,710 while the amount to be paid was $10,000. The agreement required the immediate payment of a $2,000 deposit with the balance being settled in four equal annual instalments commencing on 31 December 20X0. The charge of $2,290 represents interest of 15% per annum, calculated on the remaining balance of the liability during each accounting period. Depreciation on the plant is to be provided for at the rate of 20% per annum on a straight line basis assuming a residual value of nil.

You are required to show the breakdown of each instalment between interest and capital, using in turn each of the apportionment methods described above.

Solution

In this example, enough detail is given to use any of the apportionment methods. In an examination question, you would normally be directed to use one method specifically.

(a) **Sum-of-the-digits method**

Each instalment is allocated a digit as follows.

Instalment	*Digit*
1st (20X0)	4
2nd (20X1)	3
3rd (20X2)	2
4th (20X3)	1
	10

Or using the formula, $\frac{4 \times 5}{2} = 10$.

The $2,290 interest charges can then be apportioned.

		$
1st instalment	$2,290 × 4/10	916
2nd instalment	$2,290 × 3/10	687
3rd instalment	$2,290 × 2/10	458
4th instalment	$2,290 × 1/10	229
		2,290

The breakdown is then as follows.

	1st instalment $	*2nd instalment* $	*3rd instalment* $	*4th instalment* $
Interest	916	687	458	229
Capital repayment (balance)	1,084	1,313	1,542	1,771
	2,000	2,000	2,000	2,000

(b) **Actuarial method**

Interest is calculated as 15% of the outstanding *capital* balance at the beginning of each year. The outstanding capital balance reduces each year by the capital element comprised in each instalment. The outstanding capital balance at 1 January 20X0 is $5,710 ($7,710 fair value less $2,000 deposit).

	Total $	*Capital* $	*Interest* $
Capital balance at 1 Jan 20X0		5,710	
1st instalment (interest = $5,710 × 15%)	2,000	1,144	856
Capital balance at 1 Jan 20X1		4,566	
2nd instalment (interest = $4,566 × 15%)	2,000	1,315	685
Capital balance at 1 Jan 20X2		3,251	
3rd instalment (interest = $3,251 × 15%)	2,000	1,512	488
Capital balance at 1 Jan 20X3		1,739	
4th instalment (interest = $1,739 × 15%)	2,000	1,739	261
	8,000		2,290
Capital balance at 1 Jan 20X4		–	

6.8 Summary

IAS 17 requires various disclosures to be made in the accounts about finance leases (and hire purchase agreements). The detailed disclosures are not listed here. If you are asked a question about leases in your examination, you should remember the basic principles of:

(a) 'substance over form', and what it means

(b) leased assets (finance leases) as non-current assets in the accounts of the lessee

(c) inclusion in the accounts of the lessee of a payable for lease finance

(d) lease payments consisting partly of interest (an expense to the lessee) and partly of repayment of the lease finance debt

7 Provisions

FAST FORWARD

Under IAS 37 a provision should be recognised

– when an entity has a present obligation, legal or constructive
– it is probable that a transfer of economic benefits will be required to settle it
– a reliable estimate can be made of its amount

IAS 37 *Provisions, contingent liabilities and contingent assets* aims to ensure that appropriate **recognition criteria** and **measurement bases** are applied to provisions, contingent liabilities and contingent assets and that **sufficient information** is disclosed in the **notes** to the financial statements to enable users to understand their nature, timing and amount.

Before IAS 37, there was no accounting standard dealing with provisions. Companies wanting to show their results in the most favourable light used to make large 'one off' provisions in years where a high level of underlying profits was generated. These provisions, often known as 'big bath' provisions, were then available to shield expenditure in future years when perhaps the underlying profits were not as good.

In other words, provisions were used for profit smoothing. Profit smoothing is misleading.

Important

The key aim of IAS 37 is to ensure that **provisions are made only** where there are valid grounds for them.

IAS 37 views a provision as a liability.

Key terms

A **provision** is a **liability** of uncertain timing or amount.

A **liability** is an obligation of an entity to transfer economic benefits as a result of past transactions or events. *(IAS 37)*

The IAS distinguishes provisions from other liabilities such as trade payables and accruals. This is on the basis that for a provision there is **uncertainty** about the timing or amount of the future expenditure. Whilst uncertainty is clearly present in the case of certain accruals the uncertainty is generally much less than for provisions.

7.1 Recognition

IAS 37 states that a provision should be **recognised** as a liability in the financial statements when:

- An entity has a **present obligation** (legal or constructive) as a result of a past event
- It is probable that a **transfer of economic benefits** will be required to settle the obligation
- A **reliable estimate** can be made of the obligation

Key term

IAS 37 defines a **constructive obligation** as

'An obligation that derives from an entity's actions where:

- by an established pattern of past practice, published policies or a sufficiently specific current statement the entity has indicated to other parties that it will accept certain responsibilities; and
- as a result, the entity has created a valid expectation on the part of those other parties that it will discharge those responsibilities.'

Activity 6.4

In which of the following circumstances might a provision be recognised?

(a) On 13 December 20X9 the board of an entity decided to close down a division. The accounting date of the company is 31 December. Before 31 December 20X9 the decision was not communicated to any of those affected and no other steps were taken to implement the decision.

(b) The board agreed a detailed closure plan on 20 December 20X9 and details were given to customers and employees.

(c) A company is obliged to incur clean up costs for environmental damage (that has already been caused).

(d) A company intends to carry out future expenditure to operate in a particular way in the future.

7.2 Probable transfer of economic benefits

For the purpose of the IAS, a transfer of economic benefits is regarded as **'probable'** if the event is **more likely than not** to occur. This appears to indicate a probability of more than 50%. However, the standard makes it clear that where there is a number of similar obligations the probability should be based on considering the population as a whole, rather than one single item.

7.3 Example: transfer of economic benefits

If a company has entered into a warranty obligation then the probability of transfer of economic benefits may well be extremely small in respect of one specific item. However, when considering the population as a whole the probability of some transfer of economic benefits is quite likely to be much higher. If there is a **greater than 50% probability** of some transfer of economic benefits then a **provision** should be made for the **expected amount**.

7.4 Measurement of provisions

Important

The amount recognised as a provision should be the best estimate of the expenditure required to settle the present obligation at the balance sheet date.

The estimates will be determined by the **judgement** of the entity's management supplemented by the experience of similar transactions.

Allowance is made for **uncertainty**. Where the provision being measured involves a large population of items, the obligation is estimated by weighting all possible outcomes by their associated probabilities, ie **expected value**.

7.5 Example

Parker Co sells goods with a warranty under which customers are covered for the cost of repairs of any manufacturing defect that becomes apparent within the first six months of purchase. The company's past experience and future expectations indicate the following pattern of likely repairs.

% of goods sold	*Defects*	*Cost of repairs if all items suffered from these defects* $m
75	None	-
20	Minor	1.0
5	Major	4.0

What is the expected cost of repairs?

The cost is found using 'expected values' (75% × $nil) + (20% × $1.0m) + (5% × $4.0m) = $400,000.

Where the effect of the **time value of money** is material, the amount of a provision should be the **present value** of the expenditure required to settle the obligation. An appropriate **discount** rate should be used.

The discount rate should be a **pre-tax rate** that reflects current market assessments of the time value of money. **The discount rate(s) should not reflect risks for which future cash flow estimates have been adjusted.**

Future events which are reasonably expected to occur (eg new legislation, changes in technology) may affect the amount required to settle the entity's obligation and should be taken into account.

Gains from the expected disposal of assets should not be taken into account in measuring a provision.

Some or all of the expenditure needed to settle a provision may be expected to be recovered from a third party. If so, the **reimbursement should be recognised only when it is virtually certain that reimbursement will be received if the entity settles the obligation.**

- The reimbursement should be treated as a separate asset, and the amount recognised should not be greater than the provision itself.
- The provision and the amount recognised for reimbursement may be netted off in the income statement.

7.6 Changes in provisions

Provisions should be renewed at each balance sheet date and adjusted to reflect the current best estimate. If it is no longer probable that a transfer of economic benefits will be required to settle the obligation, the provision should be reversed.

7.7 Use of provisions

A provision should be used only for expenditures for which the provision was originally recognised. Setting expenditures against a provision that was originally recognised for another purpose would conceal the impact of two different events.

7.8 Future operating losses

Provisions should not be recognised for future operating losses. They do not meet the definition of a liability and the general recognition criteria set out in the standard.

7.9 Onerous contracts

If an entity has a contract that is onerous, the present obligation under the contract **should be recognised and measured** as a provision. An example might be vacant leasehold property.

Key term

An **onerous contract** is a contract entered into with another party under which the unavoidable costs of fulfilling the terms of the contract exceed any revenues expected to be received from the goods or services supplied or purchased directly or indirectly under the contract and where the entity would have to compensate the other party if it did not fulfil the terms of the contract.

7.10 Examples of possible provisions

It is easier to see what IAS 37 is driving at if you look at examples of those items which are possible provisions under this standard. Some of these we have already touched on.

(a) **Warranties**. These are argued to be genuine provisions as on past experience it is probable, ie more likely than not, that some claims will emerge. The provision must be estimated, however, on the basis of the class as a whole and not on individual claims. There is a clear legal obligation in this case.

(b) **Major repairs**. In the past it has been quite popular for companies to provide for expenditure on a major overhaul to be accrued gradually over the intervening years between overhauls. Under IAS 37 this is no longer possible as IAS 37 would argue that this is a mere intention to carry out repairs, not an obligation. The entity can always sell the asset in the meantime. The only solution is to treat major assets such as aircraft, ships, furnaces etc as a series of smaller assets where each part is depreciated over shorter lives. Thus any major overhaul may be argued to be replacement and therefore capital rather than revenue expenditure.

(c) **Self insurance**. A number of companies have created a provision for self insurance based on the expected cost of making good fire damage etc instead of paying premiums to an insurance company. Under IAS 37 this provision is no longer justifiable as the entity has no obligation until a fire or accident occurs. No obligation exists until that time.

(d) **Environmental contamination**. If the company has an environmental policy such that other parties would expect the company to clean up any contamination or if the company has broken current environmental legislation then a provision for environmental damage must be made.

(e) **Decommissioning or abandonment costs**. When an oil company initially purchases an oilfield it is put under a legal obligation to decommission the site at the end of its life. Prior to IAS 37 most oil companies set up the provision gradually over the life of the field so that no one year would be unduly burdened with the cost.

IAS 37, however, insists that a legal obligation exists on the initial expenditure on the field and therefore a liability exists immediately. This would appear to result in a large charge to profit and loss in the first year of operation of the field. However, the IAS takes the view that the cost of purchasing the field in the first place is not only the cost of the field itself but also the costs of putting it right again. Thus all the costs of abandonment may be capitalised.

(f) **Restructuring**. This is considered in detail below.

7.11 Provisions for restructuring

One of the main purposes of IAS 37 was to target abuses of provisions for restructuring. Accordingly, IAS 37 lays down **strict criteria** to determine when such a provision can be made.

Key term

> IAS 37 defines a **restructuring** as:
>
> A programme that is planned and is controlled by management and materially changes one of two things.
>
> - The scope of a business undertaken by an entity
> - The manner in which that business is conducted

The IAS gives the following **examples** of events that may fall under the definition of restructuring.

- The **sale or termination** of a line of business
- The **closure of business locations** in a country or region or the **relocation** of business activities from one country region to another
- **Changes in management structure**, for example, the elimination of a layer of management
- **Fundamental reorganisations** that have a material effect on the **nature and focus** of the entity's operations

The question is whether or not an entity has an obligation - legal or constructive - at the balance sheet date. For this to be the case:

- An entity must have a **detailed formal plan** for the restructuring
- It must have **raised a valid expectation** in those affected that it will carry out the restructuring by starting to implement that plan or announcing its main features to those affected by it

Important

> **A mere management decision is not normally sufficient**. Management decisions may sometimes trigger off recognition, but only if earlier events such as negotiations with employee representatives and other interested parties have been concluded subject only to management approval.

Where the restructuring involves the **sale of an operation** then IAS 37 states that no obligation arises until the entity has entered into a **binding sale agreement**. This is because until this has occurred the entity will be able to change its mind and withdraw from the sale even if its intentions have been announced publicly.

The IAS states that a restructuring provision should include only the **direct expenditures** arising from the restructuring, which are those that are both:

- **Necessarily entailed** by the restructuring; and
- Not associated with the **ongoing activities** of the entity.

The following costs should specifically **not** be included within a restructuring provision.

- **Retraining** or relocating continuing staff
- **Marketing**
- **Investment in new systems** and distribution networks

7.12 Disclosure

Disclosures for provisions fall into two parts.

- Disclosure of details of the **change in carrying value** of a provision from the beginning to the end of the year
- Disclosure of the **background** to the making of the provision and the uncertainties affecting its outcome

8 Contingencies

FAST FORWARD

An entity should not recognise a contingent asset or liability, but they may require disclosure.

Now you understand provisions it will be easier to understand contingent assets and liabilities.

Key term

IAS 37 defines a **contingent liability** as:

- A possible obligation that arises from past events and whose existence will be confirmed only by the occurrence or non-occurrence of one or more uncertain future events not wholly within the entity's control; or
- A present obligation that arises from past events but is not recognised because:
  - It is not probable that a transfer of economic benefits will be required to settle the obligation; or
  - The amount of the obligation cannot be measured with sufficient reliability.

As a rule of thumb, probable means more than 50% likely. **If an obligation is probable, it is not a contingent liability** - instead, a **provision is needed**.

8.1 Treatment of contingent liabilities

Contingent liabilities **should not be recognised in financial statements** but they **should be disclosed**. The required disclosures are:

- A brief description of the nature of the contingent liability
- An estimate of its financial effect
- An indication of the uncertainties that exist
- The possibility of any reimbursement

8.2 Contingent assets

Key term

IAS 37 defines a **contingent asset** as:

A possible asset that arises from past events and whose existence will be confirmed by the occurrence or non-occurrence of one or more uncertain future events not wholly within the entity's control.

A contingent asset must not be recognised. Only when the realisation of the related economic benefits is **virtually certain** should recognition take place. At that point, **the asset is no longer a contingent asset**!

8.3 Disclosure

A **brief description** must be provided of all material **contingent liabilities** unless they are likely to be remote. In addition, provide

- An estimate of their **financial effect**
- Details of **any uncertainties**
- The possibility of any reimbursement

Contingent assets must only be disclosed in the notes if they are **probable**. In that case a brief description of the contingent asset should be provided along with an estimate of its likely financial effect.

8.4 'Let out'

IAS 37 permits reporting entities to avoid disclosure requirements relating to provisions, contingent liabilities and contingent assets if they would be expected to **seriously prejudice** the position of the entity in dispute with other parties. However, this should only be employed in **extremely rare** cases. Details of the general nature of the provision/contingencies must still be provided, together with an explanation of why it has not been disclosed.

8.5 Flow chart

Study the flow chart, taken from IAS 37, which is a good summary of its requirements concerning provisions and contingent liabilities.

Exam focus point

If you learn this flow chart you should be able to deal with most questions you are likely to meet in an exam.

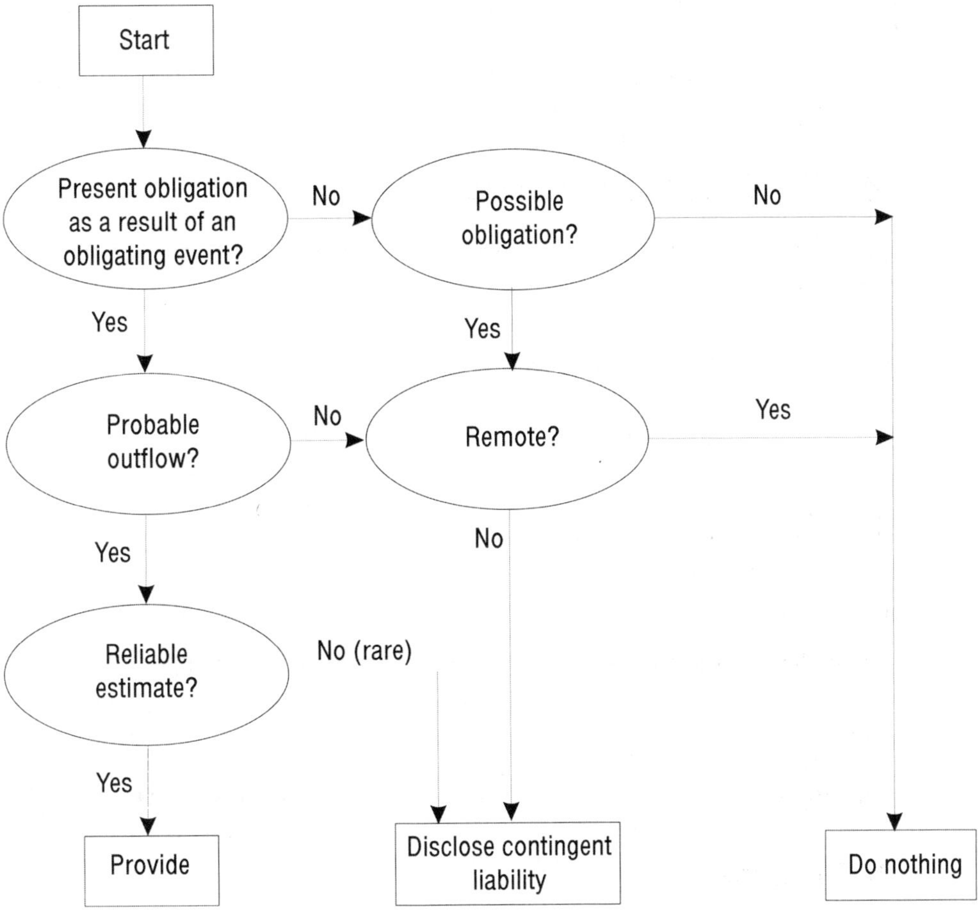

9 Events after the balance sheet date

FAST FORWARD

IAS 10 deals with **events occurring after the balance sheet date.** It distinguishes between adjusting and non-adjusting events and gives examples. You should be able to define and discuss all these terms and apply them to practical examples.

The financial statements are significant indicators of a company's success or failure. It is important, therefore, that they include all the information necessary for an understanding of the company's position.

IAS 10 (Revised) *Events after the balance sheet date* requires the provision of additional information in order to facilitate such an understanding. IAS 10 deals with events **after** the balance sheet date which may affect the position at the balance sheet date.

The standard gives the following definition.

Key term

Events occurring after the balance sheet date are those events, both favourable and unfavourable, that occur between the balance sheet date and the date on which the financial statements are authorised for issue. Two types of events can be identified.

- Those that provide evidence of conditions that existed at the balance sheet date
- Those that are indicative of conditions that arose after the balance sheet date *(IAS 10)*

Between the balance sheet date and the date the financial statements are authorised (ie for issue outside the organisation), events may occur which show that assets and liabilities at the balance sheet date should be adjusted, or that disclosure of such events should be given.

9.1 Events requiring adjustment

The standard requires adjustment of assets and liabilities in certain circumstances.

An entity shall adjust the amounts recognised in its financial statements to reflect adjusting events after the balance sheet date. An entity shall not adjust the amounts recognised in its financial statements to reflect non-adjusting events after the balance sheet date. *(IAS 10)*

An **example** of additional evidence which becomes available after the balance sheet date is where a **customer goes bankrupt, thus confirming that the trade account receivable balance at the year end is uncollectable.**

In relation to **going concern**, the standard states that, where operating results and the financial position have deteriorated after the balance sheet date, it may be necessary to reconsider whether the going concern assumption is appropriate in the preparation of the financial statements.

9.2 Events not requiring adjustment

The standard then looks at events which do **not** require adjustment.

If non-adjusting events after the balance sheet date are material, non-disclosure could influence the economic decisions of users taken on the basis of the financial statements. Accordingly, an entity shall disclose the following for each material category of non-adjusting event after the balance sheet date:

(a) the nature of the event; and
(b) an estimate of its financial effect, or a statement that such an estimate cannot be made.

(IAS 10)

The **example** given by the standard of such an event is where the **value of an investment falls between the balance sheet date and the date the financial statements are authorised** for issue. The fall in value represents circumstances during the current period, not conditions existing at the previous balance sheet date, so it is not appropriate to adjust the value of the investment in the financial statements. Disclosure is an aid to users, however, indicating 'unusual changes' in the state of assets and liabilities after the balance sheet date.

The rule for **disclosure** of events occurring after the balance sheet date which relate to conditions that arose after that date, is that disclosure should be made if non-disclosure would hinder the user's ability to make **proper evaluations** and decisions based on the financial statements. An example might be the acquisition of another business.

9.3 Dividends

Dividends on equity shares declared by the entity after the balance sheet date should not be recognised as a liability at the balance sheet date, but should be disclosed, either on the face of the balance sheet as a separate component of equity or in the notes to the financial statements.

9.4 Disclosures

The following **disclosure requirements** are given **for events** which occur after the balance sheet date which do not require adjustment. If disclosure of events occurring after the balance sheet date is required, the following information should be provided.

(a) The nature of the event
(b) An estimate of the financial effect, or a statement that such an estimate cannot be made

Activity 6.5

State whether the following events occurring after the balance sheet date require an adjustment to the assets and liabilities of the financial statements.

(a) Purchase of an investment
(b) A change in the rate of corporate tax, applicable to the previous year
(c) An increase in pension benefits
(d) Losses due to fire
(e) A bad debt suddenly being paid
(f) The receipt of proceeds of sales or other evidence concerning the net realisable value of inventory
(g) A sudden decline in the value of property held as a long-term asset

10 Reporting the substance of transactions

FAST FORWARD

There has been some concern about the use of creative accounting methods. In particular off-balance sheet financing transactions might be used to keep assets or liabilities off a company's balance sheet. Attempts have been made to restrict these practices.

10.1 Off balance sheet finance

Key term

Off balance sheet finance is the funding or refinancing of a company's operations in such a way that, under legal requirements and traditional accounting conventions, some or all of the finance may not be shown on its balance sheet.

'Off balance sheet transactions' are transactions which meet the above objective. These transactions may involve the **removal of assets** from the balance sheet, as well as liabilities, and they are also likely to have a significant impact on the income statement.

Why might company managers wish to enter into such transactions?

(a) In some countries, companies traditionally have a lower level of gearing than companies in other countries. Off balance sheet finance is used to **keep gearing low**, probably because of the views of analysts and brokers.

(b) A company may need to keep its gearing down in order to stay within the terms of **loan covenants** imposed by lenders.

(c) A quoted company with high borrowings is often expected (by analysts and others) to declare a **rights issue** in order to reduce gearing. This has an adverse effect on a company's share price and so off balance sheet financing is used to reduce gearing *and* the expectation of a rights issue.

(d) Analysts' short term views are a problem for companies **developing assets** which are not producing income during the development stage. Such companies will match the borrowings associated with such developing assets, along with the assets themselves, off balance sheet. They are brought back on balance sheet once income is being generated by the assets. This process keeps return on capital employed higher than it would have been during the development stage.

(e) In the past, groups of companies have excluded **subsidiaries** from consolidation in an off balance sheet transaction because they carry out completely different types of business and have different characteristics. The usual example is a leasing company (in say a retail group) which has a high level of gearing.

You can see from this brief list of reasons that the overriding motivation is to avoid **misinterpretation**. In other words, the company does not trust the analysts or other users to understand the reasons for a transaction and so avoids any effect such transactions might have by taking them off balance sheet. Unfortunately, the position of the company is then misstated and the user of the accounts is misled.

You must understand that not all forms of 'off balance sheet finance' are undertaken for cosmetic or accounting reasons. Some transactions are carried out to **limit or isolate risk**, to reduce interest costs and so on. In other words, these transactions are in the best interests of the company, not merely a cosmetic repackaging of figures which would normally appear in the balance sheet.

The result of the use of increasingly sophisticated off balance sheet finance transactions is a situation where the users of financial statements do not have a proper or clear view of the **state of the company's affairs**. The disclosures required by national company law and accounting standards did not in the past provide sufficient rules for disclosure of off balance sheet finance transactions and so very little of the true nature of the transaction was exposed.

Whatever the purpose of such transactions, **insufficient disclosure** creates a problem. This problem has been debated over the years by the accountancy profession and other interested parties and some progress has been made. However, company collapses during recessions have often revealed much higher borrowings than originally thought, because part of the borrowing was off balance sheet.

The main argument used for banning off balance sheet finance is that the true **substance** of the transactions should be shown, not merely the **legal form**, particularly when it is exacerbated by poor disclosure.

10.2 Substance over form

The concept of **'substance over form'** is described in IAS 17 *Leases* as follows.

'Transactions and other events are accounted for and presented in accordance with their substance and financial reality and not merely with legal form. '

An application of this principle in relation to accounting for finance leases has already been described. The legal form is that the lessor owns the leased asset, but in substance the lessee is the owner.

Another issue involving substance over form is the establishment of 'quasi subsidiaries' by a company. A **quasi-subsidiary** is an organisation that does not meet the definition of a subsidiary company, under the control of its parent company, but operates just like a subsidiary. At one time, companies did not have to include quasi-subsidiaries in their consolidated accounts ('group accounts').

Some companies used 'off balance sheet' transactions with quasi-subsidiaries to manipulate their accounts. Examples of off balance sheet transactions that were undertaken at one time are as follows.

(a) **Sale of assets**. The sale of assets to a quasi-subsidiary would be carried out to remove the associated borrowings from the balance sheet of the company, or perhaps so that the company could credit a profit in such a transaction. The asset would then be rented back to the vendor company under an operating lease (no capitalisation required by the lessee).

(b) **Purchase of companies or assets**. One reason for such a purchase through a quasi-subsidiary is if the acquired entity is expected to make losses in the near future. Post-acquisition losses can be avoided by postponing the date of acquisition to the date the holding company acquires the purchase from the quasi-subsidiary.

IAS27 Consolidated and separate financial statements contains a definition of a subsidiary based on control rather than just ownership rights, thus substantially reducing the effectiveness of this method of off-balance sheet financing. We will look at this definition in Chapter 10.

10.3 Creative accounting

Creative accounting is the **manipulation of figures for a desired result**. It can take various forms, and might make use of off balance sheet finance.

It is very rare for a company or its directors to manipulate results for the purpose of fraud. The major consideration with creative accounting is usually the effect the results will have on the share price of the company.

Analysts, brokers and economists, whose opinions affect the stock markets, are often perceived as having an outlook which is both short-term and superficial. Consequently, companies will attempt to produce the results the market expects or wants. The companies will aim for steady progress in a few key numbers and ratios and they will aim to meet the market's stated expectation.

Some examples of creative accounting are described below.

10.4 Revenue recognition and year-end cut-off

A company may issue invoices before the year end and inflate sales for the current year, when in fact they have not received firm orders for the goods.

Another example of recognising income before it should properly be recognised is where a company sells software under contract, and the sales contracts will only be realised in full over a period of time. The company might recognise the full sales value of the contract as soon as it has been secured, even though some payments from clients will fall due over several years. This is clearly imprudent, but the company might justify it by pointing to the irrevocable nature of the contract. But what if a customer should go in to liquidation? If a customer went into liquidation, no further income would be received from the contract, but the company would already have credited this non-existent income to its profits in a previous year.

10.5 Reserves

Reserves are often used to manipulate figures, and to avoid any adverse impact on the income statement. This occurs particularly in situations where an accounting standard allows a choice of treatments. Recent IASs have aimed to reduce these choices.

10.6 Examples of off balance sheet finance

Consignment goods is an arrangement where stock (or inventory) is **held by one party** (say a distributor) but is **owned by another party** (for example a manufacturer or a finance company). Consignment goods are common in the motor trade and are similar to goods sold on a 'sale or return' basis.

To identify the correct accounting treatment of consignment goods, it is necessary to identify the point at which the distributor acquired the benefits of the asset (the goods) rather than the point at which legal title was acquired. If the manufacturer has the right to require the return of goods, and if that right is likely to be exercised, then the goods are not an asset of the dealer. If the dealer is rarely required to return the goods, then this part of the transaction will have little commercial effect in practice and should be ignored for accounting purposes. The potential liability would need to be disclosed in the accounts.

Sale and leaseback transactions are arrangements under which the company sells an asset (eg a building) to another person on the terms that allow the company to repurchase the asset in certain circumstances. The key question is whether the transaction is a straightforward sale, or whether it is, in effect, a secured loan. It is necessary to look at the arrangement to determine who has the rights to the economic benefits that the asset generates, and the terms on which the asset is to be repurchased.

If the seller has the right to the benefits of the use of the asset, and the repurchase terms are such that the repurchase is likely to take place, the transaction should be accounted for as a loan.

A sale and purchase agreement is an agreement to sell an item on one date and to buy it back at an agreed price at a later date. The financial reporting issue is whether the sale and the repurchase should be treated as part of a single transaction, or whether they can be accounted for as though they are separate transactions.

Key learning points

- IAS suggests a format for the balance sheet.
- An entity must present current and non-current assets as separate classifications on the face of the balance sheet.
- Inventory must be valued at the lower of cost and net realisable value. The most commonly used methods to derive cost are FIFO and weighted average cost.
- Companies with construction contracts take credit for some of the anticipated profit before the contract has been completed. IAS11 specifies how this should be dealt with as follows:
  - Sales revenue should be debited to receivables (and credited to the income statement).
  - The amount at which contract work in progress is stated in the accounts should be cost, less cost of sales to date, including any foreseeable losses.
  - Progress billings received and receivable should first be credited to receivables and any excess to payables.
- Liabilities must be split in the balance sheet between current and non-current liabilities.
- Under finance leases
  - Assets acquired should be capitalised
  - Interest element of instalments should be charged against profit
- Operating leases are rental agreements and all instalments are charged against profit.
- Under IAS 37, a provision should be recognised
  - When an entity has a present obligation, legal or constructive,
  - It is probable that a transfer of economic benefits will be required to settle it
  - A reliable estimate can be made of its amount
- An entity should not recognise a contingent asset or liability, but they may require disclosure.
- IAS 10 deals with events occurring after the balance sheet date. IAS 10 distinguishes between adjusting and non-adjusting events.
- There has been some concern about the use of creative accounting methods. In particular off balance sheet financing transactions might be used to keep assets or liabilities off a company's balance sheet. Attempts have been made to restrict these practices.

Quick quiz

1 Which of the following are examples of current assets?

(a) Property, plant and equipment
(b) Prepayments
(c) Manufacturing licences
(d) Retained earnings

2 Provisions must be disclosed on the face of the balance sheet

True ☐

False ☐

3 Net realisable value = Selling price **less** .... **less** ....

4 Which inventory costing method is allowed under IAS 2?

(a) FIFO
(b) LIFO

5 Any expected loss on a construction contract must be recognised, in full, in the year it was identified.

True ☐

False ☐

6 (a) ....leases transfer substantially all the risks and rewards of ownership.

(b) ....leases are usually short-term rental agreements with the lessor being responsible for the repairs and maintenance of the asset.

7 A provision is a .... of .... timing or amount.

8 A programme is undertaken by management which converts the previously wholly owned chain of restaurants they ran into franchises. Is this restructuring?

9 Define contingent asset and contingent liability.

10 Define events occurring after the balance sheet date.

11 A customer goes bankrupt after the balance sheet date and his debt must be written off.

Adjusting event ☐

Non-adjusting event ☐

12 Inventory is lost in a fire after the balance sheet date.

Adjusting event ☐

Non-adjusting event ☐

Answers to quick quiz

1. b
2. True
3. Net realisable value = selling price **less** costs of completion **less** costs necessary to make the sale.
4. (a) FIFO. LIFO is not allowed.
5. True
6. (a) Finance leases

   (b) Operating leases
7. Liability of uncertain timing or amount
8. Yes. The manner in which the business is conducted has changed
9. Refer to paragraphs 8.2 and 8.1 respectively
10. Those events, unfavourable and favourable, which occur between the balance sheet date and the date on which the financial statements are authorised for issue.
11. Adjusting
12. Non-adjusting

Answers to activities

6.1

		$
A	Lower of cost (560 + 880 + 780) or NRV (660 + 740 + 960) i.e. 2,220 or 2,360	2,220
B	Lower of cost (340 + 420) or NRV(500 + 620) i.e.760 or 1,120	760
C	Lower of cost (860 + 1,720) or NRV (700 + 1,200) i.e. 2,520 or 1,900	1,900
D	Lower of cost (1,140 + 1,540) or NRV (1,320 + 1,980) I.e. 2,680 or 3,300	2,680
		7,560

6.2 There is no uncertainty involved and hence there is no justification for reducing (providing against) the value of closing inventories.

What is being suggested is obviously an attempt by management to smooth its profits so that 20X7 does not show a dip in relation to 20X6 and 20X8.

This attempted practice seeks to massage the numbers and the picture of management stewardship, rather than addressing ways to sustain sales levels through marketing, business development or enhanced trading activities, ie managing the numbers rather than managing the business activities.

6.3 *Happy contract*

(a) *40% complete*

	$'000
Income statement	
Sales revenue (40% × 300)	120
Cost of sales (40% × 225)	90
Gross profit	30
Balance sheet	
Receivables (120 – 116)	4
Construction contract in progress (90 – 90)	-

(b) *36% complete*

	$'000
Income statement	
Sales revenue (36% × 300)	108
Cost of sales (36% × 225)	81
Gross profit	27
Balance sheet	
Receivables (108 – 116 = –8)	-
Construction contract in progress (90 – 81) =	9
Payables	8

Grumpy contract

(a) *40% complete*

Working

	$'000	$'000
Total contract price		300
Less: costs to date	150	
estimated costs to completion	225	
		375
Foreseeable loss		(75)

	$'000
Income statement	
Sales revenue (40% × 300)	120
Cost of sales (40% × 375)	(150)
	(30)
Provision for future losses (bal fig)	(45)
Gross loss	(75)
Balance sheet	$'000
Receivables (120 – 116)	4
Construction contract in progress (150 – 150)	-
Provision for future losses	(45)

(b) *36% complete*

	$'000
Income statement	
Sales revenue (36% × 300)	108
Cost of sales (36% × 375)	(135)
	(27)
Provision for future losses (balancing figure)	(48)
Gross loss	(75)
Balance sheet	
Provisions: provisions for future losses*	41
*Provision for future losses	48
Less construction contract in progress (150 – 135 – 8)	7
	41

6.4 (a) No provision would be recognised as the decision has not been communicated.

(b) A provision would be made in the 20X9 financial statements.

(c) A provision for such costs is appropriate.

(d) No present obligation exists and under IAS 37 no provision would be appropriate. This is because the entity could avoid the future expenditure by its future actions, maybe by changing its method of operation.

6.5 (b), (e) and (f) require adjustment.

Reporting financial performance

7

Topic list	Syllabus reference
1 IAS 8: *Accounting policies, changes in accounting estimates and errors*	
2 IFRS 5: *Non-current assets held for sale and discontinued operations*	
3 IAS 14: *Segment reporting*	

Introduction

These topics are concerned with the way that information is presented in the financial statements and how this might affect a user's perception of the results. Of particular importance are the disclosure requirements regarding discontinued operations.

Learning objectives

On completion of this chapter you will be able to:

	Syllabus reference
• explain and appraise the meaning of an income statement which identifies discontinued operations, prior period adjustments and non-current assets held for resale	3cviii
• explain how adjustments are made for changes in accounting policy and prior period errors	3viii
• disclose assets 'held for sale'	3viii
• present information regarding discontinued operations	3viii
• identify how companies provide a segmental analysis of their results	3cviii
• explain the purpose of segmental information and appraise its usefulness	3cviii

1 IAS 8: *Accounting policies, changes in accounting estimates and errors*

FAST FORWARD

Changes in accounting policy and prior period errors should be dealt with **retrospectively**. Changes in accounting estimates should be dealt with **prospectively**.

1.1 Accounting policies

Key term

Accounting policies are the specific principles, bases, conventions, rules and practices adopted by an entity in preparing and presenting financial statements.

Accounting policies are determined by **applying the relevant IFRS or IFRIC** and considering any relevant Implementation Guidance issued by the IASB for that IFRS/IFRIC.

Where there is no applicable IFRS or IFRIC management should use its **judgement** in developing and applying an accounting policy that results in information that is **relevant** and **reliable**. Management should refer to:

(a) The requirements and guidance in IFRSs and IFRICs dealing with **similar** and **related issues**

(b) The definitions, recognition criteria and measurement concepts for assets, liabilities and expenses in the ***Framework***

Management may also consider the most recent pronouncements of **other standard setting bodies** that use a similar conceptual framework to develop standards, other accounting literature and accepted industry practices if these do not conflict with the sources above.

An entity must select and apply its accounting policies for a period **consistently** for similar transactions, other events and conditions, unless an IFRS or an IFRIC specifically requires or permits categorisation of items for which different policies may be appropriate. If an IFRS or an IFRIC requires or permits categorisation of items, an appropriate accounting policy must be selected and applied consistently to each category.

1.2 Changes in accounting policies

The same accounting policies are usually adopted from period to period, to allow users to analyse trends over time in profit, cash flows and financial position. **Changes in accounting policy will therefore be rare** and should be made only if required by one of three things.

(a) By **statute**

(b) By an **accounting standard setting body**

(c) If the change will result in a **more appropriate presentation** of events or transactions in the financial statements of the entity

The standard highlights two types of event **which do not constitute changes in accounting policy**.

(a) Adopting an accounting policy for a **new type of transaction** or event not dealt with previously by the entity.

(b) Adopting a **new accounting policy** for a transaction or event which has not occurred in the past or which was not material.

In the case of tangible non-current assets, if a policy of revaluation is adopted for the first time then this is treated, not as a change of accounting policy under IAS 8, but as a revaluation under IAS 16 *Property, plant and equipment* (see Chapter 8). The following paragraphs do not therefore apply to a change in policy to adopt revaluations.

IAS 8 requires **retrospective application**, *unless* it is **impracticable** to determine the cumulative amount of charge. Any resulting adjustment should be reported as an adjustment to the opening balance of retained earnings. Comparative information should be restated unless it is impracticable to do so.

This means that all comparative information must be restated **as if the new policy had always been in force**, with amounts relating to earlier periods reflected in an adjustment to opening reserves of the earliest period presented.

Prospective application is allowed only when it is impracticable to determine the cumulative effect of the change.

Certain **disclosures** are required when a change in accounting policy has a material effect on the current period or any prior period presented, or when it may have a material effect in subsequent periods.

(a) Reasons for the change

(b) Amount of the adjustment for the current period and for each period presented

(c) Amount of the adjustment relating to periods prior to those included in the comparative information

(d) The fact that comparative information has been restated or that it is impracticable to do so

An entity should also disclose information relevant to assessing the **impact of new IFRS** on the financial statements where these have **not yet come into force.**

1.3 Changes in accounting estimates

Estimates arise in relation to business activities because of the **uncertainties inherent within them**. Judgements are made based on the most up to date information and the use of such estimates is a necessary part of the preparation of financial statements. It does *not* undermine their reliability. Here are some examples of accounting estimates.

(a) A necessary **bad debt allowance**
(b) **Useful lives** of depreciable assets
(c) Allowance for **obsolescence of inventory**

The rule here is that the **effect of a change in an accounting estimate** should be included in the determination of net profit or loss in one of:

(a) The period of the change, if the change affects that period only
(b) The period of the change *and* future periods, if the change affects both

Changes may occur in the circumstances which were in force at the time the estimate was calculated, or perhaps additional information or subsequent developments have come to light.

An example of a change in accounting estimate which affects only the **current period** is the bad debt estimate. However, a revision in the life over which an asset is depreciated would affect both the **current and future periods**, in the amount of the depreciation expense.

Reasonably enough, the effect of a change in an accounting estimate should be included in the **same income statement classification** as was used previously for the estimate. This rule helps to ensure **consistency** between the financial statements of different periods.

The **materiality** of the change is also relevant. The nature and amount of a change in an accounting estimate that has a material effect in the current period (or which is expected to have a material effect in subsequent periods) should be disclosed. If it is not possible to quantify the amount, this impracticability should be disclosed.

1.4 Errors

Errors discovered during a current period which **relate to a prior period** may arise through:

(a) Mathematical mistakes
(b) Mistakes in the application of accounting policies
(c) Misinterpretation of facts
(d) Oversights
(e) Fraud

Most of the time these errors can be **corrected through net profit or loss for the current period**. Where they are **material** prior period errors, however, this is not appropriate. The standard considers two possible treatments.

Prior period errors: correct retrospectively.

This involves:

(a) Either restating the comparative amounts for the prior period(s) in which the error occurred,

(b) Or, when the error occurred before the earliest prior period presented, restating the opening balances of assets, liabilities and equity for that period

so that the financial statements are presented **as if the error had never occurred**.

Only where it is **impracticable** to determine the cumulative effect of an error on prior periods can an entity correct an error **prospectively**.

Various **disclosures** are required, providing information about the nature of the error and its effect on the financial results.

2 IFRS 5: *Non-current assets held for sale and discontinued operations*

FAST FORWARD

IFRS 5 requires assets 'held for sale' to be presented separately on the face of the balance sheet.

2.1 Background

IFRS 5 is the result of a short-term convergence project with the US Financial Accounting Standards Board (FASB).

IFRS 5 requires **assets** and groups of assets that are '**held for sale**' to be **presented separately** on the face of the **balance sheet** and the results of **discontinued operations** to be **presented separately** in the **income statement**. This is required so that users of financial statements will be better able to make **projections** about the financial position, profits and cash flows of the entity.

IFRS 5 does not apply to certain assets covered by other accounting standards including:

- Deferred tax assets (IAS 12)
- Investment properties accounted for in accordance with the fair value model (IAS 40)

2.2 Classification of assets held for sale

A non-current asset (or disposal group) should be classified as **held for sale** if its carrying amount will be recovered **principally through a sale transaction** rather than **through continuing use**. A number of detailed criteria must be met:

(a) The asset must be **available for immediate sale** in its present condition.
(b) Its sale must be **highly probable** (ie, significantly more likely than not).

Key term

Disposal group: a group of assets to be disposed of, by sale or otherwise, together as a group in a single transaction, and liabilities directly associated with those assets that will be transferred in the transaction. (In practice a disposal group could be a subsidiary, a cash-generating unit or a single operation within an entity.) (*IFRS 5*)

For the sale to be highly probable, the following must apply.

(a) Management must be **committed** to a plan to sell the asset.

(b) There must be an active programme to **locate a buyer.**

(c) The asset must be marketed for sale at a **price that is reasonable** in relation to its current fair value.

(d) The sale should be expected to take place **within one year** from the date of classification.

(e) It is unlikely that significant changes to the plan will be made or that the plan will be withdrawn.

An asset (or disposal group) can still be classified as held for sale, even if the sale has not actually taken place within one year. However, the delay must have been **caused by events or circumstances beyond the entity's control** and there must be sufficient evidence that the entity is still committed to sell the asset or disposal group. Otherwise the entity must cease to classify the asset as held for sale.

If an entity acquires a disposal group (eg, a subsidiary) exclusively with a view to its subsequent disposal it can classify the asset as held for sale only if the sale is expected to take place within one year and it is highly probable that all the other criteria will be met within a short time (normally three months).

An asset that is to be **abandoned** should not be classified as held for sale. This is because its carrying amount will be recovered principally through continuing use. However, a disposal group to be abandoned may meet the definition of a discontinued operation and therefore separate disclosure may be required (see below).

Activity 7.1

On 1 December 20X3, a company became committed to a plan to sell a manufacturing facility and has already found a potential buyer. The company does not intend to discontinue the operations currently carried out in the facility. At 31 December 20X3 there is a backlog of uncompleted customer orders. The company will not be able to transfer the facility to the buyer until after it ceases to operate the facility and has eliminated the backlog of uncompleted customer orders. This is not expected to occur until spring 20X4.

Required

Can the manufacturing facility be classified as 'held for sale' at 31 December 20X3?

2.3 Measurement of assets held for sale

Key terms

- **Fair value:** the amount for which an asset could be exchanged, or a liability settled, between knowledgeable, willing parties in an arm's length transaction.
- **Costs to sell:** the incremental costs directly attributable to the disposal of an asset (or disposal group), excluding finance costs and income tax expense.
- **Recoverable amount:** the higher of an asset's fair value less costs to sell and its value in use.
- **Value in use:** the present value of estimated future cash flows expected to arise from the continuing use of an asset and from its disposal at the end of its useful life.

A non-current asset (or disposal group) that is held for sale should be measured at the **lower of** its **carrying amount** and **fair value less costs to sell**. Fair value less costs to sell is equivalent to net realisable value.

An impairment loss should be recognised where fair value less costs to sell is lower than carrying amount. (see Chapter 8)

Non-current assets held for sale **should not be depreciated**, even if they are still being used by the entity.

A non-current asset (or disposal group) that is **no longer classified as held for sale** (for example, because the sale has not taken place within one year) is measured at the **lower of**:

(a) Its **carrying amount** before it was classified as held for sale, adjusted for any depreciation that would have been charged had the asset not been held for sale

(b) Its **recoverable amount** at the date of the decision not to sell

2.4 Presentation of a non-current asset or disposal group classified as held for sale

Non-current assets and disposal groups classified as held for sale should be **presented separately** from other assets in the balance sheet. The liabilities of a disposal group should be presented separately from other liabilities in the balance sheet.

(a) Assets and liabilities held for sale **should not be offset**.

(b) The **major classes** of assets and liabilities held for sale should be **separately disclosed** either on the face of the balance sheet or in the notes.

2.5 Presenting discontinued operations

FAST FORWARD

The result of **discontinued operations** should be presented separately in the income statement.

An entity should **present and disclose information** that enables users of the financial statements to evaluate the financial effects of **discontinued operations** and disposals of non-current assets or disposal groups.

Key terms

- **Discontinued operation:** a component of an entity that has either been disposed of, or is classified as held for sale, and:
  - (a) Represents a separate major line of business or geographical area of operations
  - (b) Is part of a single co-ordinated plan to dispose of a separate major line of business or geographical area of operations, or
  - (c) Is a subsidiary acquired exclusively with a view to resale.
- **Component of an entity:** operations and cash flows that can be clearly distinguished, operationally and for financial reporting purposes, from the rest of the entity.

An entity should disclose a **single amount** on the **face of the income statement** comprising the total of:

(a) The **post-tax profit or loss** of discontinued operations and

(b) The post-tax gain or loss recognised on the **measurement to fair value less costs to sell** or on the disposal of the assets or disposal group(s) constituting the discontinued operation.

An entity should also disclose an **analysis** of this single amount into:

(a) The revenue, expenses and pre-tax profit or loss of discontinued operations

(b) The related income tax expense

(c) The gain or loss recognised on the measurement to fair value less costs to sell or on the disposal of the assets of the discontinued operation

(d) The related income tax expense

This may be presented either on the face of the income statement or in the notes. If it is presented on the face of the income statement it should be presented in a section identified as relating to discontinued operations, ie separately from continuing operations. This analysis is not required where the discontinued operation is a newly acquired subsidiary that has been classified as held for sale.

An entity should disclose the **net cash flows** attributable to the operating, investing and financing activities of discontinued operations. These disclosures may be presented either on the face of the cash flow statement or in the notes. We will look at cash flow statements in chapter 10.

Gains and losses on the remeasurement of a disposal group that is not a discontinued operation but is held for sale should be included in profit or loss from continuing operations.

2.6 Illustration

The following illustration is taken from the implementation guidance to IFRS 5. Profit for the period from discontinued operations would be analysed in the notes.

As you can see the income statement is essentially the same as the example which we looked at in Chapter 5. The key difference is the distinction between continuing and discontinued operations.

XYZ GROUP
INCOME STATEMENT
FOR THE YEAR ENDED 31 DECEMBER 20X7

	20X7	*20X6*
Continuing operations	$'000	$'000
Revenue	X	X
Cost of sales	(X)	(X)
Gross profit	X	X
Other income	X	X
Distribution costs	(X)	(X)
Administrative expenses	(X)	(X)
Other expenses	(X)	(X)
Finance costs	(X)	(X)
Share of profit of associates	X	X
Profit before tax	X	X
Income tax expense	(X)	(X)
Profit for the period from continuing operations	X	X
Discontinued operations		
Profit for the period from discontinued operations	X	X
Profit for the period	X	X
Attributable to:		
Equity holders of the parent	X	X
Minority interest	X	X
	X	X

An alternative to this presentation would be to analyse the profit from discontinued operations in a separate column on the face of the income statement.

3 IAS 14: *Segment reporting*

FAST FORWARD

Segment reporting involves analysing the results of an entity showing the effect of different products and services and its operations in different geographical areas.

3.1 Background

Large entities produce a wide range of products and services, often in several different countries. Further information on how the overall results of entities are made up from each of these product or geographical areas will help the users of the financial statements. This is the reason for **segment reporting**.

(a) The entity's **past performance** will be better understood
(b) The entity's **risks and returns** may be better assessed
(c) More **informed judgements** may be made about the entity as a whole

Risks and returns of a **diversified, multi-national company** can only be assessed by looking at the individual risks and rewards attached to groups of products or services or in different geographical areas. These are subject to differing rates of profitability, opportunities for growth, future prospects and risks.

Only entities whose **equity or debt securities are publicly traded** (ie on a stock exchange) need disclose segment information. This includes entities in the process of issuing securities. Other entities that produce financial statements which comply with IASs are encouraged to disclose segment information voluntarily (in such cases IAS 14 must be followed entirely, not simply in part).

3.2 Definitions of business segment and geographical segment

These are the most important definitions in the standard, and you should be aware of the listed factors for business and geographical segments as these affect the rest of the standard.

Key terms

- A **business segment** is a distinguishable component of an entity that is engaged in providing an individual product or service or a group of related products or services and that is subject to risks and returns that are different from those of other business segments. Factors that should be considered in determining whether products and services are related include:

  (a) The nature of the products or services

  (b) The nature of the production processes

  (c) The type or class of customer for the products or services

  (d) The methods used to distribute the products or provide the services

  (e) If applicable, the nature of the regulatory environment, for example, banking, insurance, or public utilities

- A **geographical segment** is a distinguishable component of an entity that is engaged in providing products or services within a particular economic environment and that is subject to risks and returns that are different from those of components operating in other economic environments. Factors that should be considered in identifying geographical segments include:

  (a) Similarity of economic and political conditions
  (b) Relationships between operations in different geographical areas
  (c) Proximity of operations
  (d) Special risks associated with operations in a particular area
  (e) Exchange control regulations
  (f) The underlying currency risks

- A **reportable segment** is a business segment or a geographical segment identified based on the foregoing definitions for which segment information is required to be disclosed by IAS 14.

(IAS 14)

All the products or services produced by a segment will be similar with respect to a **majority of the factors** in the definition of a **business segment** (these factors are given in no particular order).

The case is similar for **geographical segments**. These may consist of one country, two or more countries or a region within a country, but they do not include operations in economic environments with significantly differing risks and returns.

IAS 14 argues that entities are organised and managed according to the predominant sources of risk. Their structure and financial reporting systems can therefore be used to identify segments. These should indicate whether the entity's risks and returns are influenced mainly by the geographical **location of its operations** or by the **location of its markets**. Either method can be used to identify geographical segments (ie either by origin or destination of sales).

There is obviously a significant level of judgement required to determine the composition of a segment. The qualitative characteristics of financial statements, as laid out in the IASB's *Framework* (see Chapter 4) should be considered.

3.3 Definitions of segment revenue, expense, result, assets and liabilities

These definitions come into play **once segments have been identified**.

Key terms

- **Segment revenue** is revenue reported in the entity's income statement that is directly attributable to a segment and the relevant portion of entity revenue that can be allocated on a reasonable basis to a segment, whether from sales to external customers or from transactions with other segments of the same entity. Segment revenue does *not* include:

  (a) Interest or dividend income, including interest earned on advances or loans to other segments, unless the segment's operations are primarily of a financial nature

  (b) Gains on sales of investments or gains on extinguishment of debt unless the segment's operations are primarily of a financial nature

- **Segment expense** is expense resulting from the operating activities of a segment that is directly attributable to the segment and the relevant portion of an expense that can be allocated on a reasonable basis to the segment, including expenses relating to sales to external customers and expenses relating to transactions with other segments of the same entity. Segment expense does not include:

  (a) Interest, including interest incurred on advances or loans from other segments, unless the segment's operations are primarily of a financial nature

  (b) Losses on sales of investments or losses on extinguishment of debt unless the segment's operations are primarily of a financial nature

  (c) Income tax expense

  (d) General administrative expenses, head office expenses, and other expenses that arise at the entity level and relate to the entity as a whole. However, costs are sometimes incurred at the entity level on behalf of a segment. Such costs are segment expenses if they relate to the segment's operating activities and they can be directly attributed or allocated to the segment on a reasonable basis

- **Segment result** is segment revenue less segment expense. Segment result is determined before any adjustments for minority interest.

- **Segment assets** are those operating assets that are employed by a segment in its operating activities and that either are directly attributable to the segment or can be allocated to the segment on a reasonable basis.

  (a) If a segment's segment result includes interest or dividend income, its segment assets include the related receivables, loans, investments, or other income-producing assets.

  (b) Segment assets do not include income tax assets.

- **Segment liabilities** are those operating liabilities that result from the operating activities of a segment and that either are directly attributable to the segment or can be allocated to the segment on a reasonable basis.

  (a) If a segment's segment result includes interest expense, its segment liabilities include the related interest-bearing liabilities.

  (b) Segment liabilities do not include income tax liabilities.

- Segment accounting policies are the accounting policies adopted for preparing and presenting the financial statements of the consolidated group or entity as well as those accounting policies that relate specifically to segment reporting. (*IAS 14*)

You can see from these definitions that only those amounts **directly attributable** to a segment should be included in the segment information.

Normally, internal financial reporting will be along these lines. Occasionally, however, amounts may be allocated to segments for management purposes which seem arbitrary or subjective. Alternatively, an entity may not allocate all items to segments which should be on a reasonable basis. In both these cases, the segment figures would **require adjustment**.

In relation to **segment assets**, if depreciation or amortisation is included as a segment expense, then the **respective asset** must be shown as a segment asset. Such assets may be shared between segments, but assets **held for the head office or for general purposes should be excluded.**

Segment liabilities do *not* include borrowings, liabilities resulting from finance leases, and other liabilities undertaken for **financing rather than operating purposes**. As with depreciation, if interest expense is included in the segment result, the related interest-bearing debt must be included in segment liabilities.

3.4 Identifying reportable segments

FAST FORWARD

IAS 14 allows management to choose their primary segment reporting format.

IAS 14 requires management to assess the dominant source and nature of an entity's risks and returns in order to assess whether the **primary segment reporting format** will be by business segment or geographical segment. The other format will then be given as a **secondary segment report**.

Dominant source and nature	Primary segment report	Secondary segment report
Business	Business	Geographical
Geographical	Geographical	Business

How is this decision made? IAS 14 states that it should be based on:

(a) An entity's internal organisational and management structure

(b) The system of internal financial reporting to the board of directors and chief executive officer

This approach is sometimes referred to as the 'management approach'.

3.5 Material segments: 10% threshold rule

There is a **materiality rule**, which we could call the 10% rule. A business or geographical segment is a reportable segment if the majority of its revenue is earned from sales to external customers *and* any of the following applies.

(a) Segment internal and external **revenue** is 10% or more of total internal and external revenue of all segments.

(b) Segment **result** (profit *or* loss) is 10% or more of the combined result of all segments in profit *or* the combined result of all segments in loss (whichever is greater in absolute amount).

(c) Segment **assets** are 10% or more of the total assets of all segments.

3.6 Disclosure of segment information

FAST FORWARD

Do not worry too much about the detailed disclosure requirements.

The disclosure requirements of IAS 14 are long and complicated, but IAS 14 gives the following illustrative example of a segmental report for a diversified multinational. This is for information only. You would not meet anything as complex as this in your exam.

	Paper products		Office products		Publishing		Other operations		Eliminations		Consolidated	
	20X2	20X1	20X2	20X1	20X2	20X1	20X2	20X1	20X2	20X1	20X2	20X1
	$m	$m	$m	$m	$m	$m	$m	$m	$m	$m	$m	$m
Revenue												
External sales	55	50	20	17	19	16	7	7				
Inter -segment sales	15	10	10	14	2	4	2	2	(29)	(30)		
Total revenue	70	60	30	31	21	20	9	9	(29)	(30)	101	90
Result												
Segment result	20	17	9	7	2	1	0	0	(1)	(1)	30	24
Unallocated corporate expenses											(7)	(9)
Operating profit											23	15
Interest expense											(4)	(4)
Interest income											2	3
Share of net profits of associates	6	5					2	2			8	7
Income taxes											(7)	(4)
Profit											22	17
Other information												
Segment assets	54	50	34	30	10	10	10	9			108	99
Investment in equity method associates	20	16					12	10			32	26
Unallocated corporate assets											35	30
Consolidated total assets											175	155
Segment liabilities	25	15	8	11	8	8	1	1			42	35
Unallocated corporate liabilities											40	55
Consolidated total liabilities											82	90
Capital expenditure	12	10	3	5	5		4	3				
Depreciation	9	7	9	7	5	3	3	4				
Non cash expenses other than depreciation	8	2	7	3	2	2	2	1				

Chapter roundup

- Changes in accounting policy should be dealt with retrospectively.
- Prior period errors should be dealt with retrospectively
- **IFRS 5** *Non-current assets held for sale and discontinued operations* requires assets 'held for sale' to be presented separately on the face of the balance sheet.
- The results of discontinued operations should be presented separately in the income statement.
- Another important aspect of reporting financial performance is **segment reporting**.
- **IAS 14** adopts a **management approach** to determining reporting segments.
- The most important **definitions** are of:
  - Business segments
  - Geographical segments
- Do not worry too much about the detailed **disclosure requirements**. These are unlikely to be of great importance in the exam.

Quick quiz

1. How should a prior period error be corrected under IAS 8?
2. Give three circumstances when a change in accounting policy might be required.
3. When can a non-current asset be classified as held for sale?
4. How should an asset held for sale be measured?
5. How does IFRS 5 define a discontinued operation?
6. What approach should normally be taken when deciding whether business or geographical segments should be the primary reporting format?

Answers to quick quiz

1 By adjusting the opening balance of retained earnings, i.e. retrospectively.

2 (a) By statute
(b) By the IASB
(c) For a more appropriate presentation

3 See Para 2.2

4 See Para 2.3

5 See Para 2.5

6 See Para 3.4

Answers to activities

7.1 The facility will not be transferred until the backlog of orders is completed; this demonstrates that the facility is not available for immediate sale in its present condition. The facility cannot be classified as 'held for sale' at 31 December 20X3. It must be treated in the same way as other items of property, plant and equipment: it should continue to be depreciated and should not be separately disclosed.

8

Non-current assets

Topic list
1 Non-current assets: basic provisions
2 Depreciation
3 Non-current asset disposals
4 IAS 16: *Property, plant and equipment*
5 IAS 40: *Investment property*
6 Intangible assets
7 Goodwill
8 IAS 36: *Impairment of assets*
9 Investments

Introduction

This is a detailed and highly examinable chapter so you should work through it carefully.

The following aspects are particularly important:

- basic provisions of IAS 16
- accounting for research and development
- goodwill

Goodwill is also dealt with in chapter 10 as it is a feature of group accounts.

Learning objectives

On completion of this chapter you will be able to:

	Syllabus reference
• describe the difference between tangible non-current assets and intangible non-current assets	3 a ii
• identify the terminology and underlying accounting methods and principles that are applied to tangible non-current assets	3 c i
• explain the meaning of depreciation, and how it is provided for in the income statement and balance sheet of a business	3 c i
• discuss the impact of revaluations on the reporting of tangible non-current assets	3 c i
• identify the terminology and underlying accounting methods and principles that are applied to intangible non-current assets	3 c ii
• explain the meaning of goodwill and how purchased goodwill is accounted for in the financial statements of a company	3 c ii
• identify how research and development costs are accounted for	3 c ii

1 Non-current assets: basic provisions

Non-current assets are long-term assets held by a business. This chapter looks at tangible and intangible non-current assets.

Tangible non-current assets are 'physical' long-term assets. The main category included in the IAS 1 Balance Sheet format is property, plant and equipment. The accounting treatment of these is dealt with in IAS 16.

Intangible non-current assets are long-term items bringing future benefits to the company, but that do not have a physical existence. They include deferred development costs and purchased goodwill as we will see later.

1.1 Valuation of non-current assets

Non-current assets are normally valued in the balance sheet at their **original cost, minus depreciation**. When a non-current asset is purchased (rather than constructed) its cost is the purchase price plus any expenses incidental to the acquisition. When a non-current asset is constructed for the company's own use, the cost will include the production or construction costs, including an amount for 'directly attributable' costs (indirect costs).

The cost of a non-current asset that has a limited economic life must be reduced by **depreciation**, that will write off the asset's cost (less any estimated residual value of the asset) in a systematic way over the expected useful life of the asset. Both tangible and intangible assets must be depreciated. However, whereas the term 'depreciation' is applied to tangible non-current assets, the term '**amortisation**' is applied to intangible non-current assets.

Freehold land does not have a limited economic life, and so does not have to be depreciated. The buildings constructed on freehold land, however, do have a limited economic life, and ought to be depreciated.

If a non-current asset suffers a **an impairment**, the fall in value must be charged as an expense in the income statement and the asset should be included in the balance sheet at its reduced value. We will look at impairment in detail in Section 8.

Non-current assets are valued at cost minus depreciation under the 'historical cost convention' of accounting. However, companies may apply **alternative accounting rules** to their assets, and **revalue non-current assets** to a current cost or current market value. As long as the company applies a consistent policy, one class of non-current assets may be revalued whilst other groups are reported at historical cost. Many companies therefore apply the alternative accounting rules to their land and buildings, and revalue these to current market value.

When a non-current asset is revalued, the increase in value should be added to a **revaluation reserve**. This is explained in the next chapter. In addition, **depreciation charges** on the asset, charged as an expense in the income statement, **must be based on the revalued amount**, rather than on the historical cost.

2 Depreciation

FAST FORWARD

The cost of a **non-current asset**, less its estimated residual value, is allocated fairly between accounting periods by means of **depreciation**. The allowance for depreciation is both:

- Charged against profit
- Deducted from the value of the non-current asset in the balance sheet.

If an asset's life extends over more than one accounting period, it earns profits over more than one period. It is a **non-current asset**.

With the exception of land held on freehold or very long leasehold, **every non-current asset eventually wears out over time**. Machines, cars and other vehicles, fixtures and fittings, and even buildings do not last for ever. When a business acquires a non-current asset, it will have some idea about how long its useful life will be, and it might decide what to do with it.

(a) Keep on using the non-current asset until it becomes **completely worn out**, useless, and worthless.

(b) **Sell off** the non-current asset at the end of its useful life, either by selling it as a second-hand item or as scrap.

Since a non-current asset has a cost, and a **limited useful life**, and its value eventually declines, it follows that a charge should be made in the income statement to reflect the use that is made of the asset by the business. This charge is called **depreciation**.

2.1 Definition of depreciation

Depreciation accounting is governed by IAS 16 *Property, plant and equipment* which we will look at in Section 2 of this chapter. However, this section will deal with some of the IAS 16 definitions concerning depreciation.

Key terms

- **Depreciation** is the result of systematic allocation of the depreciable amount of an asset over its estimated useful life. Depreciation for the accounting period is charged to net profit or loss for the period either directly or indirectly.
- **Depreciable assets** are assets which:
  - Are expected to be used during more than one accounting period
  - Have a limited useful life
  - Are held by an entity for use in the production or supply of goods and services, for rental to others, or for administrative purposes

- **Useful life** is one of two things.
  - The period over which a depreciable asset is expected to be used by the entity, or
  - The number of production or similar units expected to be obtained from the asset by the entity.
- **Depreciable amount** of a depreciable asset is the historical cost or other amount substituted for cost in the financial statements, less the estimated residual value.

(IAS 16)

An 'amount substituted for cost' will normally be a **current market value** after a revaluation has taken place.

IAS 16 requires the depreciable amount of a depreciable asset to be allocated on a **systematic basis** to each accounting period during the useful life of the asset. **Every part of an item of property, plant and equipment with a cost that is significant in relation to the total cost of the item must be depreciated separately**.

One way of defining depreciation is to describe it as a means of **spreading the cost** of a non-current asset over its useful life, and so matching the cost against the full period during which it earns profits for the business. Depreciation charges are an example of the application of the accrual assumption to calculate profits.

There are situations where, over a period, an asset has **increased in value**, ie its current value is greater than the carrying value in the financial statements. You might think that in such situations it would not be necessary to depreciate the asset. The standard states, however, that this is irrelevant, and that depreciation should still be charged to each accounting period, based on the depreciable amount, irrespective of a rise in value.

An entity is required to begin depreciating an item of property, plant and equipment when it is available for use and to continue depreciating it until it is derecognised even if it is idle during the period.

2.2 Useful life

The following factors should be considered when **estimating the useful life** of a depreciable asset.

- Expected **physical wear and tear**
- **Obsolescence**
- Legal or other **limits** on the use of the assets

Once decided, the useful life should be **reviewed at least every financial year end** and depreciation rates adjusted for the current and future periods if expectations vary significantly from the original estimates. The effect of the change should be disclosed in the accounting period in which the change takes place.

The assessment of useful life requires **judgement** based on previous experience with similar assets or classes of asset. When a completely new type of asset is acquired (ie through technological advancement or through use in producing a brand new product or service) it is still necessary to estimate useful life, even though the exercise will be much more difficult.

The standard also points out that the physical life of the asset might be longer than its useful life to the entity in question. One of the main factors to be taken into consideration is the **physical wear and tear** the asset is likely to endure. This will depend on various circumstances, including the number of shifts for which the asset will be used, the entity's repair and maintenance programme and so on. Other factors to be considered include obsolescence (due to technological advances/improvements in production/reduction in demand for the product/service produced by the asset) and legal restrictions, eg length of a related lease.

2.3 Residual value

In most cases the residual value of an asset is **likely to be immaterial**. If it is likely to be of any significant value, that value must be estimated at the date of purchase or any subsequent revaluation. The amount of residual value should be estimated based on the current situation with other similar assets, used in the same way, which are now at the end of their useful lives. Any expected costs of disposal should be offset against the gross residual value.

2.4 The total charge for depreciation: the depreciable amount

The total amount to be charged over the life of a non-current asset ('the depreciable amount') is usually its cost less any expected 'residual' sales value or disposal value at the end of the asset's life.

(a) Plant and equipment costing $20,000 which has an expected life of five years and an expected residual value of nil should be depreciated by $20,000 in total over the five-year period.

(b) Plant and equipment costing $20,000 which has an expected life of five years and an expected residual value of $3,000 should be depreciated by $17,000 in total over the five-year period.

2.5 Depreciation in the accounts

When a non-current asset is depreciated, two things must be accounted for.

(a) The **charge for depreciation** is a **cost or expense** of the accounting period.

(b) At the same time, the non-current asset is wearing out and diminishing in value, and so the value of the non-current asset in the balance sheet must be reduced by the amount of depreciation charged. The balance sheet value of the non-current asset will be its **'net book value'** which is the value net of its accumulated depreciation to date.

The amount of depreciation deducted from the cost of a non-current asset to arrive at its net book value will build up (or 'accumulate') over time, as more depreciation is charged in each successive accounting period.

For example, if plant and equipment costing $40,000 has an expected life of four years and an estimated residual value of nil, it might be depreciated by $10,000 per annum.

	Depreciation charge for the year (Income statement)	*Accumulated depreciation at end of year*	*Cost of the asset*	*Net book value at end of year*
	(A)	*(B)*	*(C)*	*(C-B)*
	$	$	$	$
At beginning of its life	-	-	40,000	40,000
Year 1	10,000	10,000	40,000	30,000
Year 2	10,000	20,000	40,000	20,000
Year 3	10,000	30,000	40,000	10,000
Year 4	10,000	40,000	40,000	0
	40,000			

At the end of year 4, the full $40,000 of depreciation charges have been made in the income statement of the four years. The net book value of the plant and equipment asset is now nil. In theory (although perhaps not in practice) the business will no longer use the plant and equipment, which would now need replacing.

2.6 Methods of depreciation

There are several different methods of depreciation. A company must select a method for each group of assets, and apply this method consistently to those assets. The choice of method should be the one that most fairly reflects the consumption of the benefits of the non-current asset over time. The depreciation methods you might need to know about are:

- Straight line method
- Reducing balance method
- Machine hour or unit method

2.7 The straight line method

This is the most commonly used method. The total depreciable amount is charged in equal instalments to each accounting period over the expected useful life of the asset. In this way, the net book value of the non-current asset declines at a steady rate, or in a 'straight line' over time.

The annual depreciation charge is calculated as:

$$\frac{\text{Cost of asset minus residual value}}{\text{Expected useful life of the asset}}$$

For example, suppose that plant and equipment costing $110,000 has an estimated life of 5 years and a residual value of $10,000. The annual depreciation charge using the straight line method would be:

$$\frac{\$(110{,}000-10{,}000)}{5\text{ years}} = \$20{,}000 \text{ per annum}$$

The cost, depreciation and book value of the non-current asset would be as follows:

	After 1 year	*After 2 years*	*After 3 years*	*After 4 years*	*After 5 years*
	$	$	$	$	$
Cost of asset	110,000	110,000	110,000	110,000	110,000
Accumulated depreciation					
Bought forward	-	20,000	40,000	60,000	80,000
Charge for the year (20%)	20,000	20,000	20,000	20,000	20,000
At the end of the year	20,000	40,000	60,000	80,000	100,000
Net book value	90,000	70,000	50,000	30,000	10,000

Since the depreciation charge per annum is the same amount every year with the straight line method, it is often convenient to state that depreciation is charged at the rate of x per cent per annum on the net cost of the asset. For example, if plant and equipment costing $50,000 is depreciated to a nil residual value over five years by the straight line method, the annual depreciation charge would be 20% of cost.

The straight line method of depreciation is a fair allocation of the total depreciable amount between the different accounting periods, provided that it is reasonable to assume that the business enjoys equal benefits from the use of the asset in every period throughout its life.

2.8 The reducing balance method

The **reducing balance method** of depreciation calculates the annual depreciation charge as a fixed percentage of the net book value of the asset, as at the end of the previous accounting period.

For example, take the plant and equipment bought for $110,000 in the above example with an estimated life of 5 years and a residual value of $10,000. To achieve this using the reducing balance method would require an annual rate of 38%.

The cost, depreciation and the net book value of the asset will be as follows:

	After 1 year	*After 2 years*	*After 3 years*	*After 4 years*	*After 5 years*
	$	$	$	$	$
Cost of asset	110,000	110,000	110,000	110,000	110,000
Accumulated depreciation					
Bought forward	-	41,800	67,716	83,785	93,747
Charge for the year (38%)	41,800	25,916	16,069	9,962	6,176
At the end of the year	41,800	67,716	83,785	93,747	99,923
Net book value	68,200	42,284	26,215	16,253	10,077

Activity 8.1

Draw a rough graph showing how the depreciation under the two above examples compare with each other, to illustrate the profile of depreciation under the straight line versus the reducing balance method.

With the reducing balance method, the annual charge for depreciation is higher in the earlier years of the asset's life, and lower in the later years. In the example above, the annual charges for years 1, 2, 3, 4 and 5 are $41,800, $25,916, $16,069, $9,962 and $6,176 respectively. The reducing balance method might therefore be used when it is considered fair to allocate a greater proportion of the total depreciable amount to the earlier years and a lower proportion to later years, on the assumption that the benefits obtained by the business from using the asset decline over time.

The reducing balance rate is calculated to bring the net book value down to the residual value at the end of the economic life. Often the rate will be rounded to a convenient percentage, and thus it may not quite work. In the above example, 40% would have given a residual value of $8,554 at the end of year 5.

2.9 Machine hour or units method

Another approach is to estimate the use that will be made of the non-current asset over its useful life, in terms of the number of hours it will be operated, or the number of units it will process. The depreciation charge is then calculated as the depreciable amount divided by the expected machine hours of use or the expected units to be processed, and expressed as a depreciation rate per hour or per unit.

The depreciation charge in any year is calculated as the actual number of hours the asset is used for multiplied by the rate per hour, or the actual number of units processed multiplied by the rate per unit.

This method is not commonly used, but it is a fair way of applying the accruals concept to the calculation of profit, where it is considered that the consumption of the asset's value relates to the use made of the asset in each accounting period.

Choosing a method of depreciation, as well as deciding on the appropriate useful life for a non-current asset, calls for the **exercise of judgement**.

(a) The **straight line method** is the simplest and the most commonly used in practice.

(b) The **reducing balance** method is an accelerated method of charging depreciation which leads to a higher charge in earlier years. Since repair and maintenance costs tend to increase as assets grow older these methods lead to a more even allocation of total non-current asset costs (depreciation plus maintenance).

(c) The **machine hour method** is suited to assets which depreciate primarily through use rather than through passing of time. Such assets might include mines and quarries, which are subject to gradual exhaustion of the minerals that they contain, and also delivery lorries, which may be argued to depreciate in accordance with the number of miles travelled.

2.10 The need for consistency

Having selected a depreciation method for a category of non-current assets, a business must apply the method consistently from one year to the next. Similarly, it is up to the business to decide what a sensible life span for a non-current asset should be, but once that life span has been chosen, it should not be changed unless something unexpected happens to the non-current asset.

A business may depreciate different categories of non-current assets in different ways. For example, if a business owns three cars, then each car would normally be depreciated in the same way (e.g. by the straight line method) but another category of asset, say, photocopiers, might be depreciated using a different method (e.g. by the machine hour method).

Activity 8.2

A company purchased a lorry at a cost of $17,000. The lorry is expected to last for five years and then be sold for scrap for $2,000. Usage over the five years is expected to be:

Year 1	200 days
Year 2	100 days
Year 3	100 days
Year 4	150 days
Year 5	40 days

Required

Work out the depreciation to be charged each year under:

(a) The straight line method
(b) The reducing balance method (using a rate of 35%)
(c) The machine hour method.

2.11 Misconceptions about depreciation

Depreciation is a process of **allocation** of the cost of a non-current asset over several accounting periods. It is worth mentioning here two common **misconceptions** about the purpose and effects of depreciation.

(a) It is sometimes thought that the net book value (NBV) of an asset should equal the current net realisable value, and that the object of charging depreciation is to reflect the fall in value of an asset over its life. This misconception is the basis of a common, but incorrect, argument that freehold properties (say) need not be depreciated in times when property values are rising. It is true that historical cost balance sheets often give a misleading impression of property when a property's net book value in the balance sheet is much below its market value. However, in such a case it is open to a business to revalue its assets. This is a separate problem from the requirement to allocate the property's cost over successive accounting periods.

(b) Another misconception is that depreciation is provided so that an asset can be replaced at the end of its useful life. This is not the case.

   (i) If there is no intention of replacing the asset, it could then be argued that there is no need to provide for any depreciation at all.

   (ii) If prices are rising, the replacement cost of the asset will exceed the amount of depreciation provided.

2.12 Depreciation is not a cash expense

Depreciation spreads the cost of a non-current asset (less its estimated residual value) over the asset's life. The cash payment for the asset will be made when, or soon after, the asset is purchased. Annual depreciation of the asset in subsequent years is not a cash expense - rather it allocates costs to those later years for a cash payment that has occurred previously. This is in line with the accruals basis of accounts preparation.

For example, suppose a business purchased some shop fittings for $6,000 on 1 July 20X5 and paid for them in cash on that date. Subsequently, depreciation may be charged at $600 per annum for ten years. So each year $600 is deducted from profits and the net book value of the fittings goes down, but no actual cash is being paid. The cash was all paid on 1 July 20X5. So annual depreciation is not a cash expense, but rather an allocation of the original cost to later years.

2.13 A fall in value of a non-current asset

When the 'market' value of a non-current asset falls so that it is worth less than the amount of its net book value **and the fall in value is expected to be permanent**, the asset should be **written down to its new low market value**. The charge in the income statement for the diminution in value of the asset during the accounting period should then be:

	$
Net book value at the beginning of the period	X
Less new reduced value	(X)
Charge for the diminution in the assets value in the period	X

This charge is like 'extra' depreciation.

3 Non-current asset disposals

FAST FORWARD

When a non-current asset is **sold**, there is likely to be a profit or loss on disposal. This is the difference between the net sale price of the asset and its net book value at the time of disposal.

Property, plant and equipment are not purchased by a business with the intention of reselling them in the normal course of trade. However, they might be sold off at some stage during their life, either when their useful life is over, or before then. A business might decide to sell off a non-current asset long before its useful life has ended.

Whenever a business sells something, it will make a profit or a loss. When non-current assets are disposed of, there will be a profit or loss on disposal. These gains or losses are reported in the income and expenses part of the income statement. They are commonly referred to as **'profit on disposal of non-current assets'** or **'loss on disposal'**.

3.1 The principles behind calculating the profit or loss on disposal

The profit or loss on the disposal of a non-current asset is the difference between:

(a) The net book value of the non-current asset at the time of its sale.
(b) Its net sale price, which is the price minus any costs of making the sale.

A profit is made when the sale price exceeds the net book value, and a loss is made when the sale price is less than the net book value.

Suppose a company purchased an asset on 1 January 20X1 for $25,000. It had an estimated life of five years and an estimated residual value of nil. The asset was eventually sold after three years on 1 January 20X4 to another trader who paid $17,500 for it.

The profit or loss on disposal, assuming that the business uses the straight line method for depreciation ($5,000 per annum), would be

	$
Cost of asset	25,000
Less accumulated depreciation (three years)	15,000
Net book value at date of disposal	10,000
Sale price	17,500
Profit on disposal	7,500

4 IAS 16: *Property, plant and equipment*

FAST FORWARD

IAS16 *Property, plant and equipment* covers the major categories of **tangible non-current assets.** As well as depreciation it looks at recognition criteria, components of cost and revaluations.

The standard gives a large number of definitions.

Key terms

- **Property, plant and equipment** are tangible assets that:
  - are held for use in the production or supply of goods or services, for rental to others, or for administrative purposes; and
  - are expected to be used during more than one period.
- **Cost** is the amount of cash or cash equivalents paid or the fair value of the other consideration given to acquire an asset at the time of its acquisition or construction.
- **Residual value** is the net amount which the entity expects to obtain for an asset at the end of its useful life after deducting the expected costs of disposal.
- **Entity specific value** is the present value of the cash flows an entity expects to arise from the continuing use of an asset and from its disposal at the end of its useful life, or expects to incur when settling a liability.
- **Fair value** is the amount for which an asset could be exchanged between knowledgeable, willing parties in an arm's length transaction.
- **Carrying amount** is the amount at which an asset is recognised in the balance sheet after deducting any accumulated depreciation and accumulated impairment losses.
- An **impairment loss** is the amount by which the carrying amount of an asset exceeds its recoverable amount. *(IAS 16)*

4.1 Recognition

In this context, recognition simply means incorporation of the item in the business's accounts, in this case as a non-current asset. The recognition of property, plant and equipment depends on two criteria.

(a) It is probable that **future economic benefits** associated with the asset will flow to the entity
(b) The cost of the asset to the entity can be **measured reliably**

These recognition criteria apply to **subsequent expenditure** as well as costs incurred initially.

Property, plant and equipment can amount to **substantial amounts** in financial statements, affecting the presentation of the company's financial position (in the balance sheet) and the profitability of the entity, through depreciation and also if an asset is wrongly classified as an expense and taken to the income statement.

Looking at the first of the two recognition criteria the **degree of certainty** attached to the flow of future economic benefits must be assessed. This should be based on the evidence available at the date of initial recognition (usually the date of purchase). The entity should thus be assured that it will receive the rewards attached to the asset and it will incur the associated risks, which will only generally be the case when the rewards and risks have actually passed to the entity. Until then, the asset should not be recognised.

Regarding the second criteria it is generally easy to measure the cost of an asset as the **transfer amount on purchase**, ie what was paid for it. **Self-constructed assets** can also be measured easily by adding together the purchase price of all the constituent parts (labour, material etc) paid to external parties.

For very **large and specialised** items, an apparently single asset should be broken down into its composite parts. This occurs where different parts have different useful lives and different depreciation rates are applied to each part e.g. an aircraft where the body and engines have different useful lives.

4.2 Initial measurement

Once an item of property, plant and equipment qualifies for recognition as an asset, it will initially be **measured at cost**.

The standard lists the components of the cost of an item of property, plant and equipment.

- **Purchase price**, less any trade discount or rebate
- **Import duties** and non-refundable purchase taxes
- **Directly attributable costs** of bringing the asset to working condition for its intended use, eg:
  - The cost of site preparation
  - Initial delivery and handling costs
  - Installation costs
  - Testing
  - Professional fees (architects, engineers)
- Initial estimate of the unavoidable cost of dismantling and removing the asset and restoring the site on which it is located

Additional guidance is given regarding 'directly attributable costs' as follows:

(a) These costs bring the asset to the location and working conditions necessary for it to be capable of operating in the manner intended by management, including those costs to test whether the asset is functioning properly.

(b) They are determined after deducting the net proceeds from selling any items produced when bringing the asset to its location and condition.

The standard also states that income and related expenses of operations that are **incidental** to the construction or development of an item of property, plant and equipment should be **recognised** in the income statement.

The following costs **will not be part of the cost** of property, plant or equipment unless they can be attributed directly to the asset's acquisition, or bringing it into its working condition.

- Administration and other general overhead costs
- Start-up and similar pre-production costs
- Initial operating losses before the asset reaches planned performance

All of these will be recognised as an **expense** rather than an asset.

The 'cost' will be the total of the construction costs (although abnormal costs, e.g. waste material, labour and other resources) should be excluded. In the case of **self-constructed assets**, the same principles are applied as for acquired assets. An example of a self-constructed asset is when a building company builds its own head office.

4.3 Measurement subsequent to initial recognition

The standard offers two possible treatments here, essentially a choice between keeping an asset recorded at **cost** or revaluing it to **fair value**.

(a) **Cost model.** Carry the asset at its cost less depreciation (and any accumulated impairment loss).

(b) **Revaluation model.** Carry the asset at a revalued amount, being its fair value at the date of the revaluation less any subsequent accumulated depreciation (and subsequent accumulated impairment losses). IAS 16 makes clear that the **revaluation model is available only if the fair value of the item can be measured reliably**.

4.4 Revaluations

FAST FORWARD

When an asset is revalued the gain is recorded in the revaluation revenue and depreciation is then charged on the revalued amount.

The **market value** of land and buildings usually represents fair value, assuming existing use and line of business. Such valuations are usually carried out by professionally qualified valuers.

In the case of **plant and equipment**, fair value can also be taken as **market value**. Where a market value is not available, however, depreciated replacement cost should be used. There may be no market value where types of plant and equipment are sold only rarely or because of their specialised nature (ie they would normally only be sold as part of an ongoing business).

The frequency of valuation depends on the **volatility of the fair values** of individual items of property, plant and equipment. The more volatile the fair value, the more frequently revaluations should be carried out. Where the current fair value is very different from the carrying value then a revaluation should be carried out.

Most importantly, when an item of property, plant and equipment is revalued, **the whole class of assets to which it belongs should be revalued.**

All the items within a class should be **revalued at the same time**, to prevent selective revaluation of certain assets and to avoid disclosing a mixture of costs and values from different dates in the financial statements. A rolling basis of revaluation is allowed if the revaluations are kept up to date and the revaluation of the whole class is completed in a short period of time.

How should any **increase in value** be treated when a revaluation takes place? The 'debit' will be the increase in value in the balance sheet, but what about the credit? IAS 16 requires the increase to be credited to a **revaluation surplus** (ie part of owners' equity), *unless* the increase is reversing a previous decrease which was recognised as an expense. To the extent that this offset is made, the increase is recognised as income; any excess is then taken to the revaluation reserve.

4.5 Example

Heap Co has a freehold property that is valued at $4m in the balance sheet, with accumulated depreciation of $250,000 on the building. The property has been revalued and its current value is now $5.6 million, but with accumulated depreciation of $400,000 on this revalued amount. The net increase in value of the asset is the increase in the total valuation ($1.6 million) minus the increase in the accumulated depreciation of $150,000. The net increase in valuation is therefore $1,450,000.

The adjustment to the **balance sheet** should be:

(a) increase the asset from $4 million to $5.6 million
(b) increase accumulated deprecation from $250,000 to $400,000
(c) increase the revaluation surplus by $1,450,000.

In future years, depreciation should be charged against profits based on the revalued amount of the building, $5.6 million.

Activity 8.3

Barney Co has an item of land carried in its books at $13,000. There has been a surge in land values in the current year and the land has been revalued to $20,000.

How will this be reflected in the balance sheet?

4.6 Depreciation

The standard states:

- The **depreciable amount** of an item of property, plant and equipment should be allocated on a systematic basis over its useful life.
- The **depreciation method** used should reflect the pattern in which the asset's economic benefits are consumed by the entity.
- The **depreciation charge** for each period should be recognised as an expense unless it is included in the carrying amount of another asset.

Land and buildings are dealt with separately even when they are acquired together because as we have already seen land normally has an unlimited life and is therefore not depreciated. In contrast buildings do have a limited life and must be depreciated. Any increase in the value of land on which a building is standing will have no impact on the determination of the building's useful life.

Depreciation is usually treated as an **expense**, but not where it is absorbed by the entity in the process of producing other assets. For example, depreciation of plant and machinery can be incurred in the production of goods for sale (inventory items). In such circumstances, the depreciation is included in the cost of the new assets produced.

A review of the **useful life** of property, plant and equipment should be carried out **at least at each financial year end** and the depreciation charge for the current and future periods should be adjusted if expectations have changed significantly from previous estimates. Changes are changes in accounting estimates and are accounted for prospectively as adjustments to future depreciation.

The **depreciation method** should also be reviewed **at least at each financial year end** and, if there has been a significant change in the expected pattern of economic benefits from those assets, the method should be changed to suit this changed pattern. When such a change in depreciation method takes place the change should be accounted for as a **change in accounting estimate** and the depreciation charge for the current and future periods should be adjusted.

4.7 Retirements and disposals

When an asset is permanently **withdrawn from use, or sold or scrapped**, and no future economic benefits are expected from its disposal, it should be withdrawn from the balance sheet.

Gains or losses are the difference between the estimated net disposal proceeds and the carrying amount of the asset. They should be recognised as income or expense in the income statement.

An entity cannot classify as revenue (ie in the top line of the income statement) a gain it realises on the disposal of an item of property, plant and equipment.

4.8 Disclosure

The standard has a list of disclosure requirements, for each class of property, plant and equipment.

(a) **Measurement bases** for determining the gross carrying amount (if more than one, the gross carrying amount for that basis in each category)

(b) **Depreciation methods** used

(c) **Useful lives** or depreciation rates used

(d) **Gross carrying amount** and accumulated depreciation (aggregated with accumulated impairment losses) at the beginning and end of the period

(e) **Reconciliation** of the carrying amount at the beginning and end of the period showing:

- (i) Additions
- (ii) Disposals
- (iii) Acquisitions through business combinations (see Chapter 10)
- (iv) Increases/decreases during the period from revaluations and from impairment losses
- (v) Impairment losses recognised in the income statement
- (vi) Impairment losses reversed in the income statement
- (vii) Depreciation
- (viii) Net exchange differences (from translation of statements of foreign entity)
- (ix) Any other movements.

The financial statements should also disclose the following.

(a) Any recoverable amounts of property, plant and equipment
(b) Existence and amounts of **restrictions on title**, and items pledged as security for liabilities
(c) Accounting policy for **the estimated costs of restoring the site**
(d) Amount of expenditures on account of **items in the course of construction**
(e) Amount of commitments to **acquisitions**

Revalued assets require further disclosures.

(a) Basis used to revalue the assets

(b) Effective date of the revaluation

(c) Whether an independent valuer was involved

(d) Nature of any indices used to determine replacement cost

(e) Carrying amount of each class of property, plant and equipment that would have been included in the financial statements had the assets been carried at cost less accumulated depreciation and accumulated impairment losses.

(f) Revaluation surplus, indicating the movement for the period and any restrictions on the distribution of the balance to shareholders.

The standard also **encourages disclosure** of additional information, which the users of financial statements may find useful.

(a) The carrying amount of temporarily idle property, plant and equipment

(b) The gross carrying amount of any fully depreciated property, plant and equipment that is still in use

(c) The carrying amount of property, plant and equipment retired from active use and held for disposal

(d) The fair value of property, plant and equipment when this is materially different from the carrying amount

The following format (with notional figures) is commonly used to disclose non-current assets movements.

	Total	*Land and buildings*	*Plant and equipment*
	$	$	$
Cost or valuation			
At 1 January 20X4	50,000	40,000	10,000
Revaluation surplus	12,000	12,000	–
Additions in year	4,000	–	4,000
Disposals in year	(1,000)	–	(1,000)
At 31 December 20X4	65,000	52,000	13,000
Depreciation			
At 1 January 20X4	16,000	10,000	6,000
Charge for year	4,000	1,000	3,000
Eliminated on disposals	(500)	–	(500)
At 31 December 20X4	19,500	11,000	8,500
Net book value			
At 31 December 20X4	45,500	41,000	4,500
At 1 January 20X4	34,000	30,000	4,000

5 IAS 40: *Investment property*

FAST FORWARD

An entity may own land or a building **as an investment** rather than for use in the business. It may therefore generate cash flows largely independently of other assets which the entity holds.

Consider the following definitions.

Key term

Investment property is property (land or a building – or part of a building – or both) held (by the owner or by the lessee under a finance lease) to earn rentals or for capital appreciation or both, rather than for:

(a) Use in the production or supply of goods or services or for administrative purposes, or
(b) Sale in the ordinary course of business

Examples of investment property include:

(a) **Land held for long-term capital appreciation** rather than for short-term sale in the ordinary course of business

(b) A **building** owned by the reporting entity (or held by the entity under a finance lease) and **leased out under an operating lease**

An accounting standard IAS 40 *Investment property* was introduced to set down special rules for these types of property.

5.1 Recognition

Investment property should be recognised as an asset when **two conditions** are met.

(a) It is **probable** that the **future economic benefits** that are associated with the investment property will **flow to the entity**.

(b) The **cost** of the investment property can be **measured reliably**.

5.2 Initial measurement

An investment property should be measured initially at its **cost,** including transaction costs.

A property interest held under a lease and classified as an investment property shall be accounted for **as if it were a finance lease**. The asset is recognised at the lower of the fair value of the property and the present value of the minimum lease payments. An equivalent amount is recognised as a liability.

5.3 Measurement subsequent to initial recognition

IAS 40 requires an entity to **choose between two models.**

- **The fair value model**
- **The cost model**

Whatever policy it chooses should be applied to **all of its investment property**.

Where an entity chooses to classify a property held under an **operating lease** as an investment property, there is **no choice**. The **fair value model must be used** for **all the entity's investment property**, regardless of whether it is owned or leased.

5.4 Fair value model

Key term

Fair value is the amount for which an asset could be exchanged between acknowledgeable, willing parties in an arm's length transaction.

(a) After initial recognition, an entity that chooses the **fair value model** should measure all of its investment property at fair value, except in the extremely rare cases where this cannot be measured reliably. In such cases it should apply the IAS 16 cost model.

(b) A gain or loss arising from a change in the fair value of an investment property should be recognised in net profit or loss for the period in which it arises.

(c) The fair value of investment property should reflect market conditions at the balance sheet date.

This is not the same as a revaluation, where increases in carrying amount above a cost-based measure are recognised as revaluation surplus. Under the fair-value model all changes in fair value are recognised in the income statement.

5.5 Cost model

The cost model is the **cost model in IAS 16.** Investment property should be measured at **depreciated cost, less any accumulated impairment losses.** An entity that chooses the cost model should **disclose the fair value of its investment property.**

5.6 Changing models

Once the entity has chosen the fair value or cost model, it should apply it to all its investment property. It **should not change from one model to the other unless the change will result in a more appropriate presentation**. IAS 40 states that it is highly unlikely that a change from the fair value model to the cost model will result in a more appropriate presentation.

5.7 Transfers

Transfers to or from investment property should **only** be made **when there is a change in use**. For example, owner occupation commences so the investment property will be treated under IAS 16 as an owner-occupied property.

When there is a transfer from investment property carried at fair value to owner-occupied property or inventories, the property's cost for subsequent accounting under IAS 16 or IAS 2 should be its fair value at the date of change of use.

Conversely, an owner-occupied property may become an investment property and need to be carried at fair value. An entity should apply IAS 16 up to the date of change of use. It should treat any difference at that date between the carrying amount of the property under IAS 16 and its fair value as a revaluation under IAS 16.

5.8 Disposals

Derecognise (eliminate from the balance sheet) an investment property on disposal or when it is permanently withdrawn from use and no future economic benefits are expected from its disposal.

Any **gain or loss** on disposal is the difference between the net disposal proceeds and the carrying amount of the asset. It should generally be **recognised as income or expense in the income statement.**

5.9 Disclosures

These relate to:

- Choice of fair value model or cost model
- Whether property interests held as operating leases are included in investment property
- Criteria for classification as investment property
- Assumptions in determining fair value
- Use of independent professional valuer (encouraged but not required)
- Rental income and expenses
- Any restrictions or obligations

An entity that adopts the fair value model must also disclose a **reconciliation** of the carrying amount of the investment property at the beginning and end of the period.

For the cost model additional disclosure relate mainly to the depreciation method. In addition, an entity which adopts the cost model **must disclose the fair value** of the investment property.

6 Intangible assets

FAST FORWARD

Intangible assets are defined by IAS 38 as non-monetary assets without physical substance. Intangible assets should initially be measured at cost, but subsequently they can be carried at **cost or at a revalued amount**.

6.1 Definition

Key term

An **intangible asset** is an identifiable non-monetary asset without physical substance. The asset must be:

(a) controlled by the entity as a result of events in the past, and
(b) something from which the entity expects future economic benefits to flow.

Examples of items that might be considered as intangible assets include computer software, patents, copyrights, motion picture films, customer lists, franchises and fishing rights. An item should not be recognised as an intangible asset, however, unless it **fully meets the definition** in the standard.

An intangible asset must be identifiable i.e distinguishable from goodwill. With non-physical items, there may be a problem with **'identifiability'**.

(a) If an intangible asset is **acquired separately through purchase**, there may be a transfer of a legal right that would help to make an asset identifiable.

(b) An intangible asset may be identifiable if it is **separable**, ie if it could be rented or sold separately. However, 'separability' is not an essential feature of an intangible asset.

Another element of the definition of an intangible asset is that it must be under the control of the entity as a result of a past event. The entity must therefore be able to enjoy the future economic benefits from the asset, and prevent the access of others to those benefits. A **legally enforceable right** is evidence of such control, but is not always a *necessary* condition.

(a) Control over **technical knowledge or know-how** only exists if it is protected by a **legal right**.

(b) The skill of employees, arising out of the benefits of **training costs**, are most unlikely to be recognisable as an intangible asset, because an entity does not control the future actions of its staff.

(c) Similarly, **market share and customer loyalty** cannot normally be intangible assets, since an entity cannot control the actions of its customers.

An item can only be recognised as an intangible asset if economic benefits are expected to flow in the future from ownership of the asset. Economic benefits may come from the **sale** of products or services, or from a **reduction in expenditures** (cost savings).

An intangible asset, when recognised initially, must be measured at **cost**. It should be recognised if, and only if **both** the following occur.

(a) It is probable that the **future economic benefits** that are attributable to the asset will **flow to the entity.**

(b) The **cost can be measured reliably**.

Management has to exercise its judgement in assessing the degree of certainty attached to the flow of economic benefits to the entity. External evidence is best.

(a) If an intangible asset is **acquired separately**, its cost can usually be measured reliably as its purchase price (including incidental costs of purchase such as legal fees, and any costs incurred in getting the asset ready for use).

(b) When an intangible asset is acquired as **part of a business combination** (ie an acquisition or takeover), the cost of the intangible asset is its fair value at the date of the acquisition.

IFRS 3 which we will look at later explains that the fair value of intangible assets acquired in business combinations can normally be measured with sufficient reliability to be **recognised separately** from goodwill.

6.2 Internally generated goodwill

Internally generated goodwill is a value attributable to a business from factors other than its tangible assets. It consists of elements such as having a strong reputation with customers for quality or giving value for money, a high and favourable public profile or a skilled work force.

Rule to learn

Internally generated goodwill may **not** be recognised as an **asset**.

The standard deliberately precludes recognition of internally generated goodwill because it requires that, for initial recognition, the cost of the asset rather than its fair value should be capable of being measured reliably and that it should be identifiable and controlled. Thus you do not recognise an asset which is subjective and cannot be measured reliably.

6.3 Research and development costs

In many companies, especially those producing food, or 'scientific' products such as medicines, or 'high technology' product, there is a large amount of expenditure on research and development (R+D). When R+D is a large item of cost its accounting treatment may have a significant influence of the profits of a business and its balance sheet valuation. The issue with R+D costs is whether these costs should be

(a) treated as an expense, and written off against profit in full in the year they are incurred, or

(b) capitalised as an intangible asset because they represent value that the business has created, and that the business will benefit from for several years into the future.

Research activities by definition do not meet the criteria for recognition under IAS 38. This is because, at the research stage of a project, it cannot be certain that future economic benefits will probably flow to the entity from the project. There is too much uncertainty about the likely success or otherwise of the project. **Research costs should therefore be written off as an expense as they are incurred**.

Examples of research costs

(a) Activities aimed at obtaining new knowledge

(b) The search for, evaluation and final selection of, applications of research findings or other knowledge

(c) The search for alternatives for materials, devices, products, processes, systems or services

(d) The formulation, design evaluation and final selection of possible alternatives for new or improved materials, devices, products, systems or services

Development costs **may qualify** for recognition as intangible assets provided that the following **strict criteria** can be demonstrated.

(a) The technical feasibility of completing the intangible asset so that it will be available for use or sale.

(b) Its intention to complete the intangible asset and use or sell it.

(c) Its ability to use or sell the intangible asset.

(d) How the intangible asset will generate probable future economic benefits. Among other things, the entity should demonstrate the existence of a market for the output of the intangible asset or the intangible asset itself or, if it is to be used internally, the usefulness of the intangible asset.

(e) Its ability to measure the expenditure attributable to the intangible asset during its development reliably.

In contrast with research costs development costs are incurred at a later stage in a project, and the probability of success should be more apparent. Examples of development costs include the following.

(a) The design, construction and testing of pre-production or pre-use prototypes and models

(b) The design of tools, jigs, moulds and dies involving new technology

(c) The design, construction and operation of a pilot plant that is not of a scale economically feasible for commercial production

(d) The design, construction and testing of a chosen alternative for new or improved materials, devices, products, processes, systems or services

6.4 Other intangibles

The standard **prohibits** the recognition of **internally generated brands**, **mastheads**, **publishing titles and customer lists** and similar items as intangible assets. These all fail to meet one or more (in some cases all) the definition and recognition criteria and in some cases are probably indistinguishable from internally generated goodwill.

6.5 Cost of an internally generated intangible asset

The costs allocated to an internally generated intangible asset should be only costs that can be **directly attributed** or allocated on a reasonable and consistent basis to creating, producing or preparing the asset for its intended use. The principles underlying the costs which may or may not be included are similar to those for other non-current assets and inventory.

The cost of an internally generated intangible asset is the sum of the **expenditure incurred from the date when** the intangible asset first **meets the recognition criteria**. If, as often happens, considerable costs have already been recognised as expenses before management could demonstrate that the criteria have been met, this earlier expenditure should not be retrospectively recognised at a later date as part of the cost of an intangible asset.

Activity 8.4

Doug Co is developing a new production process. During 20X3, expenditure incurred was $100,000, of which $90,000 was incurred before 1 December 20X3 and $10,000 between 1 December 20X3 and 31 December 20X3. Doug Co can demonstrate that, at 1 December 20X3, the production process met the criteria for recognition as an intangible asset. The recoverable amount of the know-how embodied in the process is estimated to be $50,000.

How should the expenditure be treated?

6.6 Recognition of an expense

All expenditure related to an intangible which does not meet the criteria for recognition either as an identifiable intangible asset or as goodwill arising on an acquisition should be **expensed as incurred**. The IAS gives examples of such expenditure.

- Start up costs
- Training costs
- Advertising costs
- Business relocation costs

Prepaid costs for services, for example advertising or marketing costs for campaigns that have been prepared but not launched, can still be recognised as a **prepayment**.

6.7 Measurement of intangible assets subsequent to initial recognition

The standard allows two methods of valuation for intangible assets after they have been first recognised.

Applying the **cost model**, an intangible asset should be **carried at its cost**, less any accumulated amortisation (and less any accumulated impairment losses).

The **revaluation model** allows an intangible asset to be carried at a revalued amount, which is its **fair value** at the date of revaluation, less any subsequent accumulated amortisation and any subsequent accumulated impairment losses.

(a) The fair value must be able to be measured reliably with reference to an **active market** in that type of asset.

(b) The **entire class** of intangible assets of that type must be revalued at the same time (to prevent selective revaluations).

(c) If an intangible asset in a class of revalued intangible assets cannot be revalued because there is **no active market** for this asset, the asset should be carried at its **cost less any accumulated amortisation and impairment losses**.

(d) Revaluations should be made with such **regularity** that the carrying amount does not differ from that which would be determined using fair value at the balance sheet date.

Point to note

> This treatment is **not** available for the **initial recognition** of intangible assets. This is because the cost of the asset must be reliably measured.

The guidelines state that there **will not usually be an active market** in an intangible asset; therefore the revaluation model will usually not be available. For example, although copyrights, publishing rights and film rights can be sold, each has a unique sale value. In such cases, revaluation to fair value would be inappropriate. A fair value might be obtainable however for assets such as fishing rights or quotas or taxi cab licences.

6.8 Useful life

An entity should **assess** the useful life of an intangible asset, which may be **finite or indefinite**. An intangible asset has an indefinite useful life when there is **no foreseeable limit** to the period over which the asset is expected to generate net cash inflows for the entity.

Many factors are considered in determining the useful life of an intangible asset, including: expected usage; typical product life cycles; technical, technological, commercial or other types of obsolescence; the stability of the industry; expected actions by competitors; the level of maintenance expenditure required; and legal or similar limits on the use of the asset, such as the expiry dates of related leases. Computer software and many other intangible assets normally have short lives because they are susceptible to technological obsolescence. However, uncertainty does not justify choosing a life that is unrealistically short.

The useful life of an intangible asset that arises from **contractual or other legal rights** should not exceed the period of the rights, but may be shorter depending on the period over which the entity expects to use the asset.

6.9 Amortisation period and amortisation method

An intangible asset with a finite useful life should be amortised over its **expected useful life**.

(a) Amortisation should start when the asset is **available for use**.

(b) Amortisation should cease at the earlier of the date that the asset is classified **as held for sale** in accordance with IFRS 5 *Non-current assets held for sale and discontinued operations* and the date that the asset is **derecognised**.

(c) The amortisation method used should reflect the **pattern in which the asset's future economic benefits are consumed**. If such a pattern cannot be predicted reliably, the straight-line method should be used.

(d) The amortisation charge for each period should normally be recognised **in profit or loss**.

The **residual value** of an intangible asset with a finite useful life is **assumed to be zero** unless a third party is committed to buying the intangible asset at the end of its useful life or unless there is an active market for that type of asset (so that its expected residual value can be measured) and it is probable that there will be a market for the asset at the end of its useful life.

The amortisation period and the amortisation method used for an intangible asset with a finite useful life should be **reviewed at each financial year-end**.

6.10 Intangible assets with indefinite useful lives

An intangible asset with an indefinite useful life **should not be amortised**. (IAS 36 requires that such an asset is tested for impairment at least annually.)

The useful life of an intangible asset that is not being amortised should be **reviewed each year** to determine whether it is still appropriate to assess its useful life as indefinite. Reassessing the useful life of an intangible asset as finite rather than indefinite is an indicator that the asset may be impaired and therefore it should be tested for impairment.

Activity 8.5

It may be difficult to establish the useful life of an intangible asset, and judgement will be needed. Consider how to determine the useful life of a *purchased* brand name.

Activity 8.6

List the examples given in IAS 38 of activities that might be included in either research or development.

7 Goodwill

FAST FORWARD

Purchased goodwill arising on consolidation is retained in the balance sheet as an intangible asset under IFRS 3. It must then be reviewed annually for impairment.

Goodwill is **created by good relationships** between a business and its customers.

(a) By building up a **reputation** (by word of mouth perhaps) for high quality products or high standards of service

(b) By **responding promptly and helpfully** to queries and complaints from customers

(c) Through the **personality of the staff** and their attitudes to customers

The value of goodwill to a business might be **extremely significant**. However as we have seen in Section 6, goodwill is not usually valued in the accounts of a business at all, and we should not normally expect to find an amount for goodwill in its balance sheet. For example, the welcoming smile of the bar staff may contribute more to a bar's profits than the fact that a new electronic cash register has recently been acquired. Even so, whereas the cash register will be recorded in the accounts as a non-current asset, the value of staff would be ignored for accounting purposes.

On reflection, we might agree with this omission of goodwill from the accounts of a business.

(a) The goodwill is **inherent** in the business but it has not been paid for, and it does not have an 'objective' value. We can guess at what such goodwill is worth, but such guesswork would be a matter of individual opinion, and not based on hard facts.

(b) Goodwill **changes** from day to day. One act of bad customer relations might damage goodwill and one act of good relations might improve it. Staff with a favourable personality might retire or leave to find another job, to be replaced by staff who need time to find their feet in the job, etc. Since goodwill is continually changing in value, it cannot realistically be recorded in the accounts of the business.

7.1 Purchased goodwill

There is one exception to the general rule that goodwill has no objective valuation. This is **when a business is sold**. People wishing to set up in business have a choice of how to do it – they can either buy their own long-term assets and inventory and set up their business from scratch, or they can buy up an existing business from a proprietor willing to sell it. When a buyer purchases an existing business, he will have to purchase not only its long-term assets and inventory (and perhaps take over its accounts payable and receivable too) but also the goodwill of the business.

Purchased goodwill is shown in the balance sheet because it has been paid for. It has no tangible substance, and so it is an **intangible non-current asset**.

When a business is sold, there is likely to be some purchased goodwill in the selling price. But **how is the amount of this purchased goodwill decided**?

This is not really a problem for accountants, who must simply record the goodwill in the accounts of the new business. The value of the goodwill is a **matter for the purchaser and seller to agree upon in fixing the purchase/sale price**. However, two methods of valuation are worth mentioning here.

(a) The seller and buyer agree on a price for the business **without specifically quantifying the goodwill.** The purchased goodwill will then be the difference between the price agreed and the value of the tangible net assets in the books of the new business.

(b) However, the calculation of goodwill often precedes the fixing of the purchase price and becomes a **central element of negotiation**. There are many ways of arriving at a value for goodwill and most of them are related to the profit record of the business in question.

No matter how goodwill is calculated within the total agreed purchase price, the goodwill shown by the purchaser in his accounts will be **the difference between the purchase consideration and his own valuation of the tangible net assets acquired**.

Purchased goodwill normally arises when one company (a parent company) takes over another company (a subsidiary) usually by purchasing a controlling interest in shares. This is referred to as a **business combination.** (Accounting for this situation is dealt with in Chapter 10).

Suppose, for example that a company purchases another business for $20 million. The acquired business has net assets of $15 million. The excess of the purchase price over the net assets acquired is $5 million and is purchased goodwill.

7.2 IFRS 3: *Business combinations*

IFRS 3 covers the accounting treatment of goodwill acquired in a business combination.

Goodwill acquired in a business combination is **recognised as an asset** and is initially measured at **cost**. Cost is the excess of the cost of the combination over the acquirer's interest in the net fair value of the acquiree's identifiable assets, liabilities and contingent liabilities.

After initial recognition goodwill acquired in a business combination is measured **at cost less any accumulated impairment losses**. It is **not amortised**. Instead it is tested for impairment at least annually, in accordance with IAS 36 *Impairment of assets.*

Negative goodwill arises when the acquirer's interest in the net fair value of the acquiree's identifiable assets, liabilities and contingent liabilities exceeds the cost of the business combination. IFRS 3 refers to negative goodwill as the 'excess of acquirer's interest in the net fair value of acquiree's identifiable assets, liabilities and contingent liabilities over cost'.

Negative goodwill can arise as the result of **errors** in measuring the fair value of either the cost of the combination or the acquiree's identifiable net assets. It can also arise as the result of a **bargain purchase**.

Where there is negative goodwill, an entity should first **reassess** the amounts at which it has measured both the cost of the combination and the acquiree's identifiable net assets. This exercise should identify any errors.

Any negative goodwill remaining should be **recognised immediately in profit or loss** (that is, in the income statement).

IFRS 3 requires extensive **disclosures**. These include a **reconciliation** of the carrying amount of goodwill at the beginning and end of the period, showing separately:

(a) The gross amount and accumulated impairment losses at the beginning of the period
(b) Additional goodwill recognised during the period
(c) Impairment losses recognised during the period
(d) Net exchange differences arising during the period, and
(e) The gross amount and accumulated impairment losses at the end of the period

Activity 8.7

What are the main characteristics of goodwill which distinguish it from other intangible non-current assets?

8 IAS 36: *Impairment of assets*

FAST FORWARD

Impairment is determined by comparing the **carrying amount** of the asset with its **recoverable amount**.

Assets should not be carried at above their **recoverable amount**. An entity should write down the carrying value of an asset to its recoverable amount if the carrying value of an asset is not recoverable in full. In this case the asset is said to have been **impaired**.

Key terms

- **Impairment**: a fall in the value of an asset, so that its 'recoverable amount' is now less than its carrying value in the balance sheet.
- **Carrying amount**: is the net value at which the asset is included in the balance sheet (ie after deducting accumulated depreciation and any impairment losses). *(IAS 36)*

The basic principle underlying IAS 36 is relatively straightforward. If an asset's value in the accounts is higher than its realistic value, measured as its 'recoverable amount', the asset is judged to have suffered an impairment loss. It should therefore be reduced in value, by the amount of the **impairment loss**. The amount of the impairment loss should be **written off against profit** immediately.

The main accounting issues to consider are therefore as follows.

(a) How is it possible to **identify when** an impairment loss may have occurred?
(b) How should the **recoverable amount** of the asset be measured?
(c) How should an 'impairment loss' be **reported in the accounts**?

8.1 Identifying a potentially impaired asset

An entity should assess at each balance sheet date whether there are any indications of impairment to any assets. The concept of **materiality** applies, and only material impairment needs to be identified.

If there are indications of possible impairment, the entity is required to make a formal estimate of the **recoverable amount** of the assets concerned.

IAS 36 suggests how **indications of a possible impairment** of assets might be recognised. The suggestions are based largely on common sense.

(a) **External sources of information**

(i) A fall in the asset's market value that is more significant than would normally be expected from passage of time over normal use.

(ii) A significant change in the technological, market, legal or economic environment of the business in which the assets are employed.

(iii) An increase in market interest rates or market rates of return on investments likely to affect the discount rate used in calculating value in use.

(iv) The carrying amount of the entity's net assets being more than its market capitalisation.

(b) **Internal sources of information**: evidence of obsolescence or physical damage, adverse changes in the use to which the asset is put, or the asset's economic performance

Even if there are no indications of impairment, the following assets must **always** be tested for impairment annually.

(a) An intangible asset with an **indefinite useful life**
(b) **Goodwill** acquired in a business combination

8.2 Measuring the recoverable amount of the asset

What is an asset's recoverable amount?

Key term

> The **recoverable amount of an asset** should be measured as the *higher value* of:
>
> (a) the asset's fair value less costs to sell; and
> (b) its value in use. *(IAS 36)*

An asset's fair value less costs to sell is the amount net of selling costs that could be obtained from the sale of the asset. Selling costs include sales transaction costs, such as legal expenses.

(a) If there is **an active market** in the asset, the net selling price should be based on the **market value**, or on the price of recent transactions in similar assets.

(b) If there is **no active market** in the assets it might be possible to **estimate** a net selling price using best estimates of what 'knowledgeable, willing parties' might pay in an arm's length transaction.

Net selling price **cannot** be reduced, however, by including within selling costs any **restructuring or reorganisation expenses**, or any costs that have already been recognised in the accounts as liabilities.

Key term

> The **value in use** of an asset is measured as the present value of estimated future cash flows (inflows minus outflows) generated by the asset, including its estimated net disposal value (if any) at the end of its expected useful life.

You do not need to worry about the detailed calculation of value in use but you should be aware of what it is and its relevance.

8.3 Recognition and measurement of an impairment loss

The rule for assets at historical cost is:

Rule to learn

> If the **recoverable amount** of an asset is lower than the carrying amount, the carrying amount should be reduced by the difference (ie the impairment loss) which should be charged as an expense in the income statement.

The rule for assets held at a revalued amount (such as property revalued under IAS 16) is:

Rule to learn

> The impairment loss is to be treated as a revaluation decrease under the relevant IAS.

In practice this means:

- To the extent that there is a revaluation surplus held in respect of the asset, the impairment loss should be charged to revaluation surplus.
- Any excess should be charged to the income statement.

8.4 Cash generating units.

As a basic rule, the recoverable amount of an asset should be calculated for the **asset individually**. However, there will be occasions when it is not possible to estimate such a value for an individual asset, particularly in the calculation of value in use. This is because it may be difficult to attribute cash inflows and outflows to the individual assets.

If it is not possible to calculate the recoverable amount for an individual asset, the recoverable amount of the asset's cash generating unit should be measured instead.

Key term

> A **cash generating unit** is the smallest identifiable group of assets for which independent cash flows can be identified and measured.

8.5 Accounting treatment of an impairment loss

If, and only if, the recoverable amount of an asset is less than its carrying amount in the balance sheet, an impairment loss has occurred. This loss should be **recognised immediately**.

(a) The asset's **carrying amount** should be reduced to its recoverable amount in the balance sheet.

(b) The **impairment loss** should be recognised immediately in the income statement (unless the asset has been revalued in which case the loss is treated as a revaluation decrease).

After reducing an asset to its recoverable amount, the **depreciation charge** on the asset should then be based on its new carrying amount, its estimated residual value (if any) and its estimated remaining useful life.

An impairment loss should be recognised for a **cash generating unit** if (and only if) the recoverable amount for the cash generating unit is less than the carrying amount in the balance sheet for all the assets in the unit. When an impairment loss is recognised for a cash generating unit, the loss should be allocated between the assets in the unit in the following order.

(a) First, to any assets that are obviously damaged or destroyed
(b) Next, to the **goodwill** allocated to the cash generating unit
(c) Then to all other assets in the cash-generating unit, on a **pro rata basis**

In allocating an impairment loss, the carrying amount of an asset should not be reduced below the highest of:

(a) Its fair value less costs to sell
(b) Its value in use (if determinable)
(c) Zero

Any remaining amount of an impairment loss should be recognised as a liability if required by other IASs.

8.6 Example 1: impairment loss

A company that extracts natural gas and oil has a drilling platform in the Caspian Sea. It is required by legislation of the country concerned to remove and dismantle the platform at the end of its useful life. Accordingly, the company has included an amount in its accounts for removal and dismantling costs, and is depreciating this amount over the platform's expected life.

The company is carrying out an exercise to establish whether there has been an impairment of the platform.

(a) Its carrying amount in the balance sheet is $3m.

(b) The company has received an offer of $2.8m for the platform from another oil company. The bidder would take over the responsibility (and costs) for dismantling and removing the platform at the end of its life.

(c) The present value of the estimated cash flows from the platform's continued use is $3.3m.

(d) The carrying amount in the balance sheet for the provision for dismantling and removal is currently $0.6m.

What should be the value of the drilling platform in the balance sheet, and what, if anything, is the impairment loss?

Solution

Fair value less costs to sell	=	$2.8m
Value in use	=	PV of cash flows from use less the carrying amount of the provision/liability = $3.3m – $0.6m = $2.7m
Recoverable amount	=	Higher of these two amounts, ie $2.8m
Carrying value	=	$3m
Impairment loss	=	$0.2m

The carrying value should be reduced to $2.8m

9 Investments

A company may have investments e.g. shares in another company. These would be treated as a **financial asset** under IAS 39.

This is an extremely complex standard outside the scope of your syllabus. You should assume that investments are recognised at their **cost**.

Key learning points

- This has been a long chapter with a lot to take in, so do not be surprised if it has taken you longer than you expected to work through it. Now that you have finally reached the end, you should understand the following points.
- The **cost of a non-current asset**, less its estimated residual value, is allocated fairly between accounting periods by means of **depreciation**. The **allowance** for depreciation is both:
  - Charged against profit
  - Deducted from the value of the non-current asset in the balance sheet
- When a non-current asset is **sold**, there is likely to be a profit or loss on disposal. This is the difference between the net sale price of the asset and its net book value at the time of disposal.
- IAS 16 *Property, plant and equipment* covers the major categories of **tangible non-current assets**. As well as depreciation, it also looks at recognition criteria, components of cost and revaluations.
- When a non-current asset is **revalued**, the gain is recorded in the revaluation revenue and depreciation is then charged on the revalued amount.
- An entity may own land or a building **as an investment** rather than for use in the business. It may therefore generate cash flows largely independent of other assets which the entity holds.
- IAS 40 *Investment property* defines investment property as property **held to earn rentals or for capital appreciation** or both, rather than for:
  - Use in production or supply of goods or services
  - Sale in the ordinary course of business
- Entities can choose between:
  - A **fair value model**, with changes in fair value being measured
  - A **cost model** – usual treatment under IAS 16
- **Intangible assets** are defined by **IAS 38** as non-monetary assets without physical substance. Intangible assets should initially be measured at cost, but subsequently they can be carried at **cost or at a revalued amount**.
- **Internally-generated goodwill** cannot be recognised as an asset.
- **Purchased goodwill** arising on a business combination is retained in the balance sheet as an intangible asset under **IFRS 3**. It must be reviewed for impairment annually.
- Impairment is determined by comparing the **carrying amount** of the asset with its **recoverable amount**.
- The recoverable amount of an asset is the higher of the asset's **fair value less costs to sell** and **its value in use**.
- When it is not possible to calculate the recoverable amount of a single asset, then that of its **cash generating unit** should be measured instead.
- Investments are recognised at cost.

Quick quiz

1 Define depreciation.

2 Which of the following elements can be included in the production cost of a non-current asset?

(i) Purchase price of raw materials
(ii) Architect's fees
(iii) Import duties
(iv) Installation costs

3 Market value can usually be taken as fair value.

True ☐

False ☐

4 Define impairment.

5 Investment properties must always be shown at fair value.

True ☐

False ☐

6 Intangible assets can only be recognised in a company's accounts if:

- It is probable that .... will flow to the entity
- The cost can be ....

7 What are the criteria which must be met before development expenditure can be deferred?

8 Start up costs must be expensed.

True ☐

False ☐

9 Peggy buys Phil's business for $30,000. The business assets are a bar valued at $20,000, inventories at $3,000 and receivables of $3,000. How much is goodwill valued at?

10 What method of accounting for goodwill arising on consolidation is required by IFRS 3?

Answers to quick quiz

1 See Para 2.1

2 All of them.

3 True

4 See Section 8

5 False. The cost model may be used, provided it is used consistently.

6 Future economic benefits. Measured reliably.

7 See Para 6.3

8 True

9 $30,000 – $20,000 – $3,000 – $3,000 = $4,000

10 Carry in the balance sheet at cost and review for impairment annually.

Answers to activities

8.1

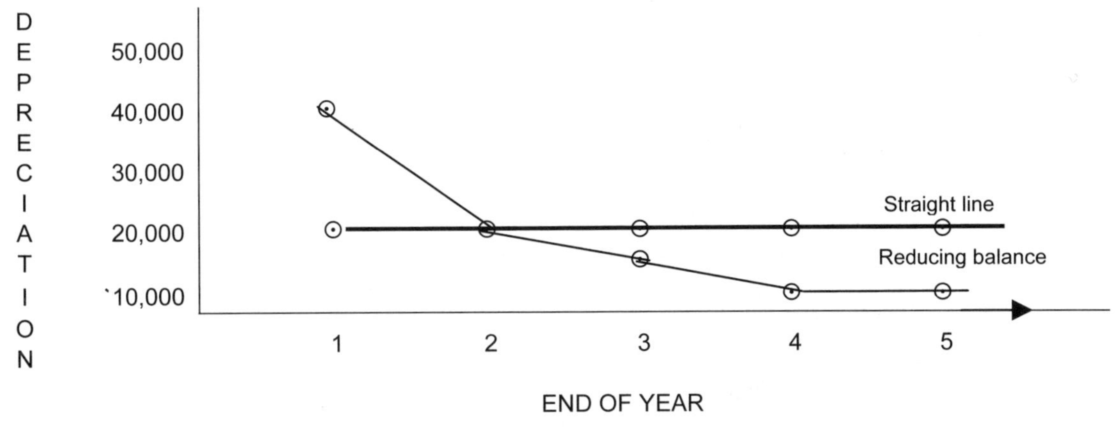

8.2 (a) Under the straight line method, depreciation for each of the five years is:

$$\text{Annual depreciation} = \frac{17{,}000 - 2{,}000}{5} = \$3{,}000$$

(b) Under the reducing balance method, depreciation for each of the five years is:

Year	*Depreciation*	
1	35% × \$17,000	= \$5,950
2	35% × (\$17,000 – \$5,950) = 35% × \$11,050	= \$3,868
3	35% × (\$11,050 – \$3,868) = 35% × \$7,182	= \$2,514
4	35% × (\$7,182 – \$2,514) = 35% × \$4,668	= \$1,634
5	Balance to bring book value down to \$2,000 = \$4,668 – \$1,634 – \$2,000	= \$1,034

(Note: in practice, it will not often be this exact ie 35% would be applied as usual)

(c) Under the machine hour method, depreciation for each of the five years is calculated as follows.

Total usage (days) = 200 + 100 + 100 + 150 + 40 = 590 days

$$\text{Depreciation per day} = \frac{£17{,}000 - £2{,}000}{590} = \$25.42$$

Year	*Usage (days)*	*Depreciation (\$) (days × \$25.42)*
1	200	5,084.00
2	100	2,542.00
3	100	2,542.00
4	150	3,813.00
5	40	1,016.80
		14,997.80

(The answer does not come to exactly \$15,000 because of the rounding carried out at the 'depreciation per day' stage of the calculation.)

8.3 In the balance sheet

- Increase land by \$7,000 (20,000 – 13,000)
- Increase revaluation surplus \$7,000.

8.4 At the end of 20X3, the production process is recognised as an intangible asset at a cost of $10,000. This is the expenditure incurred since the date when the recognition criteria were met, that is 1 December 20X3. The $90,000 expenditure incurred before 1 December 20X3 is expensed, because the recognition criteria were not met. It will never form part of the cost of the production process recognised in the balance sheet.

8.5 Factors to consider would include the following.

(a) Legal protection of the brand name and the control of the entity over the (illegal) use by others of the brand name (ie control over pirating)

(b) Age of the brand name

(c) Status or position of the brand in its particular market

(d) Ability of the management of the entity to manage the brand name and to measure activities that support the brand name (eg advertising and PR activities)

(e) Stability and geographical spread of the market in which the branded products are sold

(f) Pattern of benefits that the brand name is expected to generate over time

(g) Intention of the entity to use and promote the brand name over time (as evidenced perhaps by a business plan in which there will be substantial expenditure to promote the brand name)

8.6 IAS 38 gives these examples.

Research

- Activities aimed at obtaining new knowledge
- The search for applications of research findings or other knowledge
- The search for product or process alternatives
- The formulation and design of possible new or improved product or process alternatives

Development

- The evaluation of product or process alternatives
- The design, construction and testing of pre-production prototypes and models
- The design of tools, jigs, moulds and dies involving new technology
- The design, construction and operation of a pilot plant that is not of a scale economically feasible for commercial production

8.7 Goodwill may be distinguished from other intangible non-current assets by reference to the following characteristics.

(a) It is incapable of realisation separately from the business as a whole.

(b) Its value has no reliable or predictable relationship to any costs which may have been incurred.

(c) Its value arises from various intangible factors such as skilled employees, effective advertising or a strategic location. These indirect factors cannot be valued.

(d) The value of goodwill may fluctuate widely according to internal and external circumstances over relatively short periods of time.

(e) The assessment of the value of goodwill is highly subjective.

9

Share capital and reserves

Topic list
1 Share capital of limited companies
2 Shareholders' equity
3 Share premium account
4 Revaluation surplus
5 Reserves
6 Why statutory reserves are non-distributable
7 Retained earnings
8 Bonus issues of shares
9 Rights issues of shares
10 Disclosures in the accounts

Introduction

The topics in this chapter deal with capital transactions. A great deal of national legislation governing these transactions is concerned with the protection of creditors. Whilst local rules may vary, the overall aim is the same; to prevent companies favouring shareholders over creditors.

Learning objectives

On completion of this chapter you will be able to:

	Syllabus reference
• explain what is meant by share capital	3 c v
• identify and define the different types of share capital	3 c v
• explain the different types of statutory and non-statutory reserves	3 c v
• describe the function of the share premium account and the revaluation reserve	3 c v
• discuss the purpose and features of bonus issues and rights issues	3 c v

1 Share capital of limited companies

FAST FORWARD

Share capital consists of ordinary shares, and there may also be other classes of sharer such as preferred shares.

The proprietors' capital in a limited company consists of share capital. Share capital may be divided into several different classes. Each class of shares entitles the shareholders to different rights.

(a) All companies have ordinary shares (and may have more than one class of ordinary shares.

(b) A company may have one or more classes of preferred shares. Most classes of preferred shares entitle the shareholders to a fixed annual dividend.

Key term

Preferred shares are shares which confer certain preferential rights on their holder. These normally include the right to receive a dividend ahead of the ordinary shareholders and, in the event of the company becoming insolvent, the right to recovery of their nominal investment ahead of the ordinary shareholders.

Ordinary shares are shares which are not preferential with regard to dividend payments. Thus a holder only receives a dividend after fixed dividends have been paid to preferred shareholders. The ordinary dividend could well be higher than the preference dividend. Ordinary shareholders are the real owners (and 'risk takers'). Ordinary shares are commonly referred to as 'equity' or 'equity shares'.

Shareholders receive returns in the form of dividends. Dividends are paid out of the distributable profits of the company. Distributable profits are profits that have been 'realised' (from the sale of goods or services, from the disposal of non-current assets, from income from various sources, such as income from investments, etc).

It is usual for a company to pay dividends out of its **profits after tax** for the year. Total after-tax profits will usually be higher than the dividend payments, and the remaining profits will be retained in the business. In effect, retained profits are a way of making shareholders continue to invest in their company.

Sometimes, a company's directors might want to pay out dividends in excess of the company's after-tax profits for the year. This is permissible, provided the company has sufficient retained profits from previous years.

Under IAS 32 *Financial instruments: Presentation*, redeemable preferred shares are shown as liabilities in the balance sheet and their dividends treated as finance costs in the income statement. All other preferred shares are treated as shares and their dividends appropriated, with ordinary dividends.

Activity 9.1

Garden Gloves Co has issued 50,000 ordinary shares of 50 cents each and 20,000 7% preferred shares of $1 each. Its profits after taxation for the year to 30 September 20X5 were $8,400. The board of directors has decided to pay an ordinary dividend (i.e. a dividend on ordinary shares) which is 50% of profits after tax and preference dividend.

Required

Show the amount in total of dividends and of retained profits.

1.1 Authorised, allotted and called up share capital

FAST FORWARD

Share capital is reported in the accounts at the nominal value of the shares allotted, but only to the extent that the capital on the shares has been called up.

A distinction must be made between authorised, allotted (issued), called-up and paid-up share capital.

(a) **Authorised (or legal) capital** is the maximum amount of share capital that a company's directors are permitted to issue. The amount of authorised share capital varies from company to company, and can only be increased by agreement.

For example, a company's authorised share capital might be 5,000,000 ordinary shares of $1 each. This would then be the maximum number of shares it could issue, unless the authorised share capital were to be changed with agreement from the shareholders.

(b) **Allotted capital**, also called issued share capital, is the nominal amount of share capital that has been issued to shareholders. The amount of issued capital cannot exceed the amount of authorised capital.

In the example above, suppose the company with authorised share capital of 5,000,000 ordinary shares of $1 has allotted 4,000,000 shares. This would still give it the option to issue 1,000,000 more shares at some time in the future, without the need to increase the authorised share capital.

(c) **Called-up capital**. When shares are issued or allotted, a company does not always expect to be paid the full amount for the shares at once. It might instead call up only a part of the issue price, and wait until a later time before it calls up the remainder.

For example, if a company allots 4,000,000 ordinary shares of $1, it might call up only, say, 75 cents per share. The issued share capital would be $4,000,000, but the called up share capital would only be $3,000,000.

(d) **Paid-up capital**. Like everyone else, investors are not always prompt or reliable payers. When capital is called up, some shareholders might delay their payment (or even default on payment). Paid-up capital is the amount of called-up capital that has been paid.

For example, if a company issues 4,000,000 ordinary shares of $1 each, calls up 75 cents per share, and receives payments of $2,900,000, we would have:

	$
Allotted or issued capital	4,000,000
Called-up capital	3,000,000
Paid-up capital	2,900,000
Called-up capital not paid	100,000

The balance sheet of the company would then include called up capital not paid on the assets side, as follows:

	$
Called-up capital not paid	100,000
Cash (called-up capital paid)	2,900,000
	3,000,000
Called-up share capital	
4,000,000 ordinary shares of $1, with 75c per share called up.	3,000,000

1.2 Share capital in the balance sheet

Share capital is reported in the balance sheet at its called up value. Since most shares are issued fully paid, the called up share capital and the allotted share capital are normally the same amount. Shares are reported in different classes, for example:

Equity

	$'000
Ordinary shares of 10c each	120,000
6% preferred shares of $1	3,000
	123,000

On the face of the balance sheet, there will be a single figure for share capital, with further details in a note to the account. The further details will include the authorised share capital, and the called up share capital the number and nominal value of the shares issued. For example:

	Authorised	*Allotted, called up and fully paid*	
	Number of 50c shares	*Number of 50c shares*	*Nominal value*
	'000	'000	$'000
At the start of the year	10,000	7,000	3,500
Issued during the year	-	1,000	500
At the end of the year	10,000	8,000	4,000

1.3 The issue price for shares

The amount at which the shares are allotted/issued will often exceed their nominal value, especially in the case of a public company making a new issue of shares. For example, a company might issue 100,000 $1 shares at a price of $1.20 each. Subscribers will then pay a total of $120,000. The issued share capital of the company would be shown in its accounts at nominal value, $100,000; the excess of $20,000 is described not as share capital, but as *share premium.*

Stock market companies making a new issue of shares are likely to price the issue at an amount that reflects the current market price of the shares, which could be well in excess of the nominal value of the shares. The balance sheet shows the nominal value of issued shares, not their market value. Thus, when new shares are issued, the share premium could be very large.

1.4 The market value of shares

The nominal value of shares will be different from their market value, which is the price at which someone is prepared to purchase shares in the company from an existing shareholder. If Mr A owns 1,000 $1 shares in Z Co he may sell them to B for $5.60 each.

This transfer of existing shares does not affect Z Co's own financial position in any way whatsoever. There are no accounting entries to be made for the share sale, as the transaction is between Mr A and B.

2 Shareholders' equity

FAST FORWARD

> The net assets of a company (i.e. assets minus inabilities) are 'financed' by the shareholders' capital. The share capital is recorded in the balance sheet of a company. The rest of the capital of a company is represented by reserves.

Shareholders' equity consists of:

(a) The nominal value of issued capital (minus any amounts not yet called up on issued shares)
(b) Other equity

The share capital itself might consist of both ordinary shares and preferred shares. All reserves, however, are owned by the ordinary shareholders, who own the 'equity' in the company. We looked at share capital in detail above.

'Other equity' under IAS 1 consists of four elements.

(a) Capital paid-in in excess of par value (share premium)
(b) Revaluation surplus
(c) Reserves
(d) Retained earnings

We will look at each in turn.

3 Share premium account

FAST FORWARD

> A **share premium account** is an account into which sums received as payment for shares in excess of their nominal value must be placed.

In this context, 'premium' means the difference between the issue price of the share and its par value. The account is sometimes called 'capital paid-in in excess of par value'. When a company is first incorporated (set up) the issue price of its shares will probably be the same as their par value and so there would be no share premium. If the company does well, the market value of its shares will increase, but not the par value. The price of any new shares issued will be approximately their market value.

The difference between cash received by the company and the par value of the new shares issued is transferred to the **share premium account**. For example, if X Co issues 1,000 $1 ordinary shares at $2.60 each the book entry will be:

	$	$
Cash	2,600	
Ordinary shares		1,000
Share premium account		1,600

A share premium account only comes into being when a company issues shares at a price in excess of their nominal value. The market price of the shares, once they have been issued, has no bearing at all on the company's accounts, and so if their market price goes up or down, the share premium account would remain unaltered.

Once established, the share premium account constitutes capital of the company which cannot be paid out in dividends, ie it is a capital reserve. The share premium account will increase in value if and when new shares are issued at a price above their par value. The share premium account can be 'used' - and so decrease in value - only in certain very limited ways, which are largely beyond the scope of your basic financial accounting syllabus. One common use of the share premium account, however, is to 'finance' the issue of bonus shares, which are described later in this chapter. Other uses of this account may depend on national legislation.

Important!

The share premium account cannot be distributed as dividend under any circumstances as it is a **statutory reserve** (see Section 6).

4 Revaluation surplus

FAST FORWARD

The revaluation surplus is a statutory reserve and consists of non-distributable profits (see Section 6).

A company may revalue some of its assets. For example, a company may revalue its freehold properties from $40 million, say, to $50 million. An increase in an asset value for a company represents a gain for the company. This gain has to be included in its reserves. (The dual effect is + Assets, + Capital.) We looked at the mechanics of this in Chapter 8.

If the company continues to hold the asset, any gain on revaluation is unrealised. The company has not sold the asset, and has not earned any cash from the revaluation gain. It would therefore be inappropriate to allow the company to pay dividends out of unrealised gains. (Apart from the fact that the company might not have the cash to afford a dividend on the gain, the asset might subsequently fall in value, thus incurring a loss. It would therefore be premature to pay dividends out of unrealised gains, i.e. before the asset is actually sold and the gain is realised.)

Companies are therefore required to make a 'transfer' to a revaluation surplus, whenever it revalues a non-current asset. Both the asset and the reserve are increased by the amount of the revaluation (i.e. by the amount of the increase in the total value of the asset minus any accumulated depreciation on the asset to date.) The revaluation is taken directly to the revaluation surplus account, and is not reported as part of the company's profit for the year. The revaluation gain will be reflected in the statement of changes in equity which we looked at in chapter 5.

4.1 Disposal of a revalued asset

When an asset is disposed of, having been revalued in the past, the revaluation gain that had previously been unrealised is now realised. Since the gain is realised, the company can, if it wishes, pay dividends out of the profit (after tax).

After disposal, it is therefore inappropriate to keep an amount in the revaluation surplus for an asset the company no longer owns. The accounting treatment is as follows.

(a) The company may report a profit (or loss) on the disposal of the asset, but this is the difference between the net sales proceeds and the carrying value of the asset at the time of the disposal. The carrying value is a term for the value of the asset in the balance sheet and in the accounting records at the time. With a revalued asset, the carrying value is the revalued amount less accumulated depreciation.

(b) The rest of the realised profit on disposal is transferred directly from the revaluation surplus to the retained earnings account, without being reported as part of the profit for the year. The gain is now distributable, but it does not form part of the 'current year' profits.

Activity 9.2

A company owns a freehold property which was valued at cost $5 million minus accumulated depreciation on the building of $250,000. It was then revalued to $10 million less accumulated depreciation of $500,000. Some time later, the building was sold for $12 million. At this time, the accumulated depreciation was $700,000.

(a) How would the revaluation be accounted for?

(b) How would the disposal of the property be accounted for?

5 Reserves

FAST FORWARD

Reserves can be classified as non-statutory and statutory.

In most countries, a distinction must be made between:

(a) **Statutory reserves**, which are reserves which a company is required to set up by law, and which are not available for the distribution of dividends. We have looked at the share premium account and the revaluation surplus.

(b) **Non-statutory reserves**, which are reserves consisting of profits which are distributable as dividends, if the company so wishes

We are concerned with the latter type, which the company managers may choose to set up. These may have a specific purpose (eg plant and machinery replacement reserve) or not (eg general reserve). The creation of these reserves usually indicates a general intention not to distribute the profits involved at any future date, although legally any such reserves, being non-statutory, remain available for the payment of dividends.

Profits are transferred to these reserves by making an appropriation out of profits, usually profits for the year. Typically, you might come across the following.

	$	$
Profit after taxation		100,000
Appropriations of profit		
Dividend	60,000	
Transfer to general reserve	10,000	
		70,000
Retained profit for the year		30,000
Retained earnings b/f		250,000
Retained earnings c/f		280,000

6 Why statutory reserves are non-distributable

FAST FORWARD

Statutory reserves are non-distributable to avoid a reduction in the capital of the company.

The reason for creating statutory reserves is to **maintain the capital** of the company. This capital 'base' provides some **security for the company's creditors**, bearing in mind that the liability of shareholders is limited in the event that the company cannot repay its debts. It would be most unjust - and illegal - for a company to pay its shareholders a dividend out of its base capital when it is not even able to pay back its debts.

Another reason why statutory reserves such as the share premium account cannot be distributed as dividends is the fact that they often represent unrealised profits. A profit does arise when assets are revalued but it is not realised into cash. It is a generally accepted accounting principle that profit can only be distributed when it is realised because an unrealised profit can disappear if the value of the revalued asset subsequently drops.

7 Retained earnings

This is the **most significant reserve** and is variously described as:

(a) Retained earnings (as in IAS 1)
(b) Revenue reserve
(c) Retained profits
(d) Accumulated profits
(e) Undistributed profits
(f) Unappropriated profits

These are **profits** earned by the company and not appropriated by dividends, taxation or transfer to another reserve account.

Provided that a company is earning profits, this reserve generally increases from year to year, as most companies do not distribute all their profits as dividends. Dividends can be paid from it: even if a loss is made in one particular year, a dividend can be paid from previous years' retained earnings.

For example, if a company makes a loss of $100,000 in one year, yet has unappropriated profits from previous years totalling $250,000, it can pay a dividend not exceeding $150,000. One reason for retaining some profit each year is to enable the company to pay dividends even when profits are low (or non-existent). Another reason is usually shortage of cash.

Very occasionally, you might come across a negative balance on the retained earnings account. This would indicate that the company has retained (accumulated) losses.

8 Bonus issues of shares

FAST FORWARD

A bonus issue **capitalises** some of the reserves of the company.

A company may wish to increase the number of shares in issue without needing to raise additional finance by issuing new shares. For example, a profitable company might expand from modest beginnings over a number of years. Its profitability would be reflected in large balances on its reserves, while its original share capital might look like that of a much smaller business.

It is open to such a company to **re-classify some of its reserves as share capital**. This is purely a paper exercise which raises no funds. Any reserve may be re-classified in this way, **including a share premium account** or other statutory reserve.

Suppose for example that Bubbles Co has the following share holders' equity.

BUBBLES CO
BALANCE SHEET (EXTRACT)

	$'000	$'000
Shareholders' equity		
Share capital		
$1 ordinary shares (fully paid)		100,000
Reserves		
Share premium	100,000	
Retained earnings	200,000	
		300,000
		400,000

Bubbles decided to make a '3 for 2' bonus issue (ie issue 3 new shares for every 2 already held).

150 million new ('bonus') shares are issued to existing shareholders, so that if shareholder X previously held 20,000 shares, he will now hold 50,000. The total value of his holding should theoretically remain the same however, since the net assets of the company remain unchanged and his share of those net assets remains at 0.02% (i.e. 50,000/250,000,000; previously 20,000/100,000,000).

The company will almost certainly use up its share premium account to increase the share capital. The remaining addition to share capital would have to be 'financed' by a transfer from the retained earnings.

The share capital and reserves after the bonus issue will be:

	$ million	$ million
Shareholders' equity		
Share capital		
$1 ordinary shares (fully paid)		250
Reserves		
Share premium	0	
Retained earnings	150	
		150
		400

The total for share capital and reserves is unchanged. No new money has been raised or assets acquired by the share issue.

9 Rights issues of shares

FAST FORWARD

When a rights issue occurs, there will be an increase in both share capital (nominal value of shares issued) and share premium.

A rights issue (unlike a bonus issue) is an issue of shares for cash. Existing shareholders are offered new shares that the company is issuing, in proportion to their existing shareholding. For example, suppose that a company has 100 million shares in issue and plans to issue a further 50 million shares to raise cash. In a rights issue, it would offer existing shareholders 1 new share for every 2 shares they currently hold.

The share price in a rights issue is normally below the current market price for the shares.

Bubbles Co (above) decides to make a rights issue, shortly after the bonus issue. The terms are '2 for 5 at $2.50' (i.e. two new shares for every five already held, at a price of $2.50). Assuming that all shareholders take up their rights (which they are not obliged to), the company will issue 100 million new shares (250 million already in issue, × 2/5) to raise $250 million. This will be raised in cash. Share capital and reserves will increase by $250 million in total, of which $100 million is the nominal value of the new shares and $150 million is share premium. The balance sheet after the rights issue is as follows.

	$ million	$ million
Shareholders' equity		
Share capital		
$1 ordinary shares (fully paid) (250 million + 100 million)		350
Reserves		
Share premium (+ 150 million)	150	
Retained earnings	150	
		300
		650

Rights issues are a popular way of raising cash by issuing shares and they are cheap to administer. In addition shareholders retain control of the business as their holding is not diluted.

10 Disclosures in the accounts

FAST FORWARD

In most countries companies must include a note in their annual accounts giving details of movements on the reserve accounts during the year.

Although local rules may vary in most jurisdictions companies are required to disclose, in notes to their accounts, information about their share capital and about movements on their reserves during the year. An example of a note on reserves (based on the UK Companies Act) is shown below.

[Note number] *Reserves*

	Share premium account	*Revaluation surplus*	*General reserve*	*Retained earnings*
	$'000	$'000	$'000	$'000
At 1 January 20X5	750	240	70	1,400
On issue of shares	120	-	-	-
Retained profit for the year	-	-	-	360
Revaluation	-	80	-	-
Transfers	-	-	25	(25)
At 31 December 20X5	870	320	95	1,735

Key learning points

- Share capital consists of ordinary shares, and there may also be other classes of shares, such as preferred shares.
- Share capital is reported in the accounts at the nominal value of the shares allotted, but only to the extent that the capital on the shares has been called up.
- The net assets of a company (i.e. assets minus liabilities) are financed by the shareholders' capital. The share capital is recorded in the balance sheet of a company. The rest of the capital of a company is represented by reserves.
- A share premium account is an account into which sums received as payment in excess of their nominal value must be placed.
- The revaluation surplus is a statutory reserve and consists of non-distributable profits.
- Reserves can be classified as **non-statutory** (distributable in dividends) and **statutory** (non-distributable).
- Statutory reserves are non-distributable, to avoid a reduction in the capital of the company.
- A bonus issue **capitalises** some of the reserve of the company.
- When a rights issue occurs, there will be an increase in both share capital (nominal value of shares issued) and share premium.
- In most countries companies must include a note **in their annual accounts** giving details of movements on the reserve accounts during the year.

Quick quiz

1. What benefits do preferred shareholders normally have?
2. What is the difference between authorised and allotted share capital?
3. What is the name given to the excess paid for shares over their nominal value?
4. Why are the statutory reserves of a company non-distributable?
5. What is a bonus issue of shares?

Answers to quick quiz

1 The rights to receive a dividend ahead of the ordinary shareholders, and the right to be repaid their share capital on winding up in priority to the ordinary shareholders.

2 *Authorised* share capital is the maximum amount that the directors of the company are permitted to issue. *Allotted* share capital is the amount which has actually been issued to shareholders. It must not exceed the authorised share capital.

3 Share premium.

4 In order to maintain the capital of the company and provide some security for the company's creditors. Also because they often represent unrealised profits, which cannot be distributed.

5 An increase in the number of shares in issue without any need to raise additional finance. Therefore, some of the company's reserves are re-classified as share capital, and the shareholders will receive additional shares in proportion to their original holding.

Answers to activities

9.1

	$
Profit after tax	8,400
Preference dividend (7% of $1 × 20,000)	1,400
Earnings (profit after tax and preference dividend)	7,000
Ordinary dividend (50% of earnings)	3,500
Retained profit (also 50% of earnings)	3,500

9.2 (a) On revaluation, the changes in the accounts would be:

1 increase asset value to revalued amount, + $ 5 million
2 increase accumulated depreciation + $250,000
3 increase revaluation surplus + $4.75 million

Between the revaluation and the disposal of the asset, $200,000 of depreciation will have been charged against profits in the company's annual income statement. (This is the difference between the accumulated depreciation on disposal and the accumulated depreciation at the time of the revaluation.)

(b) On disposal, there will be a profit on disposal, reported in the income statement for the year, of $12 million less ($10 million minus $700,000) = $2,700,000. In addition, $4,750,000 would be transferred from the revaluation account to retained earnings, representing the revaluation gain that was previously unrealised but has now been realised by the disposal of the asset.

10

Group accounts

Topic list
1 Definitions
2 Content of group accounts and group structure
3 Introduction to the consolidated balance sheet
4 Minority interests
5 Dividends payable by a subsidiary
6 Goodwill arising on consolidation
7 Intra-group trading
8 Summary: consolidated balance sheet
9 Consolidated income statement
10 Summary: consolidated income statement
11 Accounting for associates
12 Joint ventures and jointly controlled entities

Introduction

Consolidation is an extremely important area of your syllabus and will be regularly examined in both Section A and B of the paper.

In this chapter we will look at the major definitions in consolidation. These are fundamental to your comprehension of the subject.

The techniques of full consolidation and the equity method are also explained. You must try to understand the underlying principles behind both of these.

Learning objectives

On completion of this chapter you will be able to:

	Syllabus reference
• identify the general characteristics of a parent company, a subsidiary, a participating interest, an associate and a long-term investment	3 c ix
• explain the meaning of minority interest, goodwill arising on consolidation, and pre-acquisition profits	3 c ix
• describe the main financial statements in the published group accounts of a public company	3 c ix
• identify, in broad terms, how the consolidated balance sheet and the income statement of a parent company and its subsidiaries are prepared	3 c ix
• discuss the methods of accounting for associates (equity method) and joint ventures	3 c ix

1 Definitions

FAST FORWARD

This chapter explains the concept of a group and introduces several important definitions.

You will probably know that most large 'companies' actually consist of several companies controlled by one central or administrative company. Together these companies are called a **group**. The controlling company, called the **parent**, will own some or all of the shares in the other companies. The other companies in a group are called **subsidiary companies** and **associated companies**.

For example, a parent company Parent Co might own all the shares of another company, Sub. The parent company's balance sheet will show its investment in Sub as a long-term investment, either at cost (less any diminution in value) or market value. The parent's own balance sheet will not disclose any details about the assets of Sub.

In some countries (eg the UK), parent companies of a group are required by law to prepare **consolidated accounts** for the group as a whole. The purpose of consolidated accounts is to show the results and financial position of the group as a whole. Consolidated accounts combine the assets and liabilities, and the profits, of all the companies in the group, and report them virtually as if the group is just a single undertaking. The legal requirement for consolidated accounts is to give users of the accounts (e.g. shareholders in the parent company) a much better understanding of the financial position and performance of the group that the parent company controls.

Group accounts (consolidated accounts) are prepared by the parent company for all the companies in the group.

We will look at some of these definitions in more detail later, but they are useful here in that they give you an overview of all aspects of group accounts.

Exam focus point

All the definitions relating to group accounts are extremely important. You must be familiar with their meaning and application.

Key terms

- **Control**. The power to govern the financial and operating policies of an entity so as to obtain benefits from its activities. *(IFRS 3, IASs 27, 28, 31)*
- **Subsidiary**. An entity that is controlled by another entity (known as the parent). *(IFRS 3, IASs 27, 28)*
- **Parent**. An entity that has one or more subsidiaries. *(IFRS 3, IAS 27)*
- **Group**. A parent and all its subsidiaries. *(IAS 27)*
- **Associate**. An entity, including an unincorporated entity such as a partnership, in which an investor has significant influence and which is neither a subsidiary nor a joint venture of the investor. *(IAS 28)*
- **Significant influence** is the power to participate in the financial and operating policy decisions of an investee or an economic activity but is not control or joint control over those policies. *(IASs 28, 31)*
- **Joint venture**. A contractual arrangement whereby two or more parties undertake an economic activity which is subject to joint control. *(IAS 31)*

1.1 Investments in subsidiaries

The important point here is **control**. In most cases, this will involve the parent company owning a majority of the ordinary shares in the subsidiary (to which normal voting rights are attached). There are circumstances, however, when the parent may own only a minority of the voting power in the subsidiary, *but* the parent still has control.

Both IFRS 3 *Business combinations* and IAS 27 *Consolidated and separate financial statements* state that control can usually be assumed to exist when the parent **owns more than half (ie over 50%) of the voting power** of an entity *unless* it can be clearly shown that **such ownership does not constitute control** (these situations will be very rare).

What about situations where this ownership criterion does not exist? IFRS 3 and IAS 27 list the following situations where control exists, even when the parent owns only 50% or less of the voting power of an entity.

(a) The parent has power over more than 50% of the voting rights by virtue of **agreement with other investors**

(b) The parent has power to **govern the financial and operating policies** of the entity by statute or under an agreement

(c) The parent has the power to **appoint or remove a majority of members of the board of directors** (or equivalent governing body)

(d) The parent has power to cast a **majority of votes at meetings of the board of directors**

IAS 27 also states that a parent loses control when it loses the power to govern the financial and operating policies of an investee. Loss of control can occur without a change in ownership levels. This may happen if a subsidiary becomes subject to the control of a government, court administrator or regulator (for example, in bankruptcy).

1.2 The requirement to consolidate

IAS 27 requires a parent to present **consolidated financial statements**, in which the accounts of the parent and subsidiary (or subsidiaries) are combined and presented **as a single entity**, unless it is able to use a permissible exemption from this requirement.

Key term

> **Consolidated financial statements**. The financial statements of a group presented as those of a single economic entity. *(IAS 27)*

When a parent issues consolidated financial statements, it should consolidate **all subsidiaries**, both foreign and domestic.

1.3 Exemption from preparing group accounts

A parent **need not present** consolidated financial statements if and only if all of the following hold:

(a) The parent is itself a **wholly-owned subsidiary** or it is a **partially owned subsidiary** of another entity and its other owners, including those not otherwise entitled to vote, have been informed about, and do not object to, the parent not presenting consolidated financial statements

(b) Its securities are **not publicly traded**

(c) It is **not in the process of issuing securities** in public securities markets; and

(d) The **ultimate or intermediate parent** publishes consolidated financial statements that comply with International Financial Reporting Standards

Where this is the case disclosure in the individual financial statements is required.

1.4 Investments in associates

This type of investment is something less than a subsidiary, but more than a simple investment (nor is it a joint venture). The key criterion here is **significant influence**. This is defined as the 'power to participate', but *not* to 'control' (which would make the investment a subsidiary).

Significant influence can be determined by the holding of voting rights (usually attached to shares) in the entity. IAS 28 I*nvestments in associates* states that if an investor holds **20% or more** of the voting power of the investee, it can be presumed that the investor has significant influence over the investee, *unless* it can be clearly shown that this is not the case.

Significant influence can be presumed *not* to exist if the investor holds **less than 20%** of the voting power of the investee, unless it can be demonstrated otherwise.

The **existence of significant influence** is evidenced in one or more of the following ways.

(a) Representation on the **board of directors** (or equivalent) of the investee
(b) Participation in the **policy making process**
(c) **Material transactions** between investor and investee
(d) Interchange of **management personnel**
(e) Provision of **essential technical information**

IAS 28 requires the use of the **equity method** of accounting for investments in associates. This method will be explained in detail in Section 11.

1.5 Accounting for investments in joint ventures

There are situations where venturers control jointly either operations or assets of the joint venture. The case of a **jointly controlled entity** will be considered in detail in Section I2.

IAS 31 *Interests in joint ventures* allows two treatments for investments in joint entities.

(a) **Either**: proportionate consolidation
(b) **Or**: equity method

1.6 Other investments

Investments which do not meet the definitions of any of the above should be accounted for according to IAS 39 *Financial instruments: recognition and measurement.* (See chapter 8).

1.7 Definitions summarised

Investment	Criteria	Required treatment in group accounts
Subsidiary	Control (> 50% rule)	Full consolidation (IAS 27)
Associate	Significant influence (20%+ rule)	Equity accounting (IAS 28)
Joint venture (jointly controlled entity)	Contractual joint control	Either: proportionate consolidation Or: equity accounting (IAS 31)
Investment which is none of the above	Asset held for accretion of wealth	As for single company accounts (IAS 39) (see Chapter 8)

2 Content of group accounts and group structure

FAST FORWARD

Group accounts show the results of the parent plus any subsidiaries as if they were a single company.

The information contained in the individual statements of a parent company and each of its subsidiaries does not give a picture of the group's total activities. A **separate set of group statements** can be prepared from the individual ones. Remember that a group has no separate (legal) existence, except for accounting purposes.

Consolidated accounts are one form of group accounts which combines the information contained in the separate accounts of a parent company and its subsidiaries as if they were the accounts of a single entity. 'Group accounts' and 'consolidated accounts' are terms often used synonymously.

In simple terms a set of consolidated accounts is prepared by **adding together** the assets and liabilities of the parent company and each subsidiary. The **whole** of the assets and liabilities of each company are included, even though some subsidiaries may be only partly owned. The 'equity and liabilities' side of the balance sheet will indicate how much of the net assets are attributable to the group and how much to outside investors in partly owned subsidiaries. These **outside investors** are known as **minority interests**.

Key term

Minority interest. That part of the profit or loss and of net assets of a subsidiary attributable to equity interests which are not owned directly, or indirectly through subsidiaries, by the parent.

(IFRS 3, IAS 27)

Minority interests should be presented in the consolidated balance sheet **within equity, separately from the parent shareholders' equity**.

Most parent companies present their own individual accounts and their group accounts in a single **package**. The package typically comprises the following.

- **Parent company financial statements**, which will include 'investments in subsidiaries undertakings' as an asset in the balance sheet, and income from subsidiaries (in dividends) in the income statement
- **Consolidated balance sheet**
- **Consolidated income statement**
- **Consolidated cash flow statement**

It may not be necessary to publish all of the parent company's financial statements, depending on local or national regulations.

Activity 10.1

Are the following companies a subsidiary or associate of P Co, or neither?

1 Bump is 75% owned by Clump, which is itself 60% owned by P Co

2 Pump is 30% owned by P Co

3 Frump is 15% owned by P Co

4 Mump is 15% owned by Stump and 45% owned by Slump. Stump and Slump are both 90% owned by P Co.

3 Introduction to the consolidated balance sheet

FAST FORWARD

Balances of the parent company and subsidiaries are added together on a line-by-line basis. Intra-group balances are cancelled out.

3.1 Basic procedure

The financial statements of a parent and its subsidiaries are **combined on a line-by-line basis** by adding together like items of assets, liabilities, equity, income and expenses.

The following steps are then taken, in order that the consolidated financial statements should **show financial information about the group as if it was a single entity**.

(a) The carrying amount of the parent's **investment in each subsidiary** and the parent's **portion of equity** of each subsidiary are **eliminated or cancelled**

(b) **Minority interests in the net income of consolidated subsidiaries** are adjusted against group income, to arrive at the net income attributable to the owners of the parent

(c) **Minority interests** in the net assets of consolidated subsidiaries should be presented separately in the consolidated balance sheet (see Section 4)

Other matters to be dealt with include the following.

(a) **Goodwill on consolidation** should be dealt with according to IFRS 3 (see Section 6)

(b) **Dividends payable** by a subsidiary must be accounted for (see Section 5)

IAS 27 states that all intragroup balances and transactions, and the resulting **unrealised profits**, should be **eliminated in full**. **Unrealised losses** resulting from intragroup transactions should also be eliminated *unless* cost can be recovered. This will be explained later in this chapter.

3.2 Cancellation

The preparation of a consolidated balance sheet, in a very simple form, consists of two procedures.

(a) Take the individual accounts of the parent company and each subsidiary and **cancel out items** which appear as an asset in one company and a liability in another.

(b) **Add together all the uncancelled assets and liabilities** throughout the group.

Items requiring cancellation may include the following.

(a) The asset **'shares in subsidiary companies'** which appears in the parent company's accounts will be matched with the liability 'share capital' in the subsidiaries' accounts.

(b) There may be **intra-group trading** within the group. For example, S Co may sell goods on credit to P Co. P Co would then be a receivable in the accounts of S Co, while S Co would be a payable in the accounts of P Co.

3.3 Example: cancellation

P Co regularly sells goods to its one subsidiary company, S Co, which it has owned since S Co's incorporation. The balance sheets of the two companies on 31 December 20X6 are given below.

P CO
BALANCE SHEET AS AT 31 DECEMBER 20X6

	$	$	$
Assets			
Non-current assets			
Tangible assets			35,000
Investment in 40,000 $1 shares in S Co at cost			40,000
			75,000
Current assets			
Inventories		16,000	
Receivables: S Co	2,000		
Other	6,000		
		8,000	
Cash at bank		1,000	
			25,000
Total assets			100,000
Equity and liabilities			
Equity			
70,000 $1 ordinary shares		70,000	
Reserves		16,000	
			86,000
Current liabilities			
Payables			14,000
Total equity and liabilities			100,000

S CO
BALANCE SHEET AS AT 31 DECEMBER 20X6

	$	$
Assets		
Non-current assets		
Tangible assets		45,000
Current assets		
Inventories	12,000	
Receivables	9,000	
		21,000
Total assets		66,000
Equity and liabilities		
Equity		
40,000 $1 ordinary shares	40,000	
Reserves	19,000	
		59,000
Current liabilities		
Bank overdraft	3,000	
Payables: P Co	2,000	
Payables: other	2,000	
		7,000
Total equity and liabilities		66,000

Required

Prepare the consolidated balance sheet of P Co at 31 December 20X6.

Solution

The cancelling items are:

(a) P Co's asset 'investment in shares of S Co' ($40,000) cancels with S Co's liability 'share capital' ($40,000);

(b) P Co's asset 'receivables: S Co' ($2,000) cancels with S Co's liability 'payables: P Co' ($2,000).

The remaining assets and liabilities are added together to produce the following consolidated balance sheet.

P CO
CONSOLIDATED BALANCE SHEET AS AT 31 DECEMBER 20X6

	$	$
Assets		
Non-current assets		
Tangible assets		80,000
Current assets		
Inventories	28,000	
Receivables	15,000	
Cash at bank	1,000	
		44,000
Total assets		124,000

Equity and liabilities		
Equity		
70,000 $1 ordinary shares	70,000	
Reserves	35,000	
		105,000
Current liabilities		
Bank overdraft	3,000	
Payables	16,000	
		19,000
Total equity and liabilities		124,000

Note the following.

(a) P Co's bank balance is **not netted off** with S Co's bank overdraft. To offset one against the other would be less informative and would conflict with the principle that assets and liabilities should not be netted off.

(b) The share capital in the consolidated balance sheet is the **share capital of the parent company alone**. This must *always* be the case, no matter how complex the consolidation, because the share capital of subsidiary companies must *always* be a wholly cancelling item.

3.4 Part cancellation

An item may appear in the balance sheets of a parent company and its subsidiary, but not at the same amounts.

(a) The parent company may have acquired **shares in the subsidiary** at a price **greater or less than their nominal value**. The asset will appear in the parent company's accounts at cost, while the liability will appear in the subsidiary's accounts at par value. This raises the issue of **goodwill**, which is dealt with later in this chapter.

(b) Even if the parent company acquired shares at par value, it **may not** have **acquired all the shares of the subsidiary** (so the subsidiary may be only partly owned). This raises the issue of **minority interests**, which are also dealt with later in this chapter.

(c) The inter-company trading balances may be out of step because of **goods or cash in transit**.

(d) One company may have **issued loan stock** of which a **proportion only** is taken up by the other company.

4 Minority interests

FAST FORWARD

In the consolidated balance sheet it is necessary to distinguish minority interests from those net assets attributable to the group and financed by shareholders' equity.

It was mentioned earlier that the total assets and liabilities of subsidiary companies are included in the consolidated balance sheet, even in the case of subsidiaries which are only partly owned. A proportion of the net assets of such subsidiaries in fact belongs to investors from outside the group (**minority interests**).

The net assets of a company are financed by share capital and reserves. The consolidation procedure for dealing with partly owned subsidiaries is to **calculate the proportion of ordinary shares, preferred shares and reserves attributable to minority interests.**

4.1 Example: minority interests

P Co has owned 75% of the share capital of S Co since the date of S Co's incorporation. Their latest balance sheets are given below.

P CO
BALANCE SHEET

	$	$
Assets		
Non-current assets		
Tangible assets	50,000	
30,000 $1 ordinary shares in S Co at cost	30,000	
		80,000
Current assets		45,000
Total assets		125,000
Equity and liabilities		
Equity		
80,000 $1 ordinary shares	80,000	
Reserves	25,000	
		105,000
Current liabilities		20,000
Total equity and liabilities		125,000

S CO
BALANCE SHEET

	$	$
Assets		
Tangible non-current assets		35,000
Current assets		35,000
Total assets		70,000
Equity and liabilities		
Equity		
40,000 $1 ordinary shares	40,000	
Reserves	10,000	
		50,000
Current liabilities		20,000
Total equity and liabilities		70,000

Required

Prepare the consolidated balance sheet.

Solution

All of S Co's net assets are consolidated despite the fact that the company is only 75% owned. The amount of net assets attributable to minority interests is calculated as follows.

	$
Minority share of share capital (25% × $40,000)	10,000
Minority share of reserves (25% × $10,000)	2,500
	12,500

Of S Co's share capital of $40,000, $10,000 is included in the figure for minority interest, while $30,000 is cancelled with P Co's asset 'investment in S Co'.

The consolidated balance sheet can now be prepared.

P GROUP
CONSOLIDATED BALANCE SHEET

	$	$
Assets		
Tangible non-current assets		85,000
Current assets		80,000
Total assets		165,000
Equity and liabilities		
Equity		
Share capital	80,000	
Reserves $(25,000 + (75% × $10,000))	32,500	
		112,500
Minority interest		12,500
		125,000
Current liabilities		40,000
Total equity and liabilities		165,000

This method of disclosure of minority interests is required by IAS 1 *Presentation of financial statements.*

4.2 Procedure

In more complicated examples the following technique is recommended for dealing with minority interests.

Step 1 **Cancel common items** in the draft balance sheets. If there is a minority interest, the subsidiary company's share capital will be a partly cancelled item. Ascertain the proportion of ordinary shares and the proportion (possibly different) of preferred shares held by the minority.

Step 2 Produce a working for the **minority interest**. Add in the amounts of preferred and ordinary share capital calculated in step 1: this completes the cancellation of the subsidiary's share capital.

Add also the minority's share of each reserve in the subsidiary company. Reserves belong to equity shareholders; the proportion attributable to minority interests therefore depends on their percentage holding of *ordinary* shares.

Step 3 Produce a **separate working for each reserve** (capital, revenue etc) found in the subsidiary company's balance sheet. The initial balances on these accounts will be taken straight from the draft balance sheets of the parent and subsidiary company.

Step 4 The closing balances in these workings can be entered directly onto the **consolidated balance sheet**.

Activity 10.2

Set out below are the draft balance sheets of P Co and its subsidiary S Co. You are required to prepare the consolidated balance sheet.

P CO

	$	$
Assets		
Non-current assets		
Tangible assets		31,000
Investment in S Co		
12,000 $1 ordinary shares at cost	12,000	
4,000 $1 preferred shares at cost	4,000	
$4,000 10% debentures at cost	4,000	
		20,000
		51,000
Current assets		21,000
Total assets		72,000
Equity and liabilities		
Equity		
Ordinary shares of $1 each	40,000	
Retained earnings	22,000	
		62,000
Current liabilities		10,000
Total equity and liabilities		72,000

S CO

	$	$
Assets		
Tangible non-current assets		34,000
Current assets		32,000
Total assets		66,000
Equity and liabilities		
Equity		
Ordinary shares of $1 each	20,000	
Preferred shares of $1 each	16,000	
Capital reserve	6,000	
Retained earnings	4,000	
		46,000
Non-current liabilities		
10% debentures		10,000
Current liabilities		10,000
Total equity and liabilities		66,000

5 Dividends payable by a subsidiary

Dividends payable by a subsidiary to the parent company should be cancelled on consolidation.

When a wholly-owned subsidiary pays a dividend out of its profits, the dividend payment has no effect on the consolidated balance sheet, because the money remains within the group. It is simply transferred from the subsidiary to the parent.

The only time that dividends paid by a subsidiary are relevant to group accounts is when there is a minority interest. When the subsidiary has declared a final dividend on or before the balance sheet date, the amount of this dividend payable to the minority interest must be reported as a current liability in the balance sheet of the group.

Suppose that a parent company P Co has one subsidiary, in which it holds 90% of the shares. The profits after tax of P Co were $5 million and the profits of its subsidiary S Co were $3 million. P Co has declared a final dividend of $4 million to its shareholders before the year end. S Co has declared a final dividend of $2 million.

(a) The total consolidated profits for the year are $5 million + $3 million, i.e. $8 million.

(b) The minority interest in the group profits is 10% of $3 million, i.e. $300,000. Of this, S Limited proposes to pay a dividend of $200,000.

(c) The group share of the profits is $5 million + 90% of $3 million, i.e. $7.7 million.

(d) In the group's balance sheet, the items reported as current liabilities are the dividend declared by P Co ($4 million) and the minority dividend of $200,000.

(e) The minority interest in the share capital and reserves of the subsidiary will have increased during the year by $100,000, which is the minority's share in the retained profits of the subsidiary.

6 Goodwill arising on consolidation

FAST FORWARD

Goodwill arising on consolidation should be recorded in the group balance sheet and reviewed for impairment each year.

When a company P Co wishes to purchase shares in a company S Co it must pay the previous owners of those shares. The most obvious form of payment would be in cash. Suppose P Co purchases all 40,000 $1 shares in S Co and pays $60,000 cash. The investment in S Co shares would appear in the balance sheet of P Co at cost, $60,000. In the balance sheet of S Co, they remain at their nominal value, $40,000.

Instead of taking cash for their shares, the former shareholders might agree to accept new shares in the purchasing company. For example, the shareholders of S Co, with a nominal value of $40,000, might agree to accept 20,000 shares of $1 in P Co in exchange for their shares. If the market value of P Co shares is $3 per share, the former shareholders would be receiving shares valued at $60,000. In the accounts of P Co, the acquisition of the shares in S Co would be recorded at $60,000 (represented, in terms of the accounting equation, by share capital of $20,000 and share premium of $40,000).

The purchase value of shares in a subsidiary, as recorded in the accounts of the parent company, will not be the same as the value of the net assets acquired, as represented by the parent company's share of the share capital and reserves of the subsidiary at the time of the acquisition.

When the cost of an investment in a subsidiary exceeds the value of the assets acquired, the difference is called **goodwill arising on consolidation** (sometimes **premium on acquisition**). It is a form of purchased goodwill. Goodwill arising on consolidation is the difference between:

(a) the purchase price for the shares, and

(b) the fair value of the net assets acquired in the subsidiary. This is represented by the share capital and the reserves of the subsidiary as at the date of the acquisition.

6.1 Goodwill and pre-acquisition profits

Up to now we have assumed that S Co had nil reserves when its shares were purchased by P Co. Assuming instead that S Co had earned profits of $8,000 in the period before acquisition, its balance sheet just before the purchase would look as follows.

	$
Total tangible assets	48,000
Share capital	40,000
Reserves	8,000
	48,000

If P Co now purchases all the shares in S Co it will acquire total tangible assets worth $48,000 at a cost of $60,000. Clearly in this case S Co's intangible assets (goodwill) are being valued at $12,000. It should be apparent that any **reserves** earned by the subsidiary **prior to its acquisition** by the parent company must be **incorporated in the cancellation** process so as to arrive at a figure for goodwill arising on consolidation. In other words, not only S Co's share capital, but also its **pre-acquisition reserves**, must be cancelled against the asset 'investment in S Co' in the accounts of the parent company. The uncancelled balance of $12,000 appears in the consolidated balance sheet.

The consequence of this is that **any pre-acquisition reserves of a subsidiary company are not aggregated with the parent company's reserves** in the consolidated balance sheet. The figure of consolidated reserves comprises the reserves of the parent company plus the **post-acquisition reserves only of subsidiary companies**. The post-acquisition reserves are simply reserves now *less* reserves at acquisition.

6.2 Example: goodwill and pre-acquisition profits

Sing Co acquired the ordinary shares of Wing Co on 31 March when the draft balance sheets of each company were as follows.

SING CO
BALANCE SHEET AS AT 31 MARCH

	$
Assets	
Non-current assets	
Investment in 50,000 shares of Wing Co at cost	80,000
Current assets	40,000
Total assets	120,000
Equity and liabilities	
Equity	
Ordinary shares	75,000
Retained earnings	45,000
Total equity and liabilities	120,000

WING CO
BALANCE SHEET AS AT 31 MARCH

	$
Current assets	60,000
Equity	
50,000 ordinary shares of $1 each	50,000
Retained earnings	10,000
	60,000

Prepare the consolidated balance sheet as at 31 March.

Solution

The technique to adopt here is to produce a new working: 'Goodwill'. A proforma working is set out below.

Goodwill

	$	$
Cost of investment		X
Share of net assets acquired as represented by:		
Ordinary share capital	X	
Share premium	X	
Retained earnings on acquisition	X	
Group share a%		(X)
		X
b% preferred shares		(X)
Goodwill		X

Applying this to our example the working will look like this.

	$	$
Cost of investment		80,000
Share of net assets acquired as represented by:		
Ordinary share capital	50,000	
Retained earnings on acquisition	10,000	
	60,000	
Group share 100%		60,000
Goodwill		20,000

SING CO
CONSOLIDATED BALANCE SHEET AS AT 31 MARCH

	$
Assets	
Non-current assets	
Goodwill arising on consolidation	20,000
Current assets	100,000
	120,000
Equity	
Ordinary shares	75,000
Retained earnings	45,000
	120,000

6.3 IFRS 3: *Business combinations*

Goodwill arising on consolidation is one form of **purchased goodwill**, and is governed by IFRS 3. As explained in Chapter 8 IFRS 3 requires that goodwill arising on consolidation should **be capitalised in the consolidated balance sheet** and **reviewed for impairment every year**.

If goodwill is impaired, its value is written down. Two key consolidation workings will be affected as follows.

Goodwill	$	$
Cost of investment		X
Share of net assets acquired as represented by		
Ordinary share capital	X	
Reserves on acquisition	X	
	X	
X Group %		(X)
Goodwill at acquisition		X
Less: goodwill impairment losses to date		**(X)**
Goodwill at balance sheet date		X

Consolidated retained earnings	$	$
	P	S
Per question	X	X
Retained earnings at acquisition		(X)
		X
S-share of part-acquisition retained earnings	X	
	X	
Less: goodwill impairment losses to date	**(X)**	
	X	

Goodwill arising on consolidation is the difference between the cost of an acquisition and the value of the subsidiary's net assets acquired.

This difference can also be **negative**: the aggregate of the fair values of the separable net assets acquired may exceed what the parent company paid for them. The treatment of this 'negative goodwill' is as follows:

(a) An entity should first **re-assess** the amounts at which it has measured both the cost of the combination and the acquiree's identifiable net assets. This exercise should **identify any errors.**

(b) Any **negative goodwill remaining** should be **recognised immediately in profit or loss**, that is in the **income statement.**

6.4 Example

The draft balance sheets of Ping Co and Pong Co on 30 June 20X4 were as follows.

PING CO
BALANCE SHEET AS AT 30 JUNE 20X4

	$	$
Assets		
Non-current assets		
Tangible assets	50,000	
20,000 ordinary shares in Pong Co at cost	30,000	
		80,000
Current assets		
Inventory	3,000	
Receivables (including $4,000 dividend declared by Pong Co)	20,000	
Cash	2,000	
		25,000
Total assets		105,000
Equity and liabilities		
Equity		
Ordinary shares of $1 each	45,000	
Capital reserves	12,000	
Retained earnings	30,000	
		87,000
Current liabilities		
Owed to Pong Co	8,000	
Trade payables	10,000	
		18,000
Total equity and liabilities		105,000

PONG CO
BALANCE SHEET AS AT 30 JUNE 20X4

	$	$
Assets		
Tangible non-current assets		40,000
Current assets		
Inventory	8,000	
Owed by Ping Co	10,000	
Receivables	7,000	
		25,000
Total assets		65,000
Equity and liabilities		
Equity		
Ordinary shares of $1 each	25,000	
Capital reserves	5,000	
Retained earnings	23,000	
		53,000
Current liabilities		
Trade payables	7,000	
Declared dividends	5,000	
		12,000
Total equity and liabilities		65,000

Ping Co acquired its investment in Pong Co on 1 July 20X1 when the revenue reserves of Pong Co stood at $6,000. There have been no changes in the share capital or capital reserves of Pong Co since that date. At 30 June 20X4 Pong Co had invoiced Ping Co for goods to the value of $2,000 which had not been received by Ping Co.

Goodwill arising on consolidation is to be capitalised. There is no impairment of goodwill.

Prepare the consolidated balance sheet of Ping Co as at 30 June 20X4.

Solution

Stage 1 Ensure parent company and subsidiary balance sheets have correctly taken account of the proposed dividends.

Ping Co has $4,000 included in receivables for its share (80%) of Pong Co's proposed dividend, so there is no adjustment to make. Similarly, Pong Co has correctly accounted for its dividend payable.

Stage 2 Agree current accounts.

Ping Co has goods in transit of $2,000 making its total inventory $3,000 + $2,000 = $5,000 and its liability to Pong Co $8,000 + $2,000 = $10,000.

Stage 3 Cancel common items: these are the current accounts between the two companies of $10,000 each and the dividends payable by Pong to Ping. This leaves a payable for the dividend owed to the minority in Pong.

Stage 4 Calculate the minority interest.

Minority interest

	$
Ordinary share capital (20% × 25,000)	5,000
Capital reserves (20% × 5,000)	1,000
Retained earnings (20% × 23,000)	4,600
	10,600

Stage 5 Calculate goodwill.

Goodwill

	$	$
Cost of investment		30,000
Share of assets acquired as represented by:		
Ordinary share capital	25,000	
Capital reserves on acquisition	5,000	
Retained earnings on acquisition	6,000	
	36,000	
Group share 80%		28,800
Goodwill		1,200

This goodwill must be capitalised in the consolidated balance sheet.

Stage 6 Calculate consolidated reserves.

Consolidated capital reserve

	$
Ping Co	12,000
Share of Pong Co's post acquisition capital reserve	–
	12,000

Consolidated retained earnings

	$
Ping Co	30,000
Share of Pong Co's post acquisition retained earnings: 80% × (23,000 – 6,000)*	13,600
	43,600

* *Note.* Post acquisition retained earnings of Pong Co are simply retained earnings now less reserves at acquisition. The working could also be presented as follows.

	Ping	*Pong*
	$	$
Retained earnings per question	30,000	23,000
Less pre-acquisition		6,000
		17,000
Share of Pong: 80% × $17,000	13,600	
	43,600	

Stage 7 Prepare the consolidated balance sheet.

PING CO
CONSOLIDATED BALANCE SHEET AS AT 30 JUNE 20X4

	$	$
Assets		
Non-current assets		
Tangible assets ($50,000 + $40,000)		90,000
Intangible asset: goodwill		1,200
Current assets		
Inventories ($5,000 + $8,000)	13,000	
Receivables ($16,000 + $7,000)	23,000	
Cash	2,000	
		38,000
Total assets		129,200
Equity and liabilities		
Equity		
Ordinary shares of $1 each	45,000	
Capital reserves	12,000	
Retained earnings	43,600	
		100,600
Minority interests		10,600
		111,200
Current liabilities		
Trade payables ($10,000 + $7,000)	17,000	
Minority dividends	1,000	
		18,000
Total equity and liabilities		129,200

It has been argued by some that the question as to whether a dividend from a subsidiary to the parent company is available for onward distribution by the parent company depends on whether receipt of the dividend can be regarded as giving rise to a **realised profit** in the financial statements of the parent company and not simply whether it derives from the pre– or post-acquisition profits of the subsidiary.

In other words if the subsidiary **recovers in value** after the distribution, the **loss in value is temporary** and need not be deducted from the cost of the investment (only permanent diminutions should be provided).

Where the investment is carried at fair value, however, it is likely that a dividend which represents a return of pre-acquisition profits would give rise to a **diminution in the value** of the investment and thus should be applied in reducing the cost (carrying value) of that investment.

6.5 Fair values

FAST FORWARD

Fair values are very important in calculating goodwill.

To understand the importance of fair values in the acquisition of a subsidiary we will look at a formal definition of goodwill.

Key term

Goodwill. Any excess of the cost of the acquisition over the acquirer's interest in the fair value of the identifiable assets and liabilities acquired as at the date of the exchange transaction.

The **balance sheet of a subsidiary company** at the date it is acquired may not be a guide to the fair value of its net assets. For example, the market value of a freehold building may have risen greatly since it was acquired, but it may appear in the balance sheet at historical cost less accumulated depreciation.

Fair value is defined as follows by IFRS 3 and various other standards – it is an important definition.

Key term

Fair value. The amount for which an asset could be exchanged, or a liability settled, between knowledgeable, willing parties in an arm's length transaction.

Until now we have calculated goodwill as the difference between the cost of the investment and the **book value** of net assets acquired by the group. If this calculation is to comply with the definition above we must ensure that the book value of the subsidiary's net assets is the same as their **fair value**.

6.6 Example: fair value adjustments

P Co acquired 75% of the ordinary shares of S Co on 1 September 20X5. At that date the fair value of S Co's non-current assets was $23,000 greater than their net book value, and the balance of retained profits was $21,000. The balance sheets of both companies at 31 August 20X6 are given below. S Co has not incorporated any revaluation in its books of account.

P CO
BALANCE SHEET AS AT 31 AUGUST 20X6

	$	$
Assets		
Non-current assets		
Tangible assets	63,000	
Investment in S Co at cost	51,000	
		114,000
Current assets		82,000
Total assets		196,000
Equity and liabilities		
Equity		
Ordinary shares of $1 each	80,000	
Retained profits	96,000	
		176,000
Current liabilities		20,000
Total equity and liabilities		196,000

S CO
BALANCE SHEET AS AT 31 AUGUST 20X6

	$	$
Assets		
Tangible non-current assets		28,000
Current assets		43,000
Total assets		71,000
Equity and liabilities		
Equity		
Ordinary shares of $1 each	20,000	
Retained profits	41,000	
		61,000
Current liabilities		10,000
Total equity and liabilities		71,000

If S Co had revalued its non-current assets at 1 September 20X5, an addition of $3,000 would have been made to the depreciation charged in the income statement for 20X5/X6.

Required

Prepare P Co's consolidated balance sheet as at 31 August 20X6.

Solution

S Co has not incorporated the revaluation in its draft balance sheet. Before beginning the consolidation workings we must therefore adjust the company's balance of profits at the date of acquisition and at the balance sheet date.

S Co adjusted balance of accumulated profits

	$	$
Balance per accounts at 1 September 20X5		21,000
Consolidation adjustment: revaluation surplus		23,000
∴ Pre-acquisition profits for consolidation purposes		44,000
Profit for year ended 31 August 20X6		
Per draft accounts $(41,000 – 21,000)	20,000	
Consolidation adjustment: increase in depreciation charge	(3,000)	
		17,000
Adjusted balance of accumulated profits at 31 August 20X6		61,000

In the consolidated balance sheet, S Co's non-current assets will appear at their revalued amount: \$(28,000 + 23,000 – 3,000) = \$48,000. The consolidation workings can now be drawn up.

1 *Minority interest*

	$
Share capital (25% × \$20,000)	5,000
Revenue reserves (25% × \$61,000)	15,250
	20,250

2 *Goodwill*

	$	$
Cost of investment		51,000
Share of net assets acquired as represented by		
Ordinary share capital	20,000	
Revenue reserves \$(21,000 + 23,000)	44,000	
	64,000	
Group share (75%)		48,000
Goodwill		3,000

3 *Accumulated profits*

	P Co $	*S Co* $
Per question	96,000	41,000
Pre acquisition profits		(21,000)
Depreciation adjustment		(3,000)
Post acquisition S Co		17,000
Group share in S Co (\$17,000 × 75%)	12,750	
Group accumulated profits	108,750	

P CO CONSOLIDATED BALANCE SHEET AS AT 31 AUGUST 20X6

	$	$
Assets		
Tangible non-current assets \$(63,000 + 48,000)	111,000	
Goodwill (W2)	3,000	
		114,000
Current assets		125,000
		239,000
Equity and liabilities		
Equity		
Ordinary shares of \$1 each	80,000	
Accumulated profits (W3)	108,750	
		188,750
Minority interest (W1)		20,250
		209,000
Current liabilities		30,000
		239,000

7 Intra-group trading

FAST FORWARD

The effects of intra-group trading should be cancelled on consolidation.

Any receivable/payable balances outstanding between the companies are cancelled on consolidation. No further problem arises if all such intra-group transactions are **undertaken at cost**, without any mark-up for profit.

However, each company in a group is a separate trading entity and may wish to treat other group companies in the same way as any other customer. In this case, a company (say A Co) may buy goods at one price and sell them at a higher price to another group company (B Co). The accounts of A Co will quite properly include the profit earned on sales to B Co; and similarly B Co's balance sheet will include inventories at their cost to B Co, ie at the amount at which they were purchased from A Co.

This gives rise to two problems.

(a) Although A Co makes a profit as soon as it sells goods to B Co, the group does not make a sale or achieve a profit until an outside customer buys the goods from B Co.

(b) Any purchases from A Co which remain unsold by B Co at the year end will be included in B Co's inventory. Their balance sheet value will be their cost to B Co, which is not the same as their cost to the group.

The objective of consolidated accounts is to present the financial position of several connected companies as that of a single entity, the group. This means that **in a consolidated balance sheet the only profits recognised should be those earned by the group** in providing goods or services to outsiders; and similarly, inventory in the consolidated balance sheet should be valued at cost to the group.

Suppose that a parent company P Co buys goods for $1,600 and sells them to a wholly owned subsidiary S Co for $2,000. The goods are in S Co's inventory at the year end and appear in S Co's balance sheet at $2,000. In this case, P Co will record a profit of $400 in its individual accounts, but from the group's point of view the figures are:

Cost	$1,600
External sales	nil
Closing inventory at cost	$1,600
Profit/loss	nil

If we add together the figures for retained reserves and inventory in the individual balance sheets of P Co and S Co the resulting figures for consolidated reserves and consolidated inventory will each be overstated by $400. A **consolidation adjustment** is therefore necessary as follows. Group reserves and group inventory are reduced by the amount of the profit unrealised by the group.

7.1 Minority interests in unrealised intra-group profits

A further problem occurs where a subsidiary company which is **not wholly owned is involved in intra-group trading** within the group. If a subsidiary S Co is 75% owned and sells goods to the parent company for $16,000 cost plus $4,000 profit, ie for $20,000 and if these items are unsold by P Co at the balance sheet date, the 'unrealised' profit of $4,000 earned by S Co and charged to P Co will be partly owned by the minority interest of S Co. As far as the minority interest of S Co is concerned, their share (25% of $4,000) amounting to $1,000 of profit on the sale of goods would appear to have been fully realised. It is only the group that has not yet made a profit on the sale.

There are three different possibilities as regards the treatment of these intra-group profits.

(a) Remove only the group's share of the profit loading

(b) **Remove the whole profit loading, charging the minority with their proportion**

(c) Remove the whole of the profit without charging the minority (to reduce group reserves by the whole profit loading)

The method given under (b) is usually considered best practice. Group inventory is still reduced by the whole amount of the unrealised profit. Group reserves are reduced by the group share and the minority interest by its share.

8 Summary: consolidated balance sheet

Purpose	To show the net assets which P controls and the ownership of those assets
Net assets	Always 100% of P net assets plus 100% of S net assets
Share capital	P only
Reason	Simply reporting to the holding company's shareholders in another form.
Reserves	100% P reserves plus the group's share of the post-acquisition retained reserves of S (less consolidation adjustments)
Reason	To show the extent to which the group actually owns total assets less liabilities
Minority interest	Minority interest share of S's consolidated net assets.
Reason	To show the extent to which other parties own net assets that are under the control of the parent company

9 Consolidated income statement

FAST FORWARD

The consolidated income statement combines the income statements of each group company. The principles applied to the consolidated balance sheet also apply to the consolidated income statement.

9.1 Simple example: consolidated income statement

P Co acquired 75% of the ordinary shares of S Co on that company's incorporation in 20X3. The summarised income statements of the two companies for the year ending 31 December 20X6 are set out below.

	P Co	*S Co*
	$	$
Sales revenue	75,000	38,000
Cost of sales	30,000	20,000
Gross profit	45,000	18,000
Administrative expenses	14,000	8,000
Profit before taxation	31,000	10,000
Taxation	10,000	2,000
Profit for the year	21,000	8,000
Retained earnings brought forward	87,000	17,000
Retained earnings carried forward	108,000	25,000

Required

Prepare the consolidated income statement.

Solution

P CO
CONSOLIDATED INCOME STATEMENT
FOR THE YEAR ENDED 31 DECEMBER 20X6

	$
Sales revenue (75 + 38)	113,000
Cost of sales (30 + 20)	50,000
Gross profit	63,000
Administrative expenses (14 + 8)	22,000
Profit before taxation	41,000
Taxation (10 + 2)	12,000
Profit after taxation	29,000
Minority interest (25% × $8,000)	2,000
Group profit for the year	27,000
Retained earnings brought forward	
(group share only: 87 + (17 × 75%))	99,750
Retained earnings carried forward	126,750

Notice how the minority interest is dealt with.

(a) Down to the line **'profit after taxation'** the **whole** of S Co's results is included without reference to group share or minority share. A **one-line adjustment** is then inserted to deduct the minority's share of S Co's profit after taxation.

(b) The minority's share ($4,250) of S Co's retained profits brought forward is **excluded**. This means that the carried forward figure of $126,750 is the figure which would appear in the balance sheet for group retained reserves.

This last point may be clearer if we revert to our **balance sheet technique** and construct the working for group reserves.

Group reserves

	$
P Co	108,000
Share of S Co's post-acquisition retained earnings (75% × $25,000)	18,750
	126,750

The minority share of S Co's reserves comprises the minority interest in the $17,000 profits brought forward plus the minority interest ($2,000) in $8,000 retained profits for the year.

Notice that a consolidated income statement **links up** with a consolidated balance sheet exactly as in the case of an individual company's accounts: the figure of retained earnings carried forward at the bottom of the income statement appears as the figure for retained earnings in the balance sheet. (*Note.* Under IAS 1 this would be shown as a movement on reserves; for convenience the reserve movements are shown here with the income statement.)

9.2 Intra-group trading

Like the consolidated balance sheet, the consolidated income statement should deal with the results of the group as those of a single entity. When one company in a group sells goods to another an identical amount is added to the sales revenue of the first company and to the cost of sales of the second. Yet as far as the entity's dealings with outsiders are concerned no sale has taken place.

The consolidated figures for sales revenue and cost of sales should represent **sales to**, and **purchases from, outsiders**. An adjustment is therefore necessary to reduce the sales revenue and cost of sales figures by the value of intra-group sales during the year.

We have also seen in an earlier chapter that any unrealised profits on intra-group trading should be excluded from the figure for group profits. This will occur whenever goods sold at a profit within the group remain in the inventory of the purchasing company at the year end. The best way to deal with this is to **calculate the unrealised profit on unsold inventories at the year end and reduce consolidated gross profit by this amount**. Cost of sales will be the balancing figure.

9.3 Example: intra-group trading

Suppose in our earlier example that S Co had recorded sales of $5,000 to P Co during 20X6. S Co had purchased these goods from outside suppliers at a cost of $3,000. One half of the goods remained in P Co's inventory at 31 December 20X6. Prepare the revised consolidated income statement.

Solution

The consolidated income statement for the year ended 31 December 20X6 would now be as follows.

	$
Sales revenue (75 + 38 – 5)	108,000
Cost of sales (balancing figure)	(46,000)
Gross profit (45 + 18 – 1*)	62,000
Administrative expenses	(22,000)
Profit before taxation	40,000
Taxation	(12,000)
Profit after taxation	28,000
Minority interest (25% × ($8,000 – $1,000*))	(1,750)
Group profit for the year	26,250
Retained earnings brought forward	99,750
Retained earnings carried forward	126,000

*Unrealised profit: ½ × ($5,000 – $3,000)

An adjustment will be made for the unrealised profit against the inventory figure in the consolidated balance sheet, as explained earlier in this chapter.

9.4 Pre-acquisition profits

As explained above, the figure for retained earnings at the bottom of the consolidated income statement must be the same as the figure for retained earnings in the consolidated balance sheet. We have seen in the previous section that retained earnings in the consolidated balance sheet comprise:

(a) The **whole of the parent company's** retained earnings

(b) A **proportion of the subsidiary company's** retained earnings. The proportion is the **group's share of post-acquisition retained earnings** in the subsidiary. From the total retained earnings of the subsidiary we must therefore **exclude** both the **minority's share** of total retained earnings and the **group's share of pre-acquisition** retained earnings.

A **similar procedure is necessary in the consolidated income statement** if it is to link up with the consolidated balance sheet. Previous examples have shown how the minority share of profits is excluded in the income statement. Their share of profits for the year is deducted from profit after tax, while the figure for profits brought forward in the consolidation schedule includes only the group's proportion of the subsidiary's profits.

In the same way, when considering examples which include pre-acquisition profits in a subsidiary, the figure for profits brought forward should include only the group's share of the post-acquisition retained profits. If the subsidiary is **acquired during the accounting year**, it is therefore necessary to apportion its profit for the year between pre-acquisition and post-acquisition elements.

9.5 Goodwill

If goodwill suffers an impairment in the accounting period administrative expenses in the consolidated income statement will be charged with the fall in value.

Activity 10.3

The following information relates to the Brodick group of companies for the year to 30 April 20X7.

	Brodick Co	*Lamlash Co*	*Corrie Co*
	$'000	$'000	$'000
Sales revenue	1,100	500	130
Cost of sales	630	300	70
Gross profit	470	200	60
Administrative expenses	105	150	20
Dividend from Lamlash Co	24	–	–
Dividend from Corrie Co	6	–	–
Profit before tax	395	50	40
Taxation	65	10	20
Profit after tax	330	40	20
Interim dividend	50	10	–
Final dividend	150	20	10
Profit for the year	130	10	10
Reserves brought forward	460	106	30
Reserves carried forward	590	116	40

Additional information

(a) The issued share capital of the group was as follows.

Brodick Co : 5,000,000 ordinary shares of $1 each.
Lamlash Co : 1,000,000 ordinary shares of $1 each.
Corrie Co : 400,000 ordinary shares of $1 each.

(b) Brodick Co purchased 80% of the issued share capital of Lamlash Co in 20X0. At that time, the revenue reserves of Lamlash amounted to $56,000.

(c) Brodick Co purchased 60% of the issued share capital of Corrie Co in 20X4. At that time, the revenue reserves of Corrie amounted to $20,000.

(d) Brodick Co recognises dividends declared by other group companies in its income statement. All dividends were declared on 30 April 20X7.

Required

Insofar as the information permits, prepare the Brodick group of companies' consolidated income statement for the year to 30 April 20X7 in accordance with IASs, and the movement on reserves.

Note. You should append a statement showing the make up of the 'reserves carried forward', and your workings should be submitted.

10 Summary: consolidated income statement

Purpose	To show the results of the group for an accounting period as if it were a single entity.
Sales revenue to profit after tax	100% P + 100% S (excluding dividend receivable from subsidiary and adjustments for inter-company transactions). Charge for impairment of goodwill during the period will be treated as an administrative expense.
Reason	To show the results of the group which were controlled by the parent company.
Intra-group sales	Strip out intra-group activity from both sales revenue and cost of sales.
Unrealised profit on inter-company sales	(a) Goods sold by P. Increase cost of sales by unrealised profit. (b) Goods sold by S. Increase cost of sales by full amount of unrealised profit and decrease minority interest by their share of unrealised profit.
Minority interests	S's profit after tax (PAT) X Less: * unrealised profit (X) X MI% X
Reason	To show the extent to which profits generated through P's control are in fact owned by other parties.
Dividends	P's only.
Reason	S's dividend is due (a) to P; and (b) to MI. P has taken in its share by including the results of S in the consolidated income statement. The MI have taken their share by being given a proportion of S's PAT. Remember: PAT = dividends + profit for the year.
Reserves carried forward	As per the balance sheet calculations.

11 Accounting for associates

FAST FORWARD

IAS 28 requires that, in consolidated accounts, **associates** should be accounted for using **equity accounting principles**.

IAS 28 requires all investments in associates to be accounted for in the consolidated accounts using the **equity method**, *unless* the investment is classified as 'held for sale' in accordance with IFRS 5 in which case it should be accounted for under IFRS 5 (see Chapter 7), or the exemption in the paragraph below applies.

Key term

- **Equity method**. A method of accounting whereby the investment is initially recorded at cost and adjusted thereafter for the post acquisition change in the investor's share of net assets of the investee. The profit or loss of the investor includes the investor's share of the profit or loss of the investee.

An investor is exempt from applying the equity method if:

(a) It is a parent exempt from preparing consolidated financial statements under IAS 27, or

(b) All of the following apply:

(i) The investor is a **wholly-owned subsidiary** or it is a **partially owned subsidiary** of another entity and its other owners, including those not otherwise entitled to vote, have been informed about, and do not object to, the investor not applying the equity method;

(ii) The investor's securities are **not publicly traded**

(iii) It is **not in the process of issuing securities** in public securities markets; and

(iv) The **ultimate or intermediate parent** publishes consolidated financial statements that comply with International Financial Reporting Standards.

If an investor that does ***not*** **issue consolidated financial statements** (ie it has no subsidiaries) but has an investment in an associate this should be included in the financial statements of the investor normally at cost.

11.1 Application of the equity method: consolidated accounts

Many of the procedures required to apply the equity method are the same as are required for full consolidation. In particular, **intra-group unrealised profits** must be excluded.

Goodwill is calculated as the difference (positive or negative) between the cost of acquisition and the investor's share of the fair values of the net identifiable assets of the associate. This should be treated as required by IFRS 3.

11.2 Equity method: income statement

The basic principle is that the investing company (X Co) should take account of its **share of the earnings** of the associate, Y Co, whether or not Y Co distributes the earnings as dividends. X Co achieves this by adding to consolidated profit the group's share of Y Co's profit after tax.

Notice the difference between this treatment and the **consolidation** of a subsidiary company's results. If Y Co were a subsidiary X Co would take credit for the whole of its sales revenue, cost of sales etc and would then make a one-line adjustment to remove any minority share.

Under equity accounting, the associated company's sales revenue, cost of sales and so on are ***not*** **amalgamated** with those of the group. Instead the group share only of the associate's profit before tax and tax charge for the year is added to the corresponding lines of the parent company and its subsidiaries. In effect, this is the corresponding treatment to the associate's parent company's treatment: the investing company is the minority interest here.

11.3 Equity method: balance sheet

A figure for **investment in associates** is shown which at the time of the acquisition must be stated at cost. This amount will increase (decrease) each year by the amount of the group's share of the associated company's profit (loss) for the year.

11.4 Example: associate

P Co, a company with subsidiaries, acquires 25,000 of the 100,000 $1 ordinary shares in A Co for $60,000 on 1 January 20X8. In the year to 31 December 20X8, A Co earns profits after tax of $24,000, from which it pays a dividend of $6,000.

How will A Co's results be accounted for in the individual and consolidated accounts of P Co for the year ended 31 December 20X8?

Solution

In the **individual accounts** of P Co, the investment will be recorded on 1 January 20X8 at cost. Unless there is an impairment in the value of the investment (see below), this amount will remain in the individual balance sheet of P Co permanently. The only entry in P Co's individual income statement will be to record dividends received. For the year ended 31 December 20X8, P Co will record the cash receipt of $1,500 ($6,000 × 25%) and record the income of $1,500.

In the **consolidated accounts** of P Co equity accounting principles will be used to account for the investment in A Co. Consolidated profit after tax will include the group's share of A Co's profit after tax (25% × $24,000 = $6,000). To the extent that this has been distributed as dividend, it is already included in P Co's individual accounts and will automatically be brought into the consolidated results. That part of the group's profit share which has not been distributed as dividend ($4,500) will be brought into consolidation.

The asset 'Investment in associates' is then stated at $64,500, being cost plus the group share of post-acquisition retained profits.

11.5 Consolidated income statement

FAST FORWARD

In the **consolidated income statement** the investing group takes credit for its share of the **after-tax** profits of associates, whether or not they are distributed as dividends.

A **consolidation schedule** may be used to prepare the consolidated income statement of a group with associates. The treatment of associates' profits in the following example should be studied carefully.

The following consolidation schedule relates to the P Co group, consisting of the parent company, an 80% owned subsidiary (S Co) and an associated company (A Co) in which the group has a 30% interest.

CONSOLIDATION SCHEDULE

	Group	*P Co*	*S Co*	*A Co*
	$'000	$'000	$'000	$'000
Sales revenue	1,400	600	800	300
Cost of sales	770	370	400	120
Gross profit	630	230	400	180
Distribution costs and administrative expenses (including depreciation, directors' emoluments etc)	290	110	180	80
	340	120	220	100
Interest receivable	30	30	–	–
	370	150	220	100
Interest payable	(20)	–	(20)	
	350	150	200	100
Group share of associated company profit	18	–	–	
(30% × 60)	368	150	200	100
Taxation	(145)	(55)	(90)	(40)
Profit after taxation	223	95	110	60
Minority interest	(22)		(22)	
	201	95	88	60
Inter-company dividends	–	20	(18)	(2)
Group profit	201	115	70	58

Note the following.

(a) **Group sales revenue, group gross profit and costs** such as depreciation etc **exclude** the sales revenue, gross profit and costs etc of **associates**.

(b) The **group share** of the associated **post-tax profits is credited** to the group income statement (here, 30% of \$60,000 = \$18,000). If the associated company had been acquired during the year, it would be necessary to deduct the pre-acquisition profits.

(c) The minority interest will only ever apply to subsidiary companies.

(d) Inter-company dividends from subsidiaries and associates should all be recorded.

11.6 Pro-forma consolidated income statement

The following is a **suggested layout** (using the figures given in the illustration above) for the consolidated income statement for a company having subsidiaries as well as associates.

	\$'000	\$'000
Revenue		1,400
Cost of sales		770
Gross profit		630
Distribution costs and administrative expenses		290
		340
Interest receivable		30
		370
Finance costs		(20)
		350
Share of profits (less losses) of associated companies		18
Profit before tax		368
Income tax expense		(145)
Profit for the year		223
Attributable to:		
Equity holders of the parent		201
Minority interest		22
		223

11.7 Consolidated balance sheet

FAST FORWARD

In the **consolidated balance sheet** the investment in associates should be shown as:

- **Group share of associates' assets other than goodwill**: plus
- **Any goodwill arising** on the acquisition of the associate.

As explained earlier, the consolidated balance sheet will contain an **asset 'Investment in associates'**. The amount at which this asset is stated will be its original cost plus the group's share of any **profits earned since acquisition** which have not been distributed as dividends.

11.8 Example: consolidated balance sheet

On 1 January 20X6 the net tangible assets of A Co amount to \$220,000, financed by 100,000 \$1 ordinary shares and revenue reserves of \$120,000. P Co, a company with subsidiaries, acquires 30,000 of the shares in A Co for \$75,000. During the year ended 31 December 20X6 A Co's profit after tax is \$30,000, from which dividends of \$12,000 are paid.

Show how P Co's investment in A Co would appear in the consolidated balance sheet at 31 December 20X6.

Solution

CONSOLIDATED BALANCE SHEET
AS AT 31 DECEMBER 20X6 (extract)

	$
Non-current assets	
Investment in associate	
Cost	75,000
Group share of post-acquisition retained profits (30% × $18,000)	5,400
	80,400

An important point to note is that this figure of $80,400 can be arrived at in a completely different way. It is the sum of:

(a) the group's share of A Co's net assets at 31 December 20X6, and
(b) the goodwill paid for the shares acquired.

This can be shown as follows.

		$	$
(a)	A Co's net assets at 31 December 20X6		
	Net assets at 1 January 20X6	220,000	
	Retained profit for year	18,000	
	Net assets at 31 December 20X6	238,000	
	Group share (30%)		71,400
(b)	Goodwill		
	Net assets acquired by group on 1 Jan 20X6 (30% × $220,000)	66,000	
	Price paid for shares	75,000	
	Goodwill		9,000
	Investment in associate per balance sheet		80,400

11.9 Associates: summary

Income statement	Include group share of associates' profit after tax as a single amount.	
Balance sheet	Interests in associates should be stated at:	$
	(a) Group share of net assets other than goodwill of associate at fair value (at the time of acquisition)	X
	(b) Goodwill on acquisition so far as it has not already been written off	X
		X

12 Joint ventures and jointly controlled entities

FAST FORWARD

Joint ventures are characterised by **joint control** evidenced by a **contractual arrangement**.

Two or more persons may decide to enter into a business venture together without wishing to form a formal long-term partnership.

Usually the venturers agree to place limitations on their activities, for example, a joint venture to manufacture and sell 'total eclipse of the sun' souvenirs could be limited by time, while a joint venture to buy and sell a bankrupt's inventory (a fairly common occurrence in practice) comes to an end when all the inventory has been sold.

Joint ventures are often found when each party can **contribute in different ways** to the venture. For example, one venturer may provide finance, another purchases or manufactures goods, while a third offers his marketing skills.

Joint ventures generally have the following characteristics.

- They are **limited by time and/or activity**
- The venturers usually **carry on their principal businesses** at the same time
- **Separate books** for the venture are **not** normally maintained
- The venturers usually agree to a **profit/ loss sharing ratio** for the purpose of the venture

IAS 31 *Interests in joint ventures* covers all types of joint ventures. It is not concerned with the accounts of the joint venture itself (if separate accounts are maintained), but rather **how the interest in a joint venture is accounted for by each joint venturer** (ie each 'partner' in the joint venture).

The assets and liabilities, income and expenses of the joint venture must be reported in the financial statements of the venturers and investors, whatever the form of the joint venture.

IAS 31 looks at the various forms of joint venture which may be undertaken and then looks at how joint ventures are dealt with in the **individual financial statements** of the venturer *and* the **group financial statements**.

12.1 Definitions

The IAS begins by listing some important definitions.

Key terms

- **Joint venture.** A contractual arrangement whereby two or more parties undertake an economic activity which is subject to joint control.
- **Control.** The power to govern the financial and operating policies of an economic activity so as to obtain benefits from its activities.
- **Joint control.** The contractually agreed sharing of control over an economic activity.
- **Significant influence.** The power to participate in the financial and operating policy decisions of an economic activity but is not control or joint control over those policies.
- **Venturer.** A party to a joint venture that has joint control over that joint venture.
- **Proportionate consolidation**. A method of accounting whereby a venturer's share of each of the assets, liabilities, income and expenses of a jointly controlled entity is combined line-by-line with similar items in the venturer's financial statements or reported as separate line items in the venturer's financial statements.
- **Equity method**. A method of accounting whereby an interest in a jointly controlled entity is initially recorded at cost and adjusted thereafter for the post acquisition change in the venturer's share of net assets of the jointly controlled entity. The income statement reflects the venturer's share of the profit or loss of the jointly controlled entity. *(IAS 31)*

12.2 Forms of joint venture

The **form and structure** of joint ventures can vary enormously. There are, however, three main types identified by the standard.

- **Jointly controlled operations**
- **Jointly controlled assets**
- **Jointly controlled entities**

We will look at each of these below. They are all usually described as joint ventures and fulfil the definition of a joint venture given above.

Whatever the form and structure, every joint venture will have **two characteristics.**

- Two (or more) venturers are bound by a **contractual arrangement**.
- The contractual relationship establishes **joint control**.

12.3 Jointly controlled operations

In this type of joint venture, there is no separate entity set up to deal with the joint venture, whether in the form of a corporation, partnership or other entity. Instead, the venturers **use their own assets and resources** for the joint venture, ie their own property, plant and equipment is used and they carry their own inventories.

The venturers also incur their own expenses and liabilities, and raise their own finance which then represents their own obligations. In these situations, the activities of the joint venture will often be performed by the venturers' staff alongside the venturers' **other similar activities**. The way that income and expenses are shared between the venturers is usually laid out in the joint venture agreement.

Activity 10.4

Can you think of an example of a situation where such a joint venture might occur?

When a joint venture in the nature of jointly controlled operations exists, IAS 31 requires a venturer to recognise the following in its financial statements.

(a) The **assets** it controls and the **liabilities** it incurs

(b) The **expenses** it incurs and the **income** it earns from the sale of goods or services by the joint venture

Separate accounts for the joint venture are not required, although the venturers may prepare management accounts for the joint venture, in order to assess its performance.

12.4 Jointly controlled assets

In this type of joint venture, the venturers have **joint control**, and often **joint ownership** of some or all of the assets in the joint venture. These assets may have been contributed to the joint venture or purchased for the purpose of the joint venture, but in any case they are **dedicated to the activities of the joint venture**. These assets are used to produce benefits for the venturers; each venturer takes a share of the output and bears a share of the incurred expenses.

As with jointly controlled operations, this type of joint venture does *not* involve setting up a corporation, partnership or any other kind of entity. The venturers **control their share of future economic benefits** through their share in the jointly controlled asset.

IAS 31 requires each venturer to recognise (ie include in their financial statements) the following in respect of its interest in jointly controlled assets.

(a) Its **share of the jointly controlled assets**, classified by their nature, eg a share of a jointly controlled oil pipeline should be classified as property, plant and equipment

(b) Any **liabilities** it has incurred, eg in financing its share of the assets

(c) Its share of any **liabilities incurred jointly** with the other venturers which relate to the joint venture

(d) Any **income** from the sale or use of its share of the joint venture's output, together with its share of any **expenses** incurred by the joint venture

(e) Any **expenses** which it has incurred in respect of its interest in the joint venture, eg those relating to financing the venturer's interest in the assets and selling its share of the output

This treatment of jointly controlled assets reflects the **substance and economic reality,** and (usually) the legal form of the joint venture. Separate accounting records need not be kept for the joint venture and financial statements for the joint venture need not be prepared. Management accounts may be produced, however, in order to monitor the performance of the joint venture.

12.5 Jointly controlled entities

FAST FORWARD

Jointly controlled entities may be accounted for using

– proportionate consolidation
– equity method.

This type of joint venture involves the setting up of a corporation, partnership or other entity. This **operates in the same way as any other entity**, except that the venturers have a contractual arrangement establishing their joint control over the economic activity of the entity.

A jointly controlled entity effectively operates as a **separate entity**: it controls the joint venture's assets, incurs liabilities and expenses and earns income. It can, as a separate entity, enter into contracts in its own name and raise finance to fund the activities of the joint venture. The venturers share the results of the jointly controlled entity, and in some cases they may also share the output of the joint venture.

The **substance** of jointly controlled entities is often similar to the joint ventures discussed above (jointly controlled assets/operations). In other circumstances, a jointly controlled entity may be set up to deal with only certain aspects of the jointly controlled operations.

As a separate entity, the jointly controlled entity must maintain its **own accounting records** and will **prepare financial statements** according to national requirements and IASs.

IAS 31 states that where a venturer prepares separate financial statements (as a single company), investments in jointly controlled entities should be *either*:

(a) accounted for at **cost**, *or*
(b) in accordance with **IAS 39**.

The same accounting treatment must be applied consistently to all jointly controlled entities.

In the consolidated financial statements of a venturer IAS 31 requires all interests in jointly controlled entities to be accounted for using *either* proportionate consolidation *or* the equity method.

12.5.1 The proportionate consolidation method

A venturer can report its interest in a jointly controlled entity in its consolidated financial statements using one of the two reporting formats for **proportionate consolidation**.

IAS 31 maintains that this treatment reflects the **substance and economic reality** of the arrangement, ie the control the venturer has over its share of future economic benefits through its share of the assets and liabilities of the venture.

The proportionate consolidation method differs from normal consolidation in that only the group share of assets and liabilities, income and expenses are brought into account. There is therefore **no minority interest**.

There are **two different formats** with which the proportionate consolidation method can be used.

(a) **Combine on a line-by-line basis** the venturer's share of each of the assets, liabilities, income and expenses of the jointly controlled entity with the similar items in the venturer's consolidated financial statements.

(b) Include in the venturer's consolidated financial statements **separate line items** for the venturer's share of the assets and liabilities, income and expenses of the jointly controlled entity.

12.5.2 Example: proportionate consolidation

Both of the above methods produce exactly the same net results and they are demonstrated in this example.

Set out below are the draft accounts of Parent Co and its subsidiaries and of Joint Venture Co. Parent Co acquired 50% of the equity capital of Joint Venture Co three years ago when the latter's reserves stood at $40,000.

SUMMARISED BALANCE SHEETS

	Parent Co & subsidiaries	*Joint Venture Co*
	$'000	$'000
Tangible non-current assets	220	170
Investment in joint venture	75	–
Current assets	100	50
Loan to Joint Venture	20	–
	415	220
Share capital ($1 shares)	250	100
Reserves	165	100
Loan from Parent Co	–	20
	415	220

SUMMARISED INCOME STATEMENTS

	Parent Co & subsidiaries	*Joint Venture Co*
	$'000	$'000
Net profit	95	80
Taxation	35	30
	60	50
Dividends payable	50	10
Retained profit	10	40

Parent Co has taken credit for the dividend receivable from Joint Venture Co.

You are required to prepare the summarised consolidated balance sheet of Parent Co, under each of the formats of proportionate consolidation described by IAS 31.

Solution: line-by-line format

PARENT CO
CONSOLIDATED BALANCE SHEET

	$'000
Tangible non-current assets (220 + (50% × 170))	305
Goodwill (W1)	5
Current assets (100 + (50% × 50))	125
Loan to joint venturer (note)	10
	445
Share capital	250
Reserves (W2)	195
	445

Note. The loan is the proportion of the $20,000 lent to the other venturer.

Workings

1 *Goodwill*

	$'000
Cost of investment	75
Share of net assets acquired (50% × 140)	70
	5

2 *Reserves*

	Parent Co & subsidiaries	*Joint Venture Co*
	$'000	$'000
Per question	165	100
Pre-acquisition		(40)
Post-acquisition		60
Group share in joint venture ($60 x 50%)	30	
Group reserves	195	

Solution: separate line method

PARENT CO
CONSOLIDATED BALANCE SHEET

	$'000	$'000
Tangible non-current assets		
Group	220	
Joint venture (170 × 50%)	85	
		305
Goodwill (as above)		5
Current assets		
Group	100	
Joint venture (50% × 50)	25	
		125
Loan to joint venturer		10
		445
Share capital		250
Reserves (as above)		195
		445

In both these cases the **consolidated income statements** would be shown in the same way.

The use of the proportionate consolidation method should be **discontinued** from the date the venturer ceases to have joint control over the entity.

12.5.3 Allowed alternative: equity method

A venturer can report its interest in a jointly controlled entity in its consolidated financial statements under the **equity method**, as used for associates. The argument for this method is that it is misleading to combine controlled items with jointly controlled items. It is also felt by some that venturers have significant influence over the entity, not merely joint control.

Key learning points

- Group accounts show the results of the parent plus any subsidiaries as if they were a single company.
- Balances of the parent company and subsidiaries are added together on a line-by-line basis. Intra-group balances are cancelled out.
- In the consolidated balance sheet it is necessary to distinguish minority interests from those net assets attributable to the group and financed by shareholders' equity.
- Dividends payable by a subsidiary to the parent company should be cancelled on consolidation.
- Goodwill arising on consolidation should be recorded in the group balance sheet and reviewed for impairment each year.
- The effects of intra-group trading should be cancelled on consolidation.
- The consolidated income statement combines the income statements of each group company. The principles applied to the consolidated balance sheet also apply to the consolidated income statement.
- IAS 28 requires that, in consolidated accounts, **associates** should be accounted for using **equity accounting principles**.
- In the **consolidated income statement** the investing group takes credit for its **share of the after-tax profits** of associates, whether or not they are distributed as dividends.
- In the **consolidated balance sheet**, the investment in associates should be shown as:
  - **Group share of the associates' assets other than goodwill**: plus
  - Any **goodwill arising on the acquisition of the associate**.
- Joint ventures are characterised by **joint control** evidenced by a **contractual arrangement.**
- **Jointly controlled entities** may be accounted for using:
  - **Proportionate consolidation**: combine items on a line by line basis, or on separate lines
  - **Equity method**: as per IAS 28

Quick quiz

1 Define a 'subsidiary'.

2 When can control be assumed?

3 What accounting treatment does IAS 27 require of a parent company?

4 When is a parent exempted from preparing consolidated financial statements?

5 What is a minority interest?

6 Chicken Co owns 80% of Egg Co. Egg Co sells goods to Chicken Co at cost plus 50%. The total invoiced sales to Chicken Co by Egg Co in the year ended 31 December 20X9 were $900,000 and, of these sales, goods which had been invoiced at $60,000 were held in inventory by Chicken Co at 31 December 20X9. What is the reduction in aggregate group gross profit?

7 What are the components making up the figure of minority interest in a consolidated balance sheet?

8 Goodwill is always positive. True or false?

9 Barley Co has owned 100% of the issued share capital of Oats Co for many years. Barley Co sells goods to Oats Co at cost plus 20%. The following information is available for the year:

Revenue	– Barley Co	$460,000
	– Oats Co	$120,000

During the year Barley Co sold goods to Oats Co for $60,000 of which $18,000 were still held in inventory by Oats at the year end.

At what amount should revenue appear in the consolidated income statement?

10 Define an associate.

11 What method of accounting is applied to (a) subsidiaries (b) associates and (c) joint ventures?

Answers to quick quiz

1 An entity that is controlled by another entity.

2 When the parent owns more than half (ie over 50%) of the voting power of an entity, **unless** it can be clearly shown that such ownership does not constitute control.

3 The accounts of parent and subsidiary are combined and presented as a single entity.

4 When the parent is itself a wholly owned subsidiary, or a partially owned subsidiary and the minority interests do not object.

5 The part of the net profit or loss and the net assets attributable to interests not owned by the parent.

6 $\$60{,}000 \times \dfrac{50}{150} = \$20{,}000$

7 The minority's share of ordinary shares, preferred shares and reserves.

8 False. Goodwill can be negative if the purchaser has 'got a bargain'.

9 Revenue: 460 + 120 – 60 = $520,000

10 An entity in which an investor has a significant influence, but which is not a subsidiary or a joint venture of the investor.

11 (a) Consolidation
(b) Equity accounting
(c) Proportionate consolidation or equity accounting

Answers to activities

10.1 1 Clump is a subsidiary of P Co Bump is also a subsidiary of P because it is a subsidiary of a subsidiary of P (i.e. a sub-subsidiary).

2 Pump is an associate.

3 The shares held by P in Frump are simply an investment.

4 Stump and Slump are both subsidiaries of P Co. Together, they hold 60% of the shares in Mump. Mump is therefore a (sub-)subsidiary of P.

10.2 Partly cancelling items are the components of P Co's investment in S Co, ie ordinary shares, preferred shares and debentures. Minorities have an interest in 75% (12,000/16,000) of S Co's preferred shares and 40% (8,000/20,000) of S Co's ordinary shares, including reserves.

You should now produce workings for minority interests, capital reserve and revenue reserve as follows.

Workings

1 *Minority interests*

		$
Ordinary share capital (40% of 20,000)		8,000
Reserves:	capital (40% × 6,000)	2,400
	revenue (40% × 4,000)	1,600
		12,000
Preferred share capital (75% × 16,000)		12,000
		24,000

2 *Capital reserve*

	$
P Co	–
Share of S Co's capital reserve (60% × 6,000)	3,600
	3,600

3 *Retained earnings*

	$
P Co	22,000
Share of S Co's retained earnings (60% × 4,000)	2,400
	24,400

The results of the workings are now used to construct the consolidated balance sheet (CBS).

P GROUP
CONSOLIDATED BALANCE SHEET

	$	$
Assets		
Tangible non-current assets		65,000
Current assets		53,000
Total assets		118,000

Equity and liabilities		
Equity		
Ordinary shares of $1 each	40,000	
Capital reserve (W2)	3,600	
Retained earnings (W3)	24,400	
		68,000
Minority interests (W1)		24,000
		92,000
Non-current liabilities		
10% debentures		6,000
Current liabilities		20,000
Total equity and liabilities		118,000

Notes

(a) S Co is a subsidiary of P Co because P Co owns 60% of its ordinary capital. It is unimportant how little of the preferred share capital is owned by P Co.

(b) As always, the share capital in the consolidated balance sheet is that of the parent company alone. The share capital in S Co's balance sheet was partly cancelled against the investment shown in P Co's balance sheet, while the uncancelled portion was credited to minority interest.

(c) The figure for minority interest comprises the interest of outside investors in the share capital and reserves of the subsidiary. The uncancelled portion of S Co's debentures is not shown as part of minority interest but is disclosed separately as a liability of the group.

10.3 BRODICK GROUP
CONSOLIDATED INCOME STATEMENT
FOR THE YEAR TO 30 APRIL 20X7

	$'000
Sales revenue (1,100 + 500 + 130)	1,730
Cost of sales (630 + 300 + 70)	1,000
Gross profit	730
Administrative expenses (105 + 150 + 20)	275
Profit before taxation	455
Tax on profit (65 + 10 + 20)	95
Profit after taxation	360
Minority interests (W1)	16
Profit for the financial year	344
Dividends (parent only)	200
Profit retained for the year	144
Reserves brought forward 1 May 20X6 (W2)	506
Reserves carried forward 30 April 20X7	650

Workings

1 *Minority interests*

	$
In Lamlash (20% × profit after tax)	8,000
In Corrie (40% × profit after tax)	8,000
	16,000

2 *Retained profits brought forward*

	Brodick Co	*Lamlash Co*	*Corrie Co*
	$'000	$'000	$'000
Per question	460	106	30
Less pre-aqn		56	20
		50	10
Share of Lamlash: 80% × 50	40		
Share of Corrie: 60% × 10	6		
	506		

10.4 There are many potential answers to this question but IAS 31 uses the example of building an aircraft. Say that Boeing is to build the body of the aircraft and the engines are to be built by Rolls Royce as specified by the airline customer for the aircraft. You can see that different parts of the manufacturing process are carried out by each of the venturers. In the Rolls Royce factory, workers will work on the engines for the Boeing plane alongside others working on engines for different aircraft.

Each venturer, Boeing and Rolls Royce, bears its own costs and takes a share of revenue from the aircraft sale. That share is decided in the contractual arrangement between the venturers.

There are many other examples which you might have thought of.

11

Cash flow statements

Topic list
1 The need for cash flow statements
2 Objective of IAS 7
3 Format of a cash flow statement
4 Example of a cash flow statement
5 Interest and dividends
6 Taxes on income
7 Disclosure
8 Reporting cash flows from operating activities
9 Preparing a cash flow statement
10 Consolidated cash flow statements
11 Interpretation of cash flow statements

Introduction

The preparation of a cashflow statement is a popular exam requirement. Such questions involve a lot of calculation but are quite mechanical so they should represent easy marks if you practise them.

You should also be prepared to explain the information which this statement provides.

Learning objectives

On completion of this chapter you will be able to:

	Syllabus reference
• explain the need for and usefulness of a cash flow statement	3 a iii
• identify why profits and cash flow are not the same	3 c x
• describe the structure of a cash flow statement in company accounts	3 a iii
• identify the terminology and the principles used in preparing a cash flow statement	3 c x
• prepare a simple cash flow statement	3 c x
• interpret a cash flow statement	4 a iv

1 The need for cash flow statements

FAST FORWARD

A cash flow statement is a useful addition to a company's financial statements as a measure of performance, because it recognises that accounting profit is not the only indicator of a company's performance.

It has been argued that 'profit' does not always give a useful or meaningful picture of a company's operations. Readers of a company's financial statements might even be **misled by a reported profit figure**.

(a) Shareholders might believe that if a company makes a profit after tax, of say, $100,000 then this is the amount which it could afford to **pay as a dividend**. Unless the company has **sufficient cash** available to stay in business and also to pay a dividend, the shareholders' expectations would be wrong.

(b) Employees might believe that if a company makes profits, it can afford to **pay higher wages** next year. This opinion may not be correct: the ability to pay wages depends on the **availability of cash**.

(c) Survival of a business entity depends not so much on profits as on its **ability to pay its debts when they fall due**. Such payments might include 'revenue' items such as material purchases, wages, interest and taxation etc, but also capital payments for new non-current assets and the repayment of loan capital when this falls due (for example on the redemption of debentures).

From these examples, it may be apparent that a company's performance and prospects depend not so much on the 'profits' earned in a period, but more realistically on liquidity or **cash flows**.

1.1 Funds flow and cash flow

Some countries, either currently or in the past, have required the disclosure of additional statements based on **funds flow** rather than cash flow. However, the definition of 'funds' can be very vague and such statements often simply require a rearrangement of figures already provided in the balance sheet and income statement. By contrast, a statement of cash flows is unambiguous and provides information which is additional to that provided in the rest of the accounts. It also lends itself to organisation by activity and not by balance sheet classification.

Cash flow statements are frequently given as an **additional statement**, supplementing the balance sheet, income statement and related notes.

2 Objective of IAS 7

FAST FORWARD

Cash flow statements concentrate on the sources and uses of cash and are a useful indicator of a company's **liquidity** and **solvency**.

The aim of IAS 7 is to provide information to users of financial statements about the entity's **ability to generate cash and cash equivalents**, as well as indicating the cash needs of the entity. The cash flow statement provides *historical* information about cash and cash equivalents, classifying cash flows between operating, investing and financing activities.

Key terms

- **Cash** comprises cash on hand and demand deposits.
- **Cash equivalents** are short-term, highly liquid investments that are readily convertible to known amounts of cash and which are subject to an insignificant risk of changes in value. *(IAS 7)*

The standard expands on the definition of cash equivalents: they are not held for investment or other long-term purposes, but rather to meet short-term cash commitments. To fulfil the above definition, an investment's **maturity date should normally be within three months from its acquisition date**. It would usually be the case then that equity investments (ie shares in other companies) are *not* cash equivalents. An exception would be where preferred shares were acquired with a very close maturity date.

Loans and other borrowings from banks are classified as investing activities. In some countries, however, **bank overdrafts** are repayable on demand and are treated as part of an entity's total cash management system. In these circumstances an overdrawn balance will be included in cash and cash equivalents. Such banking arrangements are characterised by a balance which fluctuates between overdrawn and credit.

Movements between different types of cash and cash equivalent are not included in cash flows. The investment of surplus cash in cash equivalents is part of cash management, not part of operating, investing or financing activities.

A cash flow statement should be presented as an **integral part** of an entity's financial statements. All types of entity can provide useful information about cash flows as the need for cash is universal, whatever the nature of their revenue-producing activities. Therefore **all entities are required by the standard to produce a cash flow statement.**

2.1 Benefits of cash flow information

The use of cash flow statements is very much **in conjunction** with the rest of the financial statements. Users can gain further appreciation of the change in net assets, of the entity's financial position (liquidity and solvency) and the entity's ability to adapt to changing circumstances by affecting the amount and timing of cash flows. Cash flow statements **enhance comparability** as they are not affected by differing accounting policies used for the same type of transactions or events.

Cash flow information of a historical nature can be used as an indicator of the amount, timing and certainty of future cash flows. Past forecast cash flow information can be **checked for accuracy** as actual figures emerge. The relationship between profit and cash flows can be analysed as can changes in prices over time.

3 Format of a cash flow statement

FAST FORWARD

You need to be aware of the format of the statement as laid out in IAS 7; setting out the format is an essential first stage in preparing the statement, so this format must be learnt.

IAS 7 requires cash flow statements to report cash flows during the period classified by **operating, investing and financing activities.**

The manner of presentation of cash flows between operating, investing and financing activities **depends on the nature of the entity**. By classifying cash flows between different activities in this way users can see the impact on cash and cash equivalents of each one, and their relationships with each other. We can look at each in more detail.

3.1 Operating activities

This is perhaps the key part of the cash flow statement because it shows whether, and to what extent, companies can **generate cash from their operations**. It is these operating cash flows which must, in the end pay for all cash outflows relating to other activities, ie paying loan interest, dividends and so on.

Most of the components of cash flows from operating activities will be those items which **determine the net profit or loss of the entity**, ie they relate to the main revenue-producing activities of the entity. The standard gives the following as examples of cash flows from operating activities.

(a) Cash receipts from the sale of goods and the rendering of services
(b) Cash receipts from royalties, fees, commissions and other revenue
(c) Cash payments to suppliers for goods and services
(d) Cash payments to and on behalf of employees

Certain items may be included in the net profit or loss for the period which do *not* relate to operational cash flows, for example the profit or loss on the sale of a piece of plant will be included in net profit or loss, but the cash flows will be classed as **investing**.

3.2 Investing activities

The cash flows classified under this heading show the extent of new investment in **assets which will generate future profit and cash flows**. The standard gives the following examples of cash flows arising from investing activities.

(a) Cash payments to acquire property, plant and equipment, intangibles and other non-current assets, including those relating to capitalised development costs and self-constructed property, plant and equipment

(b) Cash receipts from sales of property, plant and equipment, intangibles and other non-current assets

(c) Cash payments to acquire shares or debentures of other entities

(d) Cash receipts from sales of shares or debentures of other entities

(e) Cash advances and loans made to other parties

(f) Cash receipts from the repayment of advances and loans made to other parties

3.3 Financing activities

This section of the cash flow statement shows the share of cash which the entity's capital providers have claimed during the period. This is an indicator of **likely future interest and dividend payments**. The standard gives the following examples of cash flows which might arise under this heading.

(a) Cash proceeds from issuing shares

(b) Cash payments to owners to acquire or redeem the entity's shares

(c) Cash proceeds from issuing debentures, loans, notes, bonds, mortgages and other short or long-term borrowings

(d) Principal repayments of amounts borrowed under finance leases

Item (d) needs more explanation. Where the reporting entity uses an asset held under a finance lease, the amounts to go in the cash flow statement as financing activities are repayments of the **principal (capital)** rather than the **interest**. The interest paid will be shown under operating activities.

4 Example of a cash flow statement

CASH FLOW STATEMENT (INDIRECT METHOD)
YEAR ENDED 31 DECEMBER 20X7

	$m	$m
Cash flows from operating activities		
Profit before taxation	3,570	
Adjustments for:		
Depreciation	450	
Investment income	(500)	
Interest expense	400	
	3,920	
Increase in trade and other receivables	(500)	
Decrease in inventories	1,050	
Decrease in trade payables	(1,740)	
Cash generated from operations	2,730	
Interest paid	(270)	
Income taxes paid	(900)	
Net cash from operating activities		1,560
Cash flows from investing activities		
Purchase of property, plant and equipment	(900)	
Proceeds from sale of equipment	20	
Interest received	200	
Dividends received	200	
Net cash used in investing activities		(480)
Cash flows from financing activities		
Proceeds from issue of share capital	250	
Proceeds from long-term borrowings	250	
Dividends paid*	(1,290)	
Net cash used in financing activities		(790)
Net increase in cash and cash equivalents		290
Cash and cash equivalents at beginning of period (Note)		120
Cash and cash equivalents at end of period (Note)		410

* This could also be shown as an operating cash flow

Note: Cash and cash equivalents

Cash and cash equivalents consist of cash on hand and balances with banks, and investments in money market instruments. Cash and cash equivalents included in the cash flow statement comprise the following balance sheet amounts.

	20X7	*20X6*
	$m	$m
Cash on hand and balances with banks	40	25
Short-term investments	370	95
Cash and cash equivalents	410	120

The company has undrawn borrowing facilities of $2,000m of which only $700m may be used for future expansion.

5 Interest and dividends

Cash flows from interest and dividends received and paid should each be **disclosed separately**. Each should be classified in a consistent manner from period to period as either operating, investing or financing activities.

Dividends paid by the entity can be classified in **one of two ways**.

(a) As a **financing cash flow**, showing the cost of obtaining financial resources.

(b) As a component of **cash flows from operating activities** so that users can assess the entity's ability to pay dividends out of operating cash flows.

6 Taxes on income

Cash flows arising from taxes on income should be **separately disclosed** and should be classified as cash flows from operating activities *unless* they can be specifically identified with financing and investing activities.

Taxation cash flows are often **difficult to match** to the originating underlying transaction, so most of the time all tax cash flows are classified as arising from operating activities.

7 Disclosure

FAST FORWARD

IAS 7 requires a reconciliation of cash and cash equivalents. This should be presented as a disclosure note.

The components of cash and cash equivalents should be disclosed and a **reconciliation** should be presented, showing the amounts in the cash flow statement reconciled with the equivalent items reported in the balance sheet. This note is shown in our example in Section 4.

It is also necessary to disclose the **accounting policy** used in deciding the items included in cash and cash equivalents, in accordance with IAS 1 *Presentation of Financial Statements*, but also because of the wide range of cash management practices worldwide.

All entities should disclose, together with a **commentary by management**, any other information likely to be of importance, for example:

(a) Restrictions on the use of or access to any part of cash equivalents

(b) The amount of undrawn borrowing facilities which are available

(c) Cash flows which increased operating capacity compared to cash flows which merely maintained operating capacity

(d) Cash flows arising from each reported industry and geographical segment

8 Reporting cash flows from operating activities

FAST FORWARD

Cash flows from operating activities can be presented using the **direct** or the **indirect** method. The indirect method is normally more straightforward.

The standard offers a choice of method for this part of the cash flow statement.

(a) **Direct method:** disclose major classes of gross cash receipts and gross cash payments

(b) **Indirect method**: net profit or loss is adjusted for the effects of transactions of a non-cash nature, any deferrals or accruals of past or future operating cash receipts or payments, and items of income or expense associated with investing or financing cash flows. This is the method used in the example in Section 4.

The **direct method is the preferred method** because it discloses information, not available elsewhere in the financial statements, which could be of use in estimating future cash flows, but IAS 7 does not require it. In practice the indirect method is more commonly used, since it is quicker and easier.

8.1 Using the indirect method

This method is undoubtedly **easier** from the point of view of the preparer of the cash flow statement. The net profit or loss for the period is adjusted for the following.

(a) Changes during the period in inventories, operating receivables and payables

(b) Non-cash items, eg depreciation, provisions, profits/losses on the sales of assets

(c) Other items, the cash flows from which should be classified under investing or financing activities.

A **proforma** of such a calculation, taken from the IAS, is as follows and this method may be more common in the exam. (The proforma has been amended to reflect changes to IFRS.) We have already seen this in the example in Section 4.

	$
Cash flows from operating activities	
Profit before taxation	X
Adjustments for:	
Depreciation	X
Foreign exchange loss	X
Investment income	(X)
Interest expense	X
	X
Increase in trade and other receivables	(X)
Decrease in inventories	X
Decrease in trade payables	(X)
Cash generated from operations	X
Interest paid	(X)
Income taxes paid	(X)
Net cash from operating activities	X

It is important to understand why **certain items are added and others subtracted.** Note the following points.

(a) Depreciation is not a cash expense, but is deducted in arriving at the profit figure in the income statement. It makes sense, therefore, to eliminate it by adding it back.

(b) By the same logic, a loss on a disposal of a non-current asset (arising through underprovision of depreciation) needs to be added back and a profit deducted.

(c) An increase in inventories means less cash – you have spent cash on buying inventory.

(d) An increase in receivables means the company's customers have not paid as much, and therefore there is less cash.

(e) If we pay off payables, causing the figure to decrease, again we have less cash.

8.2 Using the direct method

The only difference when using the direct method is the way in which cashflows from operating activities are presented. (See below). The rest of the cashflow statement will be exactly the same as the example shown in Section 4. This information may be time consuming to produce hence the more frequent use of the indirect method.

	$m	$m
Cash flows from operating activities		
Cash receipts from customers	30,330	
Cash paid to suppliers and employees	(27,600)	
Cash generated from operations	2,730	
Interest paid	(270)	
Income taxes paid	(900)	
Net cash from operating activities		1,560

9 Preparing a cash flow statement

FAST FORWARD

Remember the **step-by-step preparation procedure** and use it for all the questions you practise.

In essence, preparing a cash flow statement is very straightforward. You should therefore simply learn the format and apply the steps noted in the example below. Note that the following items are treated in a way that might seem confusing, but the treatment is logical if you **think in terms of cash**.

(a) **Increase in inventory** is treated as **negative** (in brackets). This is because it represents a cash **outflow**; cash is being spent on inventory.

(b) An **increase in receivables** would be treated as **negative** for the same reasons; more receivables means less cash.

(c) By contrast an **increase in payables is positive** because cash is being retained and not used to settle accounts payable. There is therefore more of it.

9.1 Example: preparation of a cash flow statement

Kane Co's income statement for the year ended 31 December 20X2 and balance sheets at 31 December 20X1 and 31 December 20X2 were as follows.

KANE CO
INCOME STATEMENT FOR THE YEAR ENDED 31 DECEMBER 20X2

	$'000	$'000
Sales		720
Raw materials consumed	70	
Staff costs	94	
Depreciation	118	
Loss on disposal of non-current asset	18	
		300
Profit from operations		420
Interest payable		28
Profit before tax		392
Taxation		124
Profit for the year		268
Retained earnings brought forward		490
Profit for the year		268
Dividend		(72)
Retained earnings carried forward		686

KANE CO
BALANCE SHEETS AS AT 31 DECEMBER

	20X2		20X1	
	$'000	$'000	$'000	$'000
Assets				
Non-current assets				
Cost	1,596		1,560	
Depreciation	318		224	
		1,278		1,336
Current assets				
Inventory	24		20	
Trade receivables	76		58	
Bank	48		56	
		148		134
Total assets		1,426		1,470
Equity and liabilities				
Equity				
Share capital	360		340	
Share premium	36		24	
Retained earnings	686		490	
		1,082		854
Non-current liabilities				
Long-term loans		200		500
Current liabilities				
Trade payables	12		6	
Taxation	102		86	
Dividend payable	30		24	
		144		116
		1,426		1,470

During the year, the company paid $90,000 for a new piece of machinery. Proceeds received on disposal of a piece of machinery were $12,000.

Required

Prepare a cash flow statement for Kane Co for the year ended 31 December 20X2 in accordance with the requirements of IAS 7, using the indirect method.

Solution

Step 1 **Set out the proforma cash flow statement** with the headings required by IAS 7. You should leave plenty of space. Ideally, use three or more sheets of paper, one for the main statement, one for the notes and one for your workings. It is obviously essential to know the formats very well.

Step 2 Begin with the **cash flows from operating activities** as far as possible. When preparing the statement from balance sheets, you will usually have to calculate such items as depreciation, loss on sale of non-current assets, profit for the year and tax paid (see Step 4). Note that you may not be given the tax charge in the income statement. You will then have to assume that the tax paid in the year is last year's year-end provision and calculate the charge as the balancing figure.

Step 3 Calculate the cash flow figures for **dividends paid, purchase or sale of non-current assets, issue of shares and repayment of loans** if these are not already given to you (as they may be).

Step 4 If you are not given the profit figure, open up a **working for the income statement**. Using the opening and closing balances of retained earnings, the taxation charge and dividends paid and declared, you will be able to calculate profit for the year as the balancing figure to put in the cash flows from operating activities section.

Step 5 You will now be able to **complete the statement** by slotting in the figures given or calculated.

KANE CO
CASH FLOW STATEMENT FOR THE YEAR ENDED 31 DECEMBER 20X2

	$'000	$'000
Cash flows from operating activities		
Profit before tax	392	
Depreciation charges	118	
Loss on sale of tangible non-current assets	18	
Interest expense	28	
Increase in inventories	(4)	
Increase in receivables	(18)	
Increase in payables	6	
Cash generated from operations	540	
Interest paid	(28)	
Dividends paid (72 – 30 + 24)	(66)	
Tax paid (86 + 124 – 102)	(108)	
Net cash from operating activities		338
Cash flows from investing activities		
Payments to acquire tangible non-current assets	(90)	
Receipts from sales of tangible non-current assets	12	
Net cash used in investing activities		(78)
Cash flows from financing activities		
Issues of share capital (360 + 36 – 340 – 24)	32	
Long-term loans repaid (500 – 200)	(300)	
Net cash used in financing activities		(268)
Decrease in cash and cash equivalents		(8)
Cash and cash equivalents at 1.1.X2		56
Cash and cash equivalents at 31.12.X2		48

Activity 11.1

Set out below are the financial statements of Emma Co. You are the financial controller, faced with the task of implementing IAS 7 *Cash flow statements*.

EMMA CO
INCOME STATEMENT FOR THE YEAR ENDED 31 DECEMBER 20X2

	$'000
Revenue	2,553
Cost of sales	1,814
Gross profit	739
Distribution costs	125
Administrative expenses	264
Profit from operations	350
Interest received	25
Interest paid	75
Profit before tax	300
Income tax expense	140
Profit for the year	160
Dividends payable	100

EMMA CO
BALANCE SHEETS AS AT 31 DECEMBER

	20X2	*20X1*
Assets	$'000	$'000
Non-current assets		
Tangible assets	380	305
Intangible assets	250	200
Investments	–	25
Current assets		
Inventories	150	102
Receivables	390	315
Short-term investments	50	–
Cash in hand	2	1
Total assets	1,222	948
Equity and liabilities		
Equity		
Share capital ($1 ordinary shares)	200	150
Share premium account	160	150
Revaluation reserve	100	91
Retained earnings	160	100
Non-current liabilities		
Long-term loan	170	50
Current liabilities		
Trade payables	127	119
Bank overdraft	85	98
Taxation	120	110
Dividends payable	100	80
Total equity and liabilities	1,222	948

The following information is available.

(a) The proceeds of the sale of non-current asset investments amounted to $30,000.

(b) Fixtures and fittings, with an original cost of $85,000 and a net book value of $45,000, were sold for $32,000 during the year. New fixtures and fittings were purchased costing $201,000.

(c) The following information relates to tangible non-current assets.

	31.12.20X2	*31.12.20X1*
	$'000	$'000
Cost	720	595
Accumulated depreciation	340	290
Net book value	380	305

(d) 50,000 $1 ordinary shares were issued during the year at a premium of 20c per share.

(e) The short-term investments are highly liquid and are close to maturity.

Required

Prepare a cash flow statement for the year to 31 December 20X2 using the format laid out in IAS 7.

10 Consolidated cash flow statements

FAST FORWARD

Consolidated cash flow statements follow the same principles as for single company statements, with some additional complications.

Cash flows that are **internal to the group** should be eliminated in the preparation of a consolidated cash flow statement. Where a subsidiary **joins or leaves** a group during a financial year the cash flows of the group should include the cash flows of the subsidiary concerned for the same period as that for which the group's income statement includes the results of the subsidiary.

10.1 Acquisitions and disposals of subsidiaries and other business units

An entity should present separately the aggregate cash flows arising from acquisitions and from disposals of subsidiaries or other business units and classify them as **investing activities**.

Disclosure is required of the following, in aggregate, in respect of both acquisitions and disposals of subsidiaries or other business units during the period.

- Total purchase/disposal consideration
- Portion of purchase/disposal consideration discharged by means of cash/cash equivalents
- Amount of cash/cash equivalents in the subsidiary or business unit disposed of
- Amount of assets and liabilities other than cash/cash equivalents in the subsidiary or business unit acquired or disposed of, summarised by major category

The amounts shown in the cash flow statements for purchase or disposal of subsidiaries or business units will be the amounts paid or received **net** of cash/cash equivalents acquired or disposed of.

10.2 Consolidation adjustments and minority interests

The group cash flow statement should only deal with flows of cash and cash equivalents external to the group, so all intra-group cash flows should be eliminated. **Dividends paid to minority interests** should be included under the heading 'cash flow from financing' and disclosed separately.

10.3 Example: Minority interests

The following are extracts of the consolidated results for Jarvis Co for the year ended 31 December 20X8.

CONSOLIDATED INCOME STATEMENT (EXTRACT)

	$'000
Group profit before tax	90
Taxation	(30)
Profit after tax	60
Minority interest	(15)
Profit attributable to parent	45

CONSOLIDATED BALANCE SHEET (EXTRACT)

	20X1	*20X2*
	$'000	$'000
Minority interest	300	306

Calculate the dividends paid to the minority interest during the year.

Solution

The minority interest share of profit after tax represents retained profit plus dividends paid.

	$'000
Minority interest brought forward	300
Minority interest carried forward	306
	(6)
Income statement: profit	15
Dividend paid	9

10.4 Associates

When the equity method is used, only the actual cash flows from sales or purchases between the group and the associate, and investments in and dividends from the entity should be included. Dividends should be included in **operating cash flows**, where they are shown within operating profit in the income statement.

10.5 Example: Associate

The following are extracts of the consolidated results of Pripon Co for the year ended 31 December 20X8.

CONSOLIDATED INCOME STATEMENT (EXTRACT)

	$'000	$'000
Operating profit of group		150
Share of associate's profit		30
		180
Tax		75
Profit after tax		105

CONSOLIDATED BALANCE SHEET (EXTRACTS)

	20X1	*20X2*
	$'000	$'000
Investment in associate	264	276

Calculate the dividend received from the associate.

Solution

The associate profit before tax represents retained profit plus dividend plus tax.

	$'000	$'000
Investment brought forward		264
Investment carried forward		276
		(12)
Share of profit		30
Dividend from associate		18

11 Interpretation of cash flow statements

FAST FORWARD

Note that you may be expected to **analyse** or interpret a cash flow statement.

IAS 7 *Cash flow statements* was introduced on the basis that it would provide better, more comprehensive and more useful information than what was already shown in the financial statements.

So what kind of information does the cash flow statement, along with its notes, provide?

Some of the main areas where IAS 7 should provide information not found elsewhere in the financial statements are as follows.

(a) The **relationships between profit and cash** can be seen clearly and analysed accordingly.

(b) **Cash equivalents** are highlighted, giving a better picture of the liquidity of the company.

(c) **Financing inflows and outflows must be shown, rather than simply passed through reserves**.

One of the most important things to realise at this point is that it is wrong to try to assess the health or predict the death of a reporting entity solely on the basis of a single indicator. When analysing cash flow data, the **comparison should not just be between cash flows and profit, but also between cash flows over a period of time** (say three to five years).

Cash is not synonymous with profit on an annual basis, but you should also remember that the 'behaviour' of profit and cash flows will be very different. **Profit is smoothed out** through accruals, prepayments, provisions and other accounting conventions. This does not apply to cash, so the **cash flow figures** are likely to be **'lumpy'** in comparison. You must distinguish between this 'lumpiness' and the trends which will appear over time.

The **relationship between profit and cash flows will vary constantly**. Note that healthy companies do not always have reported profits exceeding operating cash flows. Similarly, unhealthy companies can have operating cash flows well in excess of reported profit. The value of comparing them is in determining the extent to which earned profits are being converted into the necessary cash flows.

Profit is not as important as the extent to which a company can **convert its profits into cash on a continuing basis.** This process should be judged over a period longer than one year. The cash flows should be compared with profits over the same periods to decide how successfully the reporting entity has converted earnings into cash.

Cash flow figures should also be considered in terms of their specific relationships with each other over time. A form of **'cash flow gearing'** can be determined by comparing operating cash flows and financing flows, particularly borrowing, to establish the extent of dependence of the reporting entity on external funding.

Other relationships can be examined.

(a) Operating cash flows and investment flows can be related to match cash recovery from investment to investment.

(b) Investment can be compared to distribution to indicate the proportion of total cash outflow designated specifically to investor return and reinvestment.

(c) A comparison of tax outflow to operating cash flow minus investment flow will establish a 'cash basis tax rate'.

The 'ratios' mentioned above can be monitored **inter- and intra-firm** and the analyses can be undertaken in monetary, general price-level adjusted, or percentage terms.

11.1 The advantages of cash flow accounting

The advantages of cash flow accounting are as follows.

(a) Survival in business depends on the **ability to generate** cash. Cash flow accounting directs attention towards this critical issue.

(b) Cash flow is **more comprehensive** than 'profit' which is dependent on accounting conventions and concepts.

(c) **Creditors** (long and short-term) are more interested in an entity's ability to repay them than in its profitability. Whereas 'profits' might indicate that cash is likely to be available, cash flow accounting is more direct with its message.

(d) Cash flow reporting provides a better means of **comparing the results** of different companies than traditional profit reporting.

(e) Cash flow reporting **satisfies the needs of all users** better.

   (i) For **management**, it provides the sort of information on which decisions should be taken (in management accounting, 'relevant costs' to a decision are future cash flows); traditional profit accounting does not help with decision-making.

   (ii) For **shareholders and auditors**, cash flow accounting can provide a satisfactory basis for stewardship accounting.

   (iii) As described previously, the information needs of **creditors and employees** will be better served by cash flow accounting.

(f) Cash flow forecasts are **easier to prepare**, as well as more useful, than profit forecasts.

(g) They can in some respects be **audited more easily** than accounts based on the accruals concept.

(h) The accruals concept is confusing, and cash flows are **more easily understood**.

(i) Cash flow accounting should be both retrospective, and also include a forecast for the future. This is of **great information value** to all users of accounting information.

(j) **Forecasts** can subsequently be **monitored** by the publication of variance statements which compare actual cash flows against the forecast.

Activity 11.2

Can you think of some possible disadvantages of cash flow accounting?

Key learning points

- **A cash flow statement** is a useful addition to a company's financial statements as a measure of performance because it recognises that accounting profit is not the only indicator of a company's performance.
- Cash flow statements concentrate on the sources and uses of cash and are a useful indicator of a company's **liquidity and solvency**.
- You need to be aware of the **format** of the statement as laid out in **IAS 7**; setting out the format is an essential first stage in preparing the statement, so this format must be learnt.
- IAS 7 requires a reconciliation of cash and cash equivalents. This should be presented as a disclosure note.
- Cash flows from operating activities can be presented using the **direct** or **indirect** method. The indirect method normally more straightforward.
- Remember the **step-by-step preparation procedure** and use it for all the questions you practise.
- Consolidated cash flow statements follow the same principles as for single company statements, with some additional complications.
- Note that you may be expected to **analyse** or **interpret** a cash flow statement.

Quick quiz

1 What is the aim of a cash flow statement?

2 The standard headings in IAS 7 *Cash flow statements* are:

- O.................. a................
- I.................. a...................
- F.................... a......................
- Net.................. in C...................... and ....

3 Cash equivalents are current asset investments which will mature or can be redeemed within three months of the year end.

True ☐

False ☐

4 Why are you more likely to encounter the indirect method as opposed to the direct method?

5 List five advantages of cash flow accounting.

Answers to quick quiz

1 To indicate an entity's ability to generate cash and cash equivalents.

2
- Operating activities
- Investing activities
- Financing activities
- Net increase (decrease) in cash and cash equivalents

3 False. See the definition in paragraph 2 if you are not sure about this.

4 The indirect method utilises figures which appear in the financial statements. The figures required for the direct method may not be readily available.

5 See paragraph 11.1

Answers to activities

11.1

EMMA CO
CASH FLOW STATEMENT FOR THE YEAR ENDED 31 DECEMBER 20X2

	$'000	$'000
Cash flows from operating activities		
Profit before tax	300	
Depreciation charge (W1)	90	
Loss on sale of tangible non-current assets (45 – 32)	13	
Profit on sale of non-current asset investments	(5)	
Interest expense (net)	50	
(Increase)/decrease in inventories	(48)	
(Increase)/decrease in receivables	(75)	
Increase/(decrease) in payables	8	
Cash generated from operations	333	
Interest paid	(75)	
Dividends paid	(80)	
Tax paid (110 + 140 – 120)	(130)	
Net cash from operating activities		48
Cash flows from investing activities		
Payments to acquire tangible non-current assets	(201)	
Payments to acquire intangible non-current assets	(50)	
Receipts from sales of tangible non-current assets	32	
Receipts from sale of non-current asset investments	30	
Interest received	25	
Net cash flows from investing activities		(164)
Cash flows from financing activities		
Issue of share capital	60	
Long-term loan	120	
Net cash flows from financing		180
Increase in cash and cash equivalents (Note)		64
Cash and cash equivalents at 1.1.X2 (Note)		(97)
Cash and cash equivalents at 31.12.X2 (Note)		(33)

NOTES TO THE CASH FLOW STATEMENT

Note: analysis of the balances of cash and cash equivalents as shown in the balance sheet

	20X2	*20X1*	*Change in year*
	$'000	$'000	$'000
Cash in hand	2	1	1
Short term investments	50	–	50
Bank overdraft	(85)	(98)	13
	(33)	(97)	64

Workings

1 *Depreciation charge*

	$'000	$'000
Depreciation at 31 December 20X2		340
Depreciation 31 December 20X1	290	
Depreciation on assets sold (85 – 45)	40	
		250
Charge for the year		90

11.2 The main disadvantages of cash accounting are essentially the advantages of accruals accounting (proper matching of related items). There is also the practical problem that few businesses keep historical cash flow information in the form needed to prepare a historical cash flow statement and so extra record keeping is likely to be necessary.

12

Other elements of corporate annual reports

Topic list
1 Notes to the financial statements
2 Management report
3 Auditors' report
4 Chairman's report
5 Operating and Financial Review
6 Summarised information
7 Interim accounts
8 Preliminary announcements
9 Environmental reporting

Introduction

This chapter looks at other information which might be included as part of an annual report. Notice that in some instances the information is a statutory requirement.

In other cases the information is provided on a voluntary basis.

Learning objectives

On completion of this chapter you will be able to:

	Syllabus reference
• describe the major features of other elements of corporate annual reports: notes to the accounts and additional financial statements, directors' report, chairman's statement, summarised information, financial reviews, interim accounts, preliminary announcements and environmental reports.	3 b i- vii

1 Notes to the financial statements

FAST FORWARD

Financial statements must be supported by **notes to the accounts**, which give additional information about figures in the accounts themselves.

1.1 Contents of notes

The notes to the financial statements will **amplify** the information given in the balance sheet, income statement and statement of changes in equity. We have already noted above the information which the IAS allows to be shown by note rather than on the face of the statements. To some extent, then, the contents of the notes will be determined by the level of detail shown on the **face of the statements**.

1.2 Structure

The notes to the financial statements should perform the following functions.

(a) Provide information about the **basis on which the financial statements were prepared** and which **specific accounting policies** were chosen and applied to significant transactions/events

(b) Disclose any information, not shown elsewhere in the financial statements, which is **required by IASs**

(c) Show any additional information that is necessary for a **fair presentation** which is not shown on the face of the financial statements

The way the notes are presented is important. They should be given in a **systematic manner** and **cross referenced** back to the related figure(s) in the balance sheet, income statement or cash flow statement.

Notes to the financial statements will amplify the information shown therein by giving the following.

(a) More **detailed analysis** or breakdowns of figures in the statements
(b) **Narrative information** explaining figures in the statements
(c) **Additional information**, eg contingent liabilities and commitments

IAS 1 suggests a **certain order** for notes to the financial statements. This will assist users when comparing the statements of different entities.

(a) Statement of **compliance** with IASs

(b) Statement of the **measurement basis** (bases) and accounting policies applied

(c) **Supporting information** for items presented on the face of each financial statement in the same order as each line item and each financial statement is presented

(d) **Other disclosures**, eg:

(i) Contingent liabilities, commitments and other financial disclosures
(ii) Non-financial disclosures

The order of specific items may have to be varied occasionally, but a systematic structure is still required.

1.3 Presentation of accounting policies

The accounting policies section should describe the following.

(a) The **measurement basis** (or bases) used in preparing the financial statements

(b) The **other accounting policies** used, as required for a proper understanding of the financial statements

This information may be shown in the notes or sometimes as a **separate component** of the financial statements.

The information on measurement bases used is obviously fundamental to an understanding of the financial statements. Where **more than one basis is used**, it should be stated to which assets or liabilities each basis has been applied.

1.4 Other disclosures

An entity must disclose in the notes:

(a) The amount of dividends proposed or declared before the financial statements were authorised for issue but not recognised as a distribution to equity holders during the period, and the amount per share

(b) The amount of any cumulative preference dividends not recognised

IAS 1 ends by listing some **specific disclosures** which will always be required if they are not shown elsewhere in the financial statements.

(a) The **domicile and legal form** of the entity, its **country of incorporation** and the **address of the registered office** (or, if different, principal place of business)

(b) A description of the **nature of the entity's operations** and its **principal activities**

(c) The name of the **parent entity** and the **ultimate parent entity** of the group

2 Management report

FAST FORWARD

In most jurisdictions, all companies apart from small companies must include a **management report** as part of their accounts.

In most jurisdictions, with the exception of small companies, all companies must include a management report in their accounts.

The management report is largely a narrative report, although certain figures must also be included. The purpose of the report is to give the users of accounts a more complete picture of the state of affairs of the company.

In principle, narrative descriptions in the management report put flesh on the bare bones of the information provided by the figures in the accounts themselves. However, in practice, the management report is often a rather dry and uninformative document. This is probably because it is often a statutory report and must be verified by the company's external auditors, whereas the chairman's report need not be.

The report must typically also show:

(a) the amount, if any, recommended for dividend

(b) the principal activities of the company in the course of the financial year, and any significant changes in those activities during the year

(c) where significant, an estimate should be provided of the difference between the book value of land held as non-current assets and its realistic market value

(d) information about the company's policy on employment of disabled persons

(e) the names of persons who were directors at any time during the financial year and their interests in shares or debentures of the company

(f) political and charitable contributions made in the year

(g) particulars of any important events affecting the company since the end of the financial year (i.e. significant events after the balance sheet date)

(h) an indication of likely future developments in the business of the company and of its subsidiaries

(i) an indication of the activities (if any) of the company and its subsidiaries in the field of research and development

(j) particulars of any purchases of its own shares by the company during the year, including reasons for the purchase

(k) in the case of public companies, a statement of the company's policy on payments to creditors.

The management report of companies employing larger numbers of staff may also be required to include details of what action has been taken to introduce, maintain or develop arrangements aimed at:

(a) providing information to employees about matters concerning them

(b) consulting with employees about decisions likely to affect their interests

(c) employee involvement, for example the availability of an employees' share option scheme

(d) achieving awareness on the part of all employees of the financial and economic factors affecting the performance of the company

3 Auditors' report

FAST FORWARD

The accounts of most limited companies must be audited and a report produced by the auditors as to whether or not the financial statements show a **true and fair view (present fairly)**.

It is the duty of the directors of a company to prepare financial statements. The role of the auditor is to perform an **independent** review of the financial statements on behalf of the shareholders. This process adds **credibility** to the financial statements.

When the annual accounts of a limited company are audited, the auditors must provide a report as to whether or not the accounts show a true and fair view of the company's results for the year and its financial position at the end of the year. The audit report is governed by auditing regulations.

Typically, auditors are able to report that they have carried out their work in accordance with auditing standards and that, in their opinion, the accounts show a **true and fair view** (or present fairly). This is described as an **unqualified audit report**.

The auditors' report covers the financial statements and the notes to the accounts In addition the auditors must consider whether the information given in the **management report** is consistent with the audited accounts. If they believe it **is not** consistent then they must state that fact in their report. Note that the cash flow statement is not mentioned outright. The report does not cover the chairman's statement.

The auditors' report is included as a part of the company's published accounts. It is normally addressed to the shareholders of the company (not to the directors).

3.1 Modified audit opinions

It is fairly unusual for an auditors' report to give a qualified opinion as to whether a company's accounts give a true and fair view of its affairs. However, there are two circumstances where this might occur: where there is a disagreement or where there is a limitation on scope.

Disagreement

(a) An adverse opinion is given where the auditors are materially in disagreement with the statements given by the company's directors in the accounts, and the auditors have concluded that the accounts would be seriously misleading.

(b) A qualified opinion or disagreement is where the auditors disagree with an item in the accounts, but they do not consider the disagreement sufficient to give an adverse opinion.

Limitations on scope

(a) Where there has been such a restriction or limitation on the work that the auditors have been able to carry out that they are unable to give an opinion on the financial statements. This might occur, for example, when a large part of the company's operations are conducted in a country to which the auditors have been unable to gain access.

(b) Where there has been a limitation on the work that the auditors have been able to carry out that they are unable to form an opinion, but the item is not so material as to justify a total disclaimer of opinion.

4 Chairman's report

FAST FORWARD

In most jurisdictions large companies include a **chairman's report** in their published financial statements.

This is **purely voluntary** as there is no statutory requirement to do so.

The chairman's report is not governed by any regulations and is often intended to present a rosy picture of the company, what it has achieved and its future prospects. Often, it is unduly optimistic.

5 Operating and Financial Review

FAST FORWARD

Listed companies may be called upon to produce an **Operating and Financial review** in their financial statements. Its purpose is to provide a framework for discussion and analysis of the business's performance and factors underlying its results and financial position.

The requirement to issue financial reviews varies from jurisdiction to jurisdiction. The following notes are based on the UK statement of best practice. (As yet, the IASB has issued no guidance on preparing an Operating and Financial Review.) This sets out the recommended approach to producing an OFR and gives details of the information that should be included if the OFR is to be useful.

FAST FORWARD The **Operating and Financial Review** should be of considerable benefit to less sophisticated users.

5.1 Objective

The objective of the review is to show:

(a) The **development and performance** of the business of the entity during the financial year;

(b) The **position** of the entity at the end of the year;

(c) The **main trends and factors underlying the development, performance and position** of the business of the entity during the financial year

(d) The main trends and factors which are likely to affect the entity's **future development**, performance and position, prepared so as to assist members to assess the strategies adopted by the entity and the potential for those strategies to succeed.

5.2 Principles

The UK guidance sets out the following principles.

(a) The OFR should set out the analysis of the business **through the eyes of the directors**.

(b) The OFR should focus on matters that are of **interest to members**. Other users will be interested in the information, but members' needs must be paramount.

(c) The OFR should have a **forward-looking orientation**, identifying those trends and factors relevant to the members' assessment of the current and future performance of the business and the progress towards the achievement of long-term business objectives. (The directors may warn readers to treat predictive information with caution.)

(d) The OFR has to **complement as well as supplement the financial statements** in order to enhance the overall corporate disclosure.

(e) The OFR should be **comprehensive and understandable**. For example, it must consider whether omitting information might influence users of financial statements.

(f) It should be **balanced and neutral** dealing evenhandedly with good and bad aspects.

(g) It should be **comparable over time**.

5.3 Information to be disclosed

The key elements of the disclosure framework are set out below.

(a) The **nature, objectives and strategies** of the business. This includes a description of the business and the external environment in which it operates, the objectives to generate and preserve value over the longer term, the directors' strategies for achieving the objectives of the business and the inclusion of other performance indicators and evidence.

(b) The **development and performance of the business**, both in the period under review and in the future. This will focus on the business segments that are relevant to an understanding of the development and performance as a whole.

(c) The **resources, risks and uncertainties and relationships** that may affect the entity's long-term value. It will analyse the main trends and factors likely to impact future prospects, and describe the resources available, the principle risks and uncertainties faced by the entity and significant relationships with stakeholders

(d) **Position of the business** including a description of the capital structure, treasury policies and objectives and liquidity of the entity (particularly cash flow), both in the period under review and the future.

To the extent necessary to meet the requirements set out above, the OFR should include information about:

(a) Environmental matters (including the impact of the business of the entity on the environment)

(b) The entity's employees

(c) Social and community issues

(d) Persons with whom the entity has contractual or other arrangements which are essential to the business of the entity

(e) Receipts from, and returns to, members of the entity in respect of shares held by them

(f) All other matters the directors consider to be relevant

5.4 Key performance indicators

An entity should provide information that enables investors to understand each key performance indicator (KPI) disclosed in the OFR.

For each KPI disclosed in the OFR:

(e) The **definition and its calculation method** should be explained.

(f) Its **purpose** should be explained.

(g) The **source of underlying data** should be disclosed and, where relevant, **assumptions** explained.

(j) **Quantification or commentary** on future targets should be provided.

(i) Where information from the financial statements has been **adjusted** for inclusion in the OFR, that fact should be highlighted and a **reconciliation** provided.

(j) Where available, **corresponding amounts** for the financial year immediately preceding the current year should be disclosed.

(k) **Any changes to KPIs** must be disclosed and the calculation method used compared to previous periods, including significant changes in the underlying accounting policies adopted in the financial statements, should be identified and explained.

6 Summarised information

FAST FORWARD

Listed companies may include a **five year summary** of their results in their published accounts. This can help interested parties to see trends and developments over the period.

The financial statements provide figures for the year just ended, and comparative figures for the previous year. It is not always sufficient, however, to assess the financial performance and financial position of a company simply on the strength of a two-year comparison.

Listed companies are often required to include a summary in their published annual report and accounts. As its name suggests, this gives abbreviated details of the company's profits and net assets and capital typically for a **five-year** period up to and including the year just ended.

The benefit to users of accounts is that the information can be used to look at trends and developments over a five-year period, instead of relying on a two-year comparison of the year just ended and the previous year.

There is not normally a set format or layout. An illustrative example is shown below.

	20X1	*20X2*	*20X3*	*20X4*	*20X5*
	$m	$m	$m	$m	$m
Revenue	10.6	11.2	13.5	14.8	17.1
Profit from operations	2.4	2.2	2.9	3.2	3.7
Profit before interest and tax	2.4	4.2	2.2	3.2	3.3
Interest	(0.2)	(0.1)	(0.3)	(0.3)	0.2
Profit before tax	2.2	4.1	1.9	2.9	3.5
Taxation	(0.6)	(1.2)	(0.6)	(0.7)	(1.2)
Profit for the year	1.6	2.9	1.3	2.2	2.3
Minority interest	(0.1)	(0.2)	(0.2)	(0.3)	(0.4)
Profit attributable to the group	1.5	2.7	1.1	1.9	1.9
Earnings per share	3.0p	5.4p	2.1p	1.6p	1.6p
	$m	$m	$m	$m	$m
Share capital and reserves	9.1	9.7	11.8	15.0	17.8
Minority interests	0.6	0.9	1.0	1.2	1.5
	9.7	10.6	12.8	16.2	19.3
Intangible assets	-	-	1.2	2.5	3.0
Tangible assets	6.3	8.0	8.5	9.9	10.8
Cash net of overdrafts	1.3	0.2	0.7	1.2	2.8
Inventory and receivables less payables and provisions	2.1	2.4	2.4	2.6	2.7
	9.7	10.6	12.8	16.2	19.3

6.1 Limitations of summarised information

In most jurisdictions it is up to the management team to decide how the information is to be summarised. Depending on exactly how the various balances are combined, a different impression of the results can be achieved. It is possible that information could be summarised in such a way that the readers of the accounts are misled.

7 Interim accounts

FAST FORWARD

Listed companies publish half-year accounts, 'interim accounts', for the first six months of their financial year. Interim accounts are much shorter than annual accounts, and contain:

(a) a brief statement of the revenue and profit for the first six months, and the amount of the interim dividend that will be paid (and the date of payment of the dividend)

(b) (usually) a chairman's statement

(c) an unaudited group income statement for the first six months of the year

(d) an unaudited group balance sheet as at the mid-year date

(e) an unaudited group cash flow statement for the six month period

(f) an unaudited group statement of the changes in equity

(g) some notes to these financial statements

Comparative figures are provided for both the first six months of the previous year and for the whole of the previous year.

Interim accounts are not audited, but they can be used to:

(a) make an assessment of how the company has performed in the first six months of the current year, compared with the first six months of the previous year

(b) make an assessment of how the company might perform in the next six months, by looking at what it achieved in the second six months of the previous year

(c) make an assessment of the financial position of the company, compared with its position at both the mid-year point in the previous year and the end of the previous year

(d) compare cash flows in the first six months of the current and the previous year

8 Preliminary announcements

FAST FORWARD

Listed companies make a **preliminary announcement** of their annual results once prepared, to publish news of the company's results and dividends as soon as they are available.

A listed company is normally required to make a preliminary announcement of its annual results without delay. Since it takes several weeks to prepare and print the published annual accounts, a preliminary announcement is used to communicate the company's annual results and dividends as soon as they are available. Note that a preliminary announcement is of **actual** results; expected results would be communicated via a profit forecast.

The announcement:

(a) must have been agreed in advance with the company's auditors

(b) must show the figures in the form of a table (or tables) and must contain at least the items of information that are included in the company's interim statement

(c) include any other additional information that is necessary for assessing the results

If the auditors' report will be qualified, this must also be revealed in the announcement.

9 Environmental reporting

FAST FORWARD

Environmental reporting involves making statements about the impact of the business's operations on the environment and any steps taken by the company to reduce any negative effects.

At the end of the 1980s there were perhaps only two or three companies in the world issuing environmental reports. Now most listed companies produce them. Worldwide there are around 20 award schemes for environmental reporting, notably the ACCA's. This section looks at environmental reporting mainly under three headings:

- The effect of environmental matters on management information and accounting
- External reporting and auditing
- Possible future developments

Let us consider the major areas of impact on (any) accountant's job caused by consideration of environmental matters.

(a) **Management accountant**

(i) Investment appraisal: evaluation of environmental costs and benefits.

(ii) Incorporating new costs, capital expenditure and so on, in to budgets and business plans.

(iii) Undertake cost/benefit analysis of any environmental improvements.

(b) **Financial accountant**

(i) The effect of revenue costs: site clean up costs, waste disposal or waste treatment costs and so on, which will affect the profit and loss account.

(ii) Gauging balance sheet impacts, particularly liabilities, contingencies, provisions *and* valuation of assets.

(iii) The effect of environmental matters, and particularly potential liabilities, on a company's relationship with bankers, insurers and major shareholders (institutional shareholders).

(iv) Environmental performance evaluation in annual reports.

(c) **Project accountant**

(i) Environmental audit of proposed takeovers, mergers and other planning matters.
(ii) Investment appraisal.

(d) **Internal auditor**: environmental audit.

(e) **Systems accountant**: effect on, and required changes to management and financial information systems.

9.1 What is environmental accounting?

The following list encompasses the major aspects of environmental accounting.

(a) Recognising and seeking to **mitigate the negative environmental effects of conventional accounting** practice.

(b) Separately **identifying environmentally related costs and revenues** within the conventional accounting systems.

(c) Devising new forms of financial and non-financial accounting systems, information systems and control systems to **encourage more environmentally benign management decisions.**

(d) Developing new forms of **performance measurement**, reporting and appraisal for both internal and external purposes.

(e) Identifying, examining and seeking to **rectify** areas in which conventional (financial) criteria and environmental criteria are in **conflict**.

(f) Experimenting with ways in which, **sustainability** may be assessed and incorporated into organisational orthodoxy.'

Accounting for the Environment Bob Gary (with Jan Bebbington and Diane Walters)

The whole environmental agenda is **constantly changing** and businesses therefore need to monitor the situation closely. Most businesses, certainly those in the UK, have generally ignored environmental matters in the past. How long will they be able to do so?

9.2 Management information and accounting

The means of codifying a company's attitude towards the environment is often the creation of a published **environmental policy document** or charter. This may be internally generated or it may be adopted from a standard environmental charter, such as the **Valdez Principles**.

The Valdez Principles

We adopt, support and will implement the principles of:

1 Protection of the biosphere
2 Sustainable use of natural resources
3 Reduction and disposal of waste
4 Wise use of energy
5 Risk reduction
6 Marketing of safe products and services
7 Damage compensation
8 Disclosure
9 Environmental directors and managers
10 Assessment and annual audit

The problem here, as with other similar principles or charters, is that the commitment required from companies is generally too high and the fear exists that the principles may have legal status which could have a severe effect on a company's liability. Other documents available which are similar to the *Valdez Principles* are:

- The International Chamber of Commerce **Business Charter for Sustainable Developments**
- The Chemical Industries Association **Responsible Care Programme**
- The Confederation of British Industry **Agenda for Voluntary Action**
- Friends of the Earth Environmental **Charter for Local Government**

Adopting such a charter is one thing; implementing and monitoring it are more important and generally more difficult to achieve.

9.3 Environmental audit

Environmental auditing is exactly what is says: auditing a business to assess its impact on the environment, or as the CBI expressed it 'the systematic examination of the interactions between any business operation and its surroundings'.

The audit will cover a range of areas and will involve the performance of different types of testing. The scope of the audit must be determined and this will depend on each individual organisation. There are, however, some aspects of the approach to environmental auditing which are worth mentioning.

(a) **Environmental Impact Assessments (EIAs)** are required, under EC directive, for all major projects which require planning permission and have a material effect on the environment. The EIA process can be incorporated into any environmental auditing strategy.

(b) **Environmental surveys** are a good way of starting the audit process, by looking at the organisation as a whole in environmental terms. This helps to identify areas for further development, problems, potential hazards and so forth.

(c) **Environmental SWOT analysis**. A 'strengths, weaknesses, opportunities, threats' analysis is useful as the environmental audit strategy is being developed. This can only be done later in the process, when the organisation has been examined in much more detail.

(d) **Environmental Quality Management (EQM).** This is seen as part of TQM (Total Quality Management) and it should be built in to an environmental management system. Such a strategy has been adopted by companies such as IBM, Dow Chemicals and by the Rhone-Poulenc Environmental Index which has indices for levels of water, air and other waste products.

(e) **Eco-audit**. The European Commission has adopted a proposal for a regulation for a voluntary community environmental auditing scheme, known as the eco-audit scheme. The scheme aims to promote improvements in company environmental performance and to provide the public with information about these improvements. Once registered, a company will have to comply with certain on-going obligations involving disclosure and audit.

(f) **Eco-labelling**. Developed in Germany, this voluntary scheme will indicate those EC products which meet the highest environmental standards, probably as the result of an EQM system. It is suggested that eco-audit *must* come before an eco-label can be given.

(g) **BS 7750 Environmental Management Systems**. BS 7750 also ties in with eco-audits and eco-labelling and with the quality BSI standard BS 5750. Achieving BS 7750 is likely to be a first step in the eco-audit process.

(h) **Supplier audits**, to ensure that goods and services bought in by an organisation meet the standards applied by that organisation.

9.4 Financial reporting

There are **no disclosure requirements relating to environmental matters under IASs**, so any disclosures tend to be **voluntary** unless environmental matters happen to fall under standard accounting principles (eg recognising liabilities).

(a) In most cases disclosure is descriptive and unquantified.

(b) There is little motivation to produce environmental information and many reasons for not doing so, including secrecy.

(c) The main factor seems to be apathy on the part of businesses but more particularly on the part of shareholders and investors. The information is not demanded, so it is not provided.

Environmental matters may be reported in the accounts of companies in the following areas.

- Contingent liabilities
- Exceptional charges
- Operating and financial review comments
- Profit and capital expenditure forecasts

The voluntary approach contrasts with the position in the United States, where the SEC/FASB accounting standards are obligatory.

While nothing is compulsory, there are a number of **published guidelines** and **codes of practice**, including:

- The *Valdez Principles*
- The Confederation of British Industry's guideline *Introducing Environmental Reporting*
- The ACCA's *Guide to Environment and Energy Reporting*
- The Coalition of Environmentally Responsible Economies (CERES) formats for environmental reports
- The Friends of the Earth *Environmental Charter for Local Government*
- The Eco Management and Audit Scheme Code of Practice
- The **Sustainability Reporting Guidelines** issued by the Global Reporting Initiative.

9.5 Example: environmental report

A good example of an environmental report is the Boots report for 1999/2000. This was published as a separate report consisting of around 20 pages. Extracts from the report are reproduced below to give you a feel for it. Note that the report is based around 'key performance indicators'. These are monitored against targets. We emphasise that this is not the only possible approach to environmental reporting.

'Environmental policy statement

We have a responsibility as a company to take proper care of the environment on behalf of our shareholders, customers, staff and the communities in which we operate. Caring for the environment is an essential part of the way we run our business.

We are committed to managing responsibly the way in which our activities affect the environment by:

- Optimising the use of energy
- Ensuring efficient use of materials
- Encouraging re-use and recycling
- Incorporating the principle of sustainable development.

By integrating environmental considerations into our everyday activities, the environment will be managed alongside other business considerations such as safety, quality and value.

Management

We will set objectives and targets for those activities which significantly affect the environment and we will measure our performance over time. Details of our progress will be published at least annually.

Environmental audits and inspections will be undertaken to monitor our progress against this policy.

Within the individual businesses there is a clear structure of responsibility devolved into each business via an appointed manager with overall environmental responsibility. At a corporate level, the Environmental Affairs team co-ordinates environmental issues for the company through the Environmental Working Party.

The company's significant impacts have been assessed and Key Performance Indicators (KPIs) have been selected to track performance over time. Data to monitor these is generated via environmental management systems that are incorporated into business systems and regularly audited.

Environmental management is integrated into everything we do from product development to the supply chain and staff training.

Key performance indicators 99/00

Energy

In 1999/2000 total company energy use decreased by 5.3 per cent, while energy efficiency improved by 10.2 per cent.

Over the last four years energy efficiency, as measured by kWh per $ thousand turnover, has improved by 12 per cent overall, maintaining a positive trend.

Transport

Commercial transport efficiency improved by 2 per cent.

Alongside the ongoing internal data verification programme, improvements to data management systems have resulted in additional transport data being reported for 1998/99. Transport efficiency over the last three years, as measured by litres of diesel consumed per $ million turnover, maintained a positive trend overall with a 2 per cent improvement recorded over the last year.

The efficiency of inventory delivery, as measured by the volume of inventory delivered per 1000 litres of fuel, reduced by 3.7 per cent at Boots The Chemists. This is due to a combination of factors, including new store openings and the closure of an old warehouse in an urban centre (see Progress against targets). The move to lower sulphur diesel for commercial fleets has also had a negative impact on fuel efficiency. Trials of alternative fuel vehicles have continued.

Carbon dioxide and global warming

In the last year, like-for-like CO2 emissions decreased by 4.4 per cent.

The main greenhouse gas associated with the company's operations is CO2 arising primarily from energy use in manufacturing and retailing, and emissions from its transport fleets. Some 84 per cent of total emissions relate to energy consumption. Similarly, around 85 per cent of transport emissions relate to commercial fleets, with around 8 per cent to company cars.

The company's modern combined heat and power (CHP) energy centre on the head office site continues to contribute to a global reduction in annual CO2 emissions of around 44,000 tonnes compared with purchasing electricity from third party suppliers. This represents a reduction in the company's total CO2 emissions of around 15 per cent each year. The saving is achieved through the re-use of waste heat from the electricity generation process to generate usable steam.

Waste

Around 26,000 tonnes of waste was recovered through recycling or incineration with heat recovery.

As the business is primarily retailing, the largest proportion of waste (91 per cent) is transit packaging and general office waste that is mainly non-hazardous. Other wastes arise from manufacturing processes, laboratories, garage and pharmacy operations.

Of the 54,000 tonnes of material identified as waste, some 26,000 tonnes (48 per cent) was recovered through recycling or incineration with heat recovery. The majority of the remaining 28,000 tonnes of waste (94 per cent) was disposed to landfill.

Quantifying the weight of non-hazardous waste is difficult due to small quantities of unweighed waste being collected from a large number of retail locations by multiple collection vehicles, and shopping centres amalgamating non-hazardous waste from a number of retailers for bulk collection. Because of this, although the company's data collection systems for waste have continued to improve, it is unlikely that year-on-year comparisons will be meaningful for some time to come.

Packaging

In the last year the company handled some 162,000 tonnes of packaging.

Minimising packaging is a complex business challenge where a number of considerations have to be balanced. These include evaluating the wide variety of roles performed by packaging (from improved keeping qualities for food and medical products to optimal shapes for efficient stacking and transportation) together with aspects such as design, quality, performance, cost and environment.

In addition, several factors mask the performance that can be directly attributed to packaging management. In particular, consumer and business demands in retailing require ongoing changes to the scale of product ranges and the general product mix within stores, which can produce conflicting trends in packaging use.

The issue will remain as a key performance indicator given its perceived environmental impact in the retail and manufacturing sectors, but it is unlikely that a valid, quantitative comparison of company performance will be developed in this area.

Water and effluent

In the last year Boots Contract Manufacturing reduced the effluent load per unit produced by more than 18 per cent.

Centralised monitoring of water consumption continued with substantial effort being put into the development of robust data management systems. This section relates mainly to Boots Contract Manufacturing, but from April 2000 the data available will include all business units and will be comparable across future years. The acquisition of historical water consumption data proved more difficult than expected, so the overall picture for the company is currently incomplete. Information has been included in the data section where meaningful.

Water conservation in Boots Contract Manufacturing, across all production areas, has again been an area of considerable focus. Improvements such as the elimination of 'once-through' water cooling systems have been implemented in key areas. Fitting improved temperature controls to a tempering belt reduced steam demand as well as saving cooling water.

Water use has been benchmarked across departments and factories to enable sharing of best practice in successful conservation strategies. A computerised data reporting system in the main factory on the Nottingham site allows water use profiles to be analysed. This has been a significant factor in bringing about change. For example, over the past four years water consumption in the factory over the Christmas shutdown period has been reduced from 60 per cent to less than 10 per cent of that on a normal working day. This experience has been shared and improved water metering is now being installed at the Airdrie factory.

In other areas external factors, such as the reduced use of preservatives in products and third party customer specifications that predefine equipment-cleaning procedures, resulted in some increased water use. Overall, water use per unit of production was reduced by 2.6 per cent against a target of 3 per cent.

Reducing waste discharged as effluent has been targeted in several key areas. Process changes have brought about material savings at Nottingham and, at Airdrie, a new system for cleaning pipes between product batches has reduced the amount of water required for this operation by 90 per cent. Together, all these initiatives reduced the loss of material to drain by more than 18 per cent (as measured by chemical oxygen demand and solids load per unit 'produced').'

Key learning points

- Financial statements must be supported by **notes to the accounts**, which give additional information about the figures in the accounts themselves.
- In most jurisdictions, all companies apart from small companies must include a **management report** as part of their accounts.
- The accounts of most limited companies must be **audited** and a report produced by the auditors as to whether the financial statements show a **true and fair view (present fairly).**
- In most jurisdictions large companies include a chairman's report in their published financial statements.
- Listed companies may be called upon to produce an **Operating and Financial Review** in their financial statements. Its purpose is to provide a framework for discussion and analysis of the business's performance and the factors underlying its results and financial position.
- Listed companies may include a **five year summary** of their results in their published accounts. This can help interested parties to see trends and developments over the period.
- Listed companies publish **half yearly interim accounts** for the first six months of their financial year.
- Listed companies make a **preliminary announcement** of their annual results once prepared, to publish news of the company's results and dividends as soon as they are available.
- **Environmental reporting** involves making statements about the impact of the businesses operations on the environment and any steps taken by the company to reduce any negative effects.

Quick quiz

1 List four types of qualified audit report

2 State at least five items that are normally included in a management report.

3 What is the purpose of an operating and financial review?

4 How might an investor carry out a trend analysis of a company's profitability?

5 What comparable figures are shown in a company's interim accounts?

6 Name four areas of company accounts where environmental matters may be reported.

Answers to quick quiz

1 Adverse opinion, qualified opinion (disagreement), total disclaimer of opinion, material disclaimer of opinion

2 See the text (Section 2).

3 To provide a clear, understandable and objective analysis of the company's performance, financial position and prospects, particularly for the benefit of "unsophisticated" users of accounts.

4 By measuring changes over the previous five-year period, taking figures from the five-year review.

5 Figures for the first six months of the previous year, and for the whole of the previous year. Balance sheet figures as at the mid-year and end-of-year dates in the previous year.

6 Contingent liabilities
Exceptional charges
Operating and financial review comments
Profit and capital expenditure forecasts

Part D

Analysis of financial statements

13

Ratio analysis

Topic list
1 Using ratios for analysis
2 The broad categories of ratios
3 Profitability and return on capital
4 Liquidity, gearing/leverage and working capital
5 Shareholders' investment ratios
6 Accounting policies and the limitations of ratio analysis
7 Public sector organisations
8 Presentation of ratio analysis

Introduction

One of the skills which the examiner is looking for in this paper is an ability to interpret financial information. One of the key tools which is used for this purpose is ratio analysis. It is essential that you can calculate the basic ratios contained in this chapter. You also need to be able to explain what they show.

Learning objectives

On completion of this chapter you will be able to:

	Syllabus reference
• compute and interpret financial ratios in respect of profitability, operating performance, liquidity, working capital management, capital structure, cash flows and stock market performance	4 a i-v
• discuss the limitations of financial ratio analysis	4 c

1 Using ratios for analysis

FAST FORWARD

Ratio analysis is a means by which users can extract information from the financial statements.

Users of company accounts try to extract information that indicates the financial performance or financial position of the company. A key problem is how to extract information that might be relied on, or that has any meaning or value. The figures in the accounts themselves might occasionally have some significance, such as when a company makes an enormous loss for the year, or has a huge cash flow deficit. More often, figures in a set of accounts don't have much meaning in themselves, and only acquire meaning when they are related to or compared with something else.

There are various comparisons that could be made:

(a) comparisons of the current year's results with the **previous year**, to establish whether performance or the financial situation has improved or worsened

(b) comparisons of the current year's results with those of similar companies in the same industry, to establish whether the company appears to be doing better or worse than **competitors**

(c) comparisons against a **'standard' or 'benchmark'** level of performance

(d) comparisons of one segment of the business operations with another segment, to establish which parts of the business appear to be performing better than others

One way of making comparisons is to relate one figure in the accounts to another, and calculate a ratio between them. A ratio calculated from the current year's accounting figures can then be compared with the ratio achieved in the previous year, or by a competitor company. Similarly, ratios can be calculated for each major segment of business operations, and the relative performance of each segment can be assessed by comparing the ratios for each.

For example, suppose that a company makes an operating profit of $7 million from sales revenue of $100 million. The ratio of profit to sales for the year is 7%. This figure in itself does not necessarily mean anything, unless it is also established that the ratio of profit to sales was 5% last year, or that the profit to sales ratio earned by a close competitor is, say, just 6%.

Exam focus point

Ratio analysis involves comparing one figure against another to produce a ratio, and assessing whether the ratio indicates a weakness or strength in the company's affairs. In an examination, you might be required to carry out one or more of these comparisons, and comment on your findings.

Calculation of ratios can often be tested in multiple choice questions.

2 The broad categories of ratios

FAST FORWARD

Accounting ratios are only one part of the accountants diagnostic kit for analysing and interpreting financial statements.

Broadly speaking, basic ratios can be grouped into five categories.

- **Profitability and return**
- **Long-term solvency and stability**
- **Short-term solvency and liquidity**
- **Efficiency (turnover ratios)**
- **Shareholders' investment ratios.**

Within each heading there are a number of standard measures or ratios that are traditionally calculated and generally accepted as meaningful indicators. However, **each individual business** must be **considered separately**, and a ratio that is meaningful for a manufacturing company may be completely meaningless for a financial institution. Avoid being **too mechanical when working out ratios.** Always be aware of the importance of **user focus**.

Further **useful insights** might also be gleaned from **companies' financial reports**.

(a) The content of any **accompanying commentary** on the accounts and other statements.

(b) A review of the **age and nature of the company's assets**.

(c) **Current and future developments** in the company's markets, at home and overseas, recent acquisitions or disposals of a subsidiary by the company.

(d) **Additional statements** and notes such as the statement of changes in equity and the statement of recognised income and expense.

(e) **Any other noticeable features** of the report and accounts, such as events after the balance sheet date, contingent liabilities, modified auditors' report, the company's taxation position, and so on.

(f) **Notes** dealing with **non-current assets**

Remember, the nature and scope of the analysis and the amount and quality of information available will depend on the circumstances and the brief provided. A shareholder may only have access to **published information**, whereas a **bank manager** is likely to be in a position to ask to see not only **financial statements**, but also documents such as **business plans**, periodic **management accounts** and **cash flow projections**.

In practice, you may be able to actually speak to management to obtain additional information. However, in an exam situation, you may have to identify what additional information might be useful and **explain tactfully** to the examiner how it might impact on your analysis and interpretation.

2.1 Industry specific performance indicators

In practice, businesses may also use a range of **industry and company specific ratios** to help them **manage the business** on a **day-to-day basis**.

Industry	Performance indicator
Hotels	Room occupancy
Accountants	Chargeable hours utilisation
Farms	Yields per acre
Hospitals	Patient waiting times
Pubs and restaurants	Till overs and unders

Motor manufacturer	Cars produced per worker
Training provider	Exam success rates
Airlines	Daily hours in air per plane

In practice, accounting firm and banks are developing **benchmarking services** for their clients whereby an individual client's **performance indicators** are shown (anonymously) alongside those of other subscribers to the **benchmarking survey**.

2.2 Holistic approach

Accounting ratios are only one part of the accountants diagnostic kit for analysing and interpreting financial statements. Other useful tools or sources of information, if available may comprise:

(a) The company's business plan
(b) Annual budgets
(c) Cash flow projections
(d) Management accounts
(e) Historic accounts figures (past trends)
(f) SWOT analysis
(g) Industry benchmark surveys
(h) Any other strategy or planning documents
(i) On line company and text search services
(j) Press releases and comments

The following diagram reinforces the importance of taking a **holistic approach** when reviewing a set of financial statements.

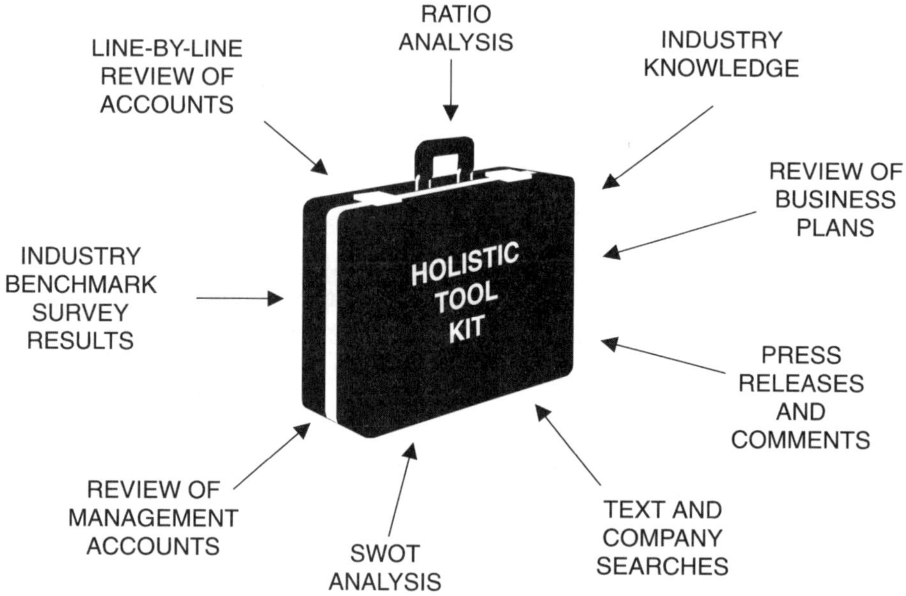

2.3 Basic ratios

The following are the **main accounting ratios** which would **traditionally** be **calculated**. However, in any question that requires you to interpret the financial statements of a company, you should **assess and select** the **most appropriate ratios** to use. Where necessary, you should also **be prepared to apply non-standard industry specific ratios** to support your interpretation.

Accounting ratio		Formula
Profitability and return		
(a)	Gross margin	$\frac{\text{Gross profit}}{\text{Revenue}} \times 100$
(b)	Net margin	$\frac{\text{Profit before interest and taxation (PBIT)}}{\text{Revenue}} \times 100$
(c)	Return on capital employed (ROCE)	$\frac{\text{Profit before interest and taxation (PBIT)}}{\text{Capital employed}} \times 100$ Shareholders' equity plus non current liabilities (where capital employed = total assets less current liabilities).
(d)	Return on equity (ROE)	$\frac{\text{Profit after tax and preferred dividends}}{\text{Equity shareholders' funds}} \times 100$
(e)	Return on gross assets	$\frac{\text{Profit before interest and taxation}}{\text{Non - current assets plus current assets}} \times 100$
(f)	Asset turnover	$\frac{\text{Revenue}}{\text{Capital employed}}$
Long term solvency and stability		
(a)	Debt ratio	$\frac{\text{Total debt}}{\text{Total assets}}$
(b)	Capital gearing	$\frac{\text{Prior charge capital}}{\text{Total capital}}$
(c)	Equity to assets ratio	$\frac{\text{Shareholders' equity}}{\text{Shareholders' equity + total prior charge capital}}$
(d)	Debt/equity ratio	$\frac{\text{Prior charge capital}}{\text{Equity shareholders' funds}}$
(e)	Interest cover	$\frac{\text{Profit before interest and tax (PBIT)}}{\text{Interest charges}}$
(f)	Cash flow ratio	$\frac{\text{Net cash inflow}}{\text{Total debts}}$
Short term solvency and liquidity		
(a)	Current ratio	$\frac{\text{Current assets}}{\text{Current liabilities}}$
(b)	Quick ratio	$\frac{\text{Current assets less inventories}}{\text{Current liabilities}}$
Efficiency		
(a)	Inventory turnover	$\frac{\text{Cost of sales}}{\text{Inventories}}$ or $\frac{\text{Inventories}}{\text{Cost of sales}} \times 365$
(b)	Accounts receivable collection period	$\frac{\text{Credit sales}}{\text{Trade receivables}}$ or $\frac{\text{Trade receivables}}{\text{Credit sales}} \times 365$
(c)	Accounts payable payment period	$\frac{\text{Purchases}}{\text{Trade payables}}$ or $\frac{\text{Trade payables}}{\text{Purchases}} \times 365$

Accounting ratio		Formula
Shareholders' investment ratios		
(a)	Earnings per share	$\frac{\text{Net profit/loss attributable to ordinary shareholders}}{\text{Weighted average number of ordinary shares outstanding during the period}}$
(b)	Dividend cover	$\frac{\text{Earnings per share}}{\text{Net dividend per (ordinary) share}}$
(c)	Price earnings (P/E) ratio	$\frac{\text{Share price}}{\text{Earnings per share}}$
(d)	Dividend yield	$\frac{\text{Dividend on the share for the year}}{\text{Current market value of the share (ex div)}} \times 100$
(e)	Earnings yield	Dividend yield × dividend cover

2.4 Example: calculating ratios

To illustrate the calculation of ratios, the following draft balance sheet and income statement figures will be used.

EARWIGO CO INCOME STATEMENT
FOR THE YEAR ENDED 31 DECEMBER 20X8

	Notes	*20X8*	*20X7*
		$	$
Revenue	1	3,095,576	1,909,051
Operating profit	1	359,501	244,229
Interest	2	17,371	19,127
Profit before taxation		342,130	225,102
Taxation		74,200	31,272
Profit for the period		267,930	193,830
Earnings per share		12.8c	9.3c
Dividends declared during the year		41,000	16,800

EARWIGO CO BALANCE SHEET
AS AT 31 DECEMBER 20X8

	Notes	*20X8*		*20X7*	
		$	$	$	$
Assets					
Non-current assets					
Tangible non-current assets			802,180		656,071
Current assets					
Inventory		64,422		86,550	
Receivables	3	1,002,701		853,441	
Cash at bank and in hand		1,327		68,363	
			1,068,450		1,008,354
Total assets			1,870,630		1,664,425
Equity and liabilities					
Equity					
Ordinary shares 10c each	5	210,000		210,000	
Share premium account		48,178		48,178	
Revenue reserve		630,721		393,791	
			888,899		651,969

	Note		
Non-current liabilities			
10% loan stock 20X4/20Y0		100,000	100,000
Current liabilities	4	881,731	912,456
Total equity and liabilities		1,870,630	1,664,425

NOTES TO THE ACCOUNTS

		20X8	20X7
1	*Sales revenue and profit*	$	$
	Sales revenue	3,095,576	1,909,051
	Cost of sales	2,402,609	1,441,950
	Gross profit	692,967	467,101
	Administration expenses	333,466	222,872
	Operating profit	359,501	244,229
	Depreciation charged	151,107	120,147
2	*Interest*		
	Payable on bank overdrafts and other loans	8,115	11,909
	Payable on loan stock	10,000	10,000
		18,115	21,909
	Receivable on short-term deposits	744	2,782
	Net payable	17,371	19,127
3	*Receivables*		
	Amounts falling due within one year		
	Trade receivables	884,559	760,252
	Prepayments and accrued income	97,022	45,729
		981,581	805,981
	Amounts falling due after more than one year		
	Trade receivables	21,120	47,460
	Total receivables	1,002,701	853,441
4	*Current liabilities*		
	Trade payables	627,018	545,340
	Accruals and deferred income	81,279	280,464
	Corporate taxes	108,000	37,200
	Other taxes	44,434	32,652
	Dividend	21,000	16,800
		881,731	912,456
5	*Called-up share capital*		
	Authorised ordinary shares of 10c each	1,000,000	1,000,000
	Issued and fully paid ordinary shares of 10c each	210,000	210,000

3 Profitability and return on capital

FAST FORWARD

Profitability ratios include:

- Return on capital employed
- Return on equity
- Profit margin
- Asset turnover
- Gross profit margin

In our example, the company made a profit in both 20X8 and 20X7, and there was an increase in profit between one year and the next:

(a) Of 52% before taxation
(b) Of 39% after taxation

Profit before taxation is generally thought to be a better figure to use than profit after taxation, because there might be unusual variations in the tax charge from year to year which would not affect the underlying profitability of the company's operations.

Another profit figure that should be calculated is PBIT, **profit before interest and tax**. This is the amount of profit which the company earned before having to pay interest to the providers of loan capital. By providers of loan capital, we usually mean longer-term loan capital, such as debentures and medium-term bank loans, which will be shown in the balance sheet as non-current liabilities.

Formula to learn

Profit before interest and tax is therefore:

(a) the profit before taxation; **plus**
(b) interest charges on long-term loan capital.

Published accounts do not always give sufficient detail on interest payable to determine how much is interest on long-term finance. We will assume in our example that the whole of the interest payable ($18,115, note 2) relates to long-term finance.

PBIT in our example is therefore:

	20X8	*20X7*
	$	$
Profit before tax	342,130	225,102
Interest payable	18,115	21,909
PBIT	360,245	247,011

This shows a 46% growth between 20X7 and 20X8.

3.1 Return on capital employed (ROCE)

It is impossible to assess profits or profit growth properly without relating them to the **amount of funds (capital) that were employed in making the profits**. The most important profitability ratio is therefore return on capital employed (ROCE), which states the profit as a percentage of the amount of capital employed.

Formula to learn

$$\text{ROCE} = \frac{\text{Profit before interest and taxation}}{\text{Capital employed}} \times 100\%$$

Capital employed = Shareholders' equity plus non-current liabilities
(*or* total assets less current liabilities)

The underlying principle is that we must **compare like with like**, and so if capital means share capital and reserves plus non-current liabilities and debt capital, profit must mean the profit earned by all this capital together. This is PBIT, since interest is the return for loan capital.

In our example, capital employed = 20X8 $1,870,630 – $881,731 = $988,899
20X7 $1,664,425 – $912,456 = $751,969

These total figures are the total assets less current liabilities figures for 20X8 and 20X7 in the balance sheet.

		20X8	*20X7*
ROCE	=	$\frac{\$360,245}{\$988,899}$	$\frac{\$247,011}{\$751,969}$
	=	36.4%	32.8%

What does a company's ROCE tell us? What should we be looking for? There are three comparisons that can be made.

(a) The **change in ROCE from one year to the next** can be examined. In this example, there has been an increase in ROCE by about 4 percentage points from its 20X7 level.

(b) The **ROCE being earned by other companies**, if this information is available, can be compared with the ROCE of this company. Here the information is not available.

(c) A comparison of the ROCE with **current market borrowing rates** may be made.

  (i) What would be the cost of extra borrowing to the company if it needed more loans, and is it earning a ROCE that suggests it could make profits to make such borrowing worthwhile?

  (ii) Is the company making a ROCE which suggests that it is getting value for money from its current borrowing?

  (iii) Companies are in a risk business and commercial borrowing rates are a good independent yardstick against which company performance can be judged.

In this example, if we suppose that current market interest rates, say, for medium-term borrowing from banks, are around 10%, then the company's actual ROCE of 36% in 20X8 would not seem low. On the contrary, it might seem high.

However, it is easier to spot a low ROCE than a high one, because there is always a chance that the company's non-current assets, especially property, are **undervalued** in its balance sheet, and so the capital employed figure might be unrealistically low. If the company had earned a ROCE, not of 36%, but of, say only 6%, then its return would have been below current borrowing rates and so disappointingly low.

3.2 Return on equity (ROE)

Return on equity gives a more restricted view of capital than ROCE, but it is based on the same principles.

Formula to learn

$$\text{ROE} = \frac{\text{Profit after tax and preferred dividend}}{\text{Ordinary share capital and other equity (equity shareholders funds)}} \times 100\%$$

In our example, ROE is calculated as follows.

	20X8	*20X7*
ROE =	$\frac{\$267,930}{\$888,899}$ = 30.1%	$\frac{\$193,830}{\$651,969}$ = 29.7%

ROE is **not a widely-used ratio**, however, because there are more useful ratios that give an indication of the return to shareholders, such as earnings per share, dividend per share, dividend yield and earnings yield, which are described later.

3.3 Analysing profitability and return in more detail: the secondary ratios

We often sub-analyse ROCE, to find out more about why the ROCE is high or low, or better or worse than last year. There are two factors that contribute towards a return on capital employed, both related to sales revenue.

(a) **Profit margin**. A company might make a high or low profit margin on its sales. For example, a company that makes a profit of 25c per $1 of sales is making a bigger return on its revenue than another company making a profit of only 10c per $1 of sales.

(b) **Asset turnover**. Asset turnover is a measure of how well the assets of a business are being used to generate sales. For example, if two companies each have capital employed of $100,000 and Company A makes sales of $400,000 per annum whereas Company B makes sales of only $200,000 per annum, Company A is making a higher revenue from the same amount of assets (twice as much asset turnover as Company B) and this will help A to make a higher return on capital employed than B. Asset turnover is expressed as 'x times' so that assets generate x times their value in annual sales. Here, Company A's asset turnover is 4 times and B's is 2 times.

Profit margin and asset turnover together explain the ROCE and if the ROCE is the primary profitability ratio, these other two are the secondary ratios. The relationship between the three ratios can be shown mathematically.

Formula to learn

Profit margin × Asset turnover = ROCE

$$\therefore \quad \frac{\text{PBIT}}{\text{Revenue}} \times \frac{\text{Revenue}}{\text{Capital employed}} = \frac{\text{PBIT}}{\text{Capital employed}}$$

In our example:

		Profit margin		*Asset turnover*		*ROCE*
(a)	20X8	$\frac{\$360,245}{\$3,095,576}$	×	$\frac{\$3,095,576}{\$988,899}$	=	$\frac{\$360,245}{\$988,899}$
		11.64%	×	3.13 times	=	36.4%
(b)	20X7	$\frac{\$247,011}{\$1,909,051}$	×	$\frac{\$1,909,051}{\$751,969}$	=	$\frac{\$247,011}{\$751,969}$
		12.94%	×	2.54 times	=	32.8%

In this example, the company's improvement in ROCE between 20X7 and 20X8 is attributable to a higher asset turnover. Indeed the profit margin has fallen a little, but the higher asset turnover has more than compensated for this.

It is also worth commenting on the change in sales revenue from one year to the next. You may already have noticed that Earwigo achieved sales growth of over 60% from $1.9 million to $3.1 million between 20X7 and 20X8. This is very strong growth, and this is certainly one of the most significant items in the income statement and balance sheet.

It might be tempting to think that a high profit margin is good, and a low asset turnover means sluggish trading. In broad terms, this is so. But there is a trade-off between profit margin and asset turnover, and you cannot look at one without allowing for the other.

(a) A **high profit margin** means a high profit per $1 of sales, but if this also means that sales prices are high, there is a strong possibility that sales revenue will be depressed, and so asset turnover lower.

(b) A **high asset turnover** means that the company is generating a lot of sales, but to do this it might have to keep its prices down and so accept a low profit margin per $1 of sales.

Consider the following.

Company A		*Company B*	
Sales revenue	$1,000,000	Sales revenue	$4,000,000
Capital employed	$1,000,000	Capital employed	$1,000,000
PBIT	$200,000	PBIT	$200,000

These figures would give the following ratios.

ROCE	=	$\frac{\$200,000}{\$1,000,000}$	= 20%	ROCE	=	$\frac{\$200,000}{\$1,000,000}$	= 20%
Profit margin	=	$\frac{\$200,000}{\$1,000,000}$	= 20%	Profit margin	=	$\frac{\$200,000}{\$4,000,000}$	= 5%
Asset turnover	=	$\frac{\$1,000,000}{\$1,000,000}$	= 1	Asset turnover	=	$\frac{\$4,000,000}{\$1,000,000}$	= 4

The companies have the same ROCE, but it is arrived at in a very different fashion. Company A operates with a low asset turnover and a comparatively high profit margin whereas company B carries out much more business, but on a lower profit margin. Company A could be operating at the luxury end of the market, whilst company B is operating at the popular end of the market.

3.4 Gross profit margin, net profit margin and profit analysis

Depending on the format of the income statement, you may be able to calculate the gross profit margin as well as the net profit margin. **Looking at the two together** can be quite informative.

For example, suppose that a company has the following summarised income statement for two consecutive years.

	Year 1	*Year 2*
	$	$
Revenue	70,000	100,000
Cost of sales	42,000	55,000
Gross profit	28,000	45,000
Expenses	21,000	35,000
Net profit	7,000	10,000

Although the net profit margin is the same for both years at 10%, the gross profit margin is not.

In year 1 it is: $\frac{\$28,000}{\$70,000}$ = 40%

and in year 2 it is: $\frac{\$45,000}{\$100,000}$ = 45%

The improved gross profit margin has not led to an improvement in the net profit margin. This is because expenses as a percentage of sales have risen from 30% in year 1 to 35% in year 2.

4 Liquidity, gearing/leverage and working capital

FAST FORWARD

Debt and gearing/leverage ratios include

- Debt ratio
- Gearing ratio/leverage
- Interest cover
- Cash flow ratio.

4.1 Long-term solvency: debt and gearing ratios

Debt ratios are concerned with **how much the company owes in relation to its size**, whether it is getting into heavier debt or improving its situation, and whether its debt burden seems heavy or light.

(a) When a company is heavily in debt banks and other potential lenders may be unwilling to advance further funds.

(b) When a company is earning only a modest profit before interest and tax, and has a heavy debt burden, there will be very little profit left over for shareholders after the interest charges have been paid. And so if interest rates were to go up (on bank overdrafts and so on) or the company were to borrow even more, it might soon be incurring interest charges in excess of PBIT. This might eventually lead to the liquidation of the company.

These are two big reasons why companies should keep their debt burden under control. There are four ratios that are particularly worth looking at, the debt ratio, gearing ratio, interest cover and cash flow ratio.

4.2 Debt ratio

Formula to learn

$$\text{Debt ratio} = \frac{\text{Total debt}}{\text{Total assets}}$$

(a) Assets consist of non-current assets at their balance sheet value, plus current assets.

(b) Debts consist of all payables, whether they are due within one year or after more than one year.

You can ignore long-term provisions and liabilities, such as deferred taxation.

There is no absolute guide to the maximum safe debt ratio, but as a very general guide, you might regard 50% as a safe limit to debt. In practice, many companies operate successfully with a higher debt ratio than this, but 50% is nonetheless a helpful benchmark. In addition, if the debt ratio is over 50% and getting worse, the company's debt position will be worth looking at more carefully.

In the case of Earwigo the debt ratio is as follows.

	20X8	*20X7*
Total debts	\$ (881,731 + 100,000)	\$ (912,456 + 100,000)
Total assets	\$1,870,630	\$1,664,425
	= 52%	= 61%

In this case, the debt ratio is quite high, mainly because of the large amount of current liabilities. However, the debt ratio has fallen from 61% to 52% between 20X7 and 20X8, and so the company appears to be improving its debt position.

4.3 Gearing/leverage

Capital gearing or leverage is concerned with a company's **long-term capital structure**. We can think of a company as consisting of non-current assets and net current assets (ie working capital, which is current assets minus current liabilities). These assets must be financed by long-term capital of the company, which is one of two things.

(a) Issued share capital which can be divided into:

(i) Ordinary shares plus other equity (eg reserves)
(ii) Preferred shares

(b) Long-term debt

Like loan capital, preferred share capital has a prior claim over profits before interest and tax, ahead of ordinary shareholders. Preferred dividends must be paid out of profits before ordinary shareholders are entitled to an ordinary dividend, and so we refer to preferred share capital and loan capital as **prior charge capital**.

The **capital gearing ratio** is a measure of the proportion of a company's capital that is prior charge capital. It is measured as follows.

Formula to learn

$$\text{Capital gearing} = \frac{\text{Total prior charge capital}}{\text{Shareholders' equity} + \text{total prior charge capital}} \times 100\%$$

(Total capital)

As with the debt ratio, there is **no absolute limit** to what a gearing ratio ought to be. A company with a gearing ratio of more than 50% is said to be high-geared (whereas low gearing means a gearing ratio of less than 50%). Many companies are high geared, but if a high geared company is becoming increasingly high geared, it is likely to have difficulty in the future when it wants to borrow even more, unless it can also boost its shareholders' capital, either with retained profits or by a new share issue.

Leverage is an alternative term for gearing; the words have the same meaning. Note that leverage (or gearing) can be looked at conversely, by calculating the proportion of total assets financed by equity, and which may be called the equity to assets ratio. It is calculated as follows.

Formula to learn

$$\text{Equity to assets ratio} = \frac{\text{Shareholders' equity}}{\text{Shareholders' equity} + \text{total prior charge capital}} \times 100\%$$

or

$$\frac{\text{Shareholders' equity}}{\text{Total assets less current liabilities}}$$

In the example of Earwigo, we find that the company, although having a high debt ratio because of its current liabilities, has a low gearing ratio. It has no preferred share capital and its only long-term debt is the 10% loan stock. The equity to assets ratio is therefore high.

		20X8	*20X7*
Gearing ratio	=	$\frac{\$100,000}{\$988,899}$	$\frac{\$100,000}{\$751,969}$
		= 10%	= 13%
Equity to assets ratio	=	$\frac{\$888,899}{\$988,899}$	$\frac{\$651,969}{\$751,969}$
		= 90%	= 87%

As you can see, the equity to assets ratio is the mirror image of gearing.

The debt/equity ratio provides similar information to the gearing ratio, and here a ratio of 100% or more would indicate high gearing.

Earwigo debt/equity ratio has improved from 15.3% in 20X7 to 11.2% in 20X8.

		20X8	*20X7*
Prior charge capital / Equity shareholders' funds	=	$\frac{\$100,000}{\$888,899}$	$\frac{\$100,000}{\$651,969}$
		= 11.2%	= 15.3%

4.4 The implications of high or low gearing/leverage

We mentioned earlier that **gearing or leverage** is, amongst other things, an attempt to **quantify the degree of risk involved in holding equity shares in a company**, risk both in terms of the company's ability to remain in business and in terms of expected ordinary dividends from the company. The problem with a highly geared company is that by definition there is a lot of debt. Debt generally carries a fixed rate of interest (or fixed rate of dividend if in the form of preferred shares), hence there is a given (and large) amount to be paid out from profits to holders of debt before arriving at a residue available for distribution to the holders of equity. The riskiness will perhaps become clearer with the aid of an example.

	Company A	*Company B*	*Company C*
	$'000	$'000	$'000
Ordinary shares	600	400	300
Revenue reserves	200	200	200
Revaluation reserve	100	100	100
	900	700	600
6% preferred shares	-	-	100
10% loan stock	100	300	300
Capital employed	1,000	1,000	1,000
Gearing ratio	10%	30%	40%
Equity to assets ratio	90%	70%	60%

Now suppose that each company makes a profit before interest and tax of $50,000, and the rate of tax on company profits is 30%. Amounts available for distribution to equity shareholders will be as follows.

	Company A	*Company B*	*Company C*
	$'000	$'000	$'000
Profit before interest and tax	50	50	50
Interest	10	30	30
Taxable profit	40	20	20
Taxation at 30%	12	6	6
Profit after tax	28	14	14
Preferred dividend	–	–	6
Available for ordinary shareholders	28	14	8

If in the subsequent year profit before interest and tax falls to $40,000, the amounts available to ordinary shareholders will become as follows.

	Company A	*Company B*	*Company C*
	$'000	$'000	$'000
Profit before interest and tax	40	40	40
Interest	10	30	30
Taxable profit	30	10	10
Taxation at 30%	9	3	3
Profit after tax	21	7	7
Preferred dividend	–	–	6
Available for ordinary shareholders	21	7	1

Note the following.

Gearing ratio	10%	30%	40%
Equity to assets ratio	90%	70%	60%
Change in PBIT	– 20%	– 20%	– 20%
Change in profit available for ordinary shareholders	– 25%	– 50%	– 87.5%

The more highly geared the company, the greater the risk that little (if anything) will be available to distribute by way of dividend to the ordinary shareholders. The example clearly displays this fact in so far as the more highly geared the company, the greater the percentage change in profit available for ordinary shareholders for any given percentage change in profit before interest and tax. The relationship similarly holds when profits increase, and if PBIT had risen by 20% rather than fallen, you would find that once again the largest percentage change in profit available for ordinary shareholders (this means an increase) will be for the highly geared company. This means that there will be greater *volatility* of amounts available for ordinary shareholders, and presumably therefore greater volatility in dividends paid to those shareholders, where a company is highly geared. That is the risk: you may do extremely well or extremely badly without a particularly large movement in the PBIT of the company.

The risk of a company's ability to remain in business was referred to earlier. Gearing or leverage is relevant to this. A highly geared company has a large amount of interest to pay annually (assuming that the debt is external borrowing rather than preferred shares). If those borrowings are **'secured'** in any way (and debentures in particular are secured), then the **holders of the debt are perfectly entitled to force the company** to **realise assets to pay their interest** if funds are not available from other sources. Clearly the more highly geared a company the more likely this is to occur when and if profits fall.

Here is a little diagram that might help to reinforce your understanding of the implications of different financial structures.

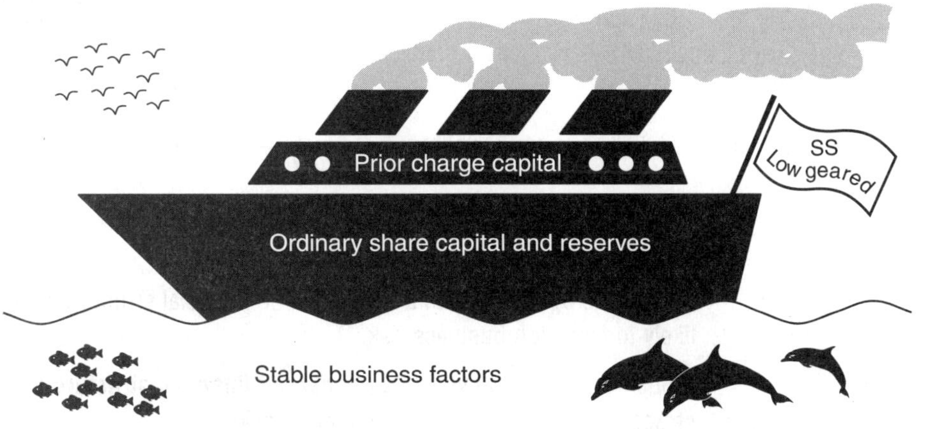

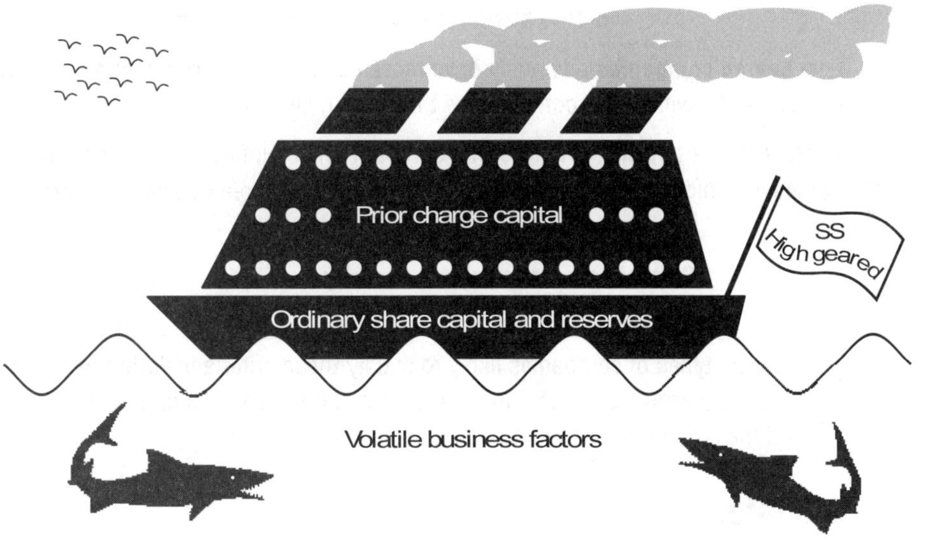

The two above scenarios can be seen within the context of four theoretical scenarios depicted in the two by two matrix below. This provides another tool which you might find useful in looking at a business.

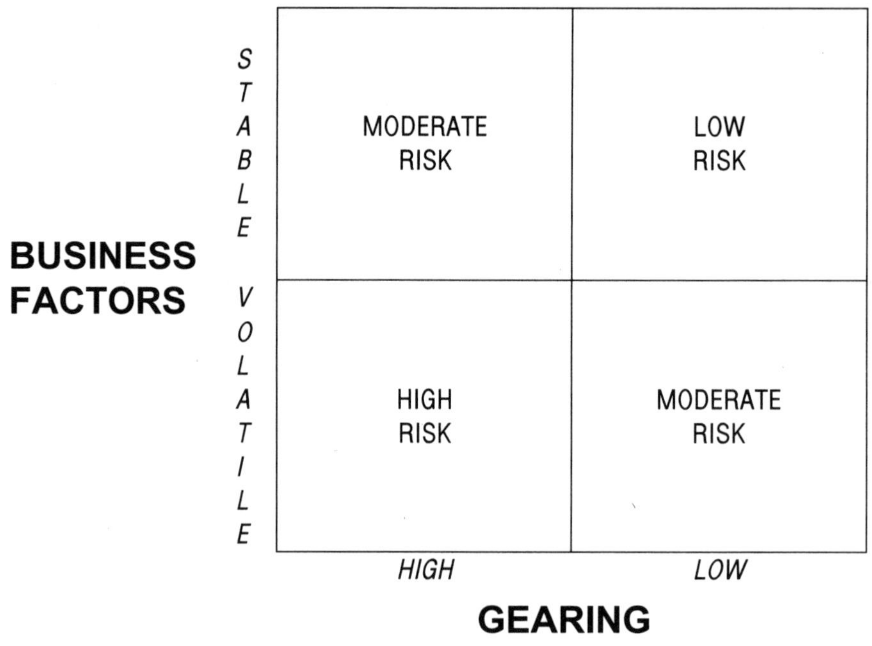

- A business operating with a highly geared financial structure and volatile business factors is likely to face high business risk.
- A business operating with a **lowly geared financial structure** and **stable business factors** structure is likely to have **low business risks**.
- **Moderate business risk** would probably be relevant to businesses with combinations of either:
  - **stable business factors** and **high gearing**.
  - **volatile business** factors and **low gearing**.

Low geared companies obviously have **more capacity** to **borrow money**. However increases in prior charge capital will in turn compromise the gearing situation!

In practice, the **gearing structure** of a company will be influenced by **company policy** as well **nature of the business**. A highly geared structure is likely to rest on three business factors.

- **Stability** of **profits**
- **Suitable assets** to provide **security**
- **Attitude** of **lenders**

Examples of types of companies likely to satisfy these criteria include property investment companies, hotels and supermarket chains. In general terms, companies in high technology industries are less likely to meet the criteria for sustaining a highly geared structure.

4.5 Interest cover

The interest cover ratio shows whether a company is earning enough profits before interest and tax to pay its interest costs comfortably, or whether its interest costs are high in relation to the size of its profits, so that a fall in PBIT would then have a significant effect on profits available for ordinary shareholders.

Formula to learn

$$\text{Interest cover} = \frac{\text{Profit before interest and tax}}{\text{Interest charges}}$$

Returning first to the example of Companies A, B and C, the interest cover was as follows.

			Company A	*Company B*	*Company C*
(a)	When PBIT was $50,000	=	$50,000 / $10,000	$50,000 / $30,000	$50,000 / $30,000
			5 times	1.67 times	1.67 times
(b)	When PBIT was $40,000	=	$40,000 / $10,000	$40,000 / $30,000	$40,000 / $30,000
			4 times	1.33 times	1.33 times

Note. Although preferred share capital is included as prior charge capital for the gearing ratio or leverage, it is usual to exclude preferred dividends from 'interest' charges. We also look at all interest payments, even interest charges on short-term debt, and so interest cover and gearing do not quite look at the same thing.

Both B and C have a low interest cover, which is a warning to ordinary shareholders that their profits are highly vulnerable, in percentage terms, to even small changes in PBIT.

Activity 13.1

Returning to the example of Earwigo in Paragraph 2.4, what is the company's interest cover?

4.6 Cash flow ratio

The cash flow ratio is the ratio of a company's **net cash inflow to its total debts**.

(a) **Net cash inflow** is the amount of cash which the company has coming into the business from its operations. A suitable figure for net cash inflow can be obtained from the cash flow statement.

(b) **Total debts** are short-term and long-term payables, including provisions. A distinction can be made between debts payable within one year and other debts and provisions.

Obviously, a company needs to be earning enough cash from operations to be able to meet its foreseeable debts and future commitments, and the cash flow ratio, and changes in the cash flow ratio from one year to the next, provide a **useful indicator of a company's cash position**.

Free cash flow is the cash flow that a company has available to do whatever it wants. There isn't an official definition of free cash flow and different definitions exists. The definition suggested here is that:

	$
Free cash flow = Net cash flow from operating activities	X
Plus/(minus): cash inflow/(outflow) from financing	X
Minus: interest payments	(X)
Minus: taxation payments	(X)
	X

Having established the amount of free cash flow, all the discretionary spending by the company can be expressed as a percentage of the free cash flow.

4.7 Short-term solvency and liquidity

FAST FORWARD

Liquidity and working capital ratios include
- Current ratio
- Quick ratio (acid test ratio)
- Accounts receivable collection period
- Inventory turnover period
- Accounts payable payment period.

Profitability is of course an important aspect of a company's performance and gearing or leverage is another. Neither, however, addresses directly the key issue of *liquidity*.

Key term

Liquidity is the amount of cash a company can put its hands on quickly to settle its debts (and possibly to meet other unforeseen demands for cash payments too).

Liquid funds consist of:

(a) Cash

(b) Short-term investments for which there is a ready market

(c) Fixed-term deposits with a bank or other financial institution, for example, a six month high-interest deposit with a bank

(d) Trade receivables (because they will pay what they owe within a reasonably short period of time)

(e) Bills of exchange receivable (because like ordinary trade receivables, these represent amounts of cash due to be received within a relatively short period of time)

In summary, **liquid assets are current asset items that will or could soon be converted into cash, and cash itself.** Two common definitions of liquid assets are:

- All current assets without exception
- All current assets with the exception of inventories

A company can obtain liquid assets from sources other than sales of goods and services, such as the issue of shares for cash, a new loan or the sale of non-current assets. But a company cannot rely on these at all times, and in general, obtaining liquid funds depends on making sales revenue and profits. Even so, profits do not always lead to increases in liquidity. This is mainly because funds generated from trading may be immediately invested in non-current assets or paid out as dividends. You should refer back to the chapter on cash flow statements to examine this issue.

The reason why a company needs liquid assets is so that it can meet its debts when they fall due. Payments are continually made for operating expenses and other costs, and so there is a **cash cycle** from trading activities of cash coming in from sales and cash going out for expenses.

4.8 The cash cycle

To help you to understand liquidity ratios, it is useful to begin with a brief explanation of the cash cycle. The cash cycle describes **the flow of cash out of a business and back into it again as a result of normal trading operations.**

Cash goes out to pay for supplies, wages and salaries and other expenses, although payments can be delayed by taking some credit. A business might hold inventory for a while and then sell it. Cash will come back into the business from the sales, although customers might delay payment by themselves taking some credit.

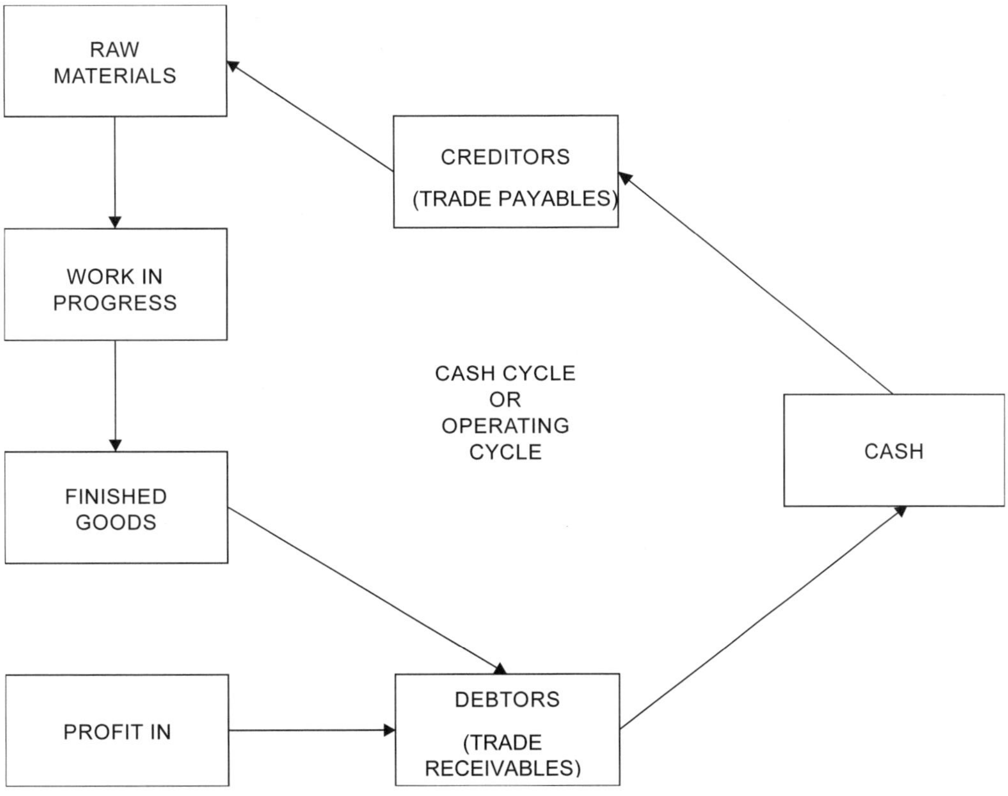

The main points about the cash cycle are as follows.

(a) The timing of cash flows in and out of a business does not coincide with the time when sales and costs of sales occur. **Cash flows out can be postponed by taking credit. Cash flows in can be delayed by having receivables.**

(b) **The time between making a purchase and making a sale also affects cash flows.** If inventories are held for a long time, the delay between the cash payment for inventory and cash receipts from selling it will also be a long one.

(c) **Holding inventories and having receivables can therefore be seen as two reasons why cash receipts are delayed.** Another way of saying this is that if a company invests in working capital, its cash position will show a corresponding decrease.

(d) Similarly, **taking credit from creditors can be seen as a reason why cash payments are delayed**. The company's liquidity position will worsen when it has to pay the suppliers, unless it can get more cash in from sales and receivables in the meantime.

The liquidity ratios and working capital turnover ratios are used to test a company's liquidity, length of cash cycle, and investment in working capital.

4.9 Liquidity ratios: current ratio and quick ratio

The 'standard' test of liquidity is the **current ratio**. It can be obtained from the balance sheet.

Formula to learn

$$\text{Current ratio} = \frac{\text{Current assets}}{\text{Current liabilities}}$$

For Earwigo this would be calculated as follows:

		20X8	*20X7*
$\frac{\text{Current assets}}{\text{Current liabilities}}$	=	$\frac{\$1,068,450}{\$881,731}$	$\frac{\$1,008,354}{\$912,456}$
		= 1.2:1	= 1.1:1

The idea behind this is that a company should have enough current assets that give a promise of 'cash to come' to meet its future commitments to pay off its current liabilities. Obviously, a **ratio in excess of 1 should be expected**. Otherwise, there would be the prospect that the company might be unable to pay its debts on time. In practice, a ratio comfortably in excess of 1 should be expected, but what is 'comfortable' varies between different types of businesses.

Companies are not able to convert all their current assets into cash very quickly. In particular, some manufacturing companies might hold large quantities of raw material inventories, which must be used in production to create finished goods inventory. These might be warehoused for a long time, or sold on lengthy credit. In such businesses, where inventory turnover is slow, most inventories are not very 'liquid' assets, because the cash cycle is so long. For these reasons, we calculate an additional liquidity ratio, known as the quick ratio or acid test ratio.

The **quick ratio**, or **acid test ratio**, is calculated as follows.

Formula to learn

$$\text{Quick ratio} = \frac{\text{Current assets less inventory}}{\text{Current liabilities}}$$

For Earwigo this would be calculated as follows:

	20X8	*20X7*
$\frac{\text{Current assets} - \text{inventory}}{\text{Current liabilities}} =$	$\frac{\$1,004,028}{\$881,731}$	$\frac{\$921,804}{\$912,456}$
	= 1.14:1	= 1.01:1

This ratio should ideally be **at least 1** for companies with a slow inventory turnover. For companies with a fast inventory turnover, a quick ratio can be comfortably less than 1 without suggesting that the company could be in cash flow trouble.

Both the current ratio and the quick ratio offer an indication of the company's liquidity position, but the absolute figures **should not be interpreted too literally**. It is often theorised that an acceptable current ratio is 1.5 and an acceptable quick ratio is 0.8, but these should only be used as a guide. Different businesses operate in very different ways. A supermarket group for example might have a current ratio of 0.52 and a quick ratio of 0.17. Supermarkets have low receivables (people do not buy groceries on credit), low cash (good cash management), medium inventories (high inventories but quick turnover, particularly in view of perishability) and very high payables.

Compare this with a manufacturing and retail organisation, with a current ratio of 1.44 and a quick ratio of 1.03. Such businesses operate with liquidity ratios closer to the standard.

What is important is the **trend** of these ratios. From this, one can easily ascertain whether liquidity is improving or deteriorating. If a supermarket has traded for the last 10 years (very successfully) with current ratios of 0.52 and quick ratios of 0.17 then it should be supposed that the company can continue in business with those levels of liquidity. If in the following year the current ratio were to fall to 0.38 and the quick ratio to 0.09, then further investigation into the liquidity situation would be appropriate. It is the relative position that is far more important than the absolute figures.

Don't forget the other side of the coin either. A current ratio and a quick ratio can get **bigger than they need to be**. A company that has large volumes of inventories and receivables might be over-investing in working capital, and so tying up more funds in the business than it needs to. This would suggest poor management of receivables (credit) or inventories by the company.

4.10 Efficiency ratios: control of receivables and inventories

A rough measure of the average length of time it takes for a company's customers to pay what they owe is the accounts receivable collection period.

Formula to learn

> The estimated average accounts receivable collection period is calculated as:
>
> $$\frac{\text{Trade receivables}}{\text{Revenue}} \times 365 \text{ days}$$

For Earwigo this would be calculated as follows:

		20X8	*20X7*
$\frac{\text{Trade receivables}}{\text{Revenue}}$	=	$\frac{\$884,559}{\$3,095,576} \times 365$	$\frac{\$760,252}{\$1,909,051} \times 365$
		= 104.3 days	= 145.4 days

The figure for sales should be taken as the sales revenue figure in the income statement. The trade receivables are not the total figure for receivables in the balance sheet, which includes prepayments and non-trade receivables. The trade receivables figure will be itemised in an analysis of the receivable total, in a note to the accounts.

The estimate of the accounts receivable collection period is **only approximate**.

(a) The balance sheet value of receivables might be abnormally high or low compared with the 'normal' level the company usually has. This may be overcome by using the average receivables balance for the current and previous year.

(b) Sales revenue in the income statement is exclusive of sales taxes, but receivables in the balance sheet are inclusive of sales tax. We are not strictly comparing like with like.

Sales are usually made on 'normal credit terms' of payment within 30 days. A collection period significantly in excess of this might be representative of poor management of funds of a business. However, some companies must allow generous credit terms to win customers. Exporting companies in particular may have to carry large amounts of receivables, and so their average collection period might be well in excess of 30 days.

The **trend of the collection period over time** is probably the best guide. If the collection period is increasing year on year, this is indicative of a poorly managed credit control function (and potentially therefore a poorly managed company).

4.11 Accounts receivable collection period: examples

Using the same types of company as examples, the collection period for each of the companies was as follows.

Company	$\frac{\text{Trade receivables}}{\text{Sales}}$	$\frac{\text{Collection period}}{(\times 365)}$	*Previous year*	$\frac{\text{Collection period}}{(\times 365)}$
Supermarket	$\frac{\$5,016K}{\$284,986K}$ =	6.4 days	$\frac{\$3,977K}{\$290,668K}$ =	5.0 days
Manufacturer	$\frac{\$458.3m}{\$2,059.5m}$ =	81.2 days	$\frac{\$272.4m}{\$1,274.2m}$ =	78.0 days
Sugar refiner and seller	$\frac{\$304.4m}{\$3,817.3m}$ =	29.3 days	$\frac{\$287.0m}{\$3,366.3m}$ =	31.1 days

The differences in collection period reflect the differences between the types of business. Supermarkets have hardly any trade receivables at all, whereas the manufacturing companies have far more. The collection periods are fairly constant from the previous year for all three companies.

4.12 Inventory turnover period

Another ratio worth calculating is the inventory turnover period. This is another estimated figure, obtainable from published accounts, which indicates the average number of days that items of inventory are held for. As with the average receivable collection period, however, it is only an approximate estimated figure, but one which should be reliable enough for comparing changes year on year.

An average of the current and previous year end inventory balances may be used.

Formula to learn

> The inventory turnover period is calculated as:
>
> $$\frac{\text{Inventory}}{\text{Cost of sales}} \times 365 \text{ days}$$

For Earwigo this would be calculated as follows:

	20X8	*20X7*
$\frac{\text{Inventory}}{\text{Cost of sales}} =$	$\frac{\$64,422}{\$2,402,609} \times 365$	$\frac{\$86,550}{\$1,441,950} \times 365$
	= 9.8 days	= 21.9 days

Earwigo has significantly refined its inventory turnover period. Depending on lead times this may lead to inventory shortages.

This is another measure of how vigorously a business is trading. A lengthening inventory turnover period from one year to the next indicates:

(a) a slowdown in trading; or

(b) a build-up in inventory levels, perhaps suggesting that the investment in inventories is becoming excessive.

Generally the **higher the inventory turnover the better**, ie the lower the turnover period the better, but several aspects of inventory holding policy have to be balanced.

(a) Lead times
(b) Seasonal fluctuations in orders
(c) Alternative uses of warehouse space
(d) Bulk buying discounts
(e) Likelihood of inventory perishing or becoming obsolete

Presumably if we add together the inventory turnover period and receivables collection period, this should give us an indication of how soon inventory is converted into cash. Both receivables collection period and inventory turnover period therefore give us a further indication of the company's liquidity.

4.13 Accounts payable payment period

Formula to learn

> **Accounts payable payment period** is ideally calculated by the formula:
>
> $$\frac{\text{Trade accounts payable}}{\text{Purchases}} \times 365 \text{ days}$$

It is rare to find purchases disclosed in published accounts and so **cost of sales serves as an approximation**. An average of the current and previous year end payables balances may be used. The payment period often helps to assess a company's liquidity; an increase is often a sign of lack of long-term finance or poor management of current assets, resulting in the use of extended credit from suppliers, increased bank overdraft and so on.

For Earwigo this would be calculated as follows:

	20X8	*20X7*
$\frac{\text{Trade accounts payable}}{\text{Purchases}} \times 365 =$	$\frac{\$627{,}018}{\$2{,}402{,}609} \times 365$	$\frac{\$545{,}340}{\$1{,}441{,}950} \times 365$
Purchases	= 95.3 days	= 138.0 days

The payment period has accelerated between 20X7 and 20X8.

Activity 13.2

Calculate liquidity and working capital ratios from the accounts of TEB Co, a business which provides service support (cleaning etc) to customers worldwide. Comment on the results of your calculations.

	20X7	*20X6*
	$m	$m
Sales revenue	2,176.2	2,344.8
Cost of sales	1,659.0	1,731.5
Gross profit	517.2	613.3
Current assets		
Inventories	42.7	78.0
Receivables (note 1)	378.9	431.4
Short-term deposits and cash	205.2	145.0
	626.8	654.4
Current liabilities		
Loans and overdrafts	32.4	81.1
Tax on profits	67.8	76.7
Dividend	11.7	17.2
Payables (note 2)	487.2	467.2
	599.1	642.2
Net current assets	27.7	12.2
Notes		
1 Trade receivables	295.2	335.5
2 Trade payables	190.8	188.1

The company in the exercise is a service company and hence it would be expected to have very low inventory and a very short inventory turnover period. The similarity of receivables collection period and payables payment period means that the company is passing on most of the delay in receiving payment to its suppliers.

Activity 13.3

(a) Calculate the operating cycle for Moribund Co for 20X2 on the basis of the following information.

	$
Inventory: raw materials	150,000
work in progress	60,000
finished goods	200,000
Purchases	500,000
Trade accounts receivable	230,000
Trade accounts payable	120,000
Revenue	900,000
Cost of goods sold	750,000

Tutorial note. You will need to calculate inventory turnover periods (total year end inventory over cost of goods sold), receivables as daily sales, and payables in relation to purchases, all converted into 'days'.

(b) List the steps which might be taken in order to improve the operating cycle.

5 Shareholders' investment ratios

FAST FORWARD

These are the ratios which help equity shareholders and other investors to **assess the value and quality of an investment in the ordinary shares of a company.**

They are:

(a) Earnings per share
(b) Dividend per share
(c) Dividend cover
(d) P/E ratio
(e) Dividend yield

The value of an investment in ordinary shares in a company **listed on a stock exchange** is its market value, and so investment ratios must have regard not only to information in the company's published accounts, but also to the current price, and the fourth and fifth ratios involve using the share price.

5.1 Earnings per share

Formula to learn

$$\text{Basic EPS} = \frac{\text{Net profit/(loss) attributable to oridinary shareholders}}{\text{Weighted average number of ordinary shares outstanding during the period}}$$

It is possible to calculate the return on each ordinary share in the year. This is the earnings per share (EPS). Earnings per share is the amount of net profit for the period that is attributable to each ordinary share which is outstanding during all or part of the period (see Chapter 5).

5.2 Dividend per share and dividend cover

The **dividend per share** in cents is self-explanatory, and clearly an item of some interest to shareholders.

Formula to learn

Dividend cover is a ratio of: $\frac{\text{Earnings per share}}{\text{Dividend per (ordinary) share}}$

It shows the **proportion of profit for the year that is available for distribution to shareholders that has been paid (or proposed) and what proportion will be retained in the business to finance future growth.** A dividend cover of 2 times would indicate that the company had paid 50% of its distributable profits as dividends, and retained 50% in the business to help to finance future operations. Retained profits are an important source of funds for most companies, and so the dividend cover can in some cases be quite high.

A **significant change** in the dividend cover from one year to the next would be worth looking at closely. For example, if a company's dividend cover were to fall sharply between one year and the next, it could be that its profits had fallen, but the directors wished to pay at least the same amount of dividends as in the previous year, so as to keep shareholder expectations satisfied.

For Earwigo this would be calculated as follows:

		20X8	20X7
$\frac{\text{Earnings per share}}{\text{Dividend per share}}$ =	=	$\frac{12.8c}{1.95c}$	$\frac{\$9.3c}{0.8c}$
		= 6.5 times	= 11.6 times

Dividend cover has fallen. This is because the dividend paid has gone up by 244.1% when net profit after tax has only increased by 38.2%.

5.3 P/E ratio

Formula to learn

P/E ratio is a ratio of: $\frac{\text{Share price}}{\text{Earnings per share}}$

A high P/E ratio indicates strong shareholder **confidence** in the company and its future, eg in profit growth, and a lower P/E ratio indicates lower confidence.

The P/E ratio of one company can be compared with the P/E ratios of:

- Other companies in the same business sector
- Other companies generally

It is often used in **stock exchange reporting** where prices are readily available.

5.4 Dividend yield

Dividend yield is the return a shareholder is currently expecting on the shares of a company.

Formula to learn

$$\text{Dividend yield} = \frac{\text{Dividend on the share for the year}}{\text{Current market value of the share (ex div)}} \times 100\%$$

(a) The dividend per share is taken as the dividend for the previous year.
(b) Ex-div means that the share price does *not* include the right to the most recent dividend.

Shareholders look for **both dividend yield and capital growth**. Obviously, dividend yield is therefore an important aspect of a share's performance.

Activity 13.4

In the year to 30 September 20X8, an advertising agency declares an interim ordinary dividend of 7.4c per share and a final ordinary dividend of 8.6c per share. Assuming an ex div share price of 315 cents, what is the dividend yield?

5.5 Earnings yield

Formula to learn

Earnings yield = Dividend yield × dividend cover.

Earnings yield is a **performance indicator** that is not given the same publicity as EPS, P/E ratio, dividend cover and dividend yield. It is measured as earnings per share, grossed up, as a percentage of the current share price. It therefore indicates what the dividend yield could be if the company paid out all its profits as dividend and retained nothing in the business.

Some companies retain a bigger proportion of their profits than others, and so the dividend yield between companies can vary for this reason. **Earnings yield overcomes the problem of comparison by assuming that all earnings are paid out as dividends.**

6 Accounting policies and the limitations of ratio analysis

FAST FORWARD The results of a company can be altered significantly by the choice of accounting policy.

6.1 The effect of choice of accounting policies

Where accounting standards allow alternative treatment of items in the accounts, then the accounting policy note should declare which policy has been chosen. It should then be applied consistently.

You should be able to think of examples of how the choice of accounting policy can affect the financial statements eg whether to revalue property in IAS 16.

6.2 Changes in accounting policy

The effect of a change of accounting policy is treated as a prior year adjustment according to IAS 8 (see Chapter 7). This just means that the comparative figures are adjusted for the change in accounting policy for comparative purposes and an adjustment is put through reserves.

Under **consistency of presentation** in IAS 1, any change in policy may only be made if it can be justified on the grounds that the new policy is preferable to the one it replaces because it will give a fairer presentation of the result and of the financial position of a reporting entity.

The problem with this situation is that the directors may be able to **manipulate the results** through change(s) of accounting policies. This would be done to avoid the effect of an old accounting policy or gain the effect of a new one. It is likely to be done in a sensitive period, perhaps when the company's profits are low or the company is about to announce a rights issue. The management would have to convince the auditors that the new policy was much better, but it is not difficult to produce reasons in such cases.

The effect of such a change is very **short-term**. Most analysts and sophisticated users will discount its effect immediately, except to the extent that it will affect any dividend (because of the effect on distributable profits). It may help to avoid breaches of banking covenants because of the effect on certain ratios.

Obviously, the accounting policy for any item in the accounts could only be changed once in quite a long period of time. Auditors would not allow another change, even back to the old policy, unless there was a wholly exceptional reason.

The managers of a company can choose accounting policies **initially** to suit the company or the type of results they want to get. Any changes in accounting policy must be justified, but some managers might try to change accounting policies just to manipulate the results.

Activity 13.5

The following are a selection of accounting ratios for a range of public companies in various industries ie

- Furniture
- Recruitment and business services
- Supermarket
- Cruise liner holidays
- Bakery shops

Review the table provided, then have a go at trying to identify which ratios relate to which industry. Write your response into the space provided at the foot of the table.

Standard ratios	*Company A*	*Company B*	*Company C*	*Company D*	*Company E*
Gross margin	8.0%	61.3%	49.6%	24.0%	-
ROCE	17.4%	26.3%	11.6%	10.1%	29.2%
Asset turnover	2.9 times	3.4 times	2.5 times	0.7 times	2.7 times
Current ratio	0.8:1	0.7:1	1.4:1	0.7:1	1.1:1
Inventory turnover	20.4 days	15.7 days	102.2 days	12.0 days	N/A
Receivables payment period	1.1 days	0.5 days	15.0 days	5.8 days	56.2 days
Payables payment period	40.0 days	54.7 days	53.7 days	30.2 days	-
Non-standard ratio					
Staff costs per employee	$17,566	$9,211	$22,279	$9,672	$24,646
Industry involved					

6.3 Limitations of ratio analysis

Ratio analysis can be helpful in extracting meaningful information from a company's accounts. However, ratio analysis has limitations that need to be understood, if the information is to be interpreted and used sensibly.

The limitations of ratio analysis are summarised in the table below.

Two-year comparisons	When ratios are used to compare the current year's results with the previous year, only two years' results are being used. The comparison might be misleading, particularly when results include unusually good or bad 'one-off' items in one of the years, that is not expected to recur.
Misleading balance sheet figures	The figures in the balance sheet may be misleading, perhaps because the position at the balance sheet date is not representative of the normal financial position of the company.
Historical cost convention	Where the historical cost convention is used, asset valuations in the balance sheet could be misleading.
Ratios are not definitive measures	Ratios need to be interpreted carefully. They can provide clues to the company's performance or financial situation, but on their own, they cannot show whether performance is good or bad.
Variations in measurement	There are no standard definitions for many ratios, which are therefore calculated in different ways by different analysts.
Out of date figures	The figures in a set of accounts are likely to be at least several months out of date, and so might not give a proper indication of the company's current performance and financial position.

Changes in the business over time	A company's operations may change considerably over time, with new businesses being acquired and existing businesses disposed of. Looking at trends in performance over time could therefore be difficult.
Comparing results of similar companies	No two companies are the same, even when they are competitors in the same industry or market. Using ratios to compare one company with another could provide misleading information.

Ratios are used as a means of condensing a company's accounts into meaningful information, but ratio analysis is largely subjective, and is more an art than a science. Provided these limitations are kept in mind, ratio analysis is nevertheless an essential tool for the interpretation of company accounts.

7 Public sector organisations

FAST FORWARD

In public sector organisations performance is measured in terms of 'best value'.

Public sector organisations are generally not-for-profit organisations, and their performance should not be measured in terms of sales turnover or profit. It is therefore usual to measure performance in public sector organisations in terms of the achievement of best value. As discussed earlier in the text, public sector organisations utilise what are called performance indicators or targets.

Two elements of measuring best value are:

(a) Monitoring efficiency performance indictors
(b) Monitoring indicators of effectiveness in achieving the organisation's objectives

Efficiency in a public sector organisation, as in a company, is a ratio of outputs obtained to input resources used. Outputs cannot be sales or profit, and has to be measured in terms of achievements that are relevant to the organisation concerned. Examples of efficiency performance indicators would therefore be:

(a) Student: teacher ratio (in schools)
(b) Patients treated per $1 of spending (in hospitals or doctors' surgeries)
(c) Cost per patient day (in hospitals)
(d) Cases handled per employee (in social work)

Effectiveness measures focus on what the organisation is attempting to achieve. Often targets will be set by the government, although targets might be set by a local government body or governing committee. To judge effectiveness, it is necessary to identify a measurable target of achievement, and monitor progress towards reaching the objective. Examples of performance indicators of effectiveness in the public sector might be:

(a) Reductions in the length of hospital waiting lists
(b) Reductions in the average length of stay in hospital per in-patient treated
(c) Reductions in the volume of street crime
(d) Increases in school examination pass rates

8 Presentation of ratio analysis

FAST FORWARD

You must realise that, however many ratios you can find to calculate, **numbers alone will not answer a question**. You **must** interpret all the information available to you and support your interpretation with ratio calculations.

Exam focus point

Examination questions on financial performance may try to simulate a real life situation. A set of accounts could be presented and you may be asked to prepare a report on them, addressed to a specific interested party, such as a bank.

You should begin your report with a heading showing who it is from, the name of the addressee, the subject of the report and a suitable date.

A good approach is often to head up a **'schedule of ratios and statistics'** which will form an appendix to the main report. Calculate the ratios in a logical sequence, dealing in turn with operating and profitability ratios, use of assets (eg turnover period for inventories, collection period for receivables), liquidity and gearing/leverage.

As you calculate the ratios you are likely to be struck by **significant fluctuations and trends**. These will form the basis of your comments in the body of the report. The report should begin with some introductory comments, setting out the scope of your analysis and mentioning that detailed figures have been included in an appendix. You should then go on to present your analysis under any categories called for by the question (eg separate sections for management, shareholders and creditors, or separate sections for profitability and liquidity).

Finally, look out for opportunities to **suggest remedial action** where trends appear to be unfavourable. Questions sometimes require you specifically to set out your advice and recommendations.

8.1 Planning your answers

This is as good a place as any to stress the importance of planning your answers. This is particularly important for 'wordy' questions. While you may feel like breathing a sigh of relief after all that number crunching, you should not be tempted to 'waffle'. The best way to avoid going off the point is to **prepare an answer plan**. This has the advantage of making you think before you write and structure your answer logically.

The following approach may be adopted when preparing an answer plan.

(a) Read the question **requirements**.

(b) **Skim through the question** to see roughly what it is about.

(c) Read through the question carefully, **underlining any key words**.

(d) Set out the **headings** for the main parts of your answer. Leave space to insert points within the headings.

(e) **Jot down points** to make within the main sections, underlining points on which you wish to expand.

(f) Write your **full answer**.

You should allow yourself the full time allocation for written answers, that is 1.8 minutes per mark. If, however, you run out of time, a clear answer plan with points in note form will earn you more marks than an introductory paragraph written out in full.

Activity 13.6

The following information has been extracted from the recently published accounts of DG.

EXTRACTS FROM THE INCOME STATEMENTS TO 30 APRIL

	20X9	*20X8*
	$'000	$'000
Sales	11,200	9,750
Cost of sales	8,460	6,825
Net profit before tax	465	320
This is after charging:		
Depreciation	360	280
Debenture interest	80	60
Interest on bank overdraft	15	9
Audit fees	12	10

BALANCE SHEETS AS AT 30 APRIL

	20X9		*20X8*	
	$'000	$'000	$'000	$'000
Assets				
Non-current assets		1,850		1,430
Current assets				
Inventory	640		490	
Receivables	1,230		1,080	
Cash	80		120	
		1,950		1,690
Total assets		3,800		3,120
Equity and liabilities				
Equity				
Ordinary share capital	800		800	
Reserves	1,245		875	
		2,045		1,675
Non-current liabilities				
10% debentures		800		600
Current liabilities				
Bank overdraft	110		80	
Payables	750		690	
Taxation	30		20	
Dividends	65		55	
		955		845
Total equity and liabilities		3,800		3,120

The following ratios are those calculated for DG, based on its published accounts for the previous year, and also the latest industry average ratios:

	DG 30 April 20X8	*Industry average*
ROCE (capital employed = equity and debentures)	16.70%	18.50%
Profit/sales	3.90%	4.73%
Asset turnover	4.29	3.91
Current ratio	2.00	1.90
Quick ratio	1.42	1.27
Gross profit margin	30.00%	35.23%
Accounts receivable collection period	40 days	52 days
Accounts payable payment period	37 days	49 days
Inventory turnover (times)	13.90	18.30
Gearing	26.37%	32.71%

Required

(a) Calculate comparable ratios (to two decimal places where appropriate) for DG for the year ended 30 April 20X9. All calculations must be clearly shown.

(b) Write a report to your board of directors analysing the performance of DG, comparing the results against the previous year and against the industry average.

Key learning points

- Ratio analysis is a means by which users can extract information from the financial statements.
- Accounting ratios are only one part of the accountant's diagnostic kit for analysing and interpreting financial statements.
- This lengthy chapter has gone into quite a lot of detail about basic ratio analysis. The ratios you should be able to calculate and/or comment on are as follows.
  - **Profitability ratios include**
    - Return on capital employed
    - Return on equity
    - Net profit margin
    - Asset turnover ratio
    - Gross profit margin
  - **Debt and gearing/leverage ratios include**
    - Debt ratio
    - Gearing ratio/leverage
    - Interest cover
    - Cash flow ratio
  - **Liquidity and working capital ratios**
    - Current ratio
    - Quick ratio (acid test ratio)
    - Accounts receivable collection period
    - Inventory turnover period
    - Accounts payable payment period
- Shareholders' investment ratios are the ratios which help equity shareholders and other investors to assess the value and quality of an investment in the ordinary shares of a company.
- The results of a company can be altered significantly by the choice of accounting policy.
- In public sector organisations performance is measured in terms of 'best value'.
- You must realise that, however many ratios you can find to calculate, **numbers alone will not answer a question**. You *must* interpret all the information available to you and support your interpretation with ratio calculations.

Quick quiz

1 List the main categories of ratio.

2 Brainstorm a list of sources of information which would be useful in interpreting a company's accounts.

3 ROCE is $\frac{\text{Profit before interest and tax}}{\text{Capital employed}} \times 100\%$

True ☐

False ☐

4 Company Q has a profit margin of 7%. Briefly comment on this.

5 The debt ratio is a company's long-term debt divided by its net assets.

True ☐

False ☐

6 The cash flow ratio is the ratio of:

A Gross cash inflow to total debt
B Gross cash inflow to net debt
C Net cash inflow to total debt
D Net cash inflow to net debt

7 List the formulae for:

(a) Current ratio (c) Accounts receivable collection period
(b) Quick ratio (d) Inventory turnover period

8 List six limitations to ratio analysis.

Answers to quick quiz

1 See Section 2.2.

2 There are a number of sources (see Section 2.2). Information on competitors and the economic climate are further items of information.

3 True

4 You should be careful here. You have very little information. This is a low margin but you need to know what industry the company operates in. 7% may be good for a major retailer.

5 False (see Section 4.2)

6 C (see Section 4.6)

7 See Sections 4.9, 4.10, 4.12.

8 Compare your list to that in paragraph 6.3.

Answers to activities

13.1 Interest payments should be taken gross, from the note to the accounts, and not net of interest receipts as shown in the income statement.

	20X8	20X7
$\frac{\text{PBIT}}{\text{Interest payable}}$	$\frac{360,245}{18,115}$	$\frac{247,011}{21,909}$
	= 20 times	= 11 times

Earwigo has more than sufficient interest cover. In view of the company's low gearing, this is not too surprising and so we finally obtain a picture of Earwigo as a company that does not seem to have a debt problem, in spite of its high (although declining) debt ratio.

13.2

	20X7	20X6
Current ratio	$\frac{626.8}{599.1} = 1.05$	$\frac{654.4}{642.2} = 1.02$
Quick ratio	$\frac{584.1}{599.1} = 0.97$	$\frac{576.4}{642.2} = 0.90$
Accounts receivable collection period	$\frac{295.2}{2,176.2} \times 365 = 49.5$ days	$\frac{335.5}{2,344.8} \times 365 = 52.2$ days
Inventory turnover period	$\frac{42.7}{1,659.0} \times 365 = 9.4$ days	$\frac{78.0}{1,731.5} \times 365 = 16.4$ days
Accounts payable payment period	$\frac{190.8}{1,659.0} \times 365 = 42.0$ days	$\frac{188.1}{1,731.5} \times 365 = 40.0$ days

The company's current ratio is a little lower than average but its quick ratio is better than average and very little less than the current ratio. This suggests that inventory levels are strictly controlled, which is reinforced by the low inventory turnover period. It would seem that working capital is tightly managed, to avoid the poor liquidity which could be caused by a long receivables collection period and comparatively high payables. The company in the exercise is a service company and hence it would be expected to have very low inventory and a very short inventory turnover period. The similarity of receivables collection period, and payables payment period meant that the company is passing on most of the delay in receiving payment to its suppliers.

13.3 (a) The operating cycle can be found as follows.

Inventory turnover period: $\frac{\text{Total closing inventory} \times 365}{\text{Cost of goods sold}}$

plus

Accounts receivable collection period: $\frac{\text{Closing trade receivables} \times 365}{\text{Sales}}$

less

Accounts payable payment period: $\frac{\text{Closing trade payables} \times 365}{\text{Purchases}}$

	20X2
Total closing inventory ($)	410,000
Cost of goods sold ($)	750,000
Inventory turnover period	199.5 days
Closing receivables ($)	230,000
Sales ($)	900,000
Receivables collection period	93.3 days
Closing payables ($)	120,000
Purchases ($)	500,000
Payables payment period	(87.6 days)
Length of operating cycle (199.5 + 93.3 – 87.6)	205.2 days

(b) The steps that could be taken to reduce the operating cycle include the following.

(i) Reducing the raw material inventory turnover period.

(ii) Reducing the time taken to produce goods. However, the company must ensure that quality is not sacrificed as a result of speeding up the production process.

(iii) Increasing the period of credit taken from suppliers. The credit period already seems very long – the company is allowed three months credit by its suppliers, and probably could not be increased. If the credit period is extended then the company may lose discounts for prompt payment.

(iv) Reducing the finished goods inventory turnover period.

(v) Reducing the receivables collection period. The administrative costs of speeding up debt collection and the effect on sales of reducing the credit period allowed must be evaluated. However, the credit period does already seem very long by the standards of most industries. It may be that generous terms have been allowed to secure large contracts and little will be able to be done about this in the short term.

13.4 The total dividend per share is (7.4 + 8.6) = 16 cents

$$\frac{16}{315} \times 100 = 5.1\%$$

13.5

Company	*Industry*
A	Supermarket chain
B	Bakery shop chain
C	Furniture retailer
D	Cruise holiday operator
E	Recruitment and business services

13.6

(a)

	20X8	*20X9*	*Industry average*
ROCE	$\frac{320+60}{2,275}=16.70\%$	$\frac{465+80}{2,845}=19.16\%$	18.50%
Profit/sales	$\frac{320+60}{9,750}=3.90\%$	$\frac{465+80}{11,200}=4.87\%$	4.73%
Asset turnover	$\frac{9,750}{2,275}=4.29x$	$\frac{11,200}{2,845}=3.94x$	3.91x
Current ratio	$\frac{1,690}{845}=2.00$	$\frac{1,950}{955}=2.04$	1.90
Quick ratio	$\frac{1,080+120}{845}=1.42$	$\frac{1,230+80}{955}=1.37$	1.27
Gross profit margin	$\frac{9,750-6,825}{9,750}=30.00\%$	$\frac{11,200-8,460}{11,200}=24.46\%$	35.23%
Accounts receivable collection period	$\frac{1,080}{9,750}\times 365=40days$	$\frac{1,230}{11,200}\times 365=40days$	52 days
Accounts payable payment period	$\frac{690}{6,825}\times 365=37days$	$\frac{750}{8,460}\times 365=32days$	49 days
Inventory Turnover (times)	$\frac{6,825}{490}=13.9x$	$\frac{8,460}{640}=13.2x$	18.30x
Gearing	$\frac{600}{2,275}=26.37\%$	$\frac{800}{2,845}=28.12\%$	32.71%

(b) (i) REPORT

To: Board of Directors
From: Accountant
Subject: Analysis of performance of DG

Date: xx/xx/xx

This report should be read in conjunction with the appendix attached which shows the relevant ratios (from part (a)).

Trading and profitability

Return on capital employed has improved considerably between 20X8 and 20X9 and is now higher than the industry average.

Net income as a proportion of sales has also improved noticeably between the years and is also now marginally ahead of the industry average. Gross margin, however, is considerably lower than in the previous year and is only some 70% of the industry average. This suggests either that there has been a change in the cost structure of DG or that there has been a change in the method of cost allocation between the periods. Either way, this is a marked change that requires investigation. The company may be in a period of transition as sales have increased by nearly 15% over the year and it would appear that new non-current assets have been purchased.

Asset turnover has declined between the periods although the 20X9 figure is in line with the industry average. This reduction might indicate that the efficiency with which assets are used has deteriorated or it might indicate that the assets acquired in 20X9 have not yet fully contributed to the business. A longer term trend would clarify the picture.

(ii) Liquidity and working capital management

The current ratio has improved slightly over the year and is marginally higher than the industry average. It is also in line with what is generally regarded as satisfactory (2:1).

The quick ratio has declined marginally but is still better than the industry average. This suggests that DG has no short term liquidity problems and should have no difficulty in paying its debts as they become due.

Receivables as a proportion of sales is unchanged from 20X8 and are considerably lower than the industry average. Consequently, there is probably little opportunity to reduce this further and there may be pressure in the future from customers to increase the period of credit given. The period of credit taken from suppliers has fallen from 37 days' purchases to 32 days' and is much lower than the industry average; thus, it may be possible to finance any additional receivables by negotiating better credit terms from suppliers.

Inventory turnover has fallen slightly and is much slower than the industry average and this may partly reflect stocking up ahead of a significant increase in sales. Alternatively, there is some danger that the inventory could contain certain obsolete items that may require writing off. The relative increase in the level of inventory has been financed by an increased overdraft which may reduce if the inventory levels can be brought down.

The high levels of inventory, overdraft and receivables compared to that of payables suggests a labour intensive company or one where considerable value is added to bought-in products.

(iii) Gearing

The level of gearing has increased only slightly over the year and is below the industry average. Since the return on capital employed is nearly twice the rate of interest on the debentures, profitability is likely to be increased by a modest increase in the level of gearing.

Signed: Accountant

14

Other techniques of financial analysis

Topic list
1 Limitations of year-on-year analysis
2 Trend analysis
3 Common size statements
4 Inter-firm analysis
5 Failure prediction models

Introduction

This chapter looks at techniques, other than ratio analysis, which can be used to help to interpret financial information. You should be aware of the benefits but also the limitations of these techniques.

Learning objectives

On completion of this chapter you will be able to:

	Syllabus reference
• describe the limitations of ratio analysis where current year's ratios are compared with the previous year	4 c
• explain the value of trend analysis, and carry out simple trend analysis	4 b
• identify the value of common size statements, and prepare such statements	4 b
• discuss the value of inter-firm comparisons, and how they might be organised	4 b
• identify the strengths and weaknesses of failure prediction models	4 b

1 Limitations of year-on-year analysis

FAST FORWARD

You need to appreciate the **limitations** of year on year analysis.

The ratios described in the previous chapter are commonly used to compare:

(a) the results in the most recent financial year with results in the previous year

(b) the results in the current year, as far as a comparison is possible, with the current annual results of similar companies

(c) occasionally, the company's financial position against an 'ideal' or desirable position

(d) the results of different business segments in the same company

In addition to the limitations of ratio analysis described in the previous chapter, year-on-year analysis has the further drawbacks that:

(a) a two-year analysis is often insufficient to obtain a complete picture of a company's financial performance and permission. There should be some longer-term analysis

(b) ratio analysis is not always clearly presented or properly summarised

(c) inter-firm comparisons are not always reliable, because of the different accounting policies used by different companies

(d) ratios are used for analysing historical performance, but do not appear to have much value for predicting the future

To overcome some of these difficulties, other techniques of analysis are sometimes used.

2 Trend analysis

FAST FORWARD

Trend analysis can be more useful, as it can highlight changes in key ratios, and it is possible to plot a trend into the future.

Instead of analysing performance between the current year and the previous year, it might be more informative to look at the picture over a five-year period, or even longer, to see whether any clear trends are discernible. Historical trends are useful because they might give a guide as to what might continue happening into the future.

Looking at the picture over a five-year or even a ten-year period might help to show whether there have been noticeable changes in some key ratios, including financial gearing, interest cover, the current and acid test ratios, and inventory and receivables turnover. If there have been noticeable changes, the possible reasons should be identified, and the likelihood of the trend continuing into the future should be considered.

Trends should also be analysed in 'top line' or 'bottom line' figures, such as sales revenue, profit after taxation, earnings per share and shareholders' funds per share. All of these should ideally continue to rise over time.

A problem with trend analysis is that even in a period of relatively low inflation, results can become distorted over time by the effects of changing price levels. Long-term trend analysis should be adjusted for inflation, so that figures are compared on a similar price level.

Suppose for example that a company has achieved the following results.

	Year 5	*Year 4*	*Year 3*	*Year 2*	*Year 1*
	$000	$000	$000	$000	$000
Revenue	4,360.7	4,250.6	4,165.0	4,123.8	3,885.0
Profit after taxation	53.8	48.0	45.7	45.9	42.8
Earnings per share	8.4c	7.6c	7.3c	7.5c	7.0c
Equity funds per share	255.5c	251.4c	249.1c	246.8c	243c

The index consumer price levels as at the end of each year are as follows

Year 1	245.9
Year 2	253.3
Year 3	268.5
Year 4	273.9
Year 5	282.0

The figures can be brought to a common price level. The most appropriate price level is probably end-of-year 5 prices. Let's assume that sales revenue, profits and earnings for each year are all at end-of-year prices. (This is a simplified assumption, because some figures will reflect an average price for the year or mid-year price. However, an assumption that all prices are at end-of-year price levels is likely to be sufficient within the context of an examination.) The figures can be brought to end-of-year 5 price levels by applying the following adjustment factors.

Year 4	*Year 3*	*Year 2*	*Year 1*
$\frac{282.0}{273.9}$	$\frac{282.0}{268.5}$	$\frac{282.0}{253.3}$	$\frac{282.0}{245.9}$
1.0296	1.0503	1.1133	1.1468

The annual figures can now be adjusted to a common price level, end-of-Year 5 prices, as follows.

	Year 5	*Year 4*	*Year 3*	*Year 2*	*Year 1*
Inflation factor	*1.0*	*1.0296*	*1.0503*	*1.1133*	*1.1468*
	$000	$000	$000	$000	$000
Revenue	4,360.7	4,376.4	4,374.5	4,591.0	4,455.3
Profit after taxation	53.8	49.4	48.0	51.1	49.1
Earnings per share	8.4c	7.8c	7.7c	8.3c	8.0c
Equity funds per share	255.5c	258.8c	261.6c	274.8c	279c

By adjusting the figures for inflation, any significant changes or trends becomes more easily discernible. In this example, the fall in revenue, profits and earnings per share in Year 3 is clear, and the fall in equity funds per share has been continuous since Year 1.

3 Common size statements

FAST FORWARD

> Common size statements compare profitability and costs by putting all income statement figures into ratio form.

Common size statements are a method of comparing profitability and costs between one year and another, or between one company or business segment and another. They simplify the comparison by putting all income statement figures into ratio form, taking sales revenue for the year as 100%. All results down to the profit after taxation figure are therefore put into a common size.

Common size statements are perhaps best explained with an illustration. Suppose that a company achieves the following results in Year 2, and comparative results for year 1 are also available.

	Year 2	*Year 1*
	$000	$000
Revenue	70,544	61,258
Cost of sales	35,978	33,700
Gross profit	34,566	27,558
Distribution costs	(5,527)	(4,915)
Administrative expenses	(14,851)	(11,139)
Total operating profit	14,188	11,504
Profit/(loss) on sale of non-current assets	709	(620)
Profit before interest and taxation	14,897	10,884
Net interest payable	(2,754)	(3,219)
Profit before taxation	12,143	7,665
Taxation	(3,122)	(2,235)
Profit for the period	9,021	5,430

These figures can be compared more easily by putting all the profit/sales ratios and cost/sales ratios into a table for comparison, as follows. Sales represent 100%, and all other figures in each column are expressed as a percentage of sales.

	Year 2	*Year 1*
	%	%
Revenue	100.0	100.0
Cost of sales	51.0	55.0
Gross profit	49.0	45.0
Distribution costs	7.8	8.0
Administrative expenses	21.1	18.2
Total operating profit	20.1	18.8
Profit/loss on sale of non-current assets	1.0	(1.0)
Profit before interest and taxation	21.1	17.8
Net interest payable	3.9	5.3
Profit before taxation	17.2	12.5
Taxation	4.4	3.6
Profit for the period	12.8	8.9

Here, the common size statement helps to clarify the year-on-year analysis. In this example, the profit for the period has gone up from 8.9% in Year 1 to 12.8% in Year 2. There was an improvement in the gross profit/sales ratio in Year 2, up from 45% to 49%, although this was largely offset by an increase in the administrative costs to sales ratio, from 18.2% to 21.1%.

If required, a common size statement could also be prepared for a balance sheet, with 100% representing the total value of each 'side' of the balance sheet.

4 Inter-firm analysis

FAST FORWARD

Inter-firm analysis can be helpful to those making investment decisions.

Making comparisons between the results of different companies in the same industry is one method of assessing how well or badly a company has performed.

Two companies might be in the same industry without being direct competitors. For example, a company with a chain of department stores will not be a direct competitor of a company with a chain of fashion stores (although they will have some overlap in the type of goods they sell). Even so, they might still be expected to show broadly the same performance, particularly in terms of sales growth, because a boom or depression in retailing tends to affect all retailers. The results of two or more companies in the same industry can be compared, and those with better accounting ratios might be judged to have performed better and to be in a better financial position.

If two companies are direct competitors, a comparison between them would be particularly interesting. Some companies have expressed a reluctance to include excessive information in their annual report and accounts, simply because they believe they would be giving away too much information unnecessarily to rivals.

To an investor, comparing the results of companies in broadly the same industry can be helpful in making a decision about which company to invest in.

A common method of inter-firm comparison is to calculate an average performance for companies in the industry, and to compare the results of individual companies against the average.

Many industries have a trade association, representing the interests of all businesses in that industry. Industries need representation on government committees, or in lobbying the government for or against changes in the law, or changes in the rules of taxation. The trade association or trade body should be regarded as a representative of all its members, who can be trusted to treat all members fairly.

Companies might therefore be willing to submit their accounting results to the trade association, and for the trade association to publish average results for the industry as a whole. Results would be expressed in terms of ratios, such as average sales growth and average profit growth, average profit/sales ratios, average gearing levels, average working capital ratios, and so on.

Where average figures are put together by a trade association, companies in the association can carry out an inter-firm comparison within their industry by comparing their own results against the published industry average.

5 Failure prediction models

FAST FORWARD

The most well known **failure prediction model** is the Z score devised in the 1950s by Altman. It is a mathematical model which combines several financial ratios into a predictor of financial failure.

Analysing financial ratios is a widely-used technique for judging a company's performance and financial position. It might be supposed that ratio analysis should be capable of providing a forecast of what is likely to happen in the future.

In particular, analysts should be interested in identifying which companies are in danger of financial collapse, because of their worsening financial situation.

Some ratios are helpful in analysing the debt position of a company, and its ability to meet its debt obligations. Significant ratios and accounting figures include:

(a) interest cover
(b) the current ratio and acid test ratio
(c) possibly, the gearing ratio
(d) the ratio of cash flow from operations to total debt

However, none of these ratios on their own provide a guide as to whether a company is in danger of financial collapse.

5.1 Z scores

The most well-known original researcher into the use of ratios to predict financial collapse was E I Altman. He researched a large number of ratios for a mixture of US companies that had failed financially and US companies that had not failed. From this research, he developed (in 1958) a mathematical model combining several financial ratios into a predictor of financial failure.

Five financial ratios were combined to produce a Z score. His formula for calculating a Z score is as follows. (It is shown here for interest. You do not have to learn it.)

Z score = 1.2A + 1.4B + 3.3C + 0.6D + 1.0E

Where

$$A = \frac{\text{working capital}}{\text{total assets}}$$

$$B = \frac{\text{retained earnings}}{\text{total assets}}$$

$$C = \frac{\text{earnings before interest and tax}}{\text{total assets}}$$

$$D = \frac{\text{market value of equity shares}}{\text{book value of total debt}}$$

(This is a form of gearing ratio)

$$E = \frac{\text{sales}}{\text{total assets}}$$

In Altman's model, a Z score of 2.7 or more indicated non-failure, and a Z score of 1.8 or less indicated a high risk of financial failure.

Altman's sample size was small, and his research was carried out on US firms in a particular range of industries. Subsequent research in different countries and in different industries has been carried out to derive failure prediction models.

It would be argued, for example, that a different failure prediction model would be needed for a UK company than for a US company. Equally, failure prediction would be different for firms in retailing compared to firms in, say, telecommunications and media.

In the UK, as an example, a failure prediction model has been developed by Taffler, which makes use of the ratios for:

(a) $\frac{\text{earning before tax}}{\text{current liabilities}}$

(b) $\frac{\text{current assets}}{\text{total liabilities}}$

(c) $\frac{\text{current liabilities}}{\text{total assets}}$

(d) $\frac{\text{sales}}{\text{total assets}}$

Activity 14.1

The results of Canute Co for the most recent financial year are as follows

	$m
Non-current assets	85
Current assets	60
	145
Share capital and reserves	80
Current liabilities	25
Long-term debt	40
	145

	$m
Sales revenue	50.0
Profit before interest and tax	14.0
Interest	(8.0)
Profit before tax	6.0
Taxation	2.0
Profit for the period	4.0
Dividends paid	1.5

Required

Assuming that all current liabilities are treated as debt, and given a market value for the company's shares of $90 million, calculate a Z score for the firm using Altman's model.

5.2 An assessment of failure prediction models

A broad assessment of failure prediction models might be made as follows.

(a) When a company suffers financial collapse and failure, it can often be seen in retrospect that its financial ratios deteriorated significantly, often very quickly, in the period leading up to the collapse. In retrospect, ratio analysis can therefore be used to explain why a company collapsed.

(b) No fully-accepted model has yet been developed for predicting business failure through ratio analysis, although some form of Z score analysis might appear to be the most promising avenue for progress.

(c) Altman's Z score model includes a ratio for the market value of equity to debt. It follows that the model cannot be used to predict the business failure of private companies, whose shares do not have a market value.

5.3 Weaknesses of corporate failure prediction models

Weaknesses of financial failure prediction models are as follows.

(a) The published financial figures of a company are always at least several months out of date when they become available to the public. Failure might occur before relevant data becomes available.

(b) All failure prediction models are based largely on historical financial records and do not properly take into consideration the general economic environment. Corporate failures are more likely to occur during a recession, for example, than during an economic upturn.

(c) Failure prediction models share the limitations of the generally accepted accounting practices by which the accounts are prepared.

(d) The definition of 'financial failure' is not clear. A company obviously fails when it goes into liquidation, but many struggling companies have been taken over or have gone through some form of rescue or reconstruction.

Key learning points

- You need to appreciate the **limitations of year on year analysis**.
- **Trend analysis** can be more useful, as it can highlight changes in key ratios, and it is possible to plot a trend into the future.
- **Common size statements** compare profitability and costs by putting all income statement figures into ratio form.
- **Inter-firm analysis** can be helpful to those making investment decisions.
- The most well-known **failure prediction model** is the Z score, devised in the 1950s by Altman. It is a mathematical model which combines several financial ratios into a predictor of financial failure.

Quick quiz

1 State three drawbacks of year on year ratio analysis.

2 Why might it be useful to look at historical trends?

3 How does Altman's Z score model work?

Answers to quick quiz

1 A two year analysis does not give a long term picture. The ratio analysis may not be properly summarised or presented. Inter-firm comparisons may hinge on different accounting policies and may not be reliable.

2 Because they can be applied to the future.

3 It applies a formula to certain financial ratios, such as working capital over total assets, and in general terms a score of 2.7 or more indicates non-failure and 1.8 or less indicates a high risk of failure.

Answer to activity

14.1 *Workings*

1 Working capital = current assets – current liabilities = 60 – 25 = 35

2 Total assets = non-current assets + current assets = 85 + 60 = 145

3 Book value of debt = long-term debt + current liabilities = 40 + 25 = 65

Ratio			*x factor*	
Working capital/total assets	35/145	= 0.2414	1.2	0.29
Retained earnings/total assets	2.5/145	= 0.0172	1.4	0.02
Earnings before interest and tax/total assets	14/145	= 0.0966	3.3	0.32
Market value of equity/book value of debt	90/65	= 1.3846	0.6	0.83
Sales/total assets	50/145	= 0.3448	1.0	0.34
Z score				1.80

This score is around the level at or below which the Z score model would predict failure.

List of key terms and index

Note: Key Terms and their page references are given in **bold.**

REVIEW FORM

BPP always appreciates feedback from the students who use our books. We would be very grateful if you would take the time to complete this feedback form, and return it to the address below.

Name: ______________________ **Address:** ______________________

____

How have you used this Text?
(Tick one box only)

☐ Home study (book only)

☐ On a course: college ______________

☐ With 'correspondence' package

☐ Other ______________

Why did you decide to purchase this Text?
(Tick one box only)

☐ Have used complementary Study Text

☐ Have used BPP Texts in the past

☐ Recommendation by friend/colleague

☐ Recommendation by a lecturer at college

☐ Saw advertising

☐ Other ______________

During the past six months do you recall seeing/receiving any of the following?
(Tick as many boxes as are relevant)

☐ Our advertisement in *ACCA Finance Matters*

☐ Our brochure with a letter through the post

Which (if any) aspects of our advertising do you find useful?
(Tick as many boxes as are relevant)

☐ Prices and publication dates of new editions

☐ Information on Text content

☐ Facility to order books off-the-page

☐ None of the above

Have you used the companion Kit for this subject? ☐ Yes ☐ No

Your ratings, comments and suggestions would be appreciated on the following areas

	Very useful	Useful	Not useful
Introductory section	☐	☐	☐
Chapter introductions	☐	☐	☐
Key terms	☐	☐	☐
Quality of explanations	☐	☐	☐
Case examples and other examples	☐	☐	☐
Questions and answers in each chapter	☐	☐	☐
Key learning points	☐	☐	☐
Quick quizzes	☐	☐	☐
List of key terms and index	☐	☐	☐

	Excellent	Good	Adequate	Poor
Overall opinion of this Text	☐	☐	☐	☐

Do you intend to continue using BPP Products? ☐ Yes ☐ No

Please note any further comments and suggestions/errors on the reverse of this page

Please return to: Pippa Riley, BPP Professional Education, FREEPOST, London, W12 8BR or e-mail pippariley@bpp.com

REVIEW FORM (continued)

Please note any further comments and suggestions/errors below